COLONEL Z

By the same authors

Operation Lucy: Most Secret
Spy Ring of the Second World War

COLONEL Z

The Secret Life of a
Master of Spies

Anthony Read and
David Fisher

VIKING

This book is dedicated to the memory of the late
Lieutenant-Colonel J. M. Langley, MBE, MC,
without whose kindness and enthusiastic help this
story of his old chief, "Uncle Claude", would
never have been written. Jimmy Langley
opened many doors for us, for which we are
eternally grateful.

We also wish to pay tribute to
the memory of Gilbert Renault-Roulier,
Colonel Rémy, our friend and adviser
in France, who died as this book
was going to press.

VIKING
Viking Penguin Inc.,
40 West 23rd Street,
New York, New York 10010, U.S.A.

First American edition
Published in 1985

LIBRARY OF CONGRESS CATALOGING IN PUBLICATION DATA
Read, Anthony.
Colonel Z.
1. Dansey, Claude Edward Marjoribanks, Sir, 1876–1947.
2. Spies—Great Britain—Biography. 3. Espionage—Great Britain—History.
I. Fisher, David. II. Title.
UB271.G72D363 1985 327.1'2'0924 [B] 83-40215
ISBN 0-670-22979-2

Printed in the United States of America
by The Book Press, Brattleboro, Vermont
Set in Times Roman

Contents

The development of British secret intelligence & security services, with particular reference to the career of Claude Dansey

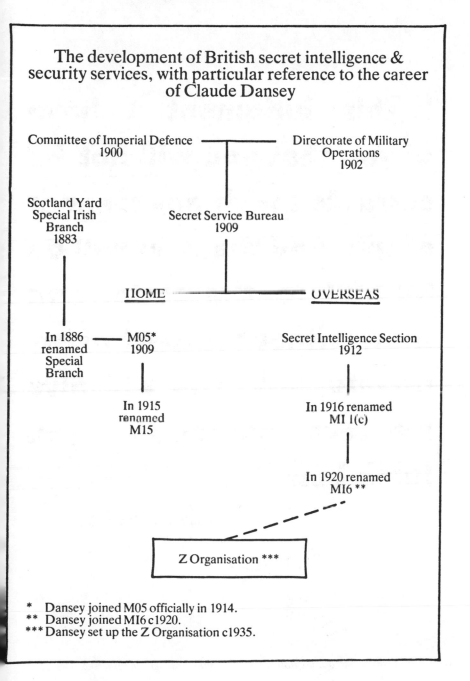

Committee of Imperial Defence
1900 ——————— Directorate of Military Operations
1902

Scotland Yard
Special Irish
Branch
1883

Secret Service Bureau
1909

HOME ————————— OVERSEAS

In 1886 —— M05*
renamed   1909
Special
Branch

Secret Intelligence Section
1912

In 1915
renamed
M15

In 1916 renamed
MI 1(c)

In 1920 renamed
MI6 **

Z Organisation ***

*   Dansey joined M05 officially in 1914.
**   Dansey joined MI6 c 1920.
*** Dansey set up the Z Organisation c1935.

" This judgment I have of you that you will not be corrupted with any manner of gift, and that you will be faithful to the State, and that, without respect of my private will, you will give me that counsel that you think best."

Elizabeth of England.

Dansey's credo: the notice he kept on the wall behind his desk.

Prologue

One day in 1942, two elderly clubmen sat in the exclusive Brooks's in St James's Street, in the heart of bomb-battered London. One leaned across and shouted into the deaf aid of his companion.

"I wonder," he yelled, "what's become of that fellow we shared a tent with, just before the relief of Mafeking?"

The other paused as he cast his mind back forty-two years to the South African war, then bellowed a response.

"You mean that fellow who used to fill stockings with sand and then go out and slug Boer sentries?"

"That's the one. Can't remember his name. Claude something."

"Dansey! If he's still alive, I'll bet he's mixed up in some dirty work somewhere."

The young Coldstream Guards captain in an adjacent chair did his best to conceal a smile. Jimmy Langley, who had escaped from the Germans in France in 1940, despite having just lost an arm at Dunkirk, knew exactly what had become of Claude Dansey: he was mixed up in some very dirty work indeed, as one of the most feared and experienced spymasters in the world. He was in charge of all operations, world-wide, for British Intelligence. He also controlled most of the intelligence and espionage organisations of the European governments in exile in London. It has been estimated that he was ultimately responsible for no less than 80,000 agents in France alone. He was the man with the power of life and death over countless spies, for when treachery was suspected Dansey alone could give the order: "Kill him."

With the exception of Naval Intelligence, which the Admiralty kept jealously to itself, Dansey was involved in just about every aspect of intelligence in the second world war. He came into contact, often abrasively, with everyone of importance in the intelligence world. Their opinions of him varied wildly. Some hated and loathed him, some worshipped him, but no one could ignore him. The reactions he provoked were always strong.

Lord Dacre (still better known as the historian Hugh Trevor-

11

Roper), who served in the Secret Intelligence Service during the war, described him to the authors as "an utter shit; corrupt, incompetent, but with a certain low cunning". This was a view shared by many.

The Duke of Portland, however, who as Victor Cavendish-Bentinck was head of the wartime Joint Intelligence Committee, recalled Dansey as "a downy old bird, very good at his job". And while one author, Charles Whiting, described him as "the most unpopular snake in the business", Philip Johns, who worked for Dansey in various senior capacities in Europe and South America, remembered him as "a wise and most experienced officer . . . his knowledge of covert activities and intelligence generally, linked with all the devious methods of subversion, was nothing less than phenomenal."

Lieutenant-Colonel J. M. Langley, who was the young Coldstream Guards officer who overheard the conversation in Brooks's Club, recalled Dansey with great affection, as did his father, who worked for him in Switzerland during the first world war. Langley himself had worked for "Uncle Claude", as Dansey was known, in both the Secret Intelligence Service and MI9, the escape and evasion organisation which brought back shot-down airmen and escaped prisoners from 1940 to 1945.*

Langley was in no doubt about Dansey's importance: "Dansey was, in fact, one of those powerful men who prefer to keep their power hidden; an *éminence grise* rather than a ruling monarch, but a highly influential personage for all that. What Dansey wanted done was done, and what he wanted undone was undone."

Even Malcolm Muggeridge, who spent the war years in the SIS and who has since been one of its most fervent critics, recalled Dansey kindly. "Everyone was scared of him. He was the only real professional in the SIS. The others at the top were all second-rate men with second-rate minds." And yet Edward Crankshaw, veteran commentator on international affairs and former intelligence officer in Moscow, described him as "the sort of man who gives spying a bad name".

If these conflicting opinions prove anything, it is surely that Lieutenant-Colonel Sir Claude Edward Marjoribanks Dansey,

---

* The family connection goes even further, for the present Mrs Langley, herself a heroine of the Belgian escape lines as Peggy Van Leer, chauffeured Dansey when she was brought out of Belgium and worked as a driver for the SIS. On one memorable occasion, she incurred the great man's wrath by depositing him at the riverside entrance – the "back door" as he regarded it – of the Savoy Hotel instead of at the main foyer.

Prologue

KCMG, Commander of the *Légion d'Honneur* of France, Chevalier of the *Ordre Léopold* of Belgium, Officer of the Legion of Merit of the United States of America, was one of the most remarkable men ever to have worked in the field of secret intelligence, yet one of the least understood. This is, perhaps, hardly surprising. The profession of espionage is one which does not encourage openness, and Dansey was a master of the art of keeping his affairs in completely watertight compartments, allowing those with whom he came into contact to see only what he wanted them to see, whether true or false.

His career was remarkable in many ways, not least because it spanned the entire hey-day of the organised British Secret Service, from its official inception, through the high points of two world wars – in both of which Dansey played a vital role – to the beginning of its inevitable decline as Britain itself ceased to be a major power.

There is a widely-held myth that the British Secret Service has existed in an unbroken line from Sir Francis Walsingham in the time of Queen Elizabeth I to the present day. It is a myth which successive governments have done little to deny, for it has always been useful to have one's enemies living in fear of unseen networks of spies. The truth, however, is far removed from the legend. Certainly, England has a long tradition of espionage and intelligence gathering, dating back far beyond Walsingham to Alfred the Great in the ninth century. But the organised and co-ordinated intelligence service which became rightly respected and feared during the two world wars only came into being at the beginning of the twentieth century. Its history before then was fragmented and spasmodic.

As late as 1895, Colonel G. A. Furse could write, in one of the first text-books on military intelligence:

> The very term "spy" conveys to our mind something dishonourable and disloyal. A spy, in the general acceptance of the term, is a low sneak who, from unworthy motives, dodges the actions of his fellow beings, to turn the knowledge he acquires to his personal account. His underhand dealings inspire us with such horror that we would blush at the very idea of having to avail ourselves of any information obtained through such an agency.

Barely five years after those words were written, Claude Dansey joined the newly-reorganised Intelligence Department of the British General Staff, in South Africa. He was then aged twenty-four,

13

and had already crammed more adventure into the five years since he had left home than most men see in a lifetime.

The writer Somerset Maugham, who was a British agent in Switzerland and Russia during the first world war, later wrote a semi-fictitious account of his experiences in his book *Ashenden*. Many of those who knew them both were convinced that Colonel R, Maugham's spymaster in the book, was based on Claude Dansey. This is how Maugham introduced him: "He was one of those men who prefer devious ways to straight, for some intricate pleasure they get in fooling their fellows."

Dansey was remarkably successful in fooling many of his fellows, and an even larger number of his enemies in Africa, Europe, Britain and the United States of America, where he operated both as an agent and later as a spymaster, and played vital roles in the creation of America's first Military Intelligence Service in 1917 and the OSS, forerunner of the present-day CIA, in the second world war.

Since he was for most of those fifty years concerned with secrecy and deception, it is impossible now to trace all his movements. He covered his tracks with consummate skill, disappearing for whole periods of time and then materialising somewhere quite different, like the White Rabbit popping in and out of an intricate and largely uncharted warren of underground tunnels. The sightings which can be recorded in this book leave many gaps, and many questions which must for ever remain unanswered. Nevertheless what we do know leaves little doubt that Claude Dansey was one of the most important, influential and colourful figures in the history of espionage and secret intelligence.

Part One

Apprenticeship

CHAPTER ONE

Adventures in Africa

Claude Dansey was born in London on 21st October 1876 at 14 Cromwell Place, a six-floor white stucco town house in the blossoming new district of South Kensington. The house is now the students' union of the Institut Français, but was then a newly-built middle-class residence. At the end of the little street, across the Cromwell Road, the Byzantine magnificence of the Natural History Museum, Waterhouse's cathedral to the teachings of Charles Darwin, was halfway to completion. Beyond it lay the gardens of the Royal Horticultural Society, the International Exhibition Buildings, the Royal Albert Hall, and the newly-unveiled Albert Memorial. As little Claude's nursemaid wheeled his baby carriage up the gentle slope of Exhibition Road to join the other nannies and their charges in Hyde Park and Kensington Gardens, he was surrounded by the outward show of Great Britain's affluence and vitality in the golden summer of Victoria's long reign.

To a child of such times, born less than three months before Disraeli proclaimed Queen Victoria Empress of India, anything seemed possible. Vast tracts of the world waited for bold Britons to explore, conquer, enlighten, plunder and generally bestow upon them the inestimable benefits of imperial rule. It was baby Claude's destiny to serve the imperial dream in various parts of the world (though not India) until his death in June 1947, coincidentally less than three months before India's independence when Queen Victoria's great-grandson relinquished the title of Emperor.

Claude was the second child and first son of Captain Edward Mashiter Dansey, an officer in the 1st Life Guards, the senior and most élite regiment in the British army, and the Honourable Eleanore Dansey, fifth daughter of the second Lord Gifford. Eventually, the Danseys had nine children, five girls and four boys,

17

all of whom survived to adulthood, when they all appear to have hated each other.

The military tradition in the Dansey family goes back at least to 1638, when William Dansey, Lord of the Manor of Little Hereford, was appointed an ensign in King Charles I's army. William, whose father and grandfather both held office as High Sheriff of Herefordshire, married the daughter of Sir Robert Dudley, Duke of Northumberland, a prominent Royalist. He quickly became a captain, fought against Cromwell's Ironsides, and for his loyalty to the King "was confined and his estates sequestered during the Usurpation". Succeeding generations of Danseys continued to be soldiers and country squires, with little to distinguish them from hundreds of other worthy families.

On his mother's side, however, Claude had a more interesting lineage, and even some royal blood. His grandmother was the eldest daughter of Lord Fitzhardinge and Frederica Charlotte, eldest daughter of the fourth Duke of Richmond, who was the great-grandson of the illegitimate son of Charles II. Lord Fitzhardinge was a member of the Berkeley family, the latest in an unbroken line stretching back to the twelfth century to live in Berkeley Castle, Gloucestershire, where an ancestor and his cronies had brutally murdered King Edward II in 1327. The Berkeleys themselves could claim some royal blood, through various marriages down the centuries.

Eleanore Dansey's grandfather, Robert Gifford (the family pronounce their name "Jifford") was a lawyer from Exeter, Devon, who entered Parliament and became, in turn, Solicitor-General, Attorney-General, Lord Chief Justice of the Court of Common Pleas, Master of the Rolls and Deputy Speaker of the House of Lords. He was created first Baron Gifford of St Leonard's, Devon, in 1824, on becoming Lord Chief Justice. His son, the second baron, appears to have been less remarkable, but two of his grandsons set the style which Claude was to follow.

The third Lord Gifford, Dansey's uncle Edric Frederick, distinguished himself by winning Britain's highest award for gallantry in action, the Victoria Cross, as a lieutenant in the 24th Regiment (South Wales Borderers) during the Ashanti wars in 1874 in what is now Ghana, West Africa. He went on to fight in the Zulu war in 1879, served on the staff of Sir Garnet Wolseley, Governor of Natal, in 1874 and 1879-80, and was then appointed Colonial Secretary for Western Australia from 1880 to 1883, when he moved to Gibraltar, also as Colonial Secretary, until 1888. His younger brother Maurice began life as an officer in the mercantile marine, but after six years at sea decided to seek adventure ashore.

18

He first became a galloper for the *Daily Telegraph*'s special correspondent in the Egyptian campaign of 1882, then moved around Africa, wherever there was trouble or excitement to be found.* Claude's childhood was unsettled. The family moved around southern England, with addresses in Henley-on-Thames, Fareham, Basingstoke and Gloucestershire as well as London, where the 1st Life Guards were stationed in Regent's Park. The moves appear to have been due less to the demands of army life than to Edward Dansey's fluctuating fortunes during the flat-racing season. Although an excellent judge of horse flesh when it came to choosing suitable mounts for the Sovereign's Escort, he proved less successful at picking winners. Indeed, most of the Dansey family seem to have found the lure of the Turf irresistible. Claude himself, as we shall see, became the manager of a racing stable during the 1920s, while his sister Margaret (Pat) Dansey lost many thousands of pounds on the horses, and according to one informant, had it not been for the generosity of the friend with whom she lived for many years, Margaret (Joan) Campbell, she might have faced a penurious old age.

Whenever he had a streak of bad luck, Dansey *père* economised by taking his family to live in France, then a sanctuary for impoverished English gentlefolk. This enabled the young Claude to gain an excellent grounding in the language. Although he could always understand French perfectly, he was often at pains in later life to give the impression that he could hardly speak a word; likewise with German and Italian. To some he was quite fluent; to others, he could barely comprehend a word   another example of Maugham's "intricate pleasure in devious ways".

Claude's education was mainly entrusted to a series of tutors until he was fourteen, when he was sent to Wellington College, forty miles outside London at Crowthorne in Berkshire – an establishment Dansey himself described as "a military institution founded in honour of the Duke of Wellington. The object of the school is primarily with a thought that students will enter the army and the education is of a military tenor". It is clear that the young Claude had every intention of following the school tradition, and with his father now installed as lieutenant-colonel of the Life

---

* The family's connection with Africa, which Claude was to further, still exists to the present day with the sixth Lord Gifford – though his views are totally opposed to those of his predecessors in the title. A lawyer like his distinguished ancestor, the current Lord Gifford is a one-time chairman of the South Kensington Labour Party and was from 1968 to 1975 chairman of the anti-colonialist Committee for Freedom for Mozambique, Angola and Guiné.

Guards, a rosy future in the premier cavalry regiment in the British army seemed assured.

But during November 1891 a considerable number of boys at Wellington reported sick with sore throats; the following month two boys died of suspected diphtheria. Some years before there had been a similar epidemic, the origin of which had been identified as the College drains. The Governors had spent over £13,000 in an attempt to rectify the problem, but now this second epidemic threatened the very survival of the school. Mere plumbing was not going to be enough to save Wellington's reputation; drastic action was required. It was therefore decided to evacuate the school to the Imperial Hotel, Malvern, a spa town noted for its cures, until such time as the Berkshire public health authorities were satisfied with the state of the College drains.

Some parents, however, amongst them Colonel and Mrs Dansey, preferred to remove their children from Wellington. Thus, instead of spending several months at the Imperial Hotel, the young Claude, then aged fifteen, was sent to a boys' school in Bruges, Belgium.

Originally called "Laurence's", the school in Bruges had been purchased in 1888 by Rev. Biscoe Wortham, a feckless and bankrupt British clergyman, who renamed the establishment the English College. Until Wortham took over as headmaster, it had been a successful and respected school, with sixty-nine pupils, producing an annual profit of just under £1,000 – a considerable sum in Victoria's day, when a servant could be paid less than £50 a year. In the hands of almost anyone else the school would have continued to prosper. But Wortham was one of those unfortunates bereft of either talent or commonsense, who seem to attract disaster. He was a born loser. His wife once complained that in six years of married life they had been forced to move no less than seventeen times – because of her husband's "misfortunes".

The son of a distinguished Hebrew lecturer at Cambridge, Wortham was married to the sister of Oscar Browning, who was a man of dubious reputation. In 1875 Browning had been dismissed from his post as housemaster at Eton on account of his prediliction for falling in love with his more attractive pupils. (George Curzon, son of Baron Scarsdale and later to become Viceroy of India, was the particular cause of his downfall.) However, cheerfully impervious to scandal, Browning moved on from Eton and became a don at King's College, Cambridge, where unabashed he continued his amorous activities. It was to be one of Browning's homosexual friends who was to prove the agent of yet another of Biscoe

Wortham's "misfortunes", and was also to cast a shadow over the young Claude Dansey's subsequent career.

Like many headmasters of his day, Wortham considered it part of his duties to censor his pupils' mail – on the principle that the sooner a moral lapse was detected the sooner it could be corrected. In October 1893 he intercepted a letter from a boy whom he described to his brother-in-law as "nice looking, well mannered, a little over sixteen, of no particular strength of character". It was clear from this letter that the boy had formed an immoral friendship with the Canadian "Robbie" Ross, a well known aesthete, twenty-four years old, who later claimed to have been Oscar Wilde's first lover. Whether this was true or not remains an open question; certainly Wilde dedicated *The Importance of Being Earnest* to him and in his will made him his literary executor. Good-looking, witty and amusing, Robert Baldwin Ross was the son of the Attorney-General of Upper Canada and, like Browning, a Kingsman himself. For a time the two men even shared the same lover, a handsome sailor named Matthew Oates.

The boy whose letter was intercepted was none other than Claude Dansey. When interrogated, he revealed that he had been seduced by Ross during a weekend he had spent in Windsor, in the company of Philip, Wortham's fourteen-year-old son. But for poor Wortham even more revelations were to follow. When he questioned Philip about the events of that fateful weekend, he was appalled to learn that Philip too had been seduced by Ross, and nor was this the only occasion on which the man had enjoyed the sexual favours of the two boys.

Sorrowfully Wortham communicated the sordid news to Colonel Dansey who was beside himself with rage. "His great desire," Wortham later complained to Browning, who no doubt took malicious delight in his brother-in-law's discomfiture, "was to punish the culprits, and it was not until the very last moment that he was convinced that [he] could not punish them without involving his own son."

Wortham did not disclose the names of Ross's "accomplices and friends", and we do not know their identities. The name of Lord Alfred Douglas, Oscar Wilde's notorious "Bosie", is mentioned in the letters, but whether or not he was implicated remains a matter for conjecture.

Colonel Dansey, determined to extract blood for this affront to the family honour, consulted the family solicitor, Sir John Wontner, who advised caution. Scandal must be avoided at any cost lest it should irreparably damage Claude's future prospects. It was vital therefore that Ross should be persuaded to return any letters that

Claude might have written to him. With this in view, Wortham arranged to meet Ross in the Hotel de Flandre, Bruges.

Wortham gained little satisfaction from the meeting. Ross was highly intelligent and by no means a weak character, as he was to prove by his support of his ex-lover: after the trial of 1895, he was one of the few who remained loyal to Oscar Wilde, never denying his intimacy with the writer and visiting him regularly in Reading jail. Ross handled Wortham with consummate skill. He pleaded ignorance of any seduction of the boys and implied that if Biscoe Wortham was considering blackmail, he had come to the wrong person. "I have no letters from [the boy Dansey]," he later wrote to Browning, "that could not be read in public." Nevertheless, he graciously agreed to return the correspondence, and the affair fizzled out.

It would be easy to exaggerate the significance of this sad little story. But we must remember that Claude was only sixteen at the time, and in the hothouse atmosphere of Victorian boys' boarding schools such occurrences were not particularly rare. Claude, of course, never mentioned the scandal to anyone, so we do not know how he regarded the matter himself, or if he felt scarred by it. One can speculate that such an experience can only have served to increase his natural secretiveness and make him determined in future to preserve the secrets of his life – an ambition in which he was remarkably successful. In addition, since his peccadillo was discovered via Wortham's censorship of his mail, it is not surprising that in later life Claude should become notorious for his refusal to commit anything to paper if he could possibly avoid it. For a future master of spies, he had learned two important lessons: always read other people's mail, and always exploit other people's weaknesses.

Colonel Dansey removed his eldest son from Biscoe Wortham's incompetent care, and nothing more was said outside the family. But it is significant that he did not encourage the boy to seek a military career in his own regiment, the Life Guards, perhaps fearing that the shadow of scandal might affect his own standing. Instead, he sent the young Claude, like some teenage remittance man, to find adventure and no doubt to prove his manhood, in foreign parts.

For the next nineteen years, Claude Dansey spent remarkably little time in Britain. His adventures began in southern Africa. No one can tell whether Claude decided on the region himself, or if he was simply sent there because of the Gifford family connections. In either case, it was an excellent choice.

—

In the British Empire of the 1890s, southern Africa was the equivalent of the American West, offering the chance not only of excitement but also of riches. As in the West, there were new frontiers to be pushed back. As in the West, there were vast open spaces to be conquered and new territories to be carved out of the wilderness in the face of hostile and frequently savage natives. And as in the West, there was gold to be found, if only by the fortunate few.

South Africa also had three important elements which were missing from the American West: the Afrikaner Boers, diamonds and Cecil Rhodes. For the moment, the Boers – white settlers of Dutch, German and Huguenot descent who had been in South Africa since 1652 – were of little importance to Dansey, though five years later they were to play a vital part in deciding his future. Diamonds, too, had only an indirect effect on him, since he does not seem to have had any interest in prospecting. But diamonds had been the making of the third element, Cecil Rhodes, and Rhodes certainly had an effect on Dansey's life and ambitions.

Cecil John Rhodes was a remarkable man by any standards. He had arrived in South Africa in 1870, a tall, thin youth aged seventeen, with curly fair hair and close-set, heavy-lidded eyes, virtually penniless and desperately sick with tuberculosis of the lungs. His ambition then was limited: to improve his health in the dry climate and make a little money, so that he could study Latin and Greek at Oxford University. Yet within a year, he was earning £100 a week in the diamond fields of Kimberley and laying the foundations of a fortune by buying up the claims of other prospectors who lost heart and gave up.

By the time he was twenty he was a rich man, well on the way to controlling the entire Kimberley mine through the company he had founded, De Beers Consolidated Mines – still the greatest name in diamonds today. He had also developed an aneurism of the aorta, and had his first heart attack when he was nineteen, but he battled on, undeterred.

He took time out to go to Oxford, as he had planned, and there he developed a dream of the whole world united into one vast federated empire, governed by the English-speaking race from Great Britain and America. He saw his own destiny in this dream as bringing the African continent under the Union Jack from the Cape to Cairo. The dream obsessed him for the rest of his life. The power and wealth he accumulated from his business interests was devoted to its realisation, which would, he believed, bring universal peace and prosperity.

By the time Claude Dansey came to Africa, Rhodes was already a legend. There were many who resented him, some even who affected to despise him. But he was a Privy Councillor, Prime Minister of the Cape and unquestionably the most powerful man in Africa, since he and his partners had almost total control of both diamond and gold production. What was more, he had pushed north into new territory, first persuading Britain to annex Bechuanaland as a protectorate and then himself taking Matabeleland and Mashonaland from the fierce Matabele tribe and consolidating them into one country, which in the year Dansey arrived he handed over to the imperial government as a ready-made colony named after him: Rhodesia. He was then forty-two years old.

Before Rhodesia became an official British colony, it was administered by a company set up by Rhodes and his friends, notably Dr Leander Starr Jameson, called the British South Africa Company. There had been one or two competitors for the exclusive Royal Charter under which the company operated. The most important of these was a group called the Exploring Company. When the British Government was reluctantly forced into granting the Charter to Rhodes, they insisted that the two companies should be merged. The chairman of the Exploring Company became a director of the BSAC. He was Lord Gifford, VC, Claude Dansey's Uncle Edric Frederick. Gifford was also heavily involved in the adjoining territory of Bechuanaland, and headed the Bechuanaland Exploration Company.

After a rather shaky start, the new country began to prosper. White settlers flowed in. By 1895 there were nearly 4,000 of them. To guard them, and to a certain extent to control them, a paramilitary force was created: the British South Africa Company Police. Later, the word "Company" was dropped from the title and it became known simply as the British South Africa Police, surviving as such until independence a century later, even though it had no connection whatever with the Union of South Africa. It was this force that the young Claude Dansey set out to join.

The British South Africa Police never quite achieved the glamour of other such forces like the Canadian "Mounties" – partly perhaps because their uniforms of slouch hats and grey shirts were less colourful – but they were nevertheless an élite force. From the beginning they were reckoned to be one of the finest semi-military bodies in the Empire, and the competition to join was keen. It could be that, far from being cajoled or persuaded to join by his illustrious relatives, Dansey may have needed their influence to gain a place. They would have been well positioned to help him, for in addition to his uncle, Lord Gifford, being on the main board of the company, his adventurous Uncle Maurice had also found his way to the new country. He had served as a scout with the column which defeated the Matabele warriors and took Bulawayo in 1893, and was now a prominent citizen in that town.

Rhodes had always pursued the policy of recruiting the sons of leading families into his columns, on the simple premise that if they got into serious difficulties their parents could be relied on to demand help from the imperial authorities, who would send regular troops to the rescue. As a result, the police force included many public school boys, younger sons of aristocratic and upper-middle-class British families and the descendants of professional officers who had not, for one reason or another, gone to Sandhurst or Woolwich.

The standard of education in the ranks was extremely high, since all recruits joined as troopers, with the possibility of rising to the highest positions. Training, military efficiency and "spit and polish" were all of a high standard, being in the hands of former warrant officers and non-commissioned officers from good regiments in the regular army. Dansey, with his military family and his time at Wellington College, fitted in perfectly and felt completely at home.

The force was organised as two small cavalry regiments, one each in Mashonaland and Matabeleland, supported by an establishment of African auxiliaries. Dansey was assigned to the Matabeleland unit, based in Bulawayo. There he received his initial training and a first experience of professional soldiering – for in its early days the force was still very much a military outfit. The toughest and most ferocious part of the training was in horsemanship, which made the normal cavalryman's training seem like a Sunday outing in Rotten Row.

Had he stayed in England and joined his father's regiment, or indeed any other unit in the British Army, Dansey would have been steered towards a life as a conventional soldier. He might have gone on to become a general, no doubt an imaginative one, but a relatively "normal" one for all that. With his love of horses and racing, inherited from his father, he would have shone at regimental point-to-point meetings, at polo and on the hunting field.

Instead, he was trained in a force which recognised the value of individual initiative and expected its young troopers to be able to work alone. The principle on which the British South Africa Police operated was that prevention is better than punishment. Peace was kept without bloodshed by constant patrolling rather than by sitting in barracks and sending out punitive expeditions after something had gone wrong. The trooper therefore spent most of his time in the saddle, riding over the open veld and supporting himself for days or weeks at a time, sometimes alone and sometimes accompanied by one or more black auxiliaries. Generally, he rode a mule, as sickness and the dreaded tsetse fly wiped out most horses in the early years. Always, he had to use his own judgement, rather than relying on the orders of senior men. It was exactly what Claude Dansey needed to prepare him for his long and unconventional career.

The journey out was in itself an enormous adventure for a young man of eighteen, away on his own for the first time. The steamship voyage of seventeen days from England to Cape Town was followed by a 900-mile journey by rail to the end of the line at the small collection of low-roofed corrugated-iron houses that made up the town of Mafeking – a name which was to pass into the English language five years later. Finally, there was an overland trek of 557 miles by stage coach, a regular wild-west vehicle with huge leather springs and a heavy undercarriage, drawn by a team of ten mules. This part of the journey took at least ten days and nights across the open, waterless veld, stopping from time to time to cook a meal with provisions brought from Mafeking, resting at night in wayside stations or friendly kraals for a few hours before pressing on with fresh mules.

Towards Bulawayo, the trail moved from open veld to a mass of fantastic, rock-strewn kopjes, the unique hillocks of southern Africa, separated by high-grass valleys, then after winding through the Mangwe Pass at the tail of the sacred Matopo Hills it emerged on to the Matabele Plateau. It was a journey which gave Dansey plenty of opportunity to study the land he was to patrol, a first introduction to the continent that was to dominate his life for the next twenty years.

He took to it immediately. Bulawayo was booming, with fine new brick buildings rising everywhere – hotels, shops, newspaper offices, even a stock exchange. The whites firmly believed the military ambitions of the Matabele had been crushed for ever, and that they could be safely employed as labourers and servants, positions they would be happy to fill. Rhodes was in his heaven, and all was right with the world.

But Rhodes's heaven was away in the south, in Cape Town, and from there the view was slightly different. All might be well for the moment in the new colony of Rhodesia, but elsewhere in southern Africa the situation was not so happy. Leaving aside the relatively small and unimportant African native states like Basutoland, Zululand and Swaziland, there were four territories in the area that was to become the Union of South Africa: two self-governing British colonies, Cape Colony and Natal, and two Boer republics, the Transvaal and Orange Free State. The Boers had settled in their territories after moving from the Cape when Britain abolished slavery throughout the Empire in 1834. They complained that without slave labour they could no longer run their farms. They covered many shades of opinion, but were totally united on two subjects: opposition to the British and an unshakeable determination to deny any political rights to Africans or people of mixed race.

The lands where they settled were inevitably areas no one else wanted – apart from any Africans who happened to be living there. But the discovery of gold in 1886 changed all that. Suddenly everybody wanted the Transvaal. Rhodes, of course, was happy to make yet another fortune in the gold mines of Johannesburg. But he had other reasons, too, for wanting the Transvaal. It was an essential part of his great dream. However, he had to choose his moment with great care. The British had tried to annex the territory ten years earlier, but had been beaten off in fierce and bloody battles. Such a reverse must not be allowed to happen again. Rhodes watched and waited.

At the end of 1895, with his nineteenth birthday behind him, Dansey was just getting used to his new life in Rhodesia. No doubt because he was still too much a new boy, he escaped being involved in one of history's more disreputable escapades – a special mission organised in the utmost secrecy by the British South Africa Company's administrator in Salisbury, Rhodes's friend Dr Jameson. On the other hand, perhaps Dansey even then was just too small to get involved.

Jameson was assembling a body of men in a remote part of Bechuanaland, in a six-mile-wide strip of land which had been set aside for the building of a railway. Rhodes had decided the time was ripe for a decisive move into the Transvaal, and had ordered Jameson to assemble a military force to stage a lightning march on Johannesburg. There it would be joined by thousands of "Uitlanders", white non-Boer immigrants, whom Rhodes judged ready to rise against the Afrikaner President Kruger, overthrow his government and install a pro-British administration in Pretoria. The Transvaal, with all its riches, could then be brought safely and easily into the imperial fold.

From the beginning, the plan went wrong. Jameson had originally intended to take 1,500 men, but could muster only 600. Still that would have to do. He had, after all, defeated the Matabele hordes with that number in 1893. The essential element in Jameson's plan was surprise. He reckoned to reach Johannesburg in a three-day dash from Pitsani, just inside the Bechuanaland frontier near Mafeking, and join up with the Uitlander revolutionaries.

On 29th December, in spite of messages telling him the Uitlanders were not ready, Jameson led his men across the frontier into the Transvaal. Unfortunately for him, news of the plot had leaked. The Boers, far from being taken by surprise, were waiting. And not a single Uitlander rode out to join the raiders. In spite of the high quality of his troops, Jameson's party had no chance against the well-organised Boers, who picked them off from cover as they rode, weary after covering 170 miles of rough country with hardly a break for rest or sleep, then surrounded them and poured bullets into their wagon square. Eventually, even Jameson saw that the position was hopeless, and he agreed to surrender. His men had suffered sixty-five casualties, sixteen of them fatal. The Boers had lost only one man. Jameson was led away, weeping, to jail in Pretoria. It was the last day of 1895, and the last day of Cecil Rhodes's power and glory.

The Jameson Raid, as the expedition was known, proved disastrous for Rhodes. He was disgraced, disowned by the British Government and forced to resign both as Prime Minister of the Cape and as Managing Director of the British South Africa Company. His personal prestige was left in tatters, never to recover. The whites in Rhodesia were shocked – their idol had been torn down and smashed.

Jan Smuts, the Boer hero, maintained that the Jameson Raid was the real declaration of war in the great Anglo-Boer conflict that was to erupt in 1899. In essence that was undoubtedly true, but for the moment peace returned to the Transvaal. The gods of war were looking slightly further north, to where the young Claude Dansey now found himself serving in a seriously depleted police force, one of a mere forty-eight whites left behind by Jameson to guard the entire country.

The Matabele saw the Boer victory as a portent. The great and apparently invincible "Dr Jim" Jameson had been soundly beaten; Rhodes himself was a broken man; many of the commanders and senior officers of the police were imprisoned in Johannesburg and Pretoria, and most of their men were with them. Now, surely, was the time to strike back to avenge the earlier defeats, and drive the white man out for ever.

The Matabele themselves had acquired the territory by conquest a mere sixty years before, when they moved north to crush the Roswi empire and seize its peoples and possessions. Their pride as conquerors had been dashed by their defeats at the hands of the company's troops, but it was not dead. It could be revived, and restored.

While the Matabele chiefs conspired and considered, natural and supernatural events combined to influence them. First, the land was struck by a severe drought. Then what crops there were were attacked by swarms of locusts. Finally, there was a terrible outbreak of rinderpest, the deadly cattle plague which had raged in Moses's Egypt. The authorities took the only course possible in an attempt to check the spread of the disease – they ordered that all suspect cattle should be slaughtered. When Dansey and his colleagues carried out the order, the Africans were incensed, seeing it as the white man's final attempt to get rid of them by starving them to death.

Mlimo, the great spirit god of the Matabele and Mashona, had through his human mouthpiece and oracle foretold the cattle plague, the drought and the locusts. Now, he ordered the tribes to rise against the white men, saying that it would rain when the blood of the whites was spilt. Strangely enough, it did exactly that, out of season, just as Mlimo had prophesied.

The Matabele rose on the night of 20th March 1896. The first casualties were three black policemen whose group was attacked by their camp fire in the hills. Soon afterwards reports began to come in from various parts of the country of settlers being hunted down by native war parties and shot, stoned, speared or bludgeoned to death. During the next ten days 122 white men, five women and three children were killed by the insurgents.

Dansey suddenly found himself involved in a war. White rule was breaking down throughout Matabeleland and the company's position was looking desperate. The bulk of the European members of the police force were still in captivity in the Transvaal. The native policemen could not be trusted to fight against their own people, and in fact many of them went over to the enemy. For the whites, there was also a shortage of horses and of arms. If ever there was an opportunity for a young man to learn the hard facts of war quickly, this was it.

The men and authorities who remained in Bulawayo were resourceful and positive. They swiftly fortified the town. Within a very short time it was impregnable to native attacks. At the same time, a Field Force 850 strong was organised by men such as Maurice Gifford, who raised and commanded two troops of cavalry which he dubbed "Gifford's Horse". Dansey, along with the other surviving police, was pressed into service.

Bulawayo was secure, as were two other strong points established by the colonists at Gwelo and Belingwe, each about ninety miles away. But the whites could not expect to defeat the Matabele by sitting tight inside their fortifications. The tribesmen had learned bitter lessons from the earlier wars and were now much tougher opponents. They knew better than to mount mass attacks in open country against prepared and well-armed positions. Now, they operated in small, highly-mobile units, choosing to fight in broken country and dense bush where the British weapons could do little damage. They had vast superiority in numbers and were armed with modern rifles as well as spears and assegais.

While Bulawayo was being made secure, the isolated colonists on their farms and mines were being slaughtered by the Matabele. In addition to their continual scouting patrols, Dansey and his colleagues had to ride in small patrols to find and rescue the settlers, fighting off native attacks on the way.

The patrols were highly successful during April, reducing the number of pioneers murdered by the rebels to thirteen, including three women and five children. On 28th April Dansey was one of 115 white men and seventy colonial Africans who inflicted a severe defeat on an impi of Matabele warriors.

The Field Force was holding its own, but its victories were local affairs and could make little impression on the situation as a whole. Towards the end of May, they met and defeated another impi, and joined up with a relief column from Salisbury, which was as yet unaffected by the rising. The column brought 150 men and much needed supplies to strengthen the garrisons. It also brought Cecil Rhodes, newly returned from England where Jameson and his chief lieutenants in the Raid were being tried and sentenced under the Foreign Enlistments Act, for preparing and mounting a military operation against a friendly state. Jameson was given fifteen months in prison. Rhodes had hurried to Salisbury as soon as he heard what was happening in his colony, and had now taken the first opportunity to travel to Bulawayo. He may have been disgraced for his part in the Jameson Raid, but he was determined to do what he could to save the country he had created.

"I am here," he told the people of Bulawayo. "You have done me the favour of giving this country my name. My return for that will be to make this country as great as I am. Your list of killed and wounded is severe in the extreme, but we shall have to hunt the Matabele in the bush and in the stones and kopjes, in a country nearly half the size of Europe." It was a formidable prospect.

The list of wounded to which Rhodes referred included Maurice Gifford, who had an arm amputated at the shoulder but insisted on continuing to lead Gifford's Horse. His courage and determination were typical of the spirit of the Field Force, but Rhodes's assessment of the size of the task facing them was realistic. Courage and determination alone were not sufficient. They needed more men, too. It was time for Rhodes to swallow his pride and ask the imperial authorities for help.

The British Government agreed. They would send assistance – as long as the company paid all the bills. Lieutenant-Colonel Herbert Plumer was ordered to raise a relief force in Mafeking and Kimberley. Volunteers rushed forward and within a short time he was able to march into Rhodesia to join up with the beleaguered forces there and create a combined strength of 2,000 whites and 600 blacks, double the number of the original defenders but still pitifully few to throw against the entire Matabele nation.

To take overall command, the government sent Lieutenant-General Sir Frederick Carrington, a veteran of previous Kaffir wars (no relation to the later Carrington who was instrumental in handing back the country to the black peoples, as the Republic of Zimbabwe). As his chief of staff, Carrington chose a thirty nine year-old cavalry officer who had impressed him during a campaign in Zululand eight years earlier, Brevet Lieutenant-Colonel Robert Baden-Powell. In doing so, he brought another vital influence into Dansey's life at a critical point.

Baden-Powell had had a varied career in India, Afghanistan, South Africa and the Gold Coast, as well as a three-year spell as intelligence officer for the Mediterranean and ADC to the Governor of Malta. He was a highly unconventional officer and a great innovator, and had done a considerable amount of spying, chiefly on his own initiative, in North Africa, Italy, Turkey, France, Germany, Russia and South Africa. On these self-financed expeditions he travelled under various guises: butterfly hunter, snipe shooter, journalist, hiker. He was an excellent artist, and always took along his sketch books and paints, with which he made pictures of military installations and anything else he thought would be valuable. He often worked under the very noses of the people he was spying on. If they became suspicious, he invited them to admire his efforts, pointing out the glorious effect of sunlight on the mountains and diverting their attention from the fortifications which just happened to be in the painting as well. On one occasion he was caught by a Prussian sentry while spying on secret operations at Spandau near Berlin. He avoided arrest by quickly pouring a bottle of brandy over his clothes and acting drunk. At the end of each vacation trip, he prepared detailed

31

reports which he presented to the War Office Intelligence Department back in London.

To us, now, such efforts seem incredibly amateurish. But, the whole system of intelligence gathering at that time depended very much on the patriotic amateur serving his country voluntarily without payment or even reimbursement of his expenses. Even at the beginning of the second world war, Dansey was still following many of the examples set by Baden-Powell over forty years before.

In Rhodesia during the Matabele Rising in 1896, however, Dansey and his fellows were involved in active fighting. With the arrival of the additional men, they were able to go on the offensive at last. But it was not easy, even with the increased numbers. Plumer lost twenty per cent of his relief force's 1,000 men within two weeks. There was talk of sending for another 5,000, but the nearest railhead was almost 600 miles away and there would be problems both of time and of supplying such large numbers, so they battled on as they were.

Dansey found himself riding out regularly on patrol, scouring the bush for the enemy and taking part in much fierce fighting. Here again, the example of Baden-Powell was an inspiration. Baden-Powell had his own very clear ideas about scouting, but he was not too proud to learn from an expert. Frederick Russell Burnham, an American scout employed by the company, passed on a number of scouting tricks which he had learned in the 1893 war against the Matabele and as a US army scout fighting in the Apache Indian wars. Baden-Powell in turn passed on his knowledge to young men such as Dansey.

Gradually, painfully, the British gained the upper hand. By mid-July the Matabele had been driven back into the shelter of their sacred hills, the Matopos, where the steep kopjes, huge boulders, secret caves and hidden ravines provided perfect cover for defenders. Even with good scouting, the region was almost impossible to storm, and the Matabele were secure. Here their kings and heroes were buried. Here their spirit gods reigned supreme. There was only one way of defeating a people holed up in such a fastness: starve them into surrender. But to do that would need a huge number of men, enough to seal off the entire region. And even then it would take a great deal of time and a great deal of money – money which the company did not have.

Rhodes, however, had other ideas. His country might be in ruins, his health failing, his political influence destroyed beyond repair, but he was still Rhodes. He went unarmed into the Matopos, met the chiefs of the Matabele, and demonstrated once again the incredible strength of his personality by emerging not with an assegai between his ribs, as many had feared, but with an agreement for peace. He also had a new name, given to him by the Matabele: Lamula 'Mkunzi, Separator of the Fighting Bulls, chief and father of his people, the Matabele. It was a truly astonishing demonstration of personal charisma.

The rebellion in Matabeleland was over. But already trouble had started in the other province, Mashonaland. Even as the Matabele were pacified, the spirit mediums of the Mashona were preaching war to the death, and with most of the troops and police away fighting the Matabele, the northern tribes took advantage of the situation to rise in open revolt. The harassed Europeans found themselves with another full-scale conflict on their hands.

Dansey and his fellows were rushed north and the British imperial authorities in Cape Town sent reinforcements. For once, they sent exactly the right sort of force: mounted infantry consisting of the cream of the army's fighting men, specially selected and trained by their battalions for irregular fighting. Dansey found himself in a unit which closely foreshadowed the special forces of the second world war. The unit operated on its own initiative and was split into subsections of four who selected their own leaders, regardless of rank.

They were good men, some 1,500 Europeans, commanded by Colonel Edwin Alderson. Even so, they had a hard time against the Mashona and it was not until November that the situation allowed Alderson and his imperial troops to be withdrawn. The fighting was not over, but the company was having to pay in full for imperial help, and the cost had already been enormous. The final job of pacification and mopping up would therefore be left to the company's police.

Dansey and his colleagues had learned the lessons of the last twelve months, becoming highly skilled guerilla fighters. Progress was slow and for the most part unspectacular, but gradually they managed to take the leaders and spirit mediums who were controlling the Mashona, and to confiscate the natives' guns. They returned to their practice of extensive patrols through the backveld, re-establishing the principle that prevention is better than repression, and by the middle of 1897, peace had been fully restored.

At that time, Dansey's short-term contract with the British South Africa Police came to an end and he had to consider what to do next. Should he stay, or should he move on, seeking fresh adventures elsewhere? He had a medal for the Matabele Campaign, was blooded as a fighting man, and had acquired an incred-

33

ible amount of experience in a very short time. Rhodesia was changing. Rhodes himself was no longer the great white hero, the police had been taken out of the control of the company as a result of the Jameson Raid and were now supervised by the High Commissioner for South Africa. The really exciting times appeared to be over. Dansey weighed up the prospects and decided: he would move on. He was, after all, approaching his twenty-first birthday, and there was the rest of the world to be explored.

CHAPTER TWO

Bandits in Borneo

Dansey made his way home in a leisurely fashion, following the example of Baden-Powell by stopping off as a tourist in places which were likely to be of interest to Britain, either as potential trouble spots or as bases occupied by enemy or rival powers. His first call was in Madagascar, the huge island off the east coast of Africa

Madagascar was a fascinating and mysterious country. The French had occupied it as a protectorate in 1890, and when Dansey arrived they had just suppressed the ruling Hova dynasty of mad black queens. He was therefore able to travel around in comparative safety, secure in the knowledge that most of the more bizarre forms of trial by ordeal had been suppressed, too. Previously, the merest suspicion of unfriendly intentions towards Queen Ranavalona could lead to such unpleasant forms of "trial" as being forced to swim a river swarming with crocodiles, or pick coins from the bottom of a large cauldron of boiling water: those who survived unharmed were considered innocent. Perhaps the most unusual of the ordeals was known as the *tanguin*, after a local fruit with a highly poisonous stone. Scrapings of the stone were wrapped in three pieces of chicken skin, which the accused was forced to swallow. If he vomited them up again, he might be innocent. If he died, he was clearly guilty. He was also guilty, however, if he failed to disgorge the pieces of skin in the right way, and would then be liable to suffer one of the Queen's choice forms of execution, which ranged from being sawn in half, through crucifixion and flaying alive, to being sewn up in uncured animal skins and left to rot inside them. The first of the three Queen Ranavalonas, some thirty years earlier, had managed to slaughter half her subjects during her reign. She was obviously a suspicious woman.

Whatever his interest in the relics of this infamous dynasty, Dansey would not have allowed them to distract his attention from

35

studying the way the French governed and garrisoned the country, for at that time they were the arch rivals and often enemies of the British, and thus a prime target for a bright young man intent on some form of military career and acutely aware of the value of good intelligence.

From Madagascar he travelled back to the mainland, to East Africa, another area of intense competition among the imperial powers, where Germany occupied what was to become Tanganyika, and Britain's own possessions included Kenya and a share, along with France, Italy and Ethiopia, of a partitioned Somaliland. A few years later, Somaliland was to become Dansey's personal responsibility, but in 1898 he must have viewed Britain's newest acquisition with very little enthusiasm, for the coastal strip was arid, furnace hot and decidedly unwelcoming. He did not stay long.

Back in Britain, opportunities for entering the regular army were limited. He obtained a militia (non-regular) commission as a second lieutenant with the Lancashire Fusiliers on 13th June 1898, but the thirty-four days he spent with part-time soldiers at the annual training camps at Altcar, near Southport, and on Salisbury Plain must have seemed extremely tame. The regulars of the 2nd Battalion of the regiment had just fought in the battle of Omdurman, and Dansey managed to get permission to travel out to Egypt to join them, and then went with them to Crete, where they were to carry out internal security duties during the brief British administration which helped the island to establish itself as an independent republic after centuries under Turkish rule.

On 9th December, a mere five months after receiving his commission, he was promoted to lieutenant. When the 2nd Battalion moved on to Malta, he stayed briefly in Crete before returning home to continue his part-time duties with the 6th, and to look impatiently around for something more exciting.

He found it 7,000 miles away on a steamy island in the China Sea, as a sub-commandant in the police force of another chartered company, the British North Borneo Company.

It was probably thanks to a Gifford family connection that the young Claude Dansey got the job in the first place. He was twenty-three years old, and a newly recruited sub-commandant in the British North Borneo Company Police – a modest enough rank in a modest enough force. Disembarking from a ship at the port of Sandakan in the British North Borneo in December 1899 Dansey had every reason to look forward to an amusing but by no means arduous time in a little-known part of the world – a typical

36

Victorian gentleman's colonial adventure. But it was to prove more than that. Within a matter of weeks Dansey was to be pitchforked into battle. Indeed, he was to lead an attack on the fort of a native rebel leader, the remarkable Mat Salleh, once described as "a figure of romance . . . sprung from a line of Malayan princes . . . a warrior: gallant, ruthless, indomitable . . . with a quest before him and a woman behind him, fighting his hopeless battle against the oncoming tide of civilisation".

The third largest island in the world, Borneo, lies on the equator to the south-east of the South-East Asian mainland. In the nineteenth century various great powers, including Britain, Austria, Holland, Italy, Spain, Portugal and even the USA, attempted to establish a presence on the island and to exploit its resources. In 1865, the Americans managed to purchase a concession from the Sultan of Sarawak, but they did not prosper, and after ten years they sold it to Baron von Overbeck, the Austrian Consul General in Hong Kong. He in turn sold out the concession to Dent Brothers, a British trading company, run by Alfred and Edward Dent.

Alfred, the elder, dreamed of creating a second East India Company, a great commercial and colonial empire in South-East Asia, based upon Borneo. It was a grandiose vision: the old East India Company had ruled India and created an empire for Britain. But it was in keeping with the spirit of the times and was by no means impractical, as the subsequent history of the company showed. With this aim in view the brothers persuaded the British Government to grant the British North Borneo Company a royal charter which, it was thought, would lend the whole enterprise an air of prestige and stability, thus attracting City investment. But the London Court of Directors of the BNBC soon grew impatient: they did not share Alfred Dent's Rhodes-like vision; they expected profits and Borneo showed no sign of producing any.

In the face of his directors' opposition Alfred Dent was forced to resign as chairman in favour of William Clark Cowie, a Scottish trader and ex-gun runner, who became first managing director, then chairman of the company. Cowie promised the shareholders expansion and increased dividends. In the event, his policies were directly responsible for landing the company in debt and for creating the climate, if not the circumstances, for the Mat Salleh revolt, which was to bring Claude Dansey out from England.

Mat (Mahommed) Salleh was the son of a Bajau mother and Datoh Butu, the Sulu chief of a village on the Sugut River. Tall, good-looking, slightly pockmarked, he was famous for his physical strength and his eloquence. Rumour also had it that as a result of performing certain magical rites he had rendered himself invulnerable to bullets. His reputation was no doubt enhanced by the fact that his senior wife, the Dayang Bandang, niece of the Sultan of Sulu, was believed to be a witch, and in accordance with local custom was not permitted to set foot on earth, but was carried everywhere in a chair. She was also alleged to have poisoned her first husband in order to marry Salleh.

Salleh's first brush with the British occurred in 1894, when a force of the company's police tried to arrest him after two Dyak merchants, who had been unwise enough to venture up the headwaters of the Sugut River, had been killed in a brawl in his kampong. Unfortunately the police were themselves coastal Dyaks and therefore distrusted by the tribes who lived upriver. Salleh, fearing for his life, refused to meet the police except in the presence of his own armed men. Not surprisingly, under the circumstances, no arrest was made. Later Salleh did meet two government officials and swore on the Koran henceforward to abide by the laws of the British – an oath he conveniently forgot as soon as he returned to the kampong.

As his influence grew, so friction between Salleh and the British increased. During the next two years Salleh's men raided government posts and villages; in retaliation the British – with noticeable lack of success – mounted a series of punitive expeditions against him.

In 1897 things came to a head, when Salleh looted and burned shops, warehouses and government buildings on the island of Gaya, inflicting $100,000 worth of damage. The company found themselves unable to retaliate. Cowie's grandiose scheme to build a railway from Brunei Bay to Sandakan had almost bankrupted the company, and there was no money left to finance any more expeditions against the rebels. Cowie was forced to opt for diplomacy. Through the Sultan of Sulu and Salleh's wife, the witch Dayang Bandang, he arranged a meeting with the rebel. Acutely conscious of his Rhodes-like role, he went unarmed and alone to the meeting, a single European amongst a horde of savages.

His first glimpse of his adversary was of a tall, thin man dressed in the height of local fashion, "in a gold cap, a smart green embroidered tunic and Sulu embroidered trousers with a red waistband".

The negotiations were a great success. Salleh accepted Cowie's offer of a full pardon in return for the rebels withdrawing to the remote Tambunan Valley, where the company would give Salleh full authority, making him in effect King in his own domain. Cowie conveniently ignored the fact that the Tambunan Valley was not the company's to give. It was the home of the Dusans, an unattractive and aggressive tribe who lived in a state of almost permanent intoxication. To make matters worse, in his oral agreement with Salleh, Cowie had promised the rebels a complete pardon, but in the written document which he sent to London, it was made clear that any escaped prisoners serving with Salleh would not qualify for the amnesty, and since half his force was composed of escapees, this represented a considerable modification of the original proposal.

However, in a matter of weeks the rebels were on the warpath once again, with attacks and murders not only in the Tambunan Valley but also on the west coast. More government posts were burned and stores looted. It was clear by now that the British were facing a large-scale native rising. The administration decided to grasp the nettle. They must send a strong force of police to break the power of the rebels once and for all. The new sub-commandant fortuitously on his way out from England would naturally be a part of the force, since he already had experience of fighting rebels.

When Claude Dansey landed at Sandakan in December 1899, he found a place which in only twenty years had grown from a tiny native village into a thriving commercial centre with a sizeable and cosmopolitan population, including many Chinese merchants from the mainland who had adopted it as their principal base in North Borneo. Sandakan boasted a port and a harbour, with godowns (warehouses) filled with goods, and a town of white-painted wooden bungalows, mostly built on stilts. It was here that Captain C. H. Harington was assembling a force of company police, to consist of 100 armed men, mostly Sikhs, led by a handful of British officers, including Dansey. Since only human transport was able to reach the remote Tambunan Valley, 500 Dusan carriers had been hired to transport the equipment and military stores, including a seven-pounder mountain gun.

Dansey can only have had two or three days to acclimatise before he set out on foot with the company's expeditionary force on 22nd December. After weeks at sea he must have found nine days hard marching in equatorial heat over some of the roughest and hilliest terrain in the world a nightmare.

Meanwhile, Salleh had not been idle. He was busy acquiring fresh supplies of gunpowder and recruiting men for his cause. He already had several hundred, and now some 300 Bajau tribesmen and 1,000 Tegaas Muruts answered his call and joined his forces. As usual his intelligence was first class: he soon knew of the company's preparations for the expedition and their objective. No doubt he had also estimated their probable time of arrival in the Tambunan Valley. He fortified the Tegaas villages and organised a chain of forts, then sat back and waited.

Captain Harington decided to use Timbau, a village two and a half miles from the government post in the valley, as his forward base, though this was only 300 yards from the nearest of Salleh's fortified villages. In fact, they were so close that they were constantly harassed, day and night, by enemy sniper fire and but for the inadequate marksmanship of the tribesmen, the expedition could have come to grief on the first day or two. Salleh's snipers ambushed the British officers while they were playing "stump cricket", and had they been better shots there can be little doubt that this would have gone down as yet another aborted expedition, and the hero of this book might have died before his career had even begun.

The idea of playing cricket in the jungle under the guns of your enemy may be highly diverting and reminiscent of G. A. Henty at his most improbable, but it does suggest that Captain Harington's force was not in a satisfactory state of military readiness. That was soon to change, however, for Harington went down with fever and handed over command to the young Sub-Commandant Dansey. It is unlikely there were any more jolly games of cricket whilst he was in charge.

Things did not go entirely Dansey's way at first. On 8th January, accompanied by a party of Dyaks, he was out posting pickets to prevent enemy snipers getting close to his lines – something Harington seems to have neglected to do – when he came upon a fort hidden in the jungle. Dansey decided to attack at once, and led a charge at the head of his Dyaks. He found the fort was too heavily defended, and much to his chagrin was forced to retreat under heavy fire, covering his withdrawal with fire from the expedition's Maxim gun.

Undeterred by this setback, runs Governor Clifford's subsequent report, "on 9th January Mr Dansey decided to attack the Tegaas village of Piasan, which lay to the N.W. of the camp at Timbau". The village "was flanked on the west by two strong forts. The fort nearest the village was selected as the main point of attack". The seven-pounder was brought up and positioned on a rise overlooking the village, so that fire could be directed on to either of the forts or the village itself, forcing the defenders to keep their heads down while the main body of police attacked the fort.

"Fort Number 1," declares the report, "was rushed in capital style by the Indian police and all white officers, viz: Messrs Dansey, Fraser, Atkinson and Douglas." However, the police did not have things all their own way. They found the Tegaas villagers had been reinforced by Bajaus from Mat Salleh's band, "and they stood their ground so well that our men were unable to force an entrance". Eventually, Dansey and his men succeeded in destroying the fort by setting fire to it. Later in the day they "rushed the second fort, which is situated on a higher hill, and this they also destroyed".

Dansey was mentioned in despatches "for the dash and skill with which the operations were conducted . . . It is not every young officer . . . who would so readily have assumed the responsibility of commanding an assault on a position so difficult to attack, or who, having done so, would have succeeded in bringing the affair to a successful issue."

The attack on Piasan set the pattern for the expedition's subsequent tactics: forts were stormed and taken one by one, although often with great difficulty. Latob, one of the most strongly fortified of the villages, was only taken after two days of shelling and fighting. But as Dansey and his men pressed relentlessly forward, Salleh's followers began to lose heart. Soon, white flags were being raised in the remaining villages; the Tegaas Muruts had had enough, and surrendered to Dansey with all their guns.

By now, Mat Salleh's position was crumbling fast. He was left with just two forts and only the Bajau tribesmen remained loyal to him. By 20th January both forts were under fire. One, under the command of Mat Jator, Salleh's chief of staff, stood on a precipice overlooking the Pelagran River. Dansey and his men began shelling it on the twenty-first, and as luck would have it the second round to hit the building set light to a roof. There was a strong wind blowing, and in no time the whole place was engulfed in flames. The defenders died or fled, and when the fire had died the British gunners were able to move in and mount the seven-pounder amongst the ruins, from where they could bombard the remaining stronghold from a range of only 800 yards.

The construction of this fort was typical of those already stormed. It consisted of three concentric walls – an outer wall six feet thick and ten feet high, with two inner walls, both equally strong, and surrounded by a stockade and a bamboo network intended to slow up any assault party. To complete the picture, the ground in front of the walls was planted with sharpened bamboo stakes.

Captain Harington was now recovered from his fever, and resumed command. He established a ring of forward posts around the stronghold, effectively cutting Salleh off from his water supply, surrounding him, and subjecting him to constant fire during the day from the Maxim, the seven-pounder and police snipers. Salleh's position was now desperate. Hoping to prevent the fires that had destroyed his other fort, he ordered his men to remove the roofs from the houses inside the compound, and live in tunnels and dug-outs carved out of the ground. Conditions deteriorated, yet he still refused to surrender, perhaps believing that his stronghold was too formidable to be taken by assault.

Had Salleh and his men withdrawn into the jungle and continued to fight a guerilla war, the British would almost certainly have been forced to retreat and relinquish any claim to the Tambunan Valley. But apart from its obvious defensive potential, the possession of a fort conferred considerable status on its owner, and Mat Salleh was never a man to reject status, no matter how it was acquired. He stayed put.

The end, when it came, was an anti-climax, with no final death-or-glory charge. On the night of 31st January a Bajau woman was captured while escaping from the fort. Under interrogation she told the police that Mat Salleh was already dead, killed by a bullet from the Maxim at noon on the previous day. With their leader dead and buried, the last of his followers intended to break out at 3 a.m. that morning. The British officers were in two minds about whether to believe her. She could be laying a trap for them. But when in the early hours of the morning a child was heard crying in a rice field, they realised she had been telling the truth. The enemy was escaping. In the darkness and the confusion, there seemed little the police could do, but the Dyaks refused to wait until light. They had old tribal scores to settle with the Bajaus who had followed Salleh, and pursued them into the jungle, killing men, women and children indiscriminately.

When Dansey and the others entered the fort at dawn, they found it deserted. The stench of death was overpowering: corpses, rotted under the blazing sun, lay everywhere. They found Mat Salleh's grave. Wrapped in a white cloth, according to Muslim custom, he was buried under the flagpole. He had been hit by a bullet in the left temple. The Dayang Bandang, his formidable wife, was alive and was taken prisoner – perhaps her witchcraft had protected her even though it had been unable to save her husband.

Claude Dansey returned with the triumphant force to Sandakan. For him, one war had ended, but another was about to start. His Borneo adventure had lasted little more than ten weeks.

CHAPTER THREE

South Africa Again

When Claude Dansey decided to join the British North Borneo Constabulary, the war in South Africa had barely started and in Britain it was generally held that it could not last long. How could a bunch of ill-educated, untrained Boer farmers hope to stand against the might of the British Army?

But Britain had been in for a series of rude shocks. The Boers might appear to be a disorganised rabble, but in fact they were skilful fighters, excellent horsemen and deadly accurate shots. Their self-contained fighting units, which they called commandos, were capable of taking on and beating British infantry who were still using the set-piece tactics of the Napoleonic wars, advancing in close order and forming squares and lines from which to fire crashing volleys of musketry. In addition, the Boers outnumbered the British: the Boer army at this stage comprised some 45,000 men, while the British had only 20,000 troops in South Africa.

By the end of the year, the disorganised rabble had inflicted a number of crushing defeats on the British, and had three towns under siege: Kimberley, where Cecil Rhodes was with the defenders; Ladysmith, where the GOC Natal, Lieutenant-General Sir George White, was trapped; and Mafeking, which was under the command of Colonel Robert Baden-Powell. It was unthinkable that Britain should lose this war. The Boers had to be taught their lesson, even though it meant sending hundreds of thousands of troops from Britain, India and other parts of the Empire.

The rallying cry was sounded, and answered in Canada, in Australia, in New Zealand – and in Lancashire. The 6th Battalion Lancashire Fusiliers volunteered for service in South Africa. The War Office accepted the offer on 5th January and ordered them to sail at the beginning of February. A message was flashed to Borneo: Dansey was to leave immediately to join his regiment in South Africa, with a regular army commission as a lieutenant. He

43

caught the first boat out of Sandakan, which took him to Ceylon, and on 21st March 1900 he was sailing out of Colombo and heading back across the Indian Ocean, a full-time professional British officer at last.

The 6th Battalion had been posted to the Orange River Station, on the border of the Orange Free State not far from Bloemfontein and some 600 miles up the railway from Cape Town. Dansey hurried to join them, arriving just in time to be selected for a special force that was being assembled further north, at Kimberley. It was an opportunity he must have leapt at, for it was the column being sent to relieve Mafeking, the last of the besieged towns.

Mafeking, in fact, had been under siege since 13th October, the first full day of the war. But it was not a very efficient siege. Regular newspaper reports were received from correspondents trapped in the town. After six months, the dusty little railway siding in the middle of nowhere had become a symbol of defiance and bravery, the very epitome of British pluck and nonchalance in the face of danger. The stiffest of all the stiff upper lips among the defenders belonged undoubtedly to the man in command, Robert Baden-Powell, rapidly becoming an international celebrity and enjoying every minute of it. He had set the style for the whole episode with his very first message to GHQ at the beginning of the siege. "All well," it read. "Four hours' bombardment. One dog killed. Baden-Powell."

In March there had been an attempt to relieve Mafeking, made by a column of Rhodesian troops under the command of Lieutenant-Colonel Herbert Plumer, the same man who four years earlier had raised a relief column in Mafeking and Kimberley to march to the rescue of Dansey and his companions during the Matabele Rising. Plumer had managed to get to within five miles of Mafeking, but he had less than 700 men and no proper guns and had been forced to withdraw with heavy losses when the Boers almost surrounded him. Baden-Powell had had to stay put, with his supplies – he said – running dangerously short.

The tide of the war, however, had begun to turn in Britain's favour at last, and Lord Roberts, the Commander-in-Chief South Africa, felt able to spare enough men and equipment to mount a proper relief operation. It was time for the siege to be ended and for B-P to emerge and receive his rewards, and Claude Dansey had the good fortune to be involved.

A flying column was being assembled at Barkly West, some twenty miles north-west of Kimberley, under the command of Colonel Bryan Mahon, an Anglo-Irishman with a reputation as a most dashing commander, newly arrived from inflicting defeats on the Queen's enemies in Egypt and the Sudan. The column was to march north towards Mafeking and rendezvous with Plumer, whose force had been strengthened by the addition of a battery of the Royal Canadian Artillery and a contingent of Queensland Mounted Infantry from Australia.

The composition of the two columns had been carefully considered to gain the maximum emotional impact throughout the Empire, for they were to represent the Empire coming to the rescue of its own. In addition to Plumer's Rhodesians, Canadians and Australians, the majority of Mahon's men were Johannesburg Uitlanders of the Imperial Light Horse and the Kimberley Mounted Corps, plus a battery of the Royal Horse Artillery – with its guns the premier regiment of the British army – two machine guns and 100 British infantrymen specially selected for the occasion from conveniently placed Fusilier battalions, twenty-five each from English, Scottish, Welsh and Irish regiments. To Dansey's delight, the 6th Battalion Lancashire Fusiliers were stationed in the right place and he had arrived at the right time with exactly the right qualifications to be an obvious candidate.

There were many reasons why Dansey would have welcomed the chance of taking part in the relief of Mafeking, quite apart from the pleasure of sharing in the glory of a moment in history. It was an opportunity to be back in the thick of the action again, as he had been in Rhodesia and Borneo. It was valuable experience for a young officer, which would look good on his record. But above all, there was the fact that he knew many of those in Mafeking and in Plumer's column, for there were many of his ex-colleagues from the British South Africa Police in both.

He would have felt equally at home with some of the officers in Mahon's column. In many ways it was like the Jameson Raid all over again, though this time the troops were marching to Mafeking rather than from it, and were going with government approval.

The column left Barkly West in the early morning of 4th May, snaking across the veld under a great cloud of dust. It covered the first 129 miles in five days, or rather five nights – because of the intense heat and lack of water *en route* Mahon chose to move mostly at night and in the very early morning. They had a brief pause in the little town of Vryburg, which had only just been evacuated by the Boers – the inhabitants barely had time to change the Vierkleur for the Union Jack before Mahon marched in – then pressed on relentlessly. Mahon had not gained the nickname "the Mahout" (the elephant driver) for nothing. He drove his men hard, covering the ground at an astonishing rate for the conditions.

Dansey was being reintroduced to the rigours of Africa with a vengeance.

On 11th May a scout from Plumer's column found them, having slipped in and out of Mafeking on the way, to report to Baden-Powell. B-P had asked for details of the size and strength of the relief column, to be sent in with a messenger. This posed a slight problem, since there was no agreed code for use between the two forces, and any message was liable to fall into Boer hands. Frank Rhodes, brother of the great Cecil, who was with the column, solved the problem in a typically British way. The message read:

"Our numbers are Naval and Military Club multiplied by ten; our guns, the number of sons in the Ward family; our supplies, the OC 9th Lancers."

Neither Plumer nor Baden-Powell found any difficulty in interpreting it: numbers, 940 (94 Piccadilly x 10); guns, 6 (the Earl of Dudley and his five brothers); supplies, few (Lieutenant-Colonel Little).

For the most part, Mahon's column, despite the impossibility of keeping its location secret thanks to the dust cloud it created, had avoided any direct contact with the Boers, partly by taking an unexpected route across country instead of following the roads or railway tracks, and partly because of the speed at which it was travelling. On 13th May, however, a force of about 900 Boers managed to get ahead of the column and attempted to ambush it. A fierce fight took place before they were driven off. The column lost five killed and twenty-six wounded or missing; the Boers lost at least twenty-two killed. Dansey escaped unharmed.

Two days later, they reached the rendezvous with Plumer's column, which had itself arrived only a few hours before, a remarkable piece of co-ordination after a combined marching distance of several hundred miles through enemy-held territory. Now, they were ready to do battle with the 2,000 or so Boers who were awaiting them eighteen miles away around Mafeking.

It was probably at this time that Dansey went out on the scouting missions, "slugging Boer sentries", as the London clubmen recalled some forty years later. Certainly Mahon sent out scouts to discover the Boer strength and disposition, and he made good use of the information they brought him. When he began his advance at dawn on the morning of 16th May, he was not only prepared for every move Commandant de la Rey made in trying to encircle the British force, but was also able to keep moving forward continuously, with only slight casualties, until he gained control of the high ground in the late afternoon and finally drove the Boers back into their positions.

That night, while everyone waited for dawn, Mahon sent out his scouts again – another opportunity for Dansey to take his loaded sock to the sentries – discovered a clear path into the town, and marched his column through under cover of darkness. When the Boers awoke next morning, they found them camped on the polo ground. It did not take long for the remaining Boers to be driven off into the bush. The siege was over, after 217 days. The twenty-three-year-old Lieutenant Dansey had notched up another valuable experience.

Mafeking may have been over, but the war was far from finished. Indeed, for Dansey it was only just beginning. Riding with Mahon's column and meeting up with Plumer's men of the British South Africa Police had brought him back into touch with the colonials he had known three or four years earlier. It had also brought him to the attention of those in authority, who no doubt realised that his talents and experience were wasted with a militia battalion of British infantry.

Before he had time to draw breath, he found himself seconded to the wildest and most glamorous of all the Uitlander outfits, the South African Light Horse, where his fellow subalterns included the Churchill brothers, Winston and Jack. Winston, in South Africa as war correspondent for the *Morning Post*, had persuaded the then Commander-in-Chief, General Redvers Buller, to allow him to enrol with the regiment after his escape from a Boer prison camp made him the most famous hero of the war, until Baden-Powell eclipsed all others. Although he was still a correspondent, he rode and fought with the "Cockyolibirds" as they were known because of the ostrich feather plumes they wore in their Boer hats.

Churchill's presence was another stroke of good fortune for Dansey, who struck up a friendship with him which, though never particularly close, would always give him direct access to the great man. Those who have ridden and fought together, sharing dangers, and hardships, often develop bonds of enduring friendship in a remarkably short time. This seems to have been the case with Dansey and Churchill. As the years rolled by, the relationship was to have a vital effect on Dansey's career on several occasions. It was a friendship which even managed to survive Dansey selling Churchill a rather poor horse – a coup which still amused Dansey in recollection in later life.

The South African Light Horse had been formed in Cape Town in November 1899 by Colonel Charles à Court, as part of a plan by

General Buller, to raise a force of colonial irregulars who could ride and shoot like the Boers. À Court found there were large numbers of refugee Uitlanders in the Cape who were disappointed at not having been able to join the Imperial Light Horse when it was formed in Natal a few weeks earlier. Buller gave him the go-ahead, and full support, though he replaced à Court's choice of commanding officer with another member of his staff, Lieutenant-Colonel Julian Byng, later to become Field Marshal Lord Byng of Vimy, one of the most successful commanders of the first world war and Governor-General of Canada from 1921 to 1926.

The SALH took the pick of the volunteers who clamoured to join. Although primarily intended as an Uitlander regiment, its only basic requirements were that a man should be able to ride and shoot, and should be physically fit. "We took fine young fellows from every mail boat that arrived," said à Court, "and we took Texas cowboys who turned up with mules from New Orleans. The scorn in the look of the cowboys when I asked them if they could ride was worth seeing. But there was one mare at our depot which no one could ride. She would go like a sheep and then suddenly begin to behave like a snake, bucking and twisting in the air until she not only unshipped her rider but got rid of her saddle and bridle, too. She was a great abater of cowboy pride. 'Well, I did expect, Captain, that the tackle would hold,' said one cowboy ruefully as he rose from the ground amidst the derisive shouts of previous victims."

Dansey managed to survive such ordeals and prove himself a worthy member of the regiment. Byng obviously thought so, for as soon as a vacancy occurred he "gave him the position of Squadron Leader, having formed a very high opinion of his qualities", a position which Dansey filled to Byng's "entire satisfaction" until the end of the campaign which marked the conclusion of the first phase of the war.

The scramble to form and train the new regiment had been hampered by shortages of rifles, transport and equipment – at one stage à Court had been reduced to inspecting cast-off greatcoats from the Metropolitan Police in a second-hand clothes shop "and wondering whether it was to be that or nothing". But within five weeks of enlisting the first recruit three squadrons had been in action at Colenso, 1,000 miles from Cape Town, as part of the first, disastrous attempt to relieve the besieged town of Ladysmith.

It was, as à Court himself described it, a "mighty fine regiment"– though it earned itself the nickname "Byng's Burglars" because of its "predatory and looting habits". Dansey must have been delighted to be a part of it, for he fitted in perfectly. Almost immediately, he found himself in action at Laing's Nek, the vital pass across the Drakensberg Mountains known as the Gibraltar of Natal, giving access from the coast to Pretoria, Johannesburg and the Transvaal.

The SALH seized and occupied Van Wyk mountain, which commanded the pass, with the loss of six killed and four wounded in a resolute attack made on them by the Boers under cover of a grass fire. From Laing's Nek the regiment rode on to the next important point on the railway at Standerton, where they surprised a Boer commando in the early morning, defeated them after a stiff fight then ate the breakfast the Boers had been preparing for themselves, before moving on again to capture a prize of eighteen railway engines, which were of great value in opening up and operating the vital rail supply line.

It was exciting soldiering, with plenty of skirmishing and scouting. By 13th September Dansey had established himself well enough to be mentioned in despatches as one of the officers and men who had "performed special acts of bravery or have been selected for, and successfully carried out, arduous reconnaissances or dangerous duties". He seemed to be assured of a successful military career as a dashing cavalry commander. But the future was beckoning him from an entirely different quarter, and by the end of the year he found himself occupied with other, more prophetic duties.

It seemed in September 1900 that the war was over. The Boer army had been smashed, President Kruger had fled over the frontier into Mozambique, and thence to Europe. The Orange Free State was now the Orange River Colony, and the annexation of the Transvaal was about to be officially announced. It had taken the British just about a year to lumber into action, avenge their earlier defeats and crush the impudent Afrikaners who had dared to challenge the imperial authority. The generals and the field marshals could sail home to collect their plaudits and rewards.

But had the war really finished? Kruger might have fled, and General Prinsloo might have surrendered, but Generals De Wet, Botha and de la Rey were still at large with 30,000 men. Field Marshal Roberts haughtily announced that he would soon starve the "banditti" into submission, and so stamp out the last dying embers of the conflict. He would, in that fateful phrase which seems to have been repeated down the years, be home for Christmas.

In the event, it was not to prove so easy. The formal war was indeed finished, the war where armies opposed each other and fought pitched battles. But a new and far more bitter war was just beginning, a war that was to set the pattern which still exists today in many parts of the globe: a guerilla war. The Boers appeared and disappeared like will-o'-the-wisps, striking hard and fast and then melting into the landscape and back into the civil population. In the first phase of the war, the commanders had had to rethink the instruction manuals, throw out the text-books and invent new styles of fighting to cope with the development of the smokeless cartridge, breech-loading rifle and quick-firing machine gun. The first phase had seen the beginning of conventional modern warfare centred on the trench, for the Boer's secret weapon had turned out to be the shovel. The second phase of the war was to mark the beginning of unconventional modern warfare. The rule book would have to be rethought all over again, after only twelve months.

One of the maxims that was quickly realised was that the guerilla's most powerful weapon is surprise. The most important weapon for those combating guerilla forces is therefore intelligence, for it is only through good use of intelligence that the element of surprise can be removed. While the army was being reorganised into columns which could be sent out to scour the countryside for guerilla forces, small enough to move fast and react quickly, yet large enough to strike powerfully, the Intelligence Department of the General Staff set about recruiting more men who had the right sort of background, experience and personal qualities to make good intelligence officers, capable of finding out by every possible means, including the use of agents and spies, where the enemy were and what they intended to do. Lieutenant C. E. M. Dansey, commanding "A" Squadron of the South African Light Horse, was an ideal candidate. On 29th November 1900 he became a member of the Intelligence Department.

The Intelligence Department had already undergone rapid and extensive development since the beginning of the war. At the start it had been desperately undermanned and desperately under-financed: in the two years before the war, the Boers spent £340,000 on their Secret Service; the British Director of Military Intelligence, Major-General Sir John Ardagh, asked for £10,000, but was given only £100, and even that was regarded as a special concession. Even so, he had been able to provide a steady stream of good intelligence. Although his department was blamed in large part for the early disasters which almost destroyed the British army in South Africa, the accusations that it had failed to warn of the true strength or intentions of the Boers were entirely without foundation. Ardagh had been detailing the dangers in a series of excellent papers since 1896, and in 1898 he had even issued a handbook on South Africa which listed with amazing accuracy the numbers of the Boers' men, guns, ammunition, equipment and spending.

The intelligence had been good. Unfortunately, no one had wanted to hear. The information had been politically inconvenient, and did not fit the preconceived ideas of those in power. It was a lesson Dansey learned well, and which greatly influenced his thinking and his actions some forty years later, when an even greater threat to peace was being ignored by the British Government.

In July 1899, while Ardagh was struggling to convince the government of the true state of affairs in South Africa, General Redvers Buller was told in great secrecy that "in the unlikely event of war" he would be given command of an expeditionary force of 10,000 men. In the meantime, he was to do nothing and say nothing to anybody, in case the Boers should be offended by military preparations. However, the head of the South African section of the Intelligence Department, Major A. E. Latham, managed to get permission to send out ten special service officers to supplement the work of the only two intelligence officers then stationed in the whole of South Africa – one each for Cape Colony and Natal. The new men included Baden-Powell, who went to Mafeking to cover the borders of the Transvaal, Bechuanaland, the Orange Free State and Rhodesia; Scott-Turner, MacInnes and O'Meara, who went to Kimberley; and Major David Henderson, who went to Ladysmith where he was joined in September by Latham himself. Baden-Powell, of course, had other duties to perform besides his intelligence function.

Their intelligence gathering activities were rigorously restricted by officials who were anxious that they do nothing which the Boers might consider "provocative" (another phrase which rings down the years and is still with us). They were not allowed to recruit agents or spies, and had to content themselves for the most part with cycling along the frontiers pretending to be tourists and making surreptitious sketches.

When the war actually started, their activities were even more restricted – for they had positioned themselves in the three towns which were promptly besieged by the Boers. The result was that when Buller arrived at Cape Town in November – without a single intelligence officer on his staff – only one of the original ten was free. The rest had all been either captured or besieged. Ironically, the only one remaining was the most junior of them all, Second-

Lieutenant A. N. Campbell of the Royal Artillery, who therefore had the distinction of becoming, for the time being at any rate, General Buller's entire intelligence staff.

Campbell was soon replaced by a more experienced man, the Hon. T. K. Murray, a local character who had been a scout in the Zulu wars. Although Murray was a civilian, he had been asked by David Henderson before he was locked away in Ladysmith, to raise a force of scouts to be known as the Corps of Guides. Buller ordered Murray to continue with this, and he enlisted a total of forty-five white men and fifty Africans, chosen for their knowledge of the Dutch and Kaffir languages and experience of veld life, including riding and shooting. They were all volunteers and were expected not only to serve without pay but also to provide their own horses, saddlery and rifles. It was the first of several such outfits, and although it was no substitute for a properly organised Field Intelligence Department it was at least a step in the right direction.

Throughout the remainder of the first phase of the war, the intelligence organisation developed and improved rapidly. When Field Marshal Lord Roberts replaced the unfortunate Buller as Commander-in-Chief South Africa he took with him not only General Herbert Kitchener from India as Chief of Staff but also Colonel George Henderson from the Staff College at Camberley to be his Head of Intelligence.

Henderson (no relation to David Henderson) was already well-known in the army as a radical thinker. He was the author of several text-books and a biography of his hero, the American Confederate general, Stonewall Jackson. He immediately set about reorganising the intelligence set-up, and when he was invalided home in the summer of 1900 he was able to hand over an efficient and successful department of some thirty officers and white subordinates, plus a network of spies, agents and scouts throughout the country, to his successor, Colonel Hume.

It was Hume, therefore, who recruited Claude Dansey into full-time intelligence work. It was Hume, too, who saw the need for further changes and developments to cope with the new situation of guerilla warfare. He wrote a paper detailing his proposals, calling for intelligence officers to be part of every column, whatever its size, as well as at divisional level, which had marked the previous limit of their use. They should be centrally co-ordinated but should control their own agents and their own small, specialised staffs. Another innovation he called for was the combining of operational intelligence and counter-intelligence in the system. In his report he stated: "Detective work in connection with rebels, although essentially for the Civil Authorities, must for obvious reasons be concluded [arranged] by the Military Authorities, and therefore by the Field Intelligence Department." Censorship of the press and of private mail must be carried out by the Field Intelligence Department, too. And he stressed the need for training intelligence personnel in peacetime.

Hume was an excellent mentor for the young Dansey. But he departed in February 1901, and it was a new DMI, David Henderson, now promoted to colonel, who had the job of putting most of his ideas into practice. Henderson, a splendid character who later founded the Royal Flying Corps and sponsored the modern Intelligence Corps, did not simply follow Hume's ideas. He added several of his own, some of which were important innovations with far-reaching effects on intelligence operations.

He set up a small branch responsible for translating captured enemy documents and Boer newspapers – appreciating that newspapers can be an extremely valuable source of information. He organised courses to instruct intelligence officers in field sketching, report writing and interrogation techniques. He started the whole field of modern signals intelligence, and introduced the use of pigeons and bicycles to speed communications, both of which were to prove valuable during the first world war. He developed the use of manned balloons for observation, not only in static positions but also on the march, with the balloon attached to a moving cart.

Signals intelligence began with small parties of men being sent out into the bush to intercept Boer heliograph messages. It developed rapidly, and when at the end of the war the British cable censor in Aden broke the cipher used in messages from General Botha in South Africa to the exiled President Kruger in Holland, the shape of things to come was clearly defined.

We do not know exactly what Dansey's duties were as a staff lieutenant in the Field Intelligence Department, though it is certain he would have been trained in all the various activities in which it was involved. A contemporary who joined the department at much the same time, Lieutenant (later Major-General) J. F. C. "Boney" Fuller, described his own experiences as bearing at least some resemblance to those of a lawman in the American West. He was given "seventy unreliable Kaffir scouts to command and the job of watching . . . 4,000 square miles of only partially pacified Orange Free State in order to find the enemy, report his whereabouts and keep him under observation". Fuller "rode the veld with his horsemen, exchanged shots with chance-met Boers, raided and searched homesteads, captured and interrogated prisoners, and guided parties of more regular troops in raids and minor assaults".

53

Dansey almost certainly had similar experiences, as well as working in several other capacities, since he stayed in the FID until it was disbanded at the end of May 1902, when the Boers finally surrendered. He could hardly have chosen a better time for his baptism, joining at the very birth of the modern Secret Service, for the reorganisation in the field was only part of the great upheaval which was taking place in the Intelligence Service as a whole, both military and civil. Many of the lessons learned in South Africa were relevant not only in terms of an army at war, but across the entire area of secret intelligence and counter-intelligence, and Dansey would be one of the men responsible for applying them.

Dansey had found his niche, and while most of the army was being hurriedly shipped home to Britain, he stayed on in South Africa. He was posted on 24th June 1902 as ADC to Brigadier-General Charles Blomfield, commander of the Harrismith District in the Orange River Colony, just over the Drakensberg Mountains from Ladysmith, where he was responsible for intelligence and counter-intelligence work, reporting to the new Directorate of Military Operations at the War Office, which now incorporated the old Intelligence Division.

Blomfield had been the commanding officer of the 2nd Battalion Lancashire Fusiliers, the unit to which Dansey had officially belonged since his secondment to the South African Light Horse and which still carried his name on its nominal roll. Dansey stayed with him in Harrismith until 20th April 1904, when MO found another use for his talents. Blomfield gave him an excellent reference when he left, summing up his character swiftly and accurately:

Lieut. C. E. Dansey has been my Aide-de-Camp from the 24th June 1902 to the present date. He has performed his duties to my entire satisfaction.

He is a man of extremely temperate habits and physically very hard and wiry.

He is most active and energetic, enterprising and resourceful and can always be relied on to carry to a successful conclusion any work he undertakes.

I can confidently recommend him in any capacity in which the qualities above mentioned are necessary or desirable qualifications for success.

Signed. Charles Blomfield
Br General Commanding
Harrismith District

Dansey was to need all the "qualities above mentioned" in his new job, for it was away to the north in British Somaliland, that arid and unwelcoming country on the Horn of Africa, where there was trouble with a rebel leader known as the Mad Mullah.

CHAPTER FOUR

The Mad Mullah

His real name was Muhammad 'Abdille Hassan. It was the British who christened him the "Mad Mullah". He was born some time between 1856 and 1864 by a watering hole in the Dulbahante country in the north-eastern part of what was to become British Somaliland Protectorate. In fact, he was not mad nor, strictly speaking, a mullah. But for twenty-one years he was to be a thorn in the side of the British, and for five of those he was to prove Dansey's most dangerous adversary to date.

One might well ask what grand strategic considerations impelled the British to lay claim to yet another hot and inhospitable land on the opposite shore of the Gulf of Aden. After all Aden itself, which controlled the approaches to the Red Sea and thus the short route to India via the Suez Canal, had been British since 1839. The reason, however, was alimental rather than political: it was all a question of food. Somaliland was Aden's larder, and in particular the principal source of mutton: each year over 70,000 head of Somali sheep were shipped across the Gulf to feed the British garrison in Aden.

But other powers were also showing an interest in the area. France, Italy and Egypt had all succeeded in establishing zones of interest in Somaliland, while Ethiopia had historical claims on the territory. In 1897, after some twelve years of discreet diplomatic scrimmaging amongst the powers, the country was duly partitioned between Britain, France, Italy and Ethiopia. As its share, Britain acquired on the Horn of Africa some 68,000 square miles of territory, roughly the shape of a ham.

Across this harsh and pitiless landscape roamed the Somali. A pastoral, nomadic people, they spent their lives in an endless quest for pasturage and water for their sheep and goats and herds of camels. Water was the conditioning factor of their lives, and it was scarce. Pools and rivers dried up two months after the rains; wells, which gave a permanent supply, lay anything from ten to 130 miles apart. Even then the water had to be hauled up in skin buckets from fifty or eighty feet below the surface, and much of it was undrinkable. In the Nogal Valley, for example, the well water was impregnated with sulphuretted hydrogen which, while not offensive to stock, could poison the herdsmen. In other places it contained chemicals in sufficient quantities to act as a violent purgative; or else it was brackish or muddy or infected.

Not surprisingly the inhabitants of such an environment were not noted for the mildness of their disposition. The Somalis were ferocious warriors constantly engaged in tribal conflicts. Their courage and indifference to pain was legendary. One case, reported by a British army doctor, is typical. A Somali warrior was severely wounded in a skirmish. The man suffered not only a gunshot wound in the spinal area but also multiple spear wounds, one of which partially disembowelled him. Nonetheless he crawled for five hours in the blazing sun, dragging some twelve feet of gut behind him. He was found, patched up, and lived to fight another day.

Over the years the British administrators and political officers came to regard the Somali with a kind of appalled admiration. A Somali, complained Brigadier-General Sir Eric Swayne, "will walk off. . . leaving two months' back pay and rations behind him, if he considers his lordly dignity insulted". Perhaps the national character was best summed up by a Bugandan policeman who once irritably observed, "each Somali his own Sultan".

Muhammad 'Abdille Hassan was typical of this race of Sultans. His religious career followed the traditional pattern. He began the study of the Koran at the age of seven; eight years later he decided to devote his life to religion; and at nineteen he was accorded the title of "Sheikh" as tribute to his religious learning and piety. In 1894, with thirteen companions, he set out on the Hadj, the pilgrimage to Mecca which every Muslim is required to make, and there he fell under the spell of a charismatic religious teacher and mystic, Sayyid Muhammad Salih, the founder of the Salihiya Order, a reformist Muslim brotherhood noted for its puritanism and strict adherence to the "Straight Path" (i.e. the laws of God). He was transformed by the experience, having been made, it is said, "to see visions of the Prophet and angels . . . the spirit which went into his head never really left him for the rest of his life".

Legend has it that the Sheikh and his thirteen Somali companions vowed on the Prophet's tomb in Mecca to wage holy war on the four infidel nations that had divided their land. The Sheikh spent the rest of his life fulfilling his vow.

He returned to Somaliland and, "in the power of the spirit", began his ministry at Berbera. He soon became embroiled in a series of bitter theological controversies with the local religious notables, most of whom were members of the older Qaadiriya Brotherhood, a less rigorous order than the Salihiya.

The Sheikh denounced smoking, the chewing of the *qaat* plant (a stimulant similar in its effect to benzedrine), the gorging of the fat of sheep's tail, and condemned all indulgence in foreign luxuries. But he won few adherents in Berbera – which is perhaps not surprising since many of the local Somali merchants were engaged in importing the very luxuries against which the Sheikh inveighed. Angered by their indifference, he took his wives and camels and trekked inland, where he was welcomed by the local tribes as an eminent man of religion. As such, he was automatically accepted as a mediator and peacemaker in inter-clan disputes. He adjusted grievances, and expounded and enforced the law of Islam with grim severity. A man found guilty of theft lost his right hand for a first offence, his left foot for the second; lips, ears, eyelids, followed for subsequent offences. From time to time the Sheikh exchanged letters discussing tribal matters with the British vice-consul in Berbera, and on occasion would send Somali wrong-doers for trial in the vice-consular court. As a result of these endeavours the Sheikh acquired great influence amongst the tribes of the interior, and for a while even basked briefly in the approbation of the British – until they heard samples of his poetry.

The Sheikh was not merely a religious and political leader but also a poet. Today he is considered the most outstanding Somali poet of the twentieth century. He once compared his own poetry to "the blinding flash of a thunderbolt".

Most of his verse is devoted to political and religious subjects, but on occasion he shows himself to be a master of invective and ridicule. In *The Road To Damnation*, a short sermon in poetic form, he contrasts his own piety with the evil lives of those who oppose him – men like those of "the Hagar lineage, with their cankered testicles" and the Iidoor people whose fate it is "to remain forever as stupid as donkeys;/ And since the day of Adam, it is their lot to trot in terror behind the infidels". No one could have accused the Sheikh of that.

He summed up his own political purposes, with classic brevity, in a poem called "The Will": "I have sought and found the Prophetic guidance/to tell the unbelieving white invaders: 'This land is not yours'."

58

The situation between the Sheikh and the British continued to fester – until the Affair of Hussain's Rifle. In retrospect it may appear a trifling matter, but it was the match that lit the fuse of revolt in Somaliland.

The facts, if such they be, are blurred and uncertain – as one suspects they were to the protagonists. Even the identity of the offending Hussain is unknown. Recent research suggests that his name was, in fact, Du'ale Hirsi. At any rate, as far as can be established, it appears that this man turned up at the Sheikh's camp and offered to sell him a rifle – a rifle which, as it happened, belonged to the British army. Now it is not clear whether the Sheikh did or did not purchase the firearm, nor is it clear whether or not he knew the rifle had been stolen. The British vice-consul in Berbera jumped to the conclusion, perhaps not unreasonably, that he did buy the gun and did know that it was not Hussain's to sell. Therefore on 23rd March 1899 he wrote to the Sheikh demanding its return. The Sheikh, annoyed by the accusation that he was guilty of receiving stolen property, wrote his reply on the back of the vice-consul's letter. For reasons that remain unclear he wrote it out twice: the same message written both large and small. "I have stolen nothing from you nor from any other person," he wrote. "Seek what you want from him who robbed you . . ."

On 1st September 1899 the British consul general received a further letter from the Sheikh. "You have oppressed our ancient religion without cause," it declared. "Whatever people obey you they are liars and slanderers." The letter concluded with the words: "Now choose for yourselves. If you want war, we accept it; if you want peace, pay the fine." The consul general retaliated by proclaiming Sayyid Muhammad 'Abdille Hassan a rebel and forbidding all men from giving him aid and succour. In addition he urged on the government of London the importance of mounting a military expedition against the trouble-maker. But war in South Africa prevented any immediate action.

First, the Sheikh (now Sayyid: an honorific title used here as "Lord" or "Master") turned his attention to the Ethiopians. The Sayyid's men had taken to looting the trading caravans which crossed the Ogaden, some of them under Ethiopian protection. Determined to punish the wrong-doers, the Ethiopian Government despatched a military expedition which after several weeks of marching and counter-marching failed to make contact with the Sayyid's men. It did, however, manage to run off with a number of camels and livestock. This so angered the Somalis that the Sayyid had no difficulty in raising a force to attack the Ethiopian post at Jigjiga, where the

Sayyid's men inflicted a heavy defeat on their adversaries.
After such a set-back the Ethiopians proposed a joint action with
the British. It was to be the first of four such joint military ventures
between 1901 and 1904, each designed to crush the power of the
Sayyid. In all they cost the British taxpayer £5,500,000 to finance,
and in military terms they were a failure. The Sayyid's men,
employing daring guerilla tactics, won a number of notable victories. At Gumburu Hill, for example, on 17th April 1903 nine British
officers and 189 men were killed.

But not even the Sayyid could hope to hold three European
governments at bay for ever with a force consisting of only a few
thousand nomads armed mostly with spears and daggers. Late in
1904, in the face of mounting losses, he decided to sue for peace.
But on his own terms. His peace initiative was preceded by a
strategic withdrawal. Accompanied by his followers, with their
flocks and herds, he prudently retreated into Italian territory
where he concluded a treaty.

The British heaved a sigh of relief. Here was a dangerous
opponent who had been, if not eliminated, then at least swept under the carpet – somebody else's carpet, which made it even better.
Nevertheless, the Sayyid still remained a free agent, still dangerous,
and still determined to liberate his country from the infidel.

But at least the British felt secure enough to withdraw their
forces to the northern coastal strip, relying on the presence of the
Dulbhante and Warsangeli tribes to provide a *cordon sanitaire*
against the Sayyid's men.

It was left to a small band of British political and intelligence
officers, assisted by a mixed force of local militia, armed police and
four companies of the King's African Rifles – some 2,000 men in all
– to counteract the Sayyid's influence amongst the tribes of the
hinterland. And that influence grew steadily. If there were few
Somalis who had heard of Muhammad 'Abdille Hassan before
1901, then his deeds against the infidel and his poems, which were
carried by word of mouth from tribe to tribe, soon made him
famous throughout the country.

This then was the situation which faced the twenty-eight-year-
old Captain Dansey when he was posted to the British Somaliland
Protectorate in 1904 as Chief Political and Intelligence Officer.
Until his arrival there had been little in the way of organised
intelligence gathering, but now all that was to change. Fresh from
South Africa, where he had learned field intelligence on active
service against the Boers and had also gained a knowledge of
counter-intelligence work during his time in Harrisburg, Dansey
was determined to put his ideas into practice. A new system of

native scouts and spies had to be organised, for without an inflow of intelligence the British forces would be operating in a fog – blind men striking at an enemy who knew every move they made. The authorities at Berbera, believing that their old adversary was now safely bottled up in Italian Somaliland, felt they had nothing more to fear. Dansey's spies were soon to prove them wrong. The Sayyid was alive and well and already on the move, and Dansey was quickly in action against his agents. Mostly Dansey's work involved routine intelligence gathering from his own agents amongst the tribes, but he was also called upon to lead various counter-intelligence operations aimed at frustrating the Sayyid's plans. A couple of examples show the pattern of such operations.

One of the Sayyid's conditions for peace which had been agreed as part of the Treaty of Illig, signed by the Italian consul general Pestalozza, was freedom to trade with whomsoever he pleased. What no one had foreseen was that the Sayyid would find a way to exploit this particular clause in order to make a demonstration of his strength amongst those tribes who had thrown in their lot with the colonial powers.

The Sayyid was entitled to send a caravan to trade in Berbera. However, it turned out that the caravan was to be escorted by a guard of no fewer than ninety armed and mounted Dervishes* – a considerably greater force than was necessary for the protection of the caravan. It was a move designed to embarrass the authorities. If the British permitted the passage of so many armed men through the territory of tribes friendly to them, next time it might be double or treble that number, and clashes would be inevitable. As it was, even ninety armed Dervishes would be enough to create panic amongst the merchants of Berbera once again, and possibly intimidate any of the clans wavering in their loyalty to the British. The Sayyid was saying to his countrymen: this I do with the permission of the infidel; think what might happen if I sent all my warriors on a *jihad* against you and your kinsfolk. The British knew that the Sayyid had to be stopped – but they could not afford bloodshed.

Dansey was ordered to intercept the caravan before it could reach Berbera. He rode out of Sheikh with thirty armed and mounted Somali militia, and in appalling heat covered 100 miles in only forty-eight hours. He came upon the Dervish caravan at Geba-geba, in the foothills at the northern end of the Nogal Valley. Meanwhile an officer with 100 additional militia was sent to back up the police in Berbera, in the event of Dansey failing to halt

---

* From the Arabic "Darwish" (sing.) "Darawish" (pl.), denoting a Muslim believer who has taken vows of poverty and austerity in the service of God.

the caravan. No one really expected him to be successful; all they hoped for was some kind of delaying action. Dansey, too, must have doubted his own chances when he came face to face with ninety armed fanatics.

However, part of the Sayyid's agreement stipulated that, in order to prevent incidents, his followers must surrender their arms before entering any of the coastal towns. Whether this argument could be stretched to cover the case of a guard for a legitimate caravan was open to question. Dansey felt that it could, and was prepared to push his luck. He politely requested the Dervishes to comply with the agreement. They refused. Dansey insisted. Voices were raised, rifles unslung, long Somali daggers unsheathed, and spears waved in the air in increasing frustration. The situation began to look ugly, or – as the report demurely puts it – the Dervishes' "manner was far from satisfactory". Although backed by a force of only thirty local militia and in the face of considerable provocation, Dansey persisted. In the end – by a mixture of threat and diplomacy, laced with extraordinary charm, a technique he was to employ often in his subsequent career – he persuaded the Dervishes to give up their rifles quietly before continuing on to Berbera. For this feat Dansey was duly mentioned in despatches; in all, during the five years he spent in Somaliland, he was to be mentioned no fewer than four times.

Another occasion involved a typical foray into the Ain Valley. Now that he had won over so many of the Warsangeli tribe to his cause, the Sayyid decided to make use of them. He encouraged them to launch a series of raids on neighbouring tribes, starting with his mother's people, the Dulbahante. Thus at one stroke he not only settled old scores – for had not the Dulbahante rejected him after he had assassinated one of their leaders? – but he was also able to extend his area of influence into the Ain Valley itself.

Once the Sayyid's intentions became clear Dansey was ordered to make a tour of the valley, the aim being to discourage any raids on the friendly tribes grazing their livestock there. At dawn, before the temperature had climbed to its usual level of well over 100°F, Dansey rode out of Sheikh at the head of a small troop of the Somali camel corps of the King's African Rifles; Richard Corfield, another political and intelligence officer, was his second in command. They made good time across the savage terrain, pressing their beasts to the limit. Eventually they reached Wadamago, where there was sweet water. There Dansey decided to set up his HQ and despatched his Somali scouts to keep watch on the enemy's movements, while his spies visited the camps of the tribes in order to glean the latest intelligence.

On 4th September there were two further raids into the Ain Valley by the Warsangeli. Alert now to the Dervishes' plans, Dansey moved south to Eil Dab two days later, thus frustrating another raid. He returned to Wadamago on the ninth. The following morning news came of a raid on the Dulbahante in the Kalindera Valley – obviously the presence of Dansey's troops had forced the Dervishes to seek other targets. Dansey retaliated by immediately sending a party under the command of another officer in pursuit of the raiders, who were soon driven off.

The whole operation – only a police action really – was successful. Dansey's handling of the situation was commended by Captain Cordeaux, Commissioner of the Somaliland Protectorate, in glowing terms: "of (his) tact and judgement in dealing with a difficult situation . . . I cannot speak too highly". What it proved to Dansey, if proof were needed, was the importance of precise intelligence work prior to taking military action. First, find out what your enemy plans, then move against him.

Nevertheless the Sayyid was not defeated: he had only suffered a temporary setback. Dervish pressure on the British and the tribes under their protection was never for a moment relaxed. He was soon probing again to find another weak spot in his adversary's defences, and once again he chose to deliver his thrust against the strategic Ain Valley.

On 2nd January 1909 Dansey received intelligence from his far-flung network of agents that two raiding parties of Dervishes had left Illig in the Italian Protectorate. One party was bound for Bohotle, the other for the Ain Valley. Dansey immediately informed his superiors, who decided to take action. A fortnight later Colonel Gough, Inspector General of the King's African Rifles, with a force of 700 men under his command, left Burao with orders to intercept the enemy forces advancing into the valley. Dansey, with Corfield as his second in command, was in charge of intelligence. Corfield graphically described their work in one of his letters home: "We have some one hundred *illalos* – that is, scouts and spies – under us, besides other scallywag irregular Somalis." He also defined their job as intelligence officers as "finding guides, locating the enemy, etc". (How inadequate that etcetera seems!)

Meanwhile, protected by a large *zariba* (a thorn hedge or fence), the British forces sat at Eil Dab and waited for orders. None were forthcoming. The arrival of reinforcements from the coast increased their number to some 2,000 men; but still there was no decision as to what precisely they should do. Weeks went by. Conditions behind the thorn hedge were hard on the troops. "The water up here," wrote Corfield, "is green and strongly impregnated with sulphuretted hydrogen . . . I am inclined to think that all foreign troops will return to Burao . . . leaving . . . Dansey and myself to carry on operations with Somali levies."

The Colonial Office, however, was suffering from a severe case of the dithers, brought on by a change of administration at Westminster. In February 1906 a Liberal government, with Sir Henry Campbell-Bannerman as Prime Minister, had taken office. They were determined to put an end to any further colonial adventures. A year later, while on a tour of British territories, Winston Churchill (then Under-Secretary of State for the Colonies) visited Somaliland. His subsequent report written for the Cabinet cut the feet from under the local British administration. Churchill advocated further withdrawal, surrendering even such posts as Sheikh, Ber and Burao, and only relying on occasional cavalry patrols to remind the tribes that the British were still there. The Mullah, he suggested, "may leave us alone. He may even die." He goes on to point out that these "wild people have always lived in anarchy and strife . . . If the worst comes to the worst, and the Mullah advances . . . we should in my opinion deal with him on the basis that if he treats the friendly tribes properly we will allow his trade to come through our posts to the sea . . . It is," he concludes, "the only (policy) which the utter poverty of the wilderness of stone and scrub, and the military strength of its fanatical inhabitants, render it worth while for a British Government to pursue."

Dansey, who had been in Burao at the time of Churchill's visit, had felt betrayed by his old comrade-in-arms. He wrote angrily to the *Morning Post*: "Mr Churchill . . . travelling in one of His Majesty's ships, appeared at Berbera. He remained there, I think, some twenty-four hours, rode nine miles away from the coast, interviewed a few coast officials and one military officer, and retired knowing all about Somaliland . . . " No doubt Dansey was not surprised at subsequent events.

At Eil Dab the troops sat behind their *zariba* waiting for the Colonial Office to make up their minds whether simply to negotiate or ignore the Sayyid, bribe him to go away, or whether to seek out his forces and destroy them. And all the time May was approaching, the month when the hot season began and the Somalis who had hired their camels to the British would demand their return.

In the end the Colonial Office decided to send Lieutenant-General Sir Reginald Wingate, ex-Governor-General of the Sudan, and General Sir Rudolf Baron von Slattin (usually known as Slattin Pasha), Inspector General of the Sudan, to Somaliland to open negotiations. The Sayyid, however, saw no advantage in reaching any political *modus vivendi* with the British, being quite happy to drag out negotiations for as long as possible. In order to demonstrate his contempt for the foreign infidels he is said to have had the bearer of General Wingate's letters to him murdered – "after the usual preliminary mutilations had been affected".

In the end so successful were the Sayyid's tactics that he was soon writing to the British demanding their withdrawal from his country – or else he would resume hostilities in earnest.

The British replied to his letter complaining of the constant raids of his Dervishes on the tribes loyal to the authorities of Berbera. Even with reinforcements, British forces were already dangerously overstretched in attempting to police an area of 68,000 square miles. Indeed, it was feared that if the Sayyid attacked in force the garrisons at Ber, Burao and Sheikh might fall. Consequently the authorities decided to reinforce the garrisons with local militia drawn from outposts like Bohotle. The pretext for the withdrawal from the latter was given as a shortage of water, but the tribes could read the writing on the wall. The Sayyid had already won; the British had caved in to his demands.

This was not true, but it suited the Sayyid to spread the word. In any case in view of the strength of his forces Britain was faced with a choice. Either they could mount a full-scale military campaign, followed probably by permanent occupation of the country, which would be extremely expensive and could well prove to be an open-ended commitment; or they could retire to the coastal zone. From there they could always make small armed forays into the interior in the hope of limiting the Sayyid's influence on the tribes, and in the not-too-distant future – as Churchill had suggested – perhaps he would die. The government in London chose the latter course. It was a sensible decision. The Sayyid was known to have between 4,000 to 6,000 armed men living near him at Illig in the Italian Protectorate; he could also call upon his adherents from amongst the tribes. In all the Sayyid could probably put into the field a force of well over 10,000 men.

Dansey did not remain behind to witness what he regarded as a sell-out and a British humiliation. As a result of his efforts over the past five years, frequently on the move, living rough in a cruel and inhospitable land, his health broke down. At the end of 1909 he left Somaliland, never to return. He feared that his career was finished, and he had already begun to look around for another job, which is perhaps why he came back to England via the Belgian Congo. He had served his apprenticeship in intelligence: his real work was about to begin.

CHAPTER FIVE

The Road to Sleepy Hollow

Claude Dansey felt badly let down by the faceless bureaucrats in Whitehall. All his dreams of a career in the army or the Colonial Service seemed to lie in ruins. He had left British Somaliland a sick man, and now an ungrateful Colonial Office proposed to cast him on to the rubbish heap. At the age of only thirty-five his career appeared finished. A bleak future on pension or half-pay stretched before him – a prospect he viewed with abhorrence. But always the fighter, ever the scourge of bureaucracy, he proceeded to bombard Lord Crewe, Churchill's successor as the Under-Secretary of State for the Colonies, with letters which were terse, indignant and acidic. He pointed out to his Lordship that in 1906 the Colonial Office had offered him "Civil permanent employment". "I was led by this offer and the use of the word permanent," he complained, "to resign my commission and prospects in the army." It was on this understanding that he had accepted the post of Chief Political and Intelligence Officer in Somaliland, which he had anticipated would be a step to some further advancement.

"I . . . spent nearly five years in Somaliland, which has injured my health considerably," he declared. But more to the point, he believed, was the fact that he had done well: he had been a success in his job: "on three occasions . . . I have received notice of the Secretary of State's appreciation of (my) services". But now the Colonial Office was insisting that "if I cannot afford to wait indefinitely and without pay for the offer of re-employment there is no course open to the Secretary of State other than to retire me with such pension or gratuity to which I may be eligible". Dansey had no stomach for sitting around, sponging on his friends and family, while he waited for the Colonial Office to move in its own mysterious way. Something had to be done. "At the age of thirty-five," he wrote, "(I am) compelled to start life again."

Sixteen months after writing that letter, which is dated 20th July

66

1910, Claude Dansey was to be found in an antechamber outside the board room of the National City Bank at 55 Wall Street, New York, awaiting an interview. The job? The post of Resident Secretary to the Executive Committee of the Sleepy Hollow Country Club.

What strange winds had blown this Colonial Service reject from the dust and heat of Somaliland to a millionaires' paradise on the banks of the Hudson River in Westchester county, New York? In July 1910 we know that Dansey was desperate to find work of any kind; yet in January 1911 he was living in a style to which he had never been accustomed and enjoying the company of men of power. How had it happened? By what miracle had he achieved this remarkable transition?

The answer is that some time between 1910 and 1911 he became a spy.

At first glance this may seem an unusual step for a man of Dansey's background, but the alternatives open to him were not particularly attractive. Frustrated in his hopes of a career in the Colonial Service and with no longer any chance of promotion in the army, he had coldly assessed his job prospects in civilian employment and concluded that they were less than brilliant. After all, what could he offer a potential employer? He spoke a few languages – French, some Somali, and he seems to have acquired a working knowledge of Afrikaans and Italian. Subsequent events suggest that he may have had at least a smattering of Portuguese and Arabic. Add to that a talent for organising networks of intelligence-gathering native scouts, plus a taste for individual action – and you have a portrait of a typical ex-officer, with no professional qualifications and no commercial experience.

Dansey was not a man who could have settled down to life as the secretary of a golf club or some worthy society. No doubt, through the Gifford family connections, a job could have been found for him in the City or in South Africa, but he always seemed loath to turn to the Giffords for help. He was, however, lucky in one respect: he was entering the profession of espionage at just the right time.

The period 1909–12 was crucial in the history of the British intelligence services. It was a time for reassessment and reorganisation. Decisions made then set the pattern in which British Intelligence still operates today.

The Boer war had stimulated what some senior officers regarded as the unseemly growth of the intelligence arm of the Directorate of Military Operations, which now boasted no fewer than six different intelligence sections. Some quarters of the army believed that all intelligence activity should be brought under stricter military control, and there were even those who held the view that espionage itself was not a suitable occupation for officers and gentlemen.

Meanwhile, in 1907, the Prime Minister, Campbell-Bannerman, had ordered the Committee of Imperial Defence to establish direct civilian political control over the armed forces. At the same time the committee were looking for ways to foster co-operation between all intelligence organisations, including their own.

In 1909, after two years spent studying the problem in the light of future British intelligence requirements, the committee made a series of recommendations. These included the establishment of a Secret Service Bureau to operate with two quite distinct and separate arms. One of these (just called the Special Intelligence Section and later MI6) would concentrate solely on gathering secret intelligence in foreign countries, whilst the other (originally named MO5) would be responsible for counter-intelligence, combating foreign (particularly Irish and German) spies operating in Britain. In 1916 this organisation was renamed MI5.

An officer from the South Staffordshire Regiment, Captain Vernon Kell, who had recently returned from service in the Far East, was offered the post of Director of MO5. Kell's health was not good. The dysentry he had picked up in China had exacerbated his childhood asthma, and there was little likelihood that he would ever return to active service with his regiment. With the end of his conventional military career in sight, Kell therefore accepted the new post.

Three years older than Claude Dansey, Vernon Kell was the son of a regular army officer and a Polish aristocrat. Thanks largely to his mother's influence, he became fluent in German, Polish, Italian and French by his teens. Later he was to master Russian as well.

MO5 began in modest enough style in a tiny, unfurnished office in Whitehall. Kell even had to apply for a chair and a table before he could start work. Files, staff, a secretary, and other necessities were not acquired until the bureau had been in operation for over a year. Kell remained its head until sacked by Churchill in May 1940.

The Special Intelligence Section was placed under the command of a Royal Naval officer, Commander (later Captain) Mansfield Smith Cumming, who already had considerable experience of espionage in various parts of the globe. Cumming was like a character out of Dornford Yates or Sapper: "a square-built man with white hair and a wooden leg". He had lost his own leg not in some naval battle but in a motor accident. He was said to have cut off the offending limb with his own penknife when trapped underneath the car. He used to disconcert visitors by sticking a knife into its wooden replacement. Cumming combined a passion for Gilbert and Sullivan with an almost adolescent relish for espionage. "It's capital sport," he told Compton Mackenzie.

The Special Intelligence Section took up residence on the top three floors at 2 Whitehall Court, a solid Victorian block overlooking the Thames. In a downstairs flat lived the playwright George Bernard Shaw, who never seems to have discovered that the commissionaires of the building were Special Branch police in disguise.

Dansey must have found it difficult to persuade Cumming or Kell to employ him. Although a dashing officer with wide experience of African intelligence work, although he had demonstrated considerable expertise in handling native agents and evaluating the information they supplied, Dansey lacked the prime requirement for the new intelligence services – money. So poor was the pay that an adequate private income was essential if one was to work for any branch of the Secret Service. And Dansey had only his army pension.

Nonetheless he was not without allies, amongst them his old comrade-in-arms from the South African war, Winston Churchill. Though they had not always seen eye to eye in the past, particularly over Churchill's damning report on British Somaliland, the link was never quite broken. Furthermore, ever since he had become Home Secretary, Churchill had taken a great personal interest in the work of MO5. He had even gone as far as to waive the legal regulations preventing its Special Intelligence Bureau from opening the mail of German agents.

Who eventually recruited Dansey remains a mystery. We do not know the precise date of his recruitment, nor the nature of his terms of employment. He probably began on a strictly amateur basis, forced to rely on his own modest financial resources, with a promise of something more permanent if he succeeded. It would have been up to him to get himself to some part of the world where British interests were considered to be at stake and to provide himself with adequate cover, and then to send back the kind of information that would interest his masters.

Dansey's travels during 1910 and 1911 were extensive, and with one exception, all were made with a view to furthering his career in secret intelligence. It is instructive to list the countries he visited.

On leaving Somaliland, he returned home via the Belgian Congo – hardly the most direct route. But the Congo, rich in rubber and minerals, was of interest to the British. He then went to British Columbia, but that seems to have been with the intention of finding suitable employment should all else fail. Later he visited Mexico, potentially oil-rich and close to the unfinished Panama Canal, and Morocco, the scene of two international crises in 1905 and 1911. And yet again he returned to the Congo.

It was there, in the real world of Conrad's "heart of darkness", that Dansey eventually discovered the road that was to lead him to Sleepy Hollow and to a lifetime spent in espionage. In the Congo he came upon Djobo Punda, the domain of the US-Belgian corporation, known as Forminière (*Société Internationale Forestière et Minière du Congo*).

The Congo was the personal fief of Leopold II, King of the Belgians: he owned it and had done so since 1879. Leopold was no ordinary monarch. He possessed all the instincts of a nineteenth-century entrepreneur: business, rather than kingship, was his true *métier*. He poured $2,500,000 of his own money into the territory, intending to exploit its natural riches – rubber, ivory, copper, etc. But the hoped-for boom never came. The Congo remained a heavy liability on the King's purse. In 1892, hoping to spread the financial load a little, he divided the country into two *domaines*: the *Domaine de la Couronne*, which remained his to do with as he pleased, and the *Domaine Privé*, which became the property of the State. Exploitation of the latter *domaine* was placed in the hands of two private companies.

By 1906 there were all the signs that the situation was changing. The Congo was at last beginning to pay off. Rubber production, for example, had reached an all-time high of just under 6,000 tons per annum, worth forty-seven million Belgian francs. However, at the same time the King's stewardship of the colony was being questioned. He was under attack from all sides. The Socialists in the Belgian Government wanted to see the colony taken out of Leopold's hands, while international opinion was horrified by reports of atrocities perpetrated on native rubber collectors by the agents employed by the companies.

The King came to the conclusion that the Congo had barely been exploited as yet: what was needed now was an injection of technical know-how and fresh capital. He turned to American sources for help.

. Leopold believed that American finance, unlike British or German, came with no political strings attached. The British pound, it was said, "always flew the Union Jack" – whereas the US dollar was only money. American capitalists, he concluded, were interested solely in business, not in politics.

Leopold had no intention of giving up control of the Congo and its profitable rubber industry to a foreign power if he could help it. What he was looking for was the kind of foreign expertise that would enable him to increase rubber production. Well versed in the mysteries of the world of international business, he knew that a rubber industry was already being established in Mexico, based on a process for extracting rubber from the guayele shrub which grows wild in the desert. The man behind the development was Irish-American multi-millionaire, Thomas Fortune Ryan, who was destined to play a vital role in Claude Dansey's career. Leopold wanted both Ryan's Mexican process and his capital. It was a laudable ambition; unfortunately, as the King was to discover, he was playing out of his league.

Ryan was a financial genius with a sense of timing and a degree of ruthlessness rarely if ever matched on Wall Street. William C. Whitney, one of his associates, described him as "the most adroit, suave and noiseless man" in US financial history. Someone else called him "the invisible man of Wall Street". Because of his speed of thought and reaction the American Press christened him "the great opportunist". He shunned the limelight, preferring to operate discreetly, without the benefit of an audience. He was one of the first men in America to employ a public relations man – who rejoiced under the name of Lemuel E. Quigg – whose job it was to keep his name *out* of the papers.

Born in 1851 on a small farm in Lovington, Nelson County, Virginia, Ryan was a big good-looking man with an open friendly face. In all the photographs of him taken in later life he looks like an amiable baritone in a barber-shop quartet, rather than an Irish Machiavelli worth several hundred million dollars.

Ryan was a curious mixture of financial buccaneer and Renaissance prince. He was frequently threatened with law suits and investigations on account of his often-piratical commercial dealings. He spent as lavishly as he earned, but not on expensive women and fine clothes – though he enjoyed both in moderation. Instead he bought works of art; he had the finest collection of mediaeval Limoges enamel in the world, and filled the garden of his home at Oak Ridge, Virginia, with sixteenth- and seventeenth-century statuary. He had a passion for oriental carpets and eighteenth-century Italian religious art. He built at least a dozen churches and cathedrals and was a major contributor to the Catholic Church in the US, to the tune of over $20 million. And he was responsible for the only million-dollar rose garden in New York.

It is a story which throws an intriguing light on his character.

71

Ryan owned a New York mansion on Fifth Avenue, where he lived with his first wife. She adored flowers – in particular, roses; they both did. But their garden was not big enough to grow as many roses as they wished. The solution to this problem for a man of Ryan's wealth was simple – he bought the house next door, knocked it down, and converted the land into a rose garden. Since the house had belonged to Charles Yerkes, the Chicago transit king who also built much of London's Tube system, and was valued at nearly $1,250,000, it turned out to be a very expensive rose garden. Admiring the marble columns which graced the magnificent staircase, Ryan decided to preserve these, and until his death in 1928, Ryan roses were trained up thirty-two white marble columns in the biggest and most beautiful garden on Fifth Avenue. Shortly after his second marriage Ryan ordered the planting of another rose garden – this time at his Oak Ridge estate, Virginia. Thus the second Mrs Ryan could breakfast on the balcony at the rear of the house and look across acres of the finest roses.

Leopold made enquiries and found out that Ryan was holidaying in Switzerland. The opportunity seemed too good to miss. The King sent a message to the multi-millionaire proposing a meeting. If he expected Ryan to jump to his command, he had misjudged his man. Ryan ignored the royal summons, but started making enquiries of his own. Never a man to permit pride to interfere with business, Leopold tried again. When a second invitation to a meeting arrived, Ryan graciously consented to see the King. What emerged from that meeting was a deal involving Forminière. The company was to be granted mining and mineral rights to more than seven million acres of the Congo and other agricultural concessions over a further two and a half million acres: in all over half the land area of the whole country, capitalised to the extent of only three million Belgian francs. Half the shares in the company would belong to the Belgian Government, the other half was to be divided equally between on the one hand the King and the Société Générale, on the other Thomas Fortune Ryan.

In order to finance the exploitation of the country Ryan, who preferred not to use his own money if he could help it, brought in several American business acquaintances – Daniel Guggenheim, Senator Nelson W. Aldrich, Harry Payne Whitney, and John Hays Hammond. It was a tight little group, drawn from what one might call the second rank of American capital, contenders rather than reigning champions. The investment paid off handsomely. The first party of American engineers sent to survey the territory discovered diamonds in several of the stream beds, and with the later development of gold and copper mining, rubber rapidly declined in economic importance. Soon Ryan was to move into the neighbouring Portuguese territory of Angola. There, while prospecting for diamonds, his experts – as he rather irritably remarked – "found oil as well".

Dansey first came to the attention of the Ryan organisation in Africa. Whether they met through Dansey's Belgian contacts or whether in some other way, we do not know. But somehow he so ingratiated himself with the organisation that he was invited to meet the multi-millionaire in person in New York. In 1911 Dansey made his own way there. He was by now a British agent.

Why the USA? Why should Britain have agents in a country known to be friendly? Both Captain Cumming and Captain Kell and their predecessors would have given the same answer – the Irish. Ever since the end of the eighteenth century, Irish revolutionary societies – dedicated to the aim of driving the British out of Ireland – had become the greatest long-term foe facing the British Secret Service. This war, for that is what it was, continued for over 200 years, and indeed is still in progress to this day.

The Irish Volunteers, the forerunners of the IRA, were formed in 1779. They attempted to form associations first with the American rebels, and later with Napoleon and the French. With the foundation of the Irish Republican Brotherhood in the USA in 1858, the situation – at least from the British point of view – took a more sinister turn. In 1865 there was an unsuccessful attempt by the Fenians, as the Brotherhood was now known in the USA, to foment a rising in Ireland. The following year a group of Irishmen invaded Canada from New York State, with the aim of establishing a secure Canadian base for operations in Ireland. Even the failure of that venture did not prevent them from planning a second invasion. Meanwhile a Fenian bombing campaign began in London. The Special Branch of Scotland Yard, originally formed to combat Irish terrorism, soon established that the dynamite used in the preparation of the bombs was American and came from Irish sources in New York.

This served to reinforce the Secret Service view that the enemy in Ireland was being backed by the Irish in America, and Thomas Fortune Ryan seemed to fit the bill to perfection. He was of Irish ancestry; he was immensely wealthy; he was known to have made huge donations to Irish charities and the Catholic Church. He could easily have been the paymaster of the Fenians. He wasn't. Indeed, there is no evidence that he was ever sympathetic to their cause; such an attitude would have been quite foreign to the man. Ryan was a businessman first and last. Politics

73

interested him only as a means of achieving his business ends: it was a weapon, not the end in itself.

The Irish connection was no doubt the reason for Dansey's presence in the USA. But it was Ryan himself – and the connections Dansey was able to make through him with people in the world of international big business – that justified it. He learned the art of pulling strings, and he learned it from a master.

Ryan's career was the epitome of the American dream. A penniless barefoot country boy, later a clerk in a dry-goods store in Baltimore, by 1900 he was worth at least $50 million. A decade later, when he met Claude Dansey, his fortune was probably three or four times that. Because of his vast wealth, and the secretive manner in which he chose to employ it, Ryan came to wield enormous political power. As always, he remained invisible: the unseen puppeteer of East Coast American politics. He was one of the angels of the Democratic Party, and helped to fund many of their political campaigns. With his old associate, William C. Whitney, at one time he held the strings that operated Tammany Hall and its notorious chief, Richard "Boss" Croker. Ryan was also known to have US senators, governors, and congressmen in his pocket "by the score". Of course, he had many enemies, amongst them Woodrow Wilson and the whole Wall Street clique. But the future President's disapproval certainly did not worry Ryan whose millions continued to grease the wheels of American politics. His political influence probably reached its peak during the first world war, when men such as Colonel House, the *éminence grise* of the White House, and William McCombs, the President's campaign manager, proved only too willing to do his bidding.

CHAPTER SIX

Private Business Matters

The job at Sleepy Hollow paid a salary of $300 a month plus luxurious accommodation and free membership of the club. As such, Dansey would be on a completely different footing from the other employees. He would be free to mix with the members as an equal.

The Sleepy Hollow Country Club began life as the country estate of a Mr Butler Wright. The property, known as "Woodlea", lay on the east side of the Albany Post Road at Scarborough-on-the-Hudson, twenty-eight miles north of New York City. Its 338 acres of hills and woodlands had been immortalised in the stories of the writer Washington Irving. "If ever I should wish for a retreat," says Diedrich Knickerbocker in Irving's *Legend of Sleepy Hollow*, "whither I might steal from the world and its distractions, and dream quietly away the remnant of a troubled life, I know of none more promising than this little valley." The observation is still true: it is a beautiful spot.

In 1892 "Woodlea" was purchased by Colonel Elliott Fitch Shepard, a native of Jamestown, New York. The colonel came from a wealthy family; his father had been president of the National Bank Note Company. He himself was a successful lawyer, member of the law firm of Strong and Shepard, and founder of the New York State Bar Association. His military rank derived from the civil war, when he had acted as aide-de-camp to General E. D. Morgan. A wealthy man in his own right, the colonel had compounded his good fortune by marrying into the Vanderbilt millions. His wife was Louisa, eldest daughter of William H. Vanderbilt, grand-daughter of the legendary Commodore.

Dissatisfied with the Butler Wright house, the Shepards decided to build a luxurious mansion of their own, one that would do justice to their exalted social and financial position. They did not have the old house demolished, but used it to accommodate servants and

75

visitors. They commissioned Stanford White, one of America's most famous architects, to build a mansion that would rival any of the great English or European country houses. White excelled himself. On a plateau overlooking the Hudson River, he created "a retreat from the world and its cares – a beautiful playground, favoured with every luxury, which nature and human artifice . . . could devise". It has been described as "one of the most sumptuous private dwellings ever built in America".

After lavishing some $2,500,000 on the house, Colonel Shepard never lived to see the building completed: he died in 1893. His widow, Louisa, lived on in the house until, finding it too vast for comfort, she leased it to a group of men as a country club. In 1910 two of the club members who lived nearby, William Rockefeller (older brother of John D. Rockefeller) and Franklin A. Vanderlip (Assistant Secretary to the US Treasury 1897–1901, later President of the National City Bank), purchased the house from Mrs Shepard at the bargain price of $600,000: about one sixth of its value. A year later, in May 1911, the two millionaires sold the property to the organisers of the Sleepy Hollow Country Club, of which they were founder members. The list of the first twenty-seven directors of the corporation which was to run the club reads like a roll call of Wall Street and Fifth Avenue aristocracy. It includes at least one Astor (John Jacob), a brace of Rockefellers (Percy and William), a Vanderlip (Franklin, of course), and such men of power and influence as A. O. Choate (investment broker), James C. Colgate (broker and banker), Oliver Harriman (railroad magnate), Samuel Sloan (banking), James A. Stillman (financier and associate of William Rockefeller), Harrison Williams (public utilities), etc. It was they who defined the aims of the club in the certificate of incorporation; " . . . to acquire . . . a club house, and grounds adjacent thereto, or convenient for use in connection therewith, and to maintain and operate the same, with stables, garage, and other accommodations for the use and convenience of its members, including the maintenance of grounds for the conduct of polo, golf and other sports . . . " There was garage space for 250 cars, including accommodation for the chauffeurs. In time the sports facilities grew to include not merely a polo field and two golf courses, but also eight tennis courts, three squash courts, four paddle tennis courts, a swimming pool, indoor and outdoor riding rings, a skeet range, and even a theatre built in the form of a Greek amphitheatre which seated an audience of 1,500 people.

Sleepy Hollow was above all a club for the rich, run by the rich, where they could relax and feel at home amongst their own kind. It proved to be even more exclusive than the Kingdom of Heaven. A

Rockefeller was more likely to get through the eye of a needle than a poor man to obtain membership of the Sleepy Hollow Country Club. It was to be Claude Dansey's home until the start of the first world war.

At 3.30 p.m. on 6th December 1911 at a meeting of the Board of Governors – Franklin A. Vanderlip in the chair – the Executive Committee announced that Captain Claude E. Dansey had been selected as Resident Secretary of the Sleepy Hollow Club for a probationary period of three months. Actually his appointment dated from the first of the month: he was already in residence at Sleepy Hollow when the governors met. The Executive Committee was merely seeking approval of its decision, which is the way of Executive Committees.

Although early on in his career Dansey had been influenced by Cecil Rhodes and the dream of imperial grandeur – an Africa British from the Cape to Cairo – which had inspired a generation of young Englishmen, he was now some fifteen years older and wiser. He had seen the African reality at first hand. He knew that such dreams would remain mere fantasy unless supported by trade and money. Britain alone simply did not possess the capital, or even the energy, to vitalise and civilise a whole continent. Fresh sources of capital must be found – capital untainted by base political ambitions which might conflict with British colonial interests. Leopold of the Belgians was therefore not alone in looking to the US for help.

Hence Dansey's interest in Ryan and the world of American big business. The Irish-American became his guru in the mysteries of high finance and the ways in which men of power could be manipulated, or at least discreetly persuaded that a particular course of action would be mutually advantageous. The example of Ryan's cunning and his passion for concealment must have encouraged Dansey's own already well-developed taste for secrecy: Dansey was learning the art of deception from a master.

Thus, with typical flair, and a degree of extraordinary good luck, Dansey had found his way into the heart of the labyrinth. There he was to discover opportunities for espionage such as few British agents can have enjoyed before or since. He was on the inside of one of the greatest commercial, political and social power centres in America. Thanks to his friendship with Thomas Fortune Ryan and contacts made through the club, he would in future be able to gain access to some of America's most powerful men and corporations.

It did not suit Ryan to be a director of the club himself. As always, he moved cautiously and circuitously. But the extent of his involvement with Sleepy Hollow can be gauged by the fact that his was the first name on the first list of members to be approved – at the same board meeting which appointed Claude Dansey as secretary. Two months later, before the expiry of his probation, at another board meeting on 7th February, held in the same bank, it was agreed "that the arrangement with Captain Dansey should be continued subject to the pleasure of the Board of Governors". Dansey's job was now secure, until such time as the board decided to get rid of him.

It is at this point, when he was taking his first steps into the twilight world of espionage, that Dansey undergoes his final metamorphosis. The dashing young officer gradually disappears and is replaced by a creature who employs stealth and deceit to achieve his ends. As he perfects his camouflage, he begins to merge with his background. He becomes harder to trace. A cloak of invisibility seems to descend on to his shoulders.

We catch a glimpse of him from time to time, but these glimpses are brief and inexplicable. What on earth was going on? What was he up to? There is, for example, the story – which he was fond of telling – of the club servants being dressed in periwigs and knee breeches. This was the garb, he assured the committee, of servants in all the best London clubs.

On another occasion it is recorded in the club minutes that Harrison Williams, one of the original directors of the corporation which set up the club, was given permission by the Executive Committee to employ Captain Dansey in a private business matter. Harrison Williams was then about forty and worth – by Sleepy Hollow standards – peanuts: a mere two million dollars or so. His subsequent career was staggering. After the war he was to win financial control of one sixth of all US public utilities, and his fortune reached the incredible figure of $680 million. He was also a believer in the old adage – if you've got it, flaunt it. "The only reason the Harrison Williamses don't live like princes," declared one wag, "is that princes can't afford to live like the Harrison Williamses." His wife was said to be the most expensively dressed woman in America. One longs to know what "private business matter" Dansey transacted for the financier. And no doubt from time to time he also did favours for other members of the club, too.

He certainly did odd jobs for Thomas Fortune Ryan. Some involved the overseeing of his interests in the Congo, but others were of a more frivolous nature. As an ex-member of the South African Light Horse and son of a colonel of the Life Guards, Claude Dansey had spent much of his early life with horses and prided himself on his judgement of horse flesh. He soon found himself involved in Ryan's racing ambitions. The multi-millionaire had set up a racing stud on his estate at Oak Ridge, Virginia. After some success on American tracks, Ryan planned an English campaign. He longed to win one of the classic races, ideally the Derby. With this end in view he turned to Dansey for advice. They discussed the choice of horse suitable for English conditions, and at the end of 1913 he instructed Dansey to make arrangements with an English trainer, the famous "Atty" Persse, for the training of a few of his best colts. But before the plan could come to fruition the first world war broke out.

Five months before the beginning of the first world war we catch another glimpse of Dansey going about his mysterious business. Not in the USA this time, but in Africa: once again he was working for Thomas Fortune Ryan.

On 9th March 1914, J. E. Bell, the new British vice-consul at Boma, a seaport on the Congo River, wrote to his superiors in the Foreign Office in London to report the arrival in the port of a Captain Dansey, who was "a former official in Somaliland under the Colonial Office". The captain was still recuperating from a bout of fever. It transpired that he had just returned from an extended tour of inspection up-country, in the Kasai, Lake Leopold and Mayumbe areas. This had been undertaken "on behalf of an American group of financiers who have invested a considerable amount of capital in undertakings in the Congo and in Africa generally and who have been contemplating the extension of their operations".

Obviously Dansey had been engaged on some kind of survey for the Ryan consortium. As an old Africa hand, and one already familiar with the Congo, he would have been invaluable to the multi-millionaire. But the reason behind his journey is unknown: we do not know why he was there. One can be sure, however, that Dansey had no intention of letting the vice-consul in on the secrets of any of his employers.

Mr Bell was impressed by the mysterious captain and found his views on the situation in the Congo "of considerable value". So valuable, indeed, that he asked him to write a short report on his journey for the British Foreign Office. The request cannot have pleased Dansey; it is doubtful if he found the irony of the situation amusing. But he was at a disadvantage. He was a sick man, and under the circumstances he could not very well refuse the suggestion. However, as Mr Bell noted to his superiors, "it will be observed that Captain Dansey does not desire to have his name published in connection with the report".

It is clear from Dansey's story, if his timetable is to be believed, that he must have been in the Congo ever since December 1913 or January 1914. Leaving Kinshasa, he travelled up the Kasai River to Djobo Punda, and thence marched along the right bank of the river until he came to the junction of the Kasai and Tshikapa rivers, where there was a Forminière exploration camp. It was staffed mostly by American mining engineers and prospectors. He stayed at the Forminière camp for at least two weeks. Then he marched south and west in the direction of the Angolan border. He implies that he did not cross the border but remained on the Belgian side, but in view of Ryan's known interests in Angola this is most unlikely. In any case he mentions entering a village where the natives spoke only Portugese, an improbable linguistic talent if the village was really in Belgian territory. Nevertheless he was not going to admit any violation of Portugese territory to a new vice-consul as keen about his job as Mr Bell. The last thing he wanted was for anyone to go poking about in his affairs.

Dansey's Congo report, like almost everything that he ever wrote, is blunt and to the point. Never a man to mince his words, he was critical of Belgian administration: "a super-abundance of fonctionnaires" but "no administration whatever, as understood in British Colonies". He was acid about Belgian relations with the natives. As he remarked to Vice-Consul Bell, "the average white man in the Congo does not know how to secure respect [from the natives] by other means than force". He attributed this to "the class of white man one finds here, his actions and ways of living are often such that no native could have respect for him". Not that he had a high opinion of the Congolese tribes themselves ("very low in the scale of native races"), and he thought it "fortunate for the Belgians that the native population is as a whole an unwarlike one". He expressed scant sympathy with Belgian complaints about the quality and reliability of native labour. "At Tshikapa," he declared, "the Americans had about 600 workmen and porters who seemed very content." He attributed this to the policy of the American manager, Mr Oliver, who had "an exceptional organisation and system of training his men". In fact, "so popular is this community that three chiefs came in proposing to move their village there".

Unlike many journeys of the period, Dansey's trip through the Congo seems to have been astonishingly trouble-free, due no doubt to the letter of recommendation he carried from M Renkin the Belgian Colonial Secretary, a letter obtained for him through the good offices of Thomas Fortune Ryan. After all, if you are the business partner of the King himself, you should be able to rely on the co-operation of his Colonial Secretary. The power of this document was sufficient to unlock all doors and free any enterprise from the web of Belgian red tape.

Dansey was back at his post at Sleepy Hollow within a few weeks of writing the report. But he was not destined to stay there long. With tension rising in Europe, events were already threatening to overwhelm the peace of the world. He handed in his notice, said his farewells to the club members and the president, Franklin A. Vanderlip, and returned to England just prior to the outbreak of the first world war. He had told the Executive Committee, of which he had been Resident Secretary for nearly three years, that he was rejoining his regiment. Actually he was ceasing to be an agent in the field and becoming an officer in the full-time staff of MO5 in London.

Part Two

The Great War

CHAPTER SEVEN

Love and MO5

When Claude Dansey returned from the USA to take up his post with MO5, under Vernon Kell, he found the British intelligence services prepared for war. For some time the Department of Military Operations had been clearing its decks for action. Ever since 1913 Major (later General) George Macdonough, then head of the department, had been talent spotting. He had compiled a register of men who possessed the kind of experience and talents he considered useful in intelligence work. These were not just fellow officers – but civilians, too, ranging from professors to businessmen, from bankers to ne'er-do-wells.

Meanwhile Kell had been building up the G (i.e. the operational) section of MO5 and extending the area of his activities. Having started with only a small office and a staff of one (himself), he had gradually acquired the services of Captains Clarke and Drake (we shall meet Reggie Drake again later), Inspector Melville of Scotland Yard, and Walter Moresby, a barrister, who handled the section's legal affairs, and of course at the outbreak of war he was joined by Dansey.

In a War Office memorandum the function of Kell's department was described as "Counter-espionage. Military policy in dealing with the civil population, including aliens". Kell interpreted his brief fairly broadly. He saw the role of his department as not merely investigating the activities of foreign agents and subversives, but also, as far as possible, in preventing such activities from occurring. Kell took the long view, and having gained the confidence of Scotland Yard, he was able to conduct operations in his own way and in his own time. He believed in keeping a known or suspected agent under surveillance, sometimes for years, until he was ready to move. An example of his ability to play the waiting game can be seen in his handling of the Karl Gustav Ernst affair.

Colonel Nicolai, the legendary head of the German Secret

Service, had placed in charge of the British section a man who had worked for many years in the United States. Gustav Steinhauer had been a detective with the famous Pinkerton Agency. Never noted for his modesty, Steinhauer boldly proclaimed himself the "Kaiser's Master Spy". While he might have been an excellent private detective, he was far too careless and flamboyant for his new profession.

Before the war Steinhauer visited Britain regularly. He was recognised at his port of entry but such was the mood of national apathy at the time concerning German espionage that he was rarely kept under surveillance – which is a pity because his contacts in Britain still remain something of a mystery. Perhaps he took time out to go to a certain barber in Caledonian Road for a shave and a haircut.

The barber in question was Karl Gustav Ernst, the son of a German surgical instrument maker. In 1909 Superintendent Quinn of Scotland Yard's Special Branch brought the activities of Ernst to the attention of Vernon Kell. A senior officer of the German Naval Intelligence Service, under surveillance for some time, had been observed calling regularly at a barber's shop at 405A Caledonian Road, London. It was a very ordinary little shop, and the area, close to Pentonville Prison, was a far cry from Mayfair or Belgravia. Kell and Superintendent Quinn found it hard to believe that the officer was merely looking for a cheap haircut. Therefore there had to be another reason. Superintendant Quinn and Kell cooperated to maintain a round-the-clock observation of the premises. At the same time Kell also applied to the Home Secretary for a warrant permitting him to intercept all mail to and from the shop in Caledonian Road.

When Kell and his staff got their hands on the correspondence, they were astonished to discover that the barber was the head of an extensive spy network, with agents all over Britain. Most of the agents were concentrated in the sea-ports. Thus they were able to supply German Naval Intelligence with up-to-date information about ship movements in and out of British ports. The information was conveyed quite openly in letters to Germany. There seems to have been little attempt to use codes or invisible ink. A regular recipient of the barber's letters was none other than Gustav Steinhauer.

Kell and his men watched and waited, until the time was ripe to move. After a while they succeeded in manipulating the flow of information to Berlin. Kell's men forged fresh letters and changed some existing ones, providing German Naval Intelligence with a stream of misinformation.

By 1914 Kell had had the barber of Caledonian Road under observation for nearly five years. Every spy in the network was identified. The only question was when to reel in the fish. As soon as it became clear that war between Britain and Germany was increasingly a possibility, not to say a probability, Kell began planning with the police forces in various parts of the country a round-up of members of the Ernst spy network. Everything awaited the declaration of war. So meticulous was Kell's planning that by the morning of 5th August, twenty-four hours after the declaration, some twenty-two German agents, including the barber himself, had been taken into custody in a series of police raids. It was an operation that established Kell's reputation. It also no doubt gave a fillip to Claude Dansey's career, too. His recruitment to MO5G coincided with Kell's mass round-up.

As the MO5 Dansey joined was still part of the Department of Military Operations, almost all members of staff were in the army. Dansey himself was officially gazetted to the Monmouthshire Regiment. Overall commander was recently promoted Colonel Macdonough. But strict compartmentalisation, which was later to beset British Intelligence, was some way off. In 1914 the department was still flexible enough to react speedily to situations as they arose, while those working in it retained a degree of mobility, able to move between sections as circumstances demanded. Foreign and home intelligence, for example, were not yet mutually exclusive fields. But inevitably, as the war progressed and the various sections multiplied, so bureaucracy blossomed, and empires were built – usually at the expense of other departments, other sections.

This internecine warfare between the various intelligence organisations, or even within the same department, at times exceeded in ferocity even the war being fought against the Germans. But all that was to come later: at first, for most of the recruits, intelligence was a strange new world. Experience was therefore at a premium. Men such as Dansey and Drake, men who had handled agents, conducted interrogations, even been spies themselves, were vitally important to the success of the British Intelligence effort.

The Aliens Restriction Act was the brainchild of Kell and Winston Churchill – a product of the period in 1910 when Churchill, as Home Secretary, had chaired a sub-committee of the Committee of Imperial Defence on which Kell sat. On the day after the declaration of war the act came into force. Under its provisions all aliens in the UK were required to register at their local police station. Those between the ages of seventeen and fifty-five were to be detained until the conclusion of the war. It was a massive task which occupied Special Branch and most of MO5G until the first Christmas of the war.

Dansey became involved in the control of aliens but in rather a different form. He was put in charge of a section which, in 1917, would be designated MI5E. Dansey's job was to oversee the entry and departure of civilians to and from Britain. As all ports were vulnerable to the entry of German agents, it was important to ensure that port security was as tight as possible.

It is, of course, a commonplace of fictional spy stories for the agent to be landed from a U-boat. As we know from Sir Roger Casement's disastrous landing on the Irish coast, this was an extremely hazardous operation. Such a landing demanded a dark night, a lonely, undefended stretch of coastline far from any habitation, and the availability of a suitable submarine. Not surprisingly most German spies attempted to make their way into Britain by more orthodox means. They travelled as bona fide passengers or crewmen aboard a ship sailing from a neutral country, of which Holland was the most easily accessible. It was however also a hot-bed of international espionage: the Germans, the British, the French – and after 1917, even the Americans – had several intelligence organisations operating in neutral Holland.

So anyone coming from Rotterdam, say, would be automatically suspect in the eyes of British counter-intelligence. The German Secret Service advised its agents to take passage aboard a ship bound for South America, one that called at some neutral port convenient to the UK, such as Vigo in northern Spain or Lisbon in Portugal. There the agent would leave the ship, claiming urgent business ashore. Later he would book another passage on another ship bound for Britain, thus ensuring that his ticket and passport would show him coming from somewhere other than Holland, the spy's playground.

Of course, the second ship would be stopped and boarded by naval control vessels based in Falmouth, Cornwall. The agent's papers would be examined and he might well be interrogated. Even if he passed this first hurdle, Tilbury – with its swarm of Scotland Yard men – awaited him. However, Colonel Nicolai and Gustav Steinhauer hoped that in the event the examination would not be so rigorous.

One German spy recruited in New York was advised to cross to San Francisco and catch a ship bound for Australia. There, equipped with an Australian passport and, perhaps, a suitable accent, he would catch a P & O liner to Britain. But even then he faced the same naval boarding party, the same Scotland Yard men; possibly even Claude Dansey. In fact, so successful did Dansey's operation become that we find in a letter from a German agent to Franz von Papen, one-time Military Attaché in the USA, which was intercepted in Switzerland, a complaint to his superior that it was almost hopeless for anyone to try and get into England.

In 1915, the year of Gallipoli and of the Battle of Loos and the Second Battle of Ypres, something odd happened to Claude Dansey – he got married. It was odd because one thinks of Dansey, that most ruthless and self-sufficient of men, as beyond the reach of such mundane entanglements. There is nothing strange in the fact that he should fall in love and wish to experience the joys of domesticity. No one has ever suggested that his sexual drives were in any way *outré* or unusual. He was a heterosexual of great charm, when he felt disposed to employ it, and throughout his life he exhibited an enviable ability to make himself attractive to women. Indeed, more than just attractive. Women, young and old, *liked* him. Even those who were in awe of him – little nineteen-year-old secretaries who worked for him in the second world war, now women in their sixties – today speak of him with genuine affection.

There is a temptation when writing of a man like Dansey, particularly in view of the nature of his profession, to ascribe subtle and machiavellian reasons for his every action. We tend to forget that spymasters are heir to the same passions that beset ordinary mortals. They fall in love and make fools of themselves, too – though it is somehow unsettling to discover that Claude Dansey was human after all.

On 20th March 1915, the marriage of Major Claude E. M. Dansey and Mrs Pauline Monroe Cory Ulman was solemnised at Hanover Square Register Office. The bride was a thirty-four-year-old American divorcee with a young daughter from her previous marriage. Pauline was the daughter of Dr David Cory, deceased, a doctor of medicine. Her first husband, Joseph Stevens Ulman, seems to have been related to J. Stevens Ulman, Special Deputy Commissioner of the New York Police, and also president of several companies. The witnesses are named as Isobel Maggridge and Dansey's father. The bridegroom's address is given as Ryder Street, Westminster; the bride's as Lower Belgrave Street, Belgravia.

Why did Dansey marry? For all the usual reasons no doubt, but there were career considerations, too. He was thirty-eight. He had at last succeeded in becoming part of the establishment in the intelligence – if not, as he might once have anticipated, in the colonial – field, and probably for the first time in many years he saw a reasonably settled future in front of him. He was now a major, with every likelihood of being brevetted lieutenant-colonel, and therefore able to offer a suitable wife both status and a measure of financial security. For men of Dansey's generation and background, marriage offered – apart from the more obvious guarantees of sexual and social acceptability – a certain aura of "steadiness", that much-admired Edwardian virtue. Certainly a marriage to an attractive, gracious and well-connected American would have done Dansey no harm.

The marriage was not, however, a success. After about fifteen years it ended in separation and eventual divorce. Dansey rarely spoke of his first wife to anyone, even his second wife, whom he married at the end of the second world war. She attributes his reticence to the fact that he was "a gentleman of the old school". However, we are inclined to believe that it is more likely to have been due to a spy's ingrained sense of secrecy. In any case, throughout his long career, Dansey always succeeded in keeping each aspect of his life in water-tight compartments. He operated on the "need to know" principle, and in Dansey's view what other people needed to know about him was no more than name, rank and number.

Nevertheless one must sympathise with Pauline Dansey. It cannot have been easy being married to a man who, by the very nature of his work, had to keep half his life obscured. Agents in the field must talk to someone, hence the importance of a wise and understanding contact. But what of the man who directs the agents, the spymaster? To whom does he talk? Like the Cabots, perhaps only to God. Most wives would object to such secrecy: perhaps Pauline did, too. Whatever may have ultimately gone wrong with the marriage, we do know that Dansey succeeded in charming his young stepdaughter, who, over sixty years later, still recalls him fondly.

One incidental product of the marriage provides a list of the members of MO5G as of March 1915. We found amongst Dansey's effects a silver cigarette box presented to him on the occasion of his marriage by the members of his section and inscribed with their names. We have succeeded in identifying most of the people:

V. G. W. Kell (Major, later Major-General, head of MI5 until 1940)

J. F. C. Carter (Major, later Lieutenant-Colonel Indian Army, head of MI5F, and eventually Assistant Commissioner of the Metropolitan Police)

H. B. Clayton (Indian Civil Service, later MI5G)

W. E. H. Cooke (unknown)
R. J. Drake (whom we have already met)
R. E. A. Elliott (Indian Civil Service)
H. S. Gladstone (Captain, later MI6H)
M. M. Haldane (later head of MI5H)
F. Hall (later head of MI5D)
F. B. Henderson (Commander RN, on attachment)
E. B. Holt-Wilson (later head of MI5F, and eventually Kell's
   second i.c. until 1940)
H. M. J. McCance (Captain, later MI5H)
W. H. Moresby (Barrister)
R. Nathan (unknown)
W. M. Rolfe (unknown)
H. C. Streatfeild (CIE, and later MI5F)
H. H. Turner (unknown)

It has (jokingly) been suggested that Dansey's marriage to an American, or at least the subsequent failure thereof, explains his alleged anti-Americanism during the second world war. Apart from the fact that he is the last man to be influenced by such frivolous and personal considerations, there is a fundamental problem in identifying Dansey's personal attitudes. Like any good spy, he was all things to all men. His opinions tended to be tailored to the company in which he found himself. If you were anti-American and he felt that he could better achieve his ends by being so himself, then he would play up to your prejudices. It was, as Somerset Maugham put it, all part of his preference for "devious ways to straight".

It is the same with his alleged misogyny. We have been told that he actually disliked women. This is certainly not true as far as his private life was concerned. But there can be no doubt that professionally he distrusted female agents, and wherever possible preferred not to use them. But this was based not on a personal dislike of the sex but rather on the experience with Edith Cavell.

Edith Cavell was a clergyman's daughter from Swardeston in Norfolk. In 1907 she became the matron of a nursing school in Belgium. When the Germans invaded in 1914, she volunteered her services to the Belgian escape line, the aim of which was to smuggle men of military age to France or Holland before they were interned or sent to forced labour in Germany. A safe house was needed for the escapees where they could be hidden until they moved down the line. The hospital seemed an ideal cover, and as such it was also used occasionally by British and French agents.

For a while things ran fairly smoothly. But trouble began when Allied soldiers, who had either escaped from POW camps or else had simply avoided capture when their positions had been overrun by the enemy, started turning up at the hospital at 149 Rue de la Culture in the hope of using the escape line themselves.

Though she may have been an excellent hospital matron, Edith Cavell was totally unsuited for intelligence work. She seemed to have had no idea of even rudimentary security procedures, and permitted Allied soldiers on the run to go drinking in the local café and even have sing-songs – in English – in the hospital. Inevitably the operation came to the attention of the German authorities, who arrested her and her head assistant on 5th August 1915.

She confessed to harbouring Allied soldiers, and on 18th August she was executed by firing squad.

In a speech at the Intelligence Corps Dinner on 20th March 1938, General Sir Walter Kirke, one-time Director of Military Intelligence, spoke respectfully of Edith Cavell and other famous women agents. "Some of those who worked for us are known the world over," he declared. It is certainly true that the Norfolk clergyman's daughter became one of the martyrs of British Intelligence. However, it is doubtful if Claude Dansey shared General Kirke's sentiments. As a result of the Cavell saga, he always questioned the value of escape networks thereafter – a view which, as we shall see, was to dominate his attitude to MI9, the British escape department in the second world war. As for Cavell herself, he would have regarded her as incompetent and unstable. She reinforced his belief in the dangers of working with amateurs – and women agents in particular. Dansey agreed with the opinions Colonel David Henderson, who had been Director of Military Intelligence when he was serving in South Africa, had expressed so memorably in his *Field Intelligence, Its Principles and Practice*, a manual published in 1904, which became the bible of modern military intelligence. He wrote:

When women are employed as secret service agents, the probability of success and the difficulty of administration are alike increased. Women are frequently very skilful in eliciting information; they require no disguise; if attractive they are likely to be welcome everywhere, and may be able to seduce from their loyalty those whose assistance or indiscretion may be of use. On the other hand, they are variable, easily offended, seldom sufficiently reticent, and apt to be reckless. Their treatment requires the most watchful discretion. Usually they will work more consistently for a person than for a principle, and a lover in the Intelligence Corps makes a useful intermediary.

Perhaps the pathetic martyrdom of Edith Cavell could have been avoided if only she had had an Intelligence Corps lover.

CHAPTER EIGHT

The Yanks Are Coming

After two and a half years of war, Dansey was one of the most senior and experienced officers in British Intelligence. If one includes his scouting days with the British South Africa Police, he had been involved in intelligence, in various capacities, for twenty-two years. During that time, he had managed to do almost every type of work: crawling past sentries in the dark of the night before battle to discover an enemy's strength and overhear his plans; running networks of spies in South Africa and Somaliland, to forestall rebel activities; posing as a tourist in order to gain information in sensitive areas as far removed from each other as Madagascar, Morocco and Mexico; watching and reporting on Irish activities in America; rounding up suspect aliens in Britain at the start of war; dealing with security and counter-espionage both in Britain and in the war zones of western Europe. The list could go on and on. Both as an agent himself and as a controller of agents, he had built up a solid store of expertise.

For nearly two years, he had held the vital position of controlling all entry to the United Kingdom, the first line of defence against enemy agents. Many men would regard such a post as marking the peak of their careers. For Claude Dansey, however, it was only a springboard.

By the spring of 1917, the Allies were in a perilous condition. Russia was wallowing in the wake of one revolution and heading inexorably for another which would take her out of the war. France was crippled by her immense losses and was beginning to lose heart. After two and a half years of grinding conflict on the Western Front in Europe, on the high seas, in the Near and Middle East and Africa, British resources of men, money and munitions were running dangerously low. The British Government was spending £5,500,000 a day on the war, supporting both herself and her allies. Without help, she would surely collapse under the burden. Her account with J. P. Morgan in New York was already overdrawn to the sum of $400 million (£80 million). By the end of the war, she was to owe the US some $4,250 million (£850 million) much of which had been incurred on behalf of other nations, debts she stood little chance of ever recovering. In the early part of 1917, though, it was still far from certain that the US Government would agree to give her credit to support these debts.

The situation was not one-sided, however. Germany and the Central Powers were in a bad way, too. The war had become like a gargantuan prize fight in which the two contestants had slugged it out, toe to toe, round after bloody round, for so long that the result depended not on which one could land a knock-out blow but on which dropped first from sheer exhaustion. But the Germans had the advantage of greater resources of food, oil and raw materials at hand in Central Europe, while the Allies were dependent on supplies brought in by sea. The odds were that the Central Powers would be able to outlast France and Britain, if they could manage to tilt the balance by achieving three vital objectives: they must engineer the collapse or withdrawal of Russia by any means possible, in order to end the fighting in the east and release men and material to the Western Front; they must prevent supplies reaching Britain and France by ship across the Atlantic; and they must either keep America out of the war or if this was not possible then at least ensure she was kept busy away from Europe.

This last objective could best be achieved by persuading Mexico to go to war with America. The prize would be the recovery of Mexico's "lost territory in Texas, New Mexico and Arizona". To this end, on 16th January 1917, the German Foreign Minister, Arthur Zimmermann, sent a coded message to the German ambassador in Washington, to be passed on "by a safe route" to the German minister in Mexico, von Eckhardt. With typical Germanic thoroughness, he sent it by three different routes, two of them by wireless and the third by the US State Department's own cable, which President Wilson allowed them to use, though he meant this permission only for messages concerning his peace efforts.

Long before the ambassador in Washington had passed on the message, in fact probably before he had even seen it, copies of all three versions landed in the in-tray of Room 40, the cryptographic section of British Naval Intelligence, at the Admiralty in London, where it was decoded as a matter of course, like all the other enemy signals picked up by the interception section.

The cryptanalysts in Room 40 had succeeded in unravelling the German military and naval ciphers unaided, but cracking the diplomatic code was another matter – until they had two pieces of luck: code books were recovered from the luggage of Wilhelm Wassmuss, the German equivalent of Lawrence of Arabia, who was operating with the tribes in Persia; and a young wireless operator and code clerk in the German radio transmitting station in Brussels fell into their hands.

This young man, Alexander Szek, was found with the help of Dansey's department. Although of Austrian parentage, he had been born and brought up in England, which entitled him to dual nationality. Two years before the war, he had gone to Brussels with his father, staying there to complete his studies when his father went back to Vienna. When the Germans took Brussels, they naturally chose to regard young Szek as being Austrian, and therefore liable to military service. Because he had been studying wireless engineering at the university, they directed him to work in the Brussels radio station.

When the British Secret Service learnt through its agents in Brussels that young Szek had been born in Croydon, just outside London, MO5 were alerted and traced a relation (his mother, or sister – this fact remains uncertain) still in England, working as a governess. Like many people with Austrian blood, she claimed to be anti-German, and Dansey's people, after applying a little pressure, persuaded her to write a letter to Szek urging him to work for the country of his birth.

Szek was extremely nervous, and was only persuaded with difficulty to steal the code, copying it out bit by bit over a three-month period. The means used to convince him of his duty could not have inspired any great confidence, because at the end he refused to hand over the final pages unless he was helped to escape. The rest of the story remains a mystery: the copied sheets of code reached England, via an agent in Holland, but Szek disappeared and was never seen or heard of again. Whether the Germans caught him and shot him, or whether, as his father claimed, the British disposed of him to prevent the Germans finding out what he had done, we shall probably never know. The code was, however, given to the men in Room 40, and the Germans continued to use it until the end of the war, unaware that it was no longer secret.

When the telegram from Zimmermann arrived in Room 40, the two cryptanalysts on duty began what they regarded as the routine task of decrypting the message. There was nothing to signify its importance. The only unusual thing about it was its length – estimated at more than 1,000 groups of numbers.

The telegram turned out to consist of two messages. The first was important enough, for it confirmed what the Allies had been expecting and dreading for some time: Germany intended to resume unrestricted submarine warfare on 1st February. This meant that any vessel from any country, including neutrals, was liable to be torpedoed without warning if found in the war zone. But it was the second message which proved all-important.

FOREIGN OFFICE TELEGRAPHS JANUARY 16:
NUMBER 1.
STRICTLY SECRET. YOURSELF TO DECIPHER.
WE INTEND TO BEGIN UNRESTRICTED U-BOAT
WARFARE ON THE FIRST OF FEBRUARY. WE
SHALL ENDEAVOUR IN SPITE OF THIS TO KEEP
THE UNITED STATES NEUTRAL. IN THE EVENT OF
THIS NOT SUCCEEDING, WE OFFER MEXICO AN
ALLIANCE ON THE FOLLOWING BASIS: MAKE WAR
TOGETHER, MAKE PEACE TOGETHER. GENEROUS
FINANCIAL SUPPORT AND AN UNDERSTANDING
ON OUR PART THAT MEXICO IS TO RECONQUER
THE LOST TERRITORIES IN TEXAS, NEW MEXICO
AND ARIZONA. THE SETTLEMENT IN DETAIL IS
LEFT TO YOU.
 YOU WILL INFORM THE PRESIDENT (OF MEXICO)
OF THE ABOVE IN THE STRICTEST SECRECY AS
SOON AS THE OUTBREAK OF WAR WITH THE
UNITED STATES IS CERTAIN AND ADD THE
SUGGESTION THAT HE SHOULD, ON HIS OWN
INITIATIVE, INVITE JAPAN TO JOIN IMMEDIATELY
AND AT THE SAME TIME MEDIATE BETWEEN
JAPAN AND OURSELVES.
 PLEASE CALL THE PRESIDENT'S ATTENTION TO
THE FACT THAT THE RUTHLESS EMPLOYMENT OF
OUR SUBMARINES NOW OFFERS THE PROSPECT
OF COMPELLING ENGLAND TO MAKE PEACE
WITHIN A FEW MONTHS. ACKNOWLEDGE
RECEIPT. ZIMMERMANN.

The Director of Naval Intelligence, now Admiral Sir Reginald "Blinker" Hall, hurriedly delivered the telegram to the Foreign Secretary, Arthur Balfour. Balfour, naturally, was overjoyed. Here was the evidence he so desperately needed to prove to President Wilson the true nature of Germany's intentions. With the soil of the United States itself threatened, surely Wilson would no longer be able to say there was nothing to choose between the war aims of Britain and Germany. He would have sent a copy of the telegram to Washington immediately, but Hall stopped him. It was vital, he reminded the Foreign Secretary, that the Germans should not know that Room 40 was breaking their codes and ciphers. Reluctantly, Balfour agreed to hold his hand until such time as Hall had arranged a suitable cover story to give the impression that Britain had come by the decoded telegram by some entirely different means.

This camouflage took Hall, with the co-operation of the other branches of the Secret Service, thirty-five days to accomplish. A British agent, known to us only as Mr H, was operating in Mexico City, where he had been living for some time, probably as far back as 1911, when Dansey made his mysterious visit there. Mr H obtained a copy of the Western Union telegram sent by the German ambassador in Washington to the minister in Mexico. The wording was sufficiently different, when decoded, to imply that the message had been obtained in Mexico, perhaps by theft after von Eckhardt had himself decoded it. Hall gave Balfour the green light.

On 24th February 1917, Balfour called on the American ambassador, Walter Hines Page, and, in what he said was "as dramatic a moment as I remember in all my life", he handed over the single sheet of paper containing the decoded message. The effect when the text of the telegram was published in America was explosive. Cries of "foul" and "forgery" from the anti-British lobby were abruptly silenced when Zimmermann himself made the extraordinary mistake of admitting it was genuine. From then on, even those newspapers which had previously been staunchly isolationist and anti-war screamed for action against Germany. Public opinion erupted in demands that the United States should enter the war immediately.

Poor, peace-loving Wilson was shattered. For another three weeks he tried vainly to find some way of avoiding the inevitable, but when three American merchant ships were sunk without warning and with heavy loss of life on 18th March, he had to admit failure. On 2nd April he spoke to a specially-convened joint session of Congress and advised them to declare war on Germany. They duly did so, on 6th April 1917.

America's long isolation from world affairs was ended. At last, she was Britain's ally, some 140 years after the two nations had parted company. There might still be some doubters in the US, but in Britain the news was received with universal elation. Now there could be no danger of the Allies losing. Arthur Balfour immediately set about organising a mission to cross the Atlantic for top-level talks. President Wilson welcomed the idea, but stated in private that he saw some dangers in the meeting and feared that some Americans might suspect "an attempt in some degree to take charge of us as an assistant of Great Britain", and therefore suggested the mission should be diplomatic rather than military. Balfour agreed, but included some military representatives in the twenty-five members of his team: for the army, General Tom Bridges, who had ridden alongside Dansey as a lieutenant in the Mafeking relief column, for the navy Admiral de Chair, and for the intelligence services the recently-promoted Lieutenant-Colonel Claude Dansey.

Dansey's inclusion was an astute move. Not only was he one of the most experienced intelligence officers in the country, but he also had an extensive knowledge and understanding (the two do not always go together) of America and a host of contacts at the very highest levels. Balfour was making his first official visit to the USA, but for Dansey it was a second home, and he could provide the rest of the mission with much-needed expertise in dealing with Americans.

The party left Euston station secretly on 10th April, heading for Greenock in Scotland, where the liner *Olympic* awaited them. They were held up for twenty-four hours at Dumfries, spending the night in the Railway Hotel because the sailing was delayed by reports of U-boat activity. Although Dansey knew that there were almost certainly no German agents in Britain – he and his colleagues in MI5 had retained their supremacy over the German espionage system – he must have been extremely concerned for their security, particularly when Balfour admitted as they left that he had completely blown their cover by giving his autograph to the lift boy. Balfour confessed in his autobiography that this "was bound to destroy my whole prestige as a master of secret diplomacy . . . I had no excuse to offer when reproached with this singular indiscretion and my authority received a shock from which it never recovered."

They eventually sailed from Greenock at midnight on 11th April and, despite storms which slowed the *Olympic*, had an uneventful crossing, passing the time with conferences and taking exercise in the ship's gymnasium until they berthed in Halifax, Nova Scotia, on the twentieth. There, they transferred to a special train for the two-day journey to Washington, being joined at New York by the President's special adviser, Colonel House. They reached Washington on Sunday, 22nd April, and drove with a cavalry escort through cheering crowds and streets decked with the Union Jack and the Stars and Stripes to the "luxurious dwelling" of Mr

Breckenridge Long, which had been put at Balfour's disposal for the duration of his visit.

Next morning, Balfour left for the White House for the first of many meetings with the President. By a happy coincidence, it was St George's Day. Dansey went his own way, to a square, domed building standing back from the road about a quarter of a mile past the army parade grounds: the War College. He had a date to keep with Major R. H. Van Deman.

CHAPTER NINE

Birth of an Intelligence Service

Ralph Van Deman is known as the father of American Military Intelligence. A tall, thin man with a heavily-lined face, looking worn and older than his years but with intense, piercing grey eyes, he reminded those who met him of Abraham Lincoln. He had a passionate belief in the importance of intelligence, and for years had struggled vainly to persuade the military authorities in America to set up a proper intelligence department.

Van Deman had started his career under General Arthur MacArthur, father of the second world war hero, in the Philippines, where he had established the Manila Information Bureau. When the organisation of the army was modernised in 1903, and a general staff was created along the lines of those being formed by European armies, Van Deman's office became part of the Second Section, which was to be an intelligence department. Van Deman had been delighted, but his joy was short-lived, for when Major-General Franklin Bell was appointed Chief of Staff he promptly merged the Second Section with the War College in Washington, supposedly as an economy measure. Bell was one of the old school of officers who despised intelligence and was determined to prevent its growth and development. He went on to destroy the section altogether, making it simply an information sub-unit of the War College, to be run by a committee, with no authority, no direct access to the staff, and virtually no budget.

Van Deman returned from duty in Asia in 1916, and was assigned to the unit. What he found horrified him. The entire intelligence organisation of the US army had been reduced to one room in the War College, where reports from attachés in embassies and legations all over the world, and from various other sources including Allied intelligence services, had piled up in what has been described as a gold mine of intelligence. It was a gold mine that had never been worked, however, for the papers and reports

101

had simply lain there, gathering dust. Not a single summary had been prepared. No information had been distributed.

Van Deman immediately set to work to try to put matters right, but it was an uphill task. He went to Bell's successor as Chief of Staff, Major-General Hugh L. Scott, to plead for the re-establishment of the Second Section, pointing out that America's involvement in the war was becoming more and more certain, and that they must be prepared. But Scott dismissed him as a nuisance, a slightly deranged man with an unwelcome obsession. For twelve months and more, Van Deman fought on, with little success. He managed to get a slight increase in his staff, but it was still pitifully inadequate. Van Deman may have been the father of American Intelligence, but it was proving to be an extremely difficult birth. He was desperately in need of a good midwife. On the morning of Monday 23rd April 1917, one walked into his office, in the unlikely shape of Claude Dansey.

According to American Intelligence mythology Van Deman's fortunes were changed by an unnamed woman author, who arrived in Washington to write a series of articles on America as arsenal of the world. Van Deman's superiors unloaded the lady on to him as something of a vindictive joke: she wanted information, he had an obsession about information, therefore he was the person to take care of her. The story goes on that the joke rebounded when the lady turned out to be a personal friend of the Secretary of War, Newton D. Baker, and that when she learned of Van Deman's trouble she spoke to Baker, who immediately called Scott and ordered him to take action. Next day, the Military Intelligence Division was formed. A nice story, but untrue, an excellent example of the sort of cover story designed to camouflage the activities of secret operators such as Dansey.

Van Deman told what actually happened in a citation he pre-pared in August 1920 when he proposed the award of the United States Distinguished Service Medal for the man who became his guide, mentor and friend.

At the time Colonel Dansey arrived in Washington the Military Intelligence of the General Staff consisted of two officers and three clerks attached to the War College Division. Efforts had been in progress for over a year to induce the War Department authorities to recognise the necessity for intelligence work and to authorise some kind of an organisation for carrying on this part of the work of a General Staff. These efforts, however, met with little interest on the part of the War Department and it was not until June 27, 1917, months after we had actually declared war, before authority was reluctantly granted to form an organisation for intelligence work and to formulate plans for co-operation with the Civil Departments of the government.

In working out our plans for the organisation of what is now the Military Intelligence Division of the General Staff Corps, the advice and assistance of Colonel Dansey was absolutely invaluable. With the hearty consent of his chief, General Bridges, he placed himself unreservedly at our disposition and he spared neither time nor labor to give us the benefit of his knowledge and experience. Not only did he give us invaluable assistance and advice in connection with organisation plans but, what was much more important and valuable at that time, exerted himself to excite and interest the Secretary of War and the Chief of Staff in the subject of Military Intelligence and probably did more than any other one man to get a hearing for those officers of the General Staff who were struggling for an opportunity to bring this most important matter to the attention of the War Department.

Dansey was putting his time at Sleepy Hollow to good use. His contacts from those years were among the most important and influential men in the land. They controlled banks and railroads and public utilities, as well as production of vital materials such as rubber, copper and oil. They were also able to pull strings for him and gain him access to men of power such as Secretary of War Baker.

Even with Dansey's considerable charm and powers of persuasion, it took some two months to obtain official approval for the establishment of an intelligence department. But Dansey and Van Deman both knew they could not wait, and began making plans immediately. Within a week of his arrival, Dansey had supplied Van Deman with a detailed description of the organisation of British Intelligence and how it operated, both in London and in the field. This supplemented and enlarged on similar information which he had given orally to the American military attaché in London, Colonel Lassiter, as early as February 1917, long before it was certain to anyone other than the intelligence services that America would definitely enter the war. It was the first time such details had ever been given to anyone other than a recognised ally. Lassiter had been duly impressed, and sent a long memo to Van Deman listing what he had been told of the structure of British Intelligence, but commenting that "it is almost impossible to get

103

anything in writing as to the detailed working of any one of the various departments, for the reason that every department has grown up very slowly around the personality of one man, and he has made his own rules".

Lassiter reveals that it was Dansey, while heading MI5E, who started the system of Passport Control Officers which was to become the standard cover for British Intelligence abroad, by attaching officers to overseas consulates to monitor the issue of visas and to investigate applicants. This achievement would be tinged with more than a little irony some twenty years later, when he was called on to form another, doubly-secret organisation because the Passport Control Officer system had been both blown and penetrated and could no longer be relied on.

Dansey, as Van Deman acknowledged, did not stint himself in feeding the Americans with both information and advice, much of it learned the hard way. One message which he came back to time after time was the overriding need for co-operation and co-ordination between the various army, General Staff and naval sections and departments in the intelligence establishment.

In the United States at that time, there were four other intelligence services all of them small and all of them limited to specific areas. The Justice Department had the infant Bureau of Investigation (later adding the prefix "Federal" to become the FBI), which had the responsibility of policing violations of federal statutes. The Treasury had the Secret Service, formed to deal with counterfeiters, which was also responsible for protecting the President, plus a few other small duties. The State Department had a small diplomatic intelligence section, though it did not run agents. The navy had a few officers assigned to intelligence work: they were known as "Aids for Information" and their duties were to supervise intelligence work concerning shipping, espionage and sabotage, surveillance of the coast, enemy submarine bases, and illegal radio stations. In the autumn of 1916, a branch Naval Intelligence office had been established in New York, and others were later set up in different cities, mainly to investigate and guard manufacturing plants which had navy contracts.

So far, the American organisations did not intrude on or interfere with each other's work. In Britain, it had taken nearly two and a half years of war to sort out the main areas of duplication and misunderstanding caused by rivalry and competition between the various arms, which had grown up piecemeal over the years. Time and energy had been wasted, and Dansey was determined to warn Van Deman of such dangers at the outset, and to advise him on the best ways of overcoming them. Van Deman took heed, as did the others, with the happy result that on 9th August he was able to write to Dansey in London telling him that

> the co-operation is as nearly perfect as anything could be. It is certainly as close and cordial as if the other departments were simply a section of the Military Intelligence Section office. I am connected with all of them by direct telephone and everything considering Military Intelligence comes here for assignment for action . . . You may not believe it is possible, but nevertheless we have combined the Navy, State and War Intelligence work under the Military Attachés in all of the neutral countries where we have military attachés.

Dansey must have been gratified but somewhat astonished at this achievement by a man who was proving to be an apt pupil, particularly as Van Deman could not resist reminding him that he had been "very skeptical" of the prospects in this area.

Of course, in warning Van Deman of the dangers of duplication, Dansey was also trying to forestall any such rivalry or confusion between the British and American services. He had, after all, come to America with the specific brief of establishing co-operation, as well as assisting and advising. He fulfilled both briefs with remarkable success. He was supported in his efforts by his chiefs in London, and by Colonel Lassiter, the American military attaché there, who wrote to the Chief of Staff:

> It is clear that without an Intelligence Service we will be like blind people fighting an enemy who sees clearly every move that we make. At the present time there is no question about it, that the Germans are fully acquainted with every move that we make. I do not presume that we have any means of our own for finding out what the Germans are doing, and unless we hasten to take advantage of the British and French machinery for acquiring information, while we are organising our own, we will certainly be at a great disadvantage.

Colonel Lassiter echoed what Dansey was telling Van Deman: "We are particularly advised to avoid duplicating Secret Service in Europe. Our Secret Service might be developed in Scandinavia but it would seem especially important to develop it in Central and South America and the Far East." To help avoid duplication, Dansey was able to tell Van Deman that if America formally requested it, and if they impressed on their people the need for absolute secrecy, military attachés in British embassies and legations would be instructed to establish "confidential relations" with their American opposite numbers, sharing secret information with them.

Many Americans saw such a move as confirmation of President Wilson's fears about Britain trying to "take charge" of his country "as an assistant". Since British Intelligence had been shamelessly intercepting and decoding US telegrams and messages for the past two years, and had been doing everything possible to influence the course of American policy, there were good reasons for such concern. After all, Dansey himself had worked in the USA as a British secret agent for three years before the outbreak of war, and it is unlikely that his interests had been confined to the Irish question.

Since the two nations were now allies, however, fighting the same war against the same enemy, it was obviously sensible for them to work hand in glove as far as possible. If there were ulterior and devious motives, there were honest ones, too. And if Britain was assuming the role of senior partner, that was only natural when she was the one with the hard-earned experience. The British leaders were also afraid – as they would be again twenty-five years later – of green Americans rushing into the intelligence world and upsetting their carefully-laid and often extremely delicate arrangements. There was no room in a modern war for the sort of naivety which President Wilson had displayed during the previous four years.

Van Deman and the Chief of the War College Division, Brigadier-General Kuhn, both welcomed the offer, even though the existing staff in American embassies and legations were not equipped to deal with intelligence matters and would need assistance. This meant getting the approval not only of the Chief of Staff for the army, but also of the State Department. Bureaucratic red tape could have made this a lengthy and tortuous process, but Dansey and Van Deman made personal contact with General Scott and Secretary Lansing, persuading them to give their direct approval for the collaboration and for the immediate appointment of assistant military attachés to be responsible for intelligence matters. Van Deman was authorised to find six suitable men who would be commissioned into the National Army, given a crash training course in Washington, then sent out to the various neutral capitals of Europe.

The most important of these were The Hague in Holland and Berne in Switzerland, where the intelligence staff in the British legation, then comprising seven officers and a number of clerks, was being enlarged. The US military attaché in Berne, Major C. W. Exton, wrote to Van Deman asking that

> some young officer of good address, and with a knowledge of French and German if possible, be sent at once to work here in conjunction with and in the offices of the British Intelligence Officer.
>
> The British Office [he went on] is thoroughly organised as a result of over two years experience, and there is really very little that we can do at present to supplement their work. They urgently request, however, that we give them this officer, and in return they say, "You will have the benefit of all the work that we are doing in this office, and you can transmit it daily to your people in France or wherever you like." . . . The British say they have plenty of funds, and that no funds are necessary on our part.

The "close and hearty co-operation" ordered by Kuhn and Scott was under way. It took several weeks for the right men to be found, and it was not until August that Van Deman was able to report that they had been commissioned and were being trained, but by then Exton could state that he was able to despatch considerable amounts of information every day to General Pershing's intelligence officer in Paris, either by telegraph or by the daily courier service. He was also telegraphing political and economic information to the Secretary of State in Washington.

While this was going on, the embassies in London and Paris were also being organised to handle intelligence in collaboration with the British and the French. Lassiter in London asked for additional staff, secure codes and ciphers, a special safe and more offices. He sought permission to rent a separate building, which he estimated would cost $5,000 a year to rent and run, since they were rapidly outgrowing their space in the embassy itself. He said the staff he needed immediately and urgently for intelligence work were:

- 1 Chief
- 1 Assistant
- 4 Officers (Intelligence Section)
- 4 Officers (Technical Section)
- 1 Surgeon
- 1 Quartermaster
- 1 NCO for recruiting
- 2 Confidential clerks from the United States
- 10 Clerks and stenographers locally employed.

In addition to the extra staff in Washington and for embassies and legations overseas, Field Intelligence had to be organised and manned, again starting totally from scratch. There was no provision in the US army as it then existed for an intelligence organisation within the GHQ in France, but the Allies were impressing on the Americans that it was essential. Again, Dansey came to the rescue, providing detailed plans of the way intelligence was organised and run at British GHQ, under the G2 staff officer.

The man chosen to be the G2 on General Pershing's staff was a young, newly-promoted lieutenant-colonel, Dennis E. Nolan. He was as keen on intelligence work as Van Deman, and the two men became enthusiastic collaborators. Following Dansey's plan, Nolan set about recruiting the men he needed for duties in France with the Corps of Intelligence Police, which later became the Counter-Intelligence Corps and eventually metamorphosed into the Intelligence and Security Corps. Initially, he wanted fifty men, who would all ideally be linguists, detectives, psychologists and social extroverts at the same time.

Nolan delegated the task of finding the men to a young lieutenant called Royden Williamson, who – under considerable pressure of time – resorted in some desperation to a method which must have made Dansey recoil in horror: he advertised for them in the newspapers! The response was from a remarkable range of men: "a delegation of Cajuns from Louisiana, a sprinkling of French Canadians, a coterie of Harvard men, a French deserter, and even an active communist". But there were enough, and after a brief training in Washington the first batch were shipped to England for further instruction at the British Intelligence School at Harrow, and thence to France. Others recruited in the same way stayed in the United States for security and counter-espionage duties across the nation.

Both for attachés and for field intelligence officers, Dansey had a great deal of useful advice, particularly concerning the use of agents. He warned them that German counter-espionage was then so well organised that it was useless to employ what he described as "the ordinary adventurer who takes to espionage whether through motives of cupidity or patriotism". Agents were, however, the chief means of collecting information and he was at pains to stress the importance of good organisation. "You can have the best agent in the world in the enemy's country," he told the American Staff, "but unless the information he collects can be gotten out regularly and with certainty, it is so much waste paper."

Dansey considered that, apart from what he called "local agents" working across the lines where possible (and it was not often possible in the trench warfare of France during the first world war), the best agents worked nowhere near the front at all. "In fact," he stated, "the further away from the front . . . the better." In this area, he favoured a particularly Danseyish stratagem, one which was to become more and more important to him during the years that lay ahead: the use of big companies and corporations to provide information and "high-class business cover" for agents planted within them.

At Dansey's suggestion, and initially with his personal help, Van Deman and his people made contact with the efficient information and intelligence departments of the large banks such as the National City Bank (in whose board room Dansey had been appointed Resident Secretary of the Sleepy Hollow Country Club and with whose directors he was on intimate terms), and J. P. Morgan and Company (with whom he had close connections through Ryan), and with large corporations such as the Standard Oil companies and the United States Steel Corporation. The success of this scheme depended largely on the confidence which the directors of the corporations concerned had in the Military Intelligence chiefs and it was invaluable for Van Deman and his successor, General Marlborough Churchill (a very distant American relative of Winston), to have someone like Claude Dansey to help establish personal contact. By the end of the war, virtually every organisation with branch offices in the US and abroad was involved.

Officially, Dansey was working from the British Embassy, as part of the mission, and he had a desk there with the military attaché, Lieutenant-Colonel M. O'Brien. But the liaison with Van Deman became so close that he was also given a desk in his office, where he could be in touch with everything that was going on. As the Intelligence Section grew and began to take shape, Dansey was called on to give lectures to them, and to the General Staff, lectures which took place behind locked doors guarded by armed soldiers. The lectures were popular and valuable. At the first, on 4th May 1917, the most enthusiastic listener seems to have been the War College Chief, Brigadier-General Kuhn, whose conversion to the cause of intelligence was obviously complete. He and Dansey became good friends, which can have done nothing to harm co-operation between the two nations, and when writing to Van Deman after he had returned to Europe, Dansey always asked to be remembered to him.

CHAPTER TEN

The Black Chamber

For six hectic weeks in May and early June 1917, Dansey interspersed his work with Van Deman with preaching the gospel of intelligence to the American staff officers who flocked to sit at his feet. He talked and lectured and advised continuously on all aspects of his craft, both positive and negative, as he called the two sides.

On the negative side, counter-intelligence, he described how the British organisation had grown from four officers and three or four clerks at the beginning of the war to some fifty officers at headquarters alone, with many others placed all over the world. The cornerstone of any counter-espionage organisation, he told the American officers, is a central registry "run in such a way that it is a pool of information, whether it concerns a German division, a suspected spy, or the pepper trade". The Central Registry of MI5 (as MO5 had now become) was used by the whole British Empire and the other Allies. It was run by one officer, supervising 130 women, and contained some 250,000 cards and 27,000 personal files or dossiers.

It is interesting to remember that this vast reservoir of information had been built up in only two and a half years in a country which had never had a centralised police force and whose people, in peacetime, were implacably opposed to the registration of personal details. If such a transformation was possible in the land which proclaimed itself "mother of the free", is it any wonder that in totalitarian countries secret police can rule with a grip of steel? Fortunately for Britain, Vernon Kell, the head of MI5, was on the side of the angels.

The police Kell made use of, principally through Sir Basil Thomson, head of the Criminal Investigation Department at Scotland Yard, were the ordinary constabularies of Britain, answerable to their local communities and not directly to central government. They were necessary, as they still are today, because MI5 and its agents have never had the power of arrest. Dansey told his American audiences that MI5 had extremely good and close relationships with the police, and could wire to any policeman in the country and get a reply direct. He was very proud of the fact that there was absolutely no red tape involved, and that although MI5 never issued orders but simply made requests, they had engaged police interest and thus obtained their willing co-operation. He had to admit, however, "You cannot expect the same point of view from them, and they often think that we ask them to do very extraordinary and unnecessary things, I have no doubt. But, on the whole, they play up to us admirably."

The only real problem with the police, Dansey reported, was over "a little refinement that they do not quite grasp. They like detection and conviction, a spy trial and the newspaper paragraph . . . In any really delicate matter we always keep our fingers on every move in the game, and see that the police do not spoil a good thing." MI5 had given up the "Detective idea" quite early in the day, realising that a dramatic conviction and a spy being shot can be far less effective than capturing a man and then making use of him either as a turned "double cross" agent, or simply by taking over his reports.

"If you catch one of their best men," he said, "and can lead them to believe that he is still loose and operating, and they continue to rely on him for their information, and use his reports, it is of infinitely greater value than having a dead man."

The "double cross" system of using enemy agents was brought to a fine art by British Intelligence in the second world war, with a special outfit known as the XX (translated for security reasons as Twenty) Committee under Sir John Masterman, a history professor borrowed from Oxford. But like so many of the famous achievements of the 1939-45 war, it had been done before, by Dansey and his fellows, during the 1914-18 conflict, when Dansey had also instructed the Americans in such niceties.

In association with this use of enemy agents, Dansey also dealt with deception, another idea which is commonly believed to have originated in the second world war, and told how the Germans had been deceived by false messages concerning the movements of the British Expeditionary Force at the beginning of the war, so that while the army was already being deployed in France, the German General Staff were convinced it was still in England.

General Kuhn confessed that he was "rather guileless" by nature, and that he had not had any idea that many of the things he was learning about were possible. He was by no means an exception in the American army of the time – Dansey reported how one influential man in Washington told him that in his opinion there was not very much you could want to know about an enemy army, once you knew it existed! It was this attitude which had made Van Deman tear his hair for so long, and it was this attitude which Dansey had to help him destroy.

One of the most delicate aspects of intelligence and counter-espionage in a democracy during wartime is the way in which individual rights and liberties – which are usually the very things being fought for – must be curtailed in the public interest. In his lectures to his American audiences, Dansey spoke of this when describing to them "two more servants of the military information service" which they would have to develop urgently: postal and cable censorship. The overt reason for these infringements of liberty and privacy was to prevent anyone unwittingly giving information in a letter or telegram which could be of use to the enemy. The censor's public job was simply to cut out any offending matter.

While the censor's basic function was undoubtedly important, Dansey and his colleagues were more concerned with stopping information being passed deliberately. Although the censors were only on the fringe of the intelligence establishment, the censorship process had proved particularly rewarding both in trapping enemy agents and in discovering vital information about the enemy's intentions.

The problem lay in spotting such messages, which were naturally disguised with great skill. "The Germans have a thousand different ways of sending a code telegram, a thousand different addresses," Dansey stated. The censors had to be carefully instructed about what to look for, and equally carefully kept in their place. They always wanted to make their own investigations rather than simply passing on anything they considered suspicious. But this did not suit MI5; they had learned to make inquiries in more devious ways, preferring where possible to play an agent rather than remove him, and make use of his messages for deception.

"Once you know a code," he explained, "such as that known as the family code, in which the message is apparently some simple thing about family matters ['Uncle Willy has had an accident, and is in hospital,' for instance would mean 'Agent X has been arrested and is in prison'] you paraphrase that telegram and let it go, or make some slight alteration and you might put the enemy on a false scent altogether."

But no matter how efficient the censorship organisation, it was useless if the intelligence department lacked the means of dealing with codes, ciphers and secret writing. Not only was America totally unequipped, it did not even operate any secure codes or ciphers of its own. The State Department codes were so old fashioned and simple they could be cracked by any decent amateur, and Dansey also had to inform Kuhn and Van Deman that photographic copies of the War Department code book were in the hands of German Intelligence, taken from a book which had been stolen during the American raid into Mexico in 1916. What was more, he told them, the Germans were intercepting all messages which passed through the transatlantic cable. The cable itself, he said, could not be tapped, but by stretching other wires alongside it for several hundred feet, telegraph operators in submarines sitting on the bottom could copy out signals by induction.

With this dismal knowledge, the Americans were forced to throw away their existing codes and ciphers and start afresh. When they wanted to inform London of the plans for the departure of the first part of the American Expeditionary Force they had to resort to a temporary expedient. They sent two messages. The first read:

President's embargo ruling should have immediate notice. Grave situation affecting international law. Statement foreshadows ruin of many neutrals. Yellow journals unifying natural excitement immensely.

The second message followed shortly afterwards. It read:

Apparently neutrals protest is sharply discounted and ignored. Isman hard hit. Blockade issue effects pretext for embargo on by products ejecting suets and vegetable oils.

Both messages were picked up and passed to the German intercepting station at Neumunster, where the German cryptanalysts examined them with care. They did not, however, break the code. The reason was psychologically brilliant – the German experts were too clever, and too sophisticated to see what was in virtually plain language right under their noses. The code was one of the simplest schoolboy ruses: the first letter of every word in the first message, and the second letter in every word in the second message spell out the answer:

Pershing sails from N.Y. June 1.

By a happy coincidence, there was a man at hand who was eager to take on the task of both preparing and breaking codes and ciphers. He was a twenty-seven-year-old telegraph clerk in the State Department code room, Herbert O. Yardley. This tall, thin-faced young man, with his high domed forehead, had a passionate interest in codes and ciphers, and had spent the previous four years trying to persuade his masters of the importance of the subject, and also of the weaknesses of America's systems. He had resorted to shock tactics by deciphering secret state messages, and had written a memorandum of over a hundred pages on the "Solution of American Diplomatic Codes", proving just how vulnerable they were. Like Van Deman, Yardley was a fanatic, and like Van Deman before the war he was regarded as something of a nuisance. But when war was declared, and he tried to get released from the State Department to join the army, he was told he was needed where he was, and would have to stay put.

Displaying the determination of the true fanatic, however, Yardley managed to get to Van Deman, and explained to him what he would like to do. His arrival, at precisely the right moment, must have seemed like a gift from heaven, and Van Deman immediately arranged that he be released from his post and commissioned as a lieutenant in the army. He was given the job of forming a cryptographic bureau which would be responsible for compiling codes and ciphers for American military and diplomatic use, solving enemy codes and ciphers, establishing secure communications systems for intelligence, and dealing with secret-ink messages. He had to find and train officers and operators not only for his own bureau in Washington but also for Nolan's department with the Expeditionary Force in France and for sub-sections in London and Paris.

All this would be a formidable task at the best of times. Now, with the added pressure of war, it must have seemed almost impossible to the young man from the State Department code room, who had no military or managerial experience whatever. Fortunately, help was at hand from the Allies, particularly from the English colonel who had his own desk in Van Deman's department. With Dansey's advice and guidance, Yardley was able to create the "Black Chamber", as his section became known. which was to outlast not only the war but also the Intelligence Department itself.

Dansey was not a specialist cryptographer, but he was aware of what was being done in Britain and France, and could provide both advice on organisation and a link with London. He could not arrange what Yardley needed most desperately – experts to come to Washington to teach their skills to Yardley's novices – for such men were needed equally desperately at home. But he could do the next best thing: have copies of hundreds of German military code and cipher intercepts sent over as examples, together with explanations of their solutions. And he could arrange for Yardley and his staff to go to London as soon as time allowed, to join in British training courses.

No doubt he also had advice to offer on recruitment, if only to prevent Yardley advertising for men. Here, they had the advantage of many letters in the War College files from people offering their services, and Yardley formed the nucleus of his section by calling on a number of scholars who seemed to have the right qualifications. By no means all of them were successful, however, though Yardley said he was "amused by their eagerness to master the principles of cryptography".

"Scholarship, I suddenly discovered, was nothing more than the capacity to absorb learning," he recorded. "These scholars were faced with a quite different problem, for there was not a great deal of learning to absorb. They would be obliged to make their own discoveries. For this reason, most of them were dismal failures."

The very first to arrive, however, was the most successful of them all. Dr John M. Manly, a small, quietly-spoken scholar, was head of the English Department of the University of Chicago. Generally, the scholars who make the best cryptographers are mathematicians, but Manly had the rare gift of what Yardley described as a "cipher brain" and "was destined to develop into the most skilful and brilliant of all our cryptographers". To Manly Yardley delegated the running of the section concerned with the breaking of enemy codes and ciphers, while he recruited an old colleague from the State Department to deal specifically with creating new ones for the War Department.

Dansey was more successful in obtaining direct help to teach the Americans about the use and detection of secret messages written in invisible ink between the lines of apparently innocuous letters or documents. Dr S. W. Collins, Britain's foremost expert in this field, travelled to Washington to lecture and instruct the chemists recruited by Yardley for his sub-section.

Collins had the advantage of addressing himself to men who, although they knew little or nothing about secret writing, were at least trained chemists. But he did not attempt to hide the difficulties. Germany led the world in chemistry at the beginning of the war, he reminded them, and had brought her scientific expertise to bear in this area, as well as many others. She had started several steps ahead, and while Britain and France had struggled to catch up, the Germans had exerted themselves to maintain and if possible increase their lead.

At the outbreak of war, Britain had been in the same situation as the Americans were now. The use and detection of secret inks was at such a primitive stage that Cumming, Chief of the SIS, always told his agents that the best secret ink was human semen. No doubt this was excellent advice for men, but one cannot help wondering how women agents managed. Although Britain and France both set up rigid postal censorship, the Germans still appeared to be getting information.

"Shortly after the declaration of war," Collins told his students, "we were stunned when we discovered, through our own under-cover agents in Germany, who had meanwhile cleverly entered the German Secret Service, that thousands of secret-ink letters were passing the censorship. The situation was critical, for we were unprepared for secret-ink espionage. We quickly gathered together many of our chemists, and began the task of matching brains with German scientists."

They were at least partly successful, making spectacular progress after a slow start, and as Dansey said, "kept the German chemists very busy inventing new means of writing with invisible inks". But the Germans did invent new methods and improvements and it was a constant struggle to keep up. In the early years, agents were caught carrying cobalt salts, potassium ferrocyanide and similar substances concealed in tubes of toothpaste, or cakes of soap. In later developments the concentration of silver, the active ingredient in the ink, was reduced to as little as one hundredth of one per cent. Since its presence could only be detected by a spectroscopic analysis, the ink could then be passed off as something else, such as a bottle of perfume.

By the time America entered the war, the Germans had moved on still further, and it was by then extremely rare for agents to carry ink in a bottle of any kind. Collins explained in his lecture:

The German chemists' technique had now developed to a point where they could conceal secret inks impregnated, without discolouring, in clothes, such as silk lingerie, handkerchiefs, soft collars, cotton gloves, silk scarves, neckties and the like. The spy had only to soak the garment in distilled water or some other prescribed solution, in order to bring out the chemicals. He then wrote his letter, using this solution as his secret ink, threw away the immediate supply of ink in solution, dried the garment and put it away for further use in the same manner. Oftentimes the spy carried or wore the impregnated garment.

There was the case of a suspect who, after a thorough search, seemed to have no ink in his possession. However, we noticed certain small, iridescent stains on his black necktie. On this we focused our attention, and soaked in distilled water a portion of the tie on which one of the stains appeared. Soon the liquid turned yellowish. Microchemical and spectroscope analysis proved the presence of silver. The ink carried by this particular spy was of a kind which no ordinary ionic reactions for silver would develop. We found the same ink impregnated in the socks of other agents, as well as in a black shoe lace and in the cloth-covered buttons of an evening-dress waistcoat.

Each of these cases called for extremely careful chemical research before the nature of the ink could be determined. And without this analysis, its appropriate developer could not be discovered.

Both Dansey and Collins told the Americans how they had caught an American journalist who had been spying for Germany, trapping him because of this secret ink. His name was George Vaux Bacon, and he operated between America, Holland and Britain. His control was a German agent in Holland called Schultz, who provided him with his instructions, in a very simple code.

Collins said:

When Bacon, in his travels, again left Holland, Schultz, who knew he was under suspicion, warned him that under no circumstances was he to take a pair of impregnated socks with him into England. He was to use only the cloth-covered buttons of his evening-dress waistcoat, which were similarly impregnated with the "P" ink. But Bacon took his socks with him. He had received them in New York, and had been given instructions to squeeze out the tops in water and use the liquid when it turned a pale whisky colour. Some of his letters he wrote in the solution of socks, some in the extract of dinner-jacket buttons.

But Dansey's men had been watching him since he re-entered England, and now they closed in. They had had their suspicions of him for some time. Dansey's officers at the ports and on the boats had observed his regular trips to Holland with growing interest until they were convinced he was up to something, though they had no hard evidence. Dansey, however, decided it was time to move.

Bacon was pulled in and searched. At first, the investigators found nothing. They might have been forced to let him go, but for a piece of incredible luck. Dansey records that he had heard something about a "new form of sympathetic ink, which had to do with venereal disease remedies. We found a large bottle of protargol, which I believe is a great venereal disease medicine. So they went through him again very, very closely, and tucked away in a corner of his vest they found a ball-pointed pen,* and when the chemists tested it they found it had been used in protargol. Then we knew we had gotten our man."

In fact, Bacon had not used protargol (or argyrol, as Collins described it) as a secret ink. He had bought it simply as an antiseptic, totally unaware that it was remarkably similar to the German secret ink. He continued to protest his innocence until Collins discovered the genuine secret ink in his socks; then he confessed. He was tried in London, and sentenced to death as a spy.

Just for a change, however, his luck turned. It was January 1917, and the British Government was very concerned not to do anything which might upset American opinion while they were trying to bring the United States into the war. Bacon's mother appealed to former President Theodore Roosevelt, and he persuaded the US Government to make strong representations on Bacon's behalf. To everyone's surprise, the British authorities listened, released him and sent him back to America, where he was sentenced to one year's imprisonment in Atlanta Penitentiary.

Dansey confessed himself puzzled by Bacon. "It is hard to say why a man of his standing should have become a spy," he said. "He was not in need of money. I think he did it out of a spirit of adventure, a good deal. He was an ideal agent from that point of view, because there was nothing to suggest that he was likely to be engaged in espionage. He had a perfectly good newspaper record and used to send his stuff back to his newspaper. It has always been a mystery why he undertook such work."

Bacon himself wrote to Yardley in 1931, claiming that his involvement in the secret world had been "nothing but a fantastic stunt designed to produce an exclusive story on espionage, if I had gotten away with it. However, I had to swear to keep what I knew to myself, so the story was never written."

---

* Not to be confused with the modern ball-point – this was the type of instrument used for signing stencils.

CHAPTER ELEVEN

Special Relationships

Dansey's stay in Washington and New York in 1917 lasted barely two months, and he was actively involved with Van Deman from London for another four or five months at the most. In that short time, however, he managed to achieve an incredible amount and was largely responsible, almost single-handed, for setting up the special relationship between the intelligence services of Britain and America which still exists today.

The French had sent a mission to the United States at much the same time as Balfour's, but it had been far less successful than the British. On the military and intelligence sides, the French officers must have known they stood no chance when Dansey, ever magnanimous, took them all to the Sleepy Hollow Country Club for a weekend as his personal guests, entertaining them generously and proprietorially. It was a particularly Danseyish way of making the situation clear to everyone.

When he returned to London, the necessary legislation and approvals from the US Government for the establishment of an intelligence service had still not been obtained. But he had given Van Deman everything he needed to know to draw up plans and lay firm foundations for an organisation that was to reach a strength of some 300 officers and 1,000 clerks by the time the war ended seventeen months later – a truly remarkable growth from the two officers and three clerks who had greeted Dansey on his arrival.

Brigadier-General Marlborough Churchill, the brilliant artillery officer and former Harvard lecturer who took over the Military Intelligence Department in Washington from June 1918, when Van Deman moved to Europe to take personal charge of American intelligence operations there, was in no doubt about the importance of Dansey's role. In a letter written after the war to Sir Basil Thomson, he said:

119

You are perfectly correct in saying that we made an honest attempt to profit by your [Britain's] experience and to benefit by your advice. Our debt to Colonel Dansey, who assisted Colonel Van Deman in the early days of our Intelligence Service, can never be exaggerated or repaid . . . all that I could do when I took over from Colonel Van Deman in June 1918 was to attempt to continue to develop the splendid service which he had built up, which was based on the British organisation and due largely to Colonel Dansey's assistance.

Dansey's job in America, however, was not simply to help the Americans with the planning and setting up of their organisation. He was also involved in active intelligence work, feeding information to Van Deman and in return receiving information from the Americans. Essentially his objective was to make sure the United States created a first-rate service and that it would then co-operate and collaborate with British Intelligence for their mutual benefit.

British Intelligence had kept an office in New York since the beginning of the war, doing the sort of work for which Dansey himself had been responsible during his time at Sleepy Hollow. This consisted mainly of finding and watching Irish and Indian troublemakers, both of whom were eager to work with the Germans against British interests. Germany was happy to provide money and arms for use in Ireland and India, in return for services in America. Since 1914 these services had come to include sabotage in docks, ships and factories; poisoning mules and horses; lacing bales of hay with steel shavings that would tear animals' guts to pieces, and tins of meat with little fish hooks that would do the same to humans; helping to smuggle messages and agents in and out of the country, and so on. The most spectacular success had been the destruction in New York harbour of some two million tons of munitions in the summer of 1916, in an explosion on Black Tom Island which had been heard a hundred miles away.

The head of the New York office from the end of 1915 was a thirty-three-year-old baronet, Sir William Wiseman, assisted by Captain Norman Thwaites, a former journalist who had been a trooper in the South African Light Horse under Dansey's command during the Boer war. Wiseman and Thwaites, though new to intelligence work, did at least know America and Americans, since they had both worked in the United States before the war. They were therefore a considerable improvement on their predecessor, who had been recommended for the post by Lord Kitchener on the strength of his work as an intelligence officer on the North-West

Frontier of India though he had never set foot in the United States.

Wiseman and Thwaites, together with Captain Guy Gaunt, the British Naval Attaché, had scored a few minor successes in counter-espionage and counter-sabotage, most notably in wrapping up the leading ring of Indian plotters. They also had a useful connection with violently anti-German Czechs and Slovaks led by a remarkable character called Emmanuel Voska, who had men everywhere, it seemed, and was in many cases well able to counterbalance the Irish influence in areas such as the docks. But the Englishmen's main value turned out to be in the diplomatic field. Thwaites had worked for several years on American newspapers, in particular for the *New York World*, the leading Democratic paper whose editor, Frank Cobb, was one of President Wilson's few close friends and confidants. Wiseman had many important contacts in business and banking from his days on Wall Street, and became a close friend of Colonel House, the President's personal adviser.

When America entered the war, the British War Office planned to post Dansey there after he had finished his immediate mission, to replace Wiseman as intelligence chief. On the face of it, it seemed an eminently sensible proposal, considering Dansey's seniority and experience. But Wiseman's special relationship with the President had advanced to such an extent that Wilson himself made a point of asking Balfour, at the end of their first meeting in the White House, to "leave Sir William Wiseman where he was".

The President's request was extremely unpopular in London. The Foreign Office objected to having the ambassador and all the normal diplomatic channels short-circuited by a young man with no background in diplomacy and no official standing in their establishment. The War Office felt that the Secret Service post was now far too important to be left to someone who was still virtually an amateur, having been in the game for less than eighteen months. However, the President had made the request personally to the Foreign Secretary, so both departments had no alternative but to agree.

In the event, it all turned out for the best. Wiseman's connection with House and Wilson proved to be of immense diplomatic value, and the special relationship which Dansey had established between the intelligence services was so strong that all they needed was a liaison officer to act more or less as a postman. Van Deman's service very quickly proved itself capable of taking care of things in America without any further help. And Dansey, having achieved what he set out to do in Washington, was of far greater value elsewhere.

Although Wiseman and Thwaites had spent time developing their diplomatic connections, they had failed to establish any sort of contact with Van Deman, nor until Dansey arrived on the scene, had they even shown any inclination to do so. Indeed it was not until he had returned to London that they approached American Intelligence.

"I am much amused," Dansey wrote to Van Deman, "to hear that directly I had gone Thwaites and Wiseman got into communication with you. It is a pity that they did not do so before. However, I think anything of value will reach you direct in future from London, and I expect their activities will be considerably curtailed shortly."

Dansey was obviously unimpressed by the performance of the British representatives, and although Wiseman tried to hold on to control of all communications, Dansey had these taken out of his hands. Wiseman had been in the habit of passing everything through the State Department, which weeded out anything it considered unimportant or inconvenient. The result was that there was a great deal which never reached Van Deman. Dansey arranged for everything from British Military Intelligence to be sent by bag through the American military attaché in London, Colonel Lassiter. At the other end, Van Deman sent his outgoing material through the new British military attaché, General Mac-Lachlan. Wiseman's wings were clipped still further when Mac-Lachlan was given jurisdiction over all intelligence matters, and his assistant attaché, Lieutenant-Colonel Arthur Murray, was made responsible for day-to-day liaison. Murray, who was a Member of Parliament and later became Lord Elibank, had been invalided home from the front, and was given a course of instruction in the Intelligence Department before being posted to Washington. No doubt Claude Dansey had a great deal of useful advice to give him.

Almost as soon as he arrived in Washington, Dansey was passing information to Van Deman about suspected enemy agents, starting with a hand-written note warning the Americans about the activities of an Imperial Russian colonel, Serge Apostoloff, who was known to deal in munitions of war for his personal gain. Dansey gave Van Deman several names of similar operators, and asked in return that he should be given copies of any cables relating to arms dealings which were intercepted by the US cable censors. Thus he established from the outset the first principle of the intelligence world: information is a commodity which can be traded.

The Russian connection was one which concerned Dansey

greatly. Apostoloff was basically just another rogue, but there were others who were something quite different. There were in America many revolutionary committees of political refugees, and Dansey warned Van Deman that these could be good cover for enemy intrigues and propaganda. A few weeks earlier, Russia had undergone the first of the revolutions which were to change the course of the country irrevocably. She was still in the war, however, on the side of the Allies. Now, the refugees who had been on the Czarist black lists were clamouring to return home, and Dansey told Van Deman he was afraid many of them were in the pay of the enemy, and hostile to the new regime in Russia.

There was one group in New York, with headquarters at 63 West 107th Street, which was financed by the New York German paper *Volkszeitung*, which in turn was known to be supported by funds from Germany. The leader of this group worked as an electrician at the Fox Film Studios, and made no secret of his revolutionary zeal. He went by the name of Leon Trotsky. Even as Dansey was warning Van Deman about him and his comrades, Trotsky was obtaining a passport and visa from the Russian consulate and setting out from New York to board a ship bound for Russia from Halifax. The Canadians were warned and stopped him, but the trusting Russian leader Kerensky cabled President Wilson and asked him to intervene. It was another of the presidential requests that could not be refused when Britain was still wooing the United States, and the British Government reluctantly gave the word to the Canadians to let Trotsky go. At the same time, General Ludendorff was passing Vladimir Ilyitch Lenin from Switzerland through Germany bound for Russia.

In May 1917, while Dansey was deeply involved in advising the Americans, a trial took place in New York which demonstrated very clearly the need for an active counter-espionage service and the value of close co-operation between the Allied services. The man on trial, Captain Franz von Rintelen, was standing in the dock by courtesy of British Intelligence. Dansey himself had had a hand in his capture.

Von Rintelen was a German naval officer who had been sent to America in April 1915, travelling through the British blockade under a false Swiss passport in the name of Emile V. Gasche, to organise espionage and sabotage and do all he could to cripple the supply of munitions to the Allies. Once he was safely in the USA, of course, he was free to revert to his own name for everyday use, only concealing his identity for certain "business" ventures. He was a charming, well-bred and handsome young man, who already knew New York from his business days before the war when he was a director of the Deutsche Bank. He had many friends and acquaintances in America and moved in the very best circles, living at the New York Yacht Club and on one occasion addressing the august Century Club in its imposing Stanford White building on West 43rd Street. Sheltered by this façade of fashionable respectability, he wrought havoc for the best part of a year and a half.

His first move was to set up an export-import business as a front, in the name of E. V. Gibbons (for some reason most of his aliases seem to have had the initials "E.V.G."; he later posed as an English wine merchant using the name Edward V. Gates) and attempted to corner almost the entire United States output of arms and ammunition, ostensibly on behalf of Russia. Then he went to work subverting labour organisations, trying to start a strike on the Atlantic coast through the Longshoreman's Union, and encouraging stoppages at the Remington arms plant, the General Electric plant at Schenectady, and at various other places concerned with manufacturing war supplies. With an American associate, David Lamar, he created the Laborers' National Peace Council, which had as its main object forcing the Federal Government to prohibit the shipment of munitions to belligerents.

On the international political front he deliberately fomented trouble between the US and Mexico, supplied money to the Irish in America who were supporting Sir Roger Casement – then in Berlin trying to raise an Irish Brigade from prisoners of war to fight against the British – and made plans for an uprising in Ireland which would be backed by U-boats off-shore and arms shipments from Germany.

Von Rintelen's most notable success, however, was in running a bomb-making plant on a German ship interned in New York harbour. With the help of Irish-American and German-American stevedores, the bombs were planted in the cargo holds of ships leaving for Europe, timed to explode several days later, when they would be on the high seas. The devices worked only too well: at least thirty-five ships were destroyed. Eventually the authorities began to close in. Amazingly, there were no federal statutes at that time covering either espionage or sabotage, but the Bureau of Investigation picked up von Rintelen's trail when he tried to buy 300,000 rifles, using one of his false names. The Secret Service was also showing an unhealthy interest in his activities, and the British Intelligence men in New York were on his tail, too. Matters became worse still when he fell out with the German military and naval attachés, who regarded him as a cuckoo in their nest and began, according to von Rintelen's own account, to scatter conspicuous clues to his identity. He had already decided it was time to leave when he received a cable recalling him to Berlin. He sailed from New York on 3rd August 1916 on the Dutch ship *Noordam*, using his false Swiss passport again, no doubt relieved to have escaped undetected.

Any feeling of security which he might have enjoyed during the voyage across the Atlantic vanished, however, when the ship was met off Falmouth by a British boarding party. (Von Rintelen himself says it was off Dover, and other accounts say the ship had to call at Southampton, but Falmouth would be the normal place for such actions.) Alerted by the German cable, and no doubt by messages from New York, Admiral Hall's Naval Intelligence Department, Dansey's section E of MI5 and Basil Thomson's police had combined forces to trap their man. The *Noordam* was held for fourteen hours, during which time the luggage of "Emile V. Gasche" and his travelling companions was searched. Incriminating documents were found at the bottom of the last trunk, and von Rintelen's identity was revealed. He was arrested and interned, and subjected to a long and careful interrogation, carried out so skilfully and so sympathetically that he co-operated fully and told everything.

When America entered the war, Britain extradited him to New York, where Dansey witnessed the conclusion of the combined operation against the German agent – he was convicted for conspiracy to foment strikes and sentenced to one year's imprisonment. Later he was charged with conspiring to defraud the United States in securing a passport, and given a further year's imprisonment; and in February 1918 he was finally charged with fire bomb conspiracy and sentenced to eighteen months' imprisonment and a fine of $2,000. President Wilson commuted this sentence in November 1920, and von Rintelen left the United States on 31st December. Subsequently, he became a close personal friend of Admiral Hall and spent a great deal of time in England. At the start of the second world war, in 1939, he offered his services to Britain, and even tried to become a British citizen, but was rejected and interned on the Isle of Man.

CHAPTER TWELVE

The Spycatcher

In 1917, Dansey's own duties in British Intelligence were princi-. pally concerned with security and counter-espionage. He was still more concerned with catching spies than with running them, though this was soon to change. Both while he was in America and during the first few months after his return to London, therefore, he was passing to Van Deman a growing number of lists of suspected enemy agents. These included details of all manner of men and women ranging from diplomats to itinerant labourers, and the Intelligence Section did its best to deal with them, establishing ever-closer links with Bruce Bielaski's Bureau of Investigation, Leland Harrison in the Office of the Counsellor at the State Department, and with the New York Police.

In New York, Van Deman set up a branch office at 302 Broadway, under the command of Nicholas Biddle, a civilian aide who was commissioned as a major and charged with maintaining close relations with Commissioner Arthur Woods. In addition to being the metropolis and therefore the centre for subversive activity, New York was also the principal port of entry to the United States. One of Biddle's main responsibilities was to follow up Dansey's warnings of enemy agents leaving neutral ports in Holland, Scandinavia and Spain, and to have them stopped or watched on their arrival.

Some of the men and women reported by Dansey were very colourful characters. Milorad Raitchvitch, for example, a one-legged stamp dealer operating a post-box for agents at his offices at 101 West 42nd Street, New York, had deserted from the Serbian army during the Balkan war and in spite of having only been a sergeant managed to pass himself off as a count in Vienna and Berlin. Frederick C. Moltke, on the other hand, was a genuine count, a Danish diplomat. He had already been quietly removed from Britain after being caught stealing the plans of London's anti-aircraft defences and persistently questioning army and naval officers on secret matters. It had been hard to prove anything, since he sent his mail out of Britain uncensored in the legation bag, but the MI5 report on him stated that it was "a sinister coincidence" that the missing anti-aircraft map had been in a room in the Admiralty where, incredible as it seems, he had been allowed to work unsupervised for two or three days. It was also reported that he had been constantly in and out of the War Office and had gone out of his way to invite officers out to dinner, where he had pumped them shamelessly. His brother, it turned out, was Danish Minister in Berlin, where he was known to be pro-German, and his wife constantly travelled between Berlin and Copenhagen. The final clincher, however, had been the state of his finances. The language of the report is delightfully quaint; "his pecuniary circumstances which had formerly been necessitous appeared to have materially altered for the better, so much so, in fact, that his expenditure was lavish and remarkable".

Moltke had been sent to Britain ostensibly to purchase munitions for the Danish Government. But the closest he came to buying anything remotely military had been to open negotiations for the purchase of six horse ambulances. Now, he had appeared in America and was dealing with the Maxim Munitions Company, trying to speed up an order for thirty million rounds of ammunition. Dansey tipped off Van Deman, and Van Deman swung into action in a particularly astute way, using a girl agent, a Miss Curtis. By the end of the year, when he decided it was time to blow the whistle on Moltke, Van Deman was able to write to Leland Harrison at the State Department asking that he should be declared an undesirable, saying that Miss Curtis had "been intimate with Moltke for the past five months" and reported him as extremely pro-German, lauding the Kaiser, from whom he had received decorations.

Moltke complained bitterly to Miss Curtis that a letter to him had been opened by the censors and five passports had been taken out. He claimed they were for Danish workmen who had been helping load the ammunition he was supposed to be buying. He tried to obtain details of a new process for making a substitute for gasoline, and when Miss Curtis mentioned that she had heard of an even more wonderful substitute, he immediately asked her to get information about it. He also tried to persuade her to provide him with accurate information about Liberty motors for aircraft, through a friend of hers, Caleb Bragg, the record-breaking aviator who was one of the organisers of the Wright-Martin Aeroplane

127

Company. The Intelligence Department made a set of fake plans to be sold to Moltke, but had to abandon the scheme when he became suspicious. The time had come to have him expelled.

It does not sound as though it had been a particularly arduous mission for Miss Curtis: Van Deman reported to the State Department that Moltke's finances were still improving and that he had squandered money right and left on expensive presents and high living.

Anthony J. Brogan was an Irishman living in America whom Dansey described as "exceptionally dangerous" and "one of the most important German agents". He must have been a man of enormous charm, for his domestic and romantic affairs were incredibly tangled. His wife in New York, Cecelia, managed his real-estate business, the Cantique Development Syndicate, in the Cameron Building at 185 Madison Avenue, but seems to have been particularly innocent. She knew hardly anything about him, supposing he was a naturalised American citizen as he had told her he had voted in the USA. When questioned about him she even said with some relish that she believed he was away in Europe on "some mysterious mission" and seemed quite content to wait for him. In addition to the trusting Cecelia, there was also Mary Smith who lived elsewhere in New York and had two children by him; a young lady called May O'Connor, who travelled through Europe with him as his wife; and Mrs Rose Sutton Parker, married to a major with the US Expeditionary Force, who was his lover both in America and in Europe.

Brogan claimed he had been born in Oil City, Pennsylvania, the son of an Irish immigrant, but the records show that he had in fact been born in County Clare, Ireland, in 1876 – the same year that Claude Dansey had made his appearance in the more comfortable surroundings of South Kensington – and had not arrived in the US until 1889. He gained a place at Notre Dame University, Indiana, graduated in 1901 with the degree of Bachelor of Literature, entered government service in the Philippines, where he became a postmaster at the military station of Imus (and first met Rose Sutton Parker), then later District Supervisor. In 1905, he travelled through China and Japan to Germany, and the University of Freiberg. In 1906, he returned to the US and became involved in Irish rebel politics.

Dansey had been aware of the Irishman since his own days at the Sleepy Hollow Country Club, for Brogan had then been owner and publisher of a newspaper, *The Irish American*, and had started his

128

real-estate company, which did no real-estate business but was a cover for his activities as a rebel agent. In 1915, he sold *The Irish American* to the German military attaché, Franz von Papen, and set off for Europe with the proceeds.

For some time, Brogan had been in regular communication with Sir Roger Casement, whom he had met in New York in 1914. Casement had stayed then with John Quinn, an eminent lawyer and patron of the arts, who was also a friend and associate of Thomas Fortune Ryan, advising him on his art purchases. It is safe to assume that Dansey also knew Quinn, and that Quinn may have told him something of Casement's plans, for although a fervent supporter of the Irish cause, Quinn was devoted to the idea that Ireland should and would gain Home Rule by constitutional rather than violent means. Certainly, Dansey was concerned with stopping Casement, who was not only issuing rabid anti-British propaganda but also actively encouraging an uprising in Ireland, and trying – vainly as it turned out – to raise a force from Irish prisoners of war in Germany to fight against Britain.

Early in 1916 Brogan arrived safely in Italy with May O'Connor, and slipped through Switzerland into Germany, where he met Casement in Berlin. Rose Parker said he took $60,000 to Casement from New York, presumably the proceeds from the sale of his newspaper to the Germans, who did not, incidentally, continue to publish it. Then, with knowledge of Casement's plans, he travelled to London, and into Dansey's sights again. At that time, Dansey did not know that Brogan and O'Connor had been into Germany, and in any case they had American passports and were thus still neutral citizens. Nevertheless, he had them hauled in and questioned. Although May O'Connor had various notes in her baggage which were highly critical of conditions in England, there was nothing that could be proved, and the two were "allowed" to leave England bound for Buenos Aires.

South America would have been a good safe place for Brogan, but the Irish-American had other ideas. When the ship stopped at Vigo in Spain, he and his "wife" disembarked and made for Madrid. From there he wrote to his real wife in New York telling her that the leaders of the German party in Spain were looking after him and providing all his needs, and instructing her to destroy all his papers, many of which were from Casement.

Brogan's days as a secret agent were over, however. As Dansey pointed out to Van Deman, when he presented him with Brogan's dossier in June 1917, the Irishman was *brûlé*; the Germans would not continue to use him. He had also walked into a trap. Dansey had told the State Department about certain irregularities in

129

Brogan's passport, that he had engaged in highly dubious activities, had on two occasions aided persons to secure fraudulent passports, and that the woman travelling with him was not his lawful wife. Brogan left May O'Connor, who was sick, in Madrid and made a little excursion into Italy, an Allied nation. To his horror he was instantly arrested as a suspected German agent, held in jail for three weeks and then returned to Spain, where his passport was taken away at the frontier. He tried to get Rose Parker, who arrived in Barcelona by a strange coincidence at the same time as he was there, to obtain fresh passports from the American consul, but his charm must have failed him for once – she promptly reported him to the consul, and when he threatened her she went back to her husband in Paris and reported him again, to Colonel Nolan and US Intelligence.

It had been a particularly smooth checkmate. Did Dansey really believe Brogan would go all the way to Buenos Aires – from where he would presumably have been free to move back north and cause further trouble? Or had he counted on the ship's call at Vigo being just too tempting to resist? Either way, the result was certain: for Anthony J. Brogan the war was over. He was trapped in Spain, out of harm's way like a wasp in a bottle, and there he would stay until the American authorities chose to pull out the stopper by giving him back his passport.

While Brogan was being ensnared, the man for whom he had travelled to Europe had met a far more tragic end. Roger Casement had been captured after landing from a U-boat on Banna Strand, Tralee Bay, on 29th April 1916, ironically trying to prevent a rising, since he knew the promised German help would not be forthcoming in sufficient strength. Whether Dansey had any hand in catching him is not known. Admiral Hall and Naval Intelligence were certainly involved, and so were Basil Thomson and his branch of Scotland Yard. As usual, their activities were at least partially public, while the men of MI5 remained invisible, though they must have had at least a hand in the affair and should by rights have had the main responsibility. In any event, Casement was arrested, taken to London, tried and hanged as a traitor to the Empire he had served for so many years, in the Congo and elsewhere. The execution was one of the biggest political blunders of the whole war, for it instantly turned Casement into a martyr, despite Hall's highly successful efforts to blacken his character beyond redemption by circulating his black diaries, which included lurid details of his homosexual activities.

The way the government dealt with Casement went completely against everything Dansey tried to teach and practise: when you take an enemy agent, always try to make use of him for your own purposes – once he is dead, he is of no value whatever.

Among the other cases in America with which Dansey was connected there are two which stand out. In one, a man who travelled with a Russian passport in the name of Pablo Waberski, was in reality a German naval lieutenant called Lothar Witzke. Dansey's report described him and his partner, the German spy chief in Mexico, Kurt Jahnke, as the most savage and dangerous sabotage combination in existence. British Intelligence believed Witzke had been responsible for the Black Tom explosion in New York harbour, the most spectacular piece of sabotage in the entire war. Both men were now in Mexico, planning Witzke's next assignments.

Acting on Dansey's tip off, Van Deman sent an agent into Mexico, where he managed to become friendly with the pair – not such a difficult feat, since Jahnke lived and operated quite openly in the pro-German surroundings south of the border. When Witzke slipped back into the United States, Van Deman's men were waiting for him. He was arrested, but denied everything, and it looked as though it would be impossible to prove any charges against him. His only suspicious possession was a sheet of paper covered in numbers, which could have been a code. The paper was given to Herbert Yardley, who soon managed to decipher the message, which was addressed to all German consuls in Mexico, signed by the German minister, von Eckhardt, and read: "Strictly Secret. The bearer of this is a subject of the Empire who travels as a Russian under the name of Pablo Waberski. He is a German secret agent. Please furnish him on request protection and assistance, also advance him on demand up to one thousand pesos of Mexican gold and send his code telegrams to this embassy as official consular dispatches."

Witzke was tried as a spy, and sentenced to be hanged, the only German agent in America to receive the death sentence in the first world war. President Wilson reprieved him, however, and after the war he was released, went home to Germany and was decorated with the Iron Cross, First and Second Class, for his work in the United States. Although he never denied it, his part in the Black Tom explosion remained unproved.

The final American case in which Dansey was involved was that of Madame Maria de Victorica, "the beautiful blonde woman of Antwerp". Victorica was a tall, strikingly attractive lady aged about thirty-five, who had been born into the Prussian aristocracy as daughter of Baron Hans von Kretschman, a general, noted author of military treaties and friend of Prince von Bulow, the German Foreign Minister. Through von Bulow she was introduced to Colonel Walter Nicolai, head of the Kaiser's Secret Intelligence Service, who saw the potential of this lovely woman with several academic degrees and outstanding abilities as a linguist, and hired her as a secret agent in about 1910. That, at least, is the story. The truth was not quite so salubrious: Maria de Victorica was a heroin addict. Whether she took to the drug because of her profession, or whether she was persuaded to become a spy because of her addiction, no one knows. It is not impossible that Nicolai could have deliberately started her on heroin in order to increase her dependence on him. Other spymasters have certainly used drugs both as persuaders and as bribes; Dansey himself did so in Europe – though only on his enemies – in both world wars, as we shall see.

Maria had worked successfully in various countries, marrying Manuel Gustave Victorica, an Argentine citizen who was also a German agent. British Intelligence had been searching for Maria since first picking up her trail in Antwerp in 1914, but she had eluded them. She might have continued to do so, but for the clumsiness of a German courier.

Dansey's men in Spain reported that an unnamed German agent was on his way to New York, carrying a message and $10,000 to one of two addresses on Long Island. Dansey passed the message on to Van Deman, who arranged for the houses to be watched and all mail to be intercepted. The occupants of the houses had both gone away, destination unknown, but eventually a letter did arrive for one of them. It was checked and found to be innocent. The trail seemed to be going cold, when a second letter arrived. This time, there was definitely something odd, for although the envelope, posted in New York, was addressed to a man, the letter inside was undoubtedly to a woman. It was checked, and found to contain writing in secret ink.

The man who had posted the letter had thoughtfully put a genuine return address on the back of the envelope: a lodging house in New York City. Although he had put a false name, it was not difficult to find him. He turned out to be a steward on a Norwegian ship, and after hard questioning confessed that he had acted as a courier, bringing two letters into America, which he had then posted. He said he did not know anything about the contents of the letters, but realised that he must have inadvertently switched them when he made out new envelopes, to replace the original ones. He had carried them in his boots, he explained, and they had become worn and crumpled. Thus, the letter to the woman should have gone to the other address, which fortunately he could remember.

The address he gave them was that of an innocent elderly widow, who was unwittingly being used as a post box. She had received other letters that did not belong to her, and had once opened one. She could not remember much about it, except for a name: Victorica.

Now, the hunt was on in earnest. The secret writing on the letter contained directives from Germany for the destruction of munitions plants and docks in the United States, blowing up vital mineral mines, beginning espionage operations in Brazil, which had just declared war on Germany, and details of codes and cover addresses. Obviously, the person for whom the letter was intended was the head of the German organisation in the United States, presumably replacing von Rintelen. But his or her identity still remained unknown.

At this point, the co-operation between British and American Intelligence which Dansey had taken so much trouble to establish began to bear fruit. London confirmed that they had been hunting "the beautiful blonde woman of Antwerp" – though they did not know her name – since the beginning of the war, and that the French had just caught a spy believed to be associated with her. His name was Manuel Gustav Victorica. Further checking through MI5's now unrivalled central records revealed that Dansey's port and immigration control people had noted as a matter of routine that a woman called Maria de Victorica had passed through, on an Argentine passport, heading for New York in January 1917. They had a full description of her, as well as her name, so Van Deman arranged for a thorough check by the police of every fashionable hotel and boarding house in New York.

The result was infuriating. She had checked into the Knickerbocker Hotel on 21st January, the day she arrived, but had suddenly left on 3rd February, leaving no forwarding address. Her trail was picked up again, however, without too much difficulty, for she had gone straight to the Waldorf Astoria, where she had stayed until 21st February, when again she had suddenly checked out. It may have been coincidence that the first time she moved was the day when diplomatic relations were broken between Germany and the USA, and the second time was immediately after the arrest of a leading saboteur, "Dynamite Charlie" Wunnenberg. In any event, she then took an expensive apartment at the Spencer Arms, paying rent in advance until 20th June. After only nine days, however, she had disappeared again, and this time there was no further trace.

British Intelligence, however, offered yet another clue, through its cable censorship, which produced a copy of an apparently innocent telegram sent on 4th February to a banking firm in New York, with instructions for someone called Victorica. When decoded, the instructions turned out to be for her to withdraw $35,000 and put it in a secure place because of the danger of war with America. The bank had paid the money over in cash on 20th February, and since then had not seen or heard from the lady whom they described as "a stunning blonde". They did, however, have one possible address for her, that of a foreign mission in New York which often acted as a poste restante. There the hunters found several letters waiting for her, mostly without stamps, indicating that they had been smuggled into America and delivered by hand. Some of them were nearly a year old: the lady had presumably been afraid to call for them. This did not mean, however, that she had not received the messages, since it was normal for several copies of such instructions to be sent to different addresses simultaneously, in case the cover was breached.

The new letters revealed an astonishing range of activities, showing that Victorica was involved in all sorts of sabotage and espionage. There were names and cover addresses in Holland, Sweden and Denmark as well as those of people in America. Suitable sites were to be found for secret supply dumps on the American coast for German U-boats, showing that the Germans had planned submarine bases there as early as 13th February 1917, as well as other bases on the coast of Spain, thus accounting for the incredibly long range of the U-boats which were sinking so much shipping in the Atlantic. And there were plans for the importing of Germany's newest and most powerful explosive, which they called "tetra" (tetra-nitro-cellulose).

This last was the most bizarre of all the facts revealed by the letters, for they showed that Victorica was making use of unsuspecting Catholic priests to obtain religious statues for her from a manufacturer in Zurich, Switzerland. What the priests did not know was that the statues were filled with tetra instead of plaster!

The letters did not give any further indication of where Victorica was to be found, but there were other names mentioned and Van Deman decided to have them all placed under constant surveillance. After a while, one of his agents noticed that the schoolgirl cousin of one of the people on the list was a very devout churchgoer, visiting St Patrick's Cathedral on Fifth Avenue at precisely the same time on the same day each week. Next time she went, he followed her in, noting that she was carrying a folded newspaper under her arm. She knelt in prayer for a little while, then rose and walked away, leaving the newspaper behind. As the agent watched, a man went to the same pew, also carrying a newspaper, which he skilfully switched with the one the girl had left. When he left the cathedral the agent followed him, through the city, on to a train and all the way to Long Beach, Long Island. At the Nassau Hotel, he went into the lounge, sat down and smoked a cigarette. When he left, an elegant blonde woman moved into his place and took possession of the newspaper. The hunt was up.

Maria de Victorica was registered at the hotel as "Marie de Vussier". The folded newspaper contained more than $20,000 which had been smuggled into the country for her to use in running her network. She was arrested on a presidential warrant, and later indicted for conspiracy to commit espionage. But she was never brought to trial. During her questioning, deprived of the drug on which she depended, she collapsed and was rushed to the prison ward in Bellevue Hospital. Although the American authorities treated her with every consideration, her condition steadily deteriorated until she died, two years later.

By the time the beautiful blonde spy was caught, Dansey had long moved on to other things. When he returned to London on 16th June 1917, the British ambassador in Washington, Sir Cecil Spring Rice, cabled the War Office and the Foreign Office telling them to do nothing about sending a permanent military mission to Washington until they had spoken to Dansey. Perhaps he, like Van Deman and others, was hoping Dansey would be sent back as its head.

Meanwhile, the desk which Dansey had occupied in Van Deman's office was now being used by Henry L. Stimson, who had already served in President Taft's Cabinet, and was later to be Secretary of State under President Hoover and then Secretary of War under Franklin D. Roosevelt. The intention of the US General Staff was that Stimson would go to London to represent Van Deman, while Dansey went to Washington for British Intelligence. Before this plan could be put into effect, however, orders came down "from the top" (i.e. the President himself) that for purely political reasons, Stimson was to stay in Washington. His fame in intelligence annals rests, therefore, on his decision as Secretary of State in 1929 to close down Yardley's Black Chamber, with the immortal words "Gentlemen do not read each other's mail" – and then as Secretary of War having to order its reconstitution, along with the OSS, when America entered the second world war!

CHAPTER THIRTEEN

Holland and Switzerland

Van Deman and Ambassador Spring Rice were not alone in wanting to have Dansey in Washington on a permanent basis. Newton D. Baker, the American Secretary of War, personally wrote to General Bridges saying that Dansey had been "of the greatest assistance in the formation of an Intelligence Section of the General Staff of our Army, and it is earnestly requested that, if consistent with the instructions of your Government, he be allowed to remain in the United States after the departure of your Mission, for the purpose of further aiding the General Staff with his advice and assistance".

Baker concluded his letter: "I assure you that such action on your part will be highly appreciated by our Government." It was a powerful plea, but not powerful enough. Dansey's skills and talents were desperately needed elsewhere. He was to be given a new job, one he considered the most difficult he had ever faced: he was to be responsible for Holland.

When the Germans had swept into Belgium in 1914, they had by-passed Holland, leaving it isolated, an island bounded on the one side by the might of Germany and on the other by the North Sea. The Dutch were not signatories of the Treaty of London which guaranteed Belgian neutrality, and therefore felt no moral obligation to go to the defence of their neighbour. The Dutch trusted none of the great powers and felt the conflict to be no concern of theirs. Of course, there were Dutch men and women who nursed pro-German or pro-Allied sentiments. Nevertheless the attitude of the Dutch political parties as a whole can best be summed up in the words of the Dutch historian who wrote: "We were too good to fatten other people's ambitions with our blood." Or, put another way, a plague on both your houses.

Neutrality in time of war is a policy rarely appreciated by the belligerents, who cannot understand how anyone can doubt the justice of their cause. They therefore tend to regard any convenient neutral country as a potential battle ground for their secret services. America provided one such arena until it entered the war in April 1917; but Holland, more central to the conflict, was the principal espionage playground for the whole war. Any intelligence coming from Dutch sources tended to have direct bearing on the military situation in France and Belgium – in particular, the train-watching service. This provided intelligence concerning German troop movements to the front. Agents counted troop trains, and, if possible, identified the various German regiments from their insignias. It was known that it took twenty-four trains to transport a German division; a whole army corps required twice that number of trains.

The Allies had their problems: how to co-ordinate their intelligence-gathering efforts. Each Allied government, French, British, Belgian – and after 1917, the Americans, too – ran their own Dutch espionage networks: some, indeed, ran more than one. Even the Russians had what has been described as a nebulous organisation which was based partly in Paris and partly in Holland, though its purpose and method of operation remains a mystery; nor is it known if it ever performed any useful function. In any case, the imperial Russian service was not trusted by the other Allied organisations.

The British boasted no fewer than three quite distinct networks, sending back intelligence to four different centres – GHQ (France), War Office (London), SIS (Whitehall Court) and Folkestone. There was minimal co-operation between these various sections, and at times they competed so fiercely with each other that their effectiveness was compromised. This problem was recognised as early as November 1914, when the first efforts were made to co-ordinate the various sections through a central bureau at Folkestone, but competition remained a perennial problem.

The official British Secret Service in Holland was headed by Captain Tinsley, known as T. He operated from the office of the British consul general, Ernest Maxxse, in Rotterdam, and his direct superior was the head of the Secret Service in London, Captain Mansfield Cumming, RN, known as C. T's organisation was responsible for counter-intelligence, obtaining commercial intelligence, news of contraband or the shipment of forbidden articles to the enemy, etc., as well as providing military information.

Secondly, there was the W. L. Bureau. The initials have no particular significance, being telegraphese for the surname of the head of the bureau, Major B. A. Wallinger. Like C, Wallinger had a wooden leg but ran his department from Lower Sloane Street in London, not Whitehall Court. It is not recorded if Wallinger, like Cumming, was given to stabbing at his wooden stump with a paperknife. On Wallinger's staff was a recently recruited lieutenant new to intelligence work: Sigismund Payne Best, who was to remain in espionage long after the war and would later work for Claude Dansey in his Z Organisation in Holland. The W. L. Bureau supplied intelligence to Colonel Walter Kirke at GHQ, France.

The C.F. section was the third British espionage service operating through the Netherlands. Again the initials seem to have no particular significance. They could stand for *chemin de fer*, which would be appropriate since the basic function of the section was train-watching, or else they stood for Cameron-Folkestone. Major A. C. Cameron ran the section from Folkestone, this being the port used by all cross-Channel boats to and from Holland. He also had a branch office in Paris, where he used to recruit Belgian and French train-watchers.

Back at GHQ, to which the C. F. section, like the W. L. Bureau, forwarded the results of its intelligence-gathering activities, a large room had been taken over by train experts and a railway map of Germany, Holland, Belgium and northern France was painted on the floor. Models representing troop trains were placed on the painted railway lines to help the experts assess the strategic implications of the different train movements. Was the 15th Bavarian Army Corps being sent to a particular part of the front? If so, did it mean that there was going to be a new enemy offensive?

Both W. L. and C. F. sections recruited their own teams of couriers, agents and *passeurs* (line-crossers). And both were in competition with each other, though in this case competition did not lead to greater efficiency but merely to confusion.

The job of *passeur* was extremely hazardous. The Germans had blazed a 300-metre-wide strip along most of the Dutch/Belgian and Dutch/German border. Down the centre of this strip they built an electrified fence, carrying a charge of some 20,000 volts, and on either side of this barrier they installed barbed wire. Anyone crossing the border had first to negotiate the barbed wire, then the high voltage fence, and then still more wire. To make matters even more tricky, the fence was not live twenty-four hours a day: the juice was switched on and off in order to confuse any potential infiltrators.

A *passeur* specialised in getting through this obstacle. The tools of his trade consisted of a couple of sticks notched at both ends, rubber gloves and boots. The technique was to hook two electrified wires into the notches of the stick and then force the wires apart, thus creating a gap through which a man could crawl. The rubber gloves and boots were needed to prevent the electrical charge from earthing itself and barbecuing the *passeur*. Sometimes if a party wished to cross the frontier, then a barrel, minus both ends, acted as a makeshift tunnel through the wire.

Of course this was not the only way to get across the border into Belgium. Best recalls bribing the German frontier guards and their superiors with quantities of cocaine and morphine. He claims to have received official permission from no less a person than Lloyd George himself to purchase drugs for this purpose. However, we are inclined to think it more likely that Best bought the drugs illegally on the black market with intelligence funds. A friend of Best's, a cigarette manufacturer, disguised the drugs in packets of cigarettes in order to make it easier to smuggle them across the border. Needless to say, this use of drugs was not lost on Claude Dansey, who would turn it to more sinister ends in the second world war.

When it came to passing simple messages across the frontier, other techniques were devised. Carrier pigeons had been employed in South Africa, but proved even more successful in Europe where they encountered fewer natural predators. The only danger was that because of the shortage of food they were often eaten by their own handlers. There were also experiments in the use of small gas-filled balloons designed to float over the wire. However, since the balloons were always at the mercy of the prevailing winds, they turned out to have only limited application. There was even an attempt to use model aircraft, the sort powered by a rubber band, but this too seems to have been equally ineffective. Wireless sets, traditionally part of the equipment of the agent, were in those days bulky and heavy and therefore difficult to transport, particularly through the electrified fence.

Without doubt the most ingenious system of assembling information was devised by Best himself. With the connivance of the Roman Catholic hierarchy in Belgium, he used church offertory boxes as letter drops. Messages, written in invisible ink on banknotes, were deposited by his Belgian agents in the offertory boxes, then later taken to a central office in Antwerp where they were decoded and taken to Best in Holland. There was nothing very mysterious about the ink: it was easily made. All you needed to do was to dip your pen in the liquid used to fill Leclanche electric batteries which were in common use on the Continent for powering electric door bells. In order to reveal the message written on the banknote, you heated it – with an ordinary household iron.

The British sent this flow of intelligence material to London via special couriers who travelled on the cross-Channel steamers from Rotterdam to Parkston (Felixstowe). Joseph Crozier, a French banker who was the *Deuxième Bureau* man in Rotterdam, tells of taking sackloads of intelligence reports on similar steamers bound for France. Since the ships were always in danger of German attack, or at the very least of being stopped and boarded, the security of the whole operation was a constant nightmare. The sacks, as Crozier discovered, were virtually unsinkable when thrown overboard, even when the sacking itself was punched full of holes. His solution was to bribe the firemen on the steamers to keep his sacks in the stokehold. At any sign of trouble they were to throw them into the boiler where they would be immediately incinerated.

British Intelligence adopted a system of specially weighted sacks, but seem either never to have tested them properly, or else by 1916 had become so complacent about security that they no longer considered the bags at risk.

During the night of 22nd – 23rd June 1916, near the Schouwen Bank Light Vessel, a German torpedo boat intercepted the SS *Brussels*, one of the Great Eastern Railway's vessels, *en route* from Rotterdam, and escorted her into Zeebrugge. The *Brussels* was carrying a cargo of foodstuffs from Holland plus a large number of passengers – mostly refugees – amongst whom were several British couriers loaded down with intelligence reports. These, of course, fell into German hands.

It was a disaster of the first magnitude. The Germans had not only temporarily broken the link between London and the Dutch-based networks, but since most of the captured material was in its original form (i.e. it was not in code), the enemy had no difficulty in reading it. "The transmission of agents' reports in original," wrote Colonel Drake, who had been critical of the system from the first, "is a danger to the lives of those agents which it is unfair to ask them to incur." Although the agents operated under code names, a good counter-intelligence officer could guess their whereabouts and identify them from the nature of the information they gave.

For the Germans this remarkable intelligence coup came as a complete surprise. It was not the result of brilliant machiavellian plotting: the Germans intercepted the SS *Brussels* largely on account of her skipper's gold watch.

On 2nd March 1915, in the same waters where he was later to be boarded by the enemy, Captain Charles Fryatt, the skipper of the SS *Brussels*, had attempted to ram a German submarine, the U33. For this exploit Captain Fryatt became an overnight hero in the

Press, and as a result, was presented with a gold watch by the chairman of the Great Eastern Railway Company, Lord Claud Hamilton. The watch bore the inscription, "For courage and skilful seamanship on March 2nd 1915".

Fryatt made the most of his hour of fame. He was given to boasting of his exploits in the dockside bars of Rotterdam, and if anyone doubted, he would show them his gold watch with its corroboratory inscription. It was to prove his death warrant.

Once in Zeebrugge, the captured crew and stewardesses of the SS *Brussels* were interned by the Germans. Five weeks later it was decided that Captain Fryatt should face a German court martial. The grounds were simple. "Fryatt," declared the German War Council, "did not form part of the enemy armed forces . . . [Therefore] . . . his attempt to sink the German submarine constituted an act of *franc tireur* which the law of war punishes with death."

The trial did not last long. In the face of the evidence provided by the accused's gold watch, the defence was hamstrung. The court brought in a verdict of death. That afternoon, on 28th July 1916, Captain Fryatt died in front of a German firing squad.

In death Captain Fryatt became even more famous than in life. He became the subject of a British propaganda campaign equal to that which surrounded the execution of Edith Cavell in 1915. The *New York Times* described Fryatt's execution as "deliberate murder", while the *New York Herald* declared it to be "the crowning German atrocity".

The story of the SS *Brussels* was to be repeated only three months later, on 23rd September, when several Dutch coastal vessels were stopped and boarded by the Germans and escorted into Zeebrugge for further examination. A second intelligence débâcle was in the offing. Couriers and mails were taken off the ships. True, this time at least there had been some attempt to dispose of the incriminating material before it fell into German hands. But once again, either through ill-luck or incompetence or a combination of the two, security procedures were not carried out: the "FO bag was not provided with proper sinkers and floated!"

Obviously such sloppiness could no longer be tolerated. The incidents, writes Captain Burge, "led to the reorganisation of the Secret Service in Holland, a task which involved a prolonged and careful scrutiny of the conditions and requirements by the various branches concerned both in England, Holland and France".

The process began with an enquiry, held the following February, into both the SS *Brussels* and the other incident. Like most such enquiries, it produced a compromise which satisfied nobody and only partially solved the basic problems. The conclusions of the conference were simple:

All reports from GHQ organisations (i.e. W. L. and C. F. services) were to be collected and taken to a clearing house in Holland controlled by T (who was responsible to Cumming at Whitehall Court). These reports were then to be despatched to the military attaché in The Hague, Major Oppenheim, to be edited and forwarded to London, presumably in code. A Captain Verdon was to be appointed by GHQ to act as assistant military attaché and help Major Oppenheim in his task of sifting and evaluating the information. But Captain Verdon was to have no personal dealings with agents. A liaison officer was to be sent to the Military Intelligence Directorate from GHQ, France.

There were two advantages to the new arrangement. Firstly, it gave GHQ the chance of overseeing the assembly of information at an early stage, and secondly, it encouraged practical liaison between London and GHQ.

By now it was clear to everyone that from the security point of view, Holland leaked like a bucket without a bottom. Something had to be done to protect agents and sources of information: security had to be tightened. The whole Dutch network needed overhauling. But who was to do it? London deliberated for some time and looked around for a suitable intelligence supremo for the job. He would have to be a man who combined vast practical experience of spying in a neutral country plus a wide knowledge of counter-intelligence work: the ideal poacher turned game-keeper, in fact.

In July 1917, four months after the enquiry, London gave the task of reorganising the Secret Service in Holland to Claude Dansey. He was to transfer from MI5, the Security Service, to MI1C, the Secret Intelligence Service.

Dansey had no illusions about the difficulties facing him in Holland. He knew he was stepping into a scorpion's nest of espionage and intrigue, where "low class agents (sell) the same information and (draw) pay from more than one service", as he complained in another letter to Van Deman. "The 'professionals' in Holland have now brought their competition to such a pitch, that nearly every third man is a Secret Service agent working for one of the belligerents, if not for both."

As usual Dansey had no illusions about the trustworthiness of agents. "If they find an allied service is getting better information than they do, some of them are not above giving information to the Germans about their successful competitors," he observed.

No one knew better than Claude Dansey that espionage, like rotten meat, always attracted the more dubious elements. Crooks and fantasists, con-men and clowns, as well as dedicated patriots, abounded in Dansey's twilight world.

Even senior British officers, it seems – if Best is to be believed – were not immune from the general corruption. He accused T himself (Captain Tinsley), acting in concert with the commercial and military attachés, of extorting money from certain Dutch firms by threatening to put them on a black list of companies co-operating with the enemy. Once a firm was placed on the list it had no chance of ever working again for the Allies – a threat which could have devastating consequences particularly for, say, a shipping company. Best claims that Smits, the salvage tug company, paid T and his associates 100,000 guilders to stay off this black list. Whether or not his accusation was correct it is clear from several sources that T was not held in high esteem in British Intelligence circles.

The fact that Holland was neutral did not mean that life was safe for any agent, whether Allied or German. The country was full of refugees, mostly Belgian and French, as well as an estimated 10,000 deserters from the various armies, not to mention escaped prisoners of war; apart from Switzerland there was really nowhere else escaped Allied soldiers could aim for.

At Rotterdam and Sneidam there were two camps housing Russian escapees. Perhaps their presence explains the activities of the "nebulous" Russian Intelligence organisation which operated there and in Paris.

Life during the first world war was not easy in Holland. There was considerable unemployment – small by today's standards but worrying in a country which had averaged under four per cent unemployment until 1914. The cost of living was high. There were frequent shortages of such staples as coffee, tea, fruit, cocoa, meat, fats, and especially bread. The economy was stagnant. In order to survive, the Netherlands needed a reliable supply of raw materials at stable prices – a forlorn hope in time of war, when they found themselves being exploited by the belligerents. Germany, for example, sold them coal at three times the usual price.

Smuggling, particularly by Dutch soldiers garrisoning the eastern border with Germany, was the only growth industry in Holland. In 1913 there were just under 5,000 convictions for smuggling in the judicial tribunals of the Dutch boundary districts; in 1917 the number of convictions had risen to over 40,000, and it was generally accepted that this was only the tip of an immense iceberg.

It is hardly surprising therefore that in such a climate there was no shortage of men prepared to do almost anything for a few guilders.

Best himself was kidnapped from his home by German agents, or Dutchmen working for the Germans, disguised as police officers, and he was only saved by the quick-wittedness of his butler who telephoned police headquarters to check on the number plate of the car used by the supposed police. The car was eventually traced to the docks and Best was found drugged in a cellar.

By the same token, rough justice was meted out to traitors. There was, according to Best, "only one sentence for a man who betrayed anyone, and that was death . . . Anyone who worked for the W. L. service who . . . behaved in a treacherous manner, was perfectly certain to be killed." He himself seems to have executed about four such traitors. "You're responsible for the lives of a whole lot of people," he explained, "and unless you have the reputation of being just but severe, you're bound to be lost."

Dansey was determined to stamp his authority on Allied Intelligence operations in Holland. The French went their own way, but then they were always difficult. But he certainly had no intention of permitting the fledgling American Secret Service to muddy the already murky waters, as the American military attaché in Holland threatened to do. Dansey complained to Van Deman that the attaché "had become a target for a great many very undesirable agents, amongst whom were many who had been discharged from either the French, British or Belgian services".

Dansey backed up his complaint with a plea from Colonel French, second-in-command to Major-General Macdonough, the head of British Military Intelligence. The colonel asked him to say to Colonel Van Deman "that he hoped that all your military attachés in neutral countries may be instructed not only to collaborate with ours, but to hold their hands about starting any new systems of Secret Service. This applies particularly to Holland."

The last thing Dansey needed was more competition in the Dutch intelligence market, especially from a country, albeit an ally, with vast funds at her disposal. Information in a neutral country cost money and usually went to the highest bidder.

The Americans, probably rightly, ignored the British plea. They did start a "new system of Secret Service" in Holland, but on a relatively modest scale, and at the same time co-operated with existing Allied networks. Needless to say, however, the problem of co-operation was not resolved overnight. Indeed it remained a vexed question until the end of the war. As late as August 1918 an inter-Allied conference, chaired by Major-General Macdonough, was called to re-examine the whole subject. The subsequent report advised setting up a commission in Holland, to be headed by Major-General Boucabeille, the French military attaché (and also senior Allied officer) in The Hague. The commission, it was hoped, would be able to arbitrate between the conflicting demands of the different networks. But the war ended before the usefulness of the new body could be evaluated. Certainly on paper it seems to have been little more than a talking shop, a toothless watchdog of the interests of individual Allied countries.

Holland was not to be the only neutral country in which Dansey was to operate. In view of his by now extensive field experience in this area, he was also ordered to take over responsibility for British espionage networks in Switzerland.

Switzerland in the first world war has been immortalised in Somerset Maugham's volume of short stories, *Ashenden*, which he wrote about his experience while working as an agent for British Intelligence. After a stint as an ambulance driver in France Maugham's old complaint, TB, which dogged him for so much of his early life, flared up again and he was forced to resign from the ambulance service. Seeking for somewhere to recuperate and regain his health, he applied for a visa to Switzerland. He was then approached by Sir John Wallinger, brother of Major Wallinger of the W. L. Section. Since he was going to Switzerland, would he care to serve his country as a spy?

As instructed, Maugham took a room in a hotel in Geneva and ostensibly set about writing plays, but at the same time he was making contact with various Allied agents. Every week he had to find his way secretly into France with the information he had acquired. He chose to use the steamer across Lake Geneva at whose western end the city of Geneva lies, to Thonon on the French side of the lake. The French officials had orders not to stamp his passport, so that it would appear to the Swiss that he had not actually left the country at all but merely taken a round trip to Vevey or Lausanne at the north-east corner of the lake.

It has been suggested that the character of Colonel R in the *Ashenden* stories is based on Sir John Wallinger, but we believe that the character is an amalgam of Wallinger and Dansey, whom the novelist almost certainly met through one of the Wallinger brothers. There is no doubt that Colonel R's dialogue in *Ashenden* captures some of the sardonic tone of Dansey's authentic utterances. "If you do well," he tells the narrator, Ashenden, "you'll get no thanks and if you get into trouble you'll get no help." It is a line Dansey used on several occasions to his agents. At another point in one of the stories Colonel R confides to the narrator; "a lot of nonsense is talked about the value of human life" – a view Dansey also shared. Maugham (Ashenden) neatly sums up Colonel R: "What a shrewd, unscrupulous old thing was R! He took no risks; he trusted nobody; he made use of his instruments, but high or low, had no opinion of them."

When Dansey was appointed to the Swiss post, he immediately recruited a man to act for him and provide a liaison between the British Embassy in Berne and Whitehall Court, the SIS London office. He chose a barrister who had occupied the same position with Major Stewart Menzies, Colonel Drake's second-in-command at General Haig's GHQ in France. The barrister was Frederick Oswald Langley, the father of Colonel Jimmy Langley, who was to be Dansey's man running MI9, the escape organisation in the second world war.

Langley Senior had a distinguished war record. He had gone to France with the South Staffordshires, Vernon Kell's old regiment. There he had won an MC and been twice mentioned in despatches. But whilst undergoing yet another tour of front-line duty, he was caught in a German bombardment. A shell made a direct hit on a dug-out he was in, and he was buried alive for seventy-two hours. This experience left him shell-shocked and he was declared unfit for further duty at the front. It was at this point that he was recruited by Menzies, who was a friend of the family.

As assistant military attaché in Berne, Switzerland, working for Dansey, Langley made many friends, particularly amongst the US Legation staff. One of Langley's official American contacts was a twenty-four-year-old third secretary in charge of intelligence. His name was Allen Dulles, who thirty-six years later would become head of the CIA.

Allen W. Dulles joined the State Department in 1916. His first posting was to Vienna, where he frequently acted as a courier taking diplomatic pouches to the US Legation in Switzerland. The following year, when the US entered the war, he was posted to Berne. When Dulles approached the harassed first secretary of the Legation to find out the nature of his duties, the man had no time to waste on junior third secretaries: the place was swarming with new arrivals all trying to find out what they were supposed to be doing. "I guess the best thing for you is to take charge of intelligence," he told Dulles, adding that the place was swarming with spies. Dulles soon discovered that he spoke no less than the truth.

Dulles took a room at the Palace Bellevue Hotel in Berne and plunged in to this new clandestine world with great enthusiasm.

Berne "is *the Diplomatic* and *Spy* center", he wrote excitedly to his mother. Before long he was able to give her more details of his work. "Those [Americans] coming from Germany now are, of course, open to suspicion; and some undoubtedly are, if not German agents, at any rate disloyal. I have had some very interesting encounters with persons whom I have had good reason to suspect belonged to each of these classes." Sometimes, he said, the work was "so 'story-book like' that one wonders whether the incidents are real – and not a chapter of [E. Phillips] Oppenheim". Nevertheless Dulles came to the conclusion that "there is a chance to do as much here as if one were shooting personally a whole regiment of Bosche (sic)".

Switzerland in wartime was, as always, the country where deals were done, where the belligerents from both sides could meet, talk and frequently double cross each other. Obscure espionage games were played by various intelligence agencies, including the Japanese, who for reasons now totally obscure were engaged in spying on their British allies rather than on the German enemy. It was the country in which the victims of the conflict – exiled Czechs, Slovaks, Slavs, Croats, etc. – could meet and dream their hopeless dreams and plan their phantom wars of national liberation in the hope of some future utopia. One of those champions of the seemingly hopeless cause, then exiled in Zurich, was Lenin. His contact with Dulles was brief and unsatisfactory, but it was to provide Dulles years later with a cautionary tale which he used to tell new recruits to the Agency.

The Bolshevik leader had made contact with the US consul in Zurich, James McNally, and on occasion supplied him with up-to-date, accurate information about conditions inside Russia. The consul duly passed all this on to the Legation, who chose to ignore it – largely because they did not trust McNally, whose daughter was known to be married to a German naval officer. It was felt that McNally might have divided loyalties. When late one afternoon the telephone rang, Dulles – who was duty officer – answered it. Lenin was excited and emotional and wanted to speak to someone in authority; the matter was desperately urgent. However, everyone else had gone home, and Dulles himself had a date with a girl which he had no intention of missing. He therefore told the man to come back tomorrow. Tomorrow, insisted Lenin, would be too late. But Dulles was adamant. As it turned out, Lenin was right. He left Switzerland that night for Russia and a role in twentieth-century history.

Claude Dansey would never have made a mistake like that. With him the business of espionage always came first.

147

One of Dulles's most reliable informants was the exiled Czech leader, Jan Masaryk; one of the disasters – not Dulles's fault – was also Czech: a girl who was employed by the US Legation and allowed access to the code room. The British informed Dulles that she was a German spy; and to him fell the distasteful task of delivering this Czech Mata Hari into the hands of her enemies. He took her out to dinner one evening and then walked her home, where two British agents were waiting for her. He never saw her again: like the characters in Lewis Carroll's "Hunting of the Snark", she "suddenly and silently vanished away". If the agents were Dansey's men and Dansey had turned his thumb down, then her chances of survival were slim.

Dansey found Switzerland to his liking. He understood the Swiss: they both shared an appreciation of the power and use of money. This is not to say that Dansey was avaricious, or even interested in money for its own sake: he was not. But espionage in peacetime or in a neutral country is an expensive business. Money is needed to grease palms, as well as the wheels of intrigue: agents have to be paid, information purchased, officials bribed, etc. Dansey had become a master of the art of conducting intelligence work under these conditions.

Thanks to his Sleepy Hollow connections, thanks perhaps above all to his friendship with Thomas Fortune Ryan, he now had the inside track to the international business and financial community, and for the rest of his life he was to exploit this for all he was worth. Thereafter, Dansey always regarded Switzerland as his personal fief, and woe betide any other agency that dared to interfere with his operations there. So sure was he of his Swiss base, that just before the second world war, at a time when he knew he was in the running to take over the job of C, the head of the British Secret Service, he made Zurich his headquarters, and from there ran the various branches of his highly secret Z Organisation. For Dansey Switzerland had become home.

Part Three

The Twenty-Year Truce
1919–39

CHAPTER FOURTEEN

The Game of Foxes and the Sport of Kings

The end of the war brought abrupt changes in the intelligence world as a whole and in the career of Claude Dansey in particular. The two decades of uneasy peace before hostilities were resumed were to see his career pass through a series of developments as remarkable as any he had already experienced: first, reverting to his old role as a secret agent operating in high places; then returning to the full-time staff in an important official position; suffering disgrace and exile; creating his own semi-private, double-secret organisation; and finally achieving a position in which he controlled virtually the whole of Allied Intelligence.

In November 1918, however, before he could begin his post-war progress, there was a great deal of clearing up to be done, along with the transformation of the Secret Intelligence Service into an instrument which could cope with the politics of peace. Dansey and his fellows found themselves required to use their skills against their allies, as the winners started squabbling over the share-out of the spoils. Britain and France, especially, reverted immediately to their mutual jealousies and suspicions as they jockeyed for power and influence in the remains of the two great empires which had finally crumbled during the war: the Austro-Hungarian in central Europe and the Ottoman in the Middle East.

Dansey was to become involved in both areas. He began in the Balkans, where national boundaries were traditionally fluid and national pride and duplicity had always gone hand in hand. States had changed sides with bewildering rapidity during the war, either to keep pace with the varying fortunes of the main belligerents or where governments had fallen and been replaced by others with different allegiances. Often, as in Greece and Romania, for example, the rulers had totally different sympathies from those of their peoples. In such circumstances, it was not going to be easy to decide exactly who should be classed as a loser having to pay a forfeit of territory, and who should be regarded as one of the winners, eligible to receive the prizes.

Britain, France, Italy and America all had troops in the Balkans, supposedly helping to establish and maintain the peace. But their governments were also keen to gain influence. Inevitably they began to line up friends and potential puppets, almost always in opposition to each other. Some impression of the goings-on can be gauged from a report received by the Foreign Office in London in 1919, which stated that the Italians were "making a vigorous bid for the friendship of Romania", and that there was friction between the Italians on the one hand and the British and French on the other, because Italy had sent the battleship *Andrea Doria* into the Black Sea on a ceremonial visit to celebrate an Italian victory, when in fact it had been British and French armies which had fought and won in Serbia and Bulgaria. At the same time, the report said, the French and Italians were working hard t)gether to strengthen the Romanian belief that Britain and America were wholly responsible for the "harsh attitude" of the Peace Conference towards her! An added complication, if one were needed, was the threat of international Bolshevism from Russia stirring up the always volatile internal politics of the Balkan countries.

In such a situation, there was obviously great need for an intelligence organisation to try to keep track of what everyone was up to. But such an organisation did not exist. Someone would have to be found to organise it – and who better than Claude Dansey?

The choice of Dansey was hardly surprising. The general in charge of British forces in the Balkans was none other than Tom Bridges, Dansey's old friend from South Africa and the American mission. He knew as well as anyone Dansey's expertise in creating intelligence systems from scratch. In addition, Dansey already had some knowledge of the politics of the area, since his stomping ground in Switzerland had been the home of numerous important Balkan exiles. His agents had sent back many reports on their activities and ambitions.

Dansey travelled out to Salonika and set about establishing the much-needed *apparat*, bustling about the region and taking particular interest in territory which was disputed, such as Dobruja, the province on the Black Sea around the port of Constanza, to which both Romania and Bulgaria laid vociferous claim. All the Allies wanted to woo Romania, which was then a leading oil producer from its fields at Ploesti. But there was a problem: who was to be classed as a winner and who as a loser? After an initial two years of neutrality Romania had entered the war on the Allied side, but had been swiftly and soundly beaten and then occupied by

Germany. Having joined the Russians in signing an armistice with the Central Powers late in 1917, it had officially relinquished its position as one of the Allies.

The Romanians are essentially a Latin people, and it was possible to deal with them and even to understand them. Their rivals the Bulgarians were completely different. After three years on the side of the Central Powers they had seen the error of their ways and switched to the Allied cause just in time, hoping to pick up pieces of Ottoman and Austro-Hungarian territory. Now they claimed that their defection had broken the Central Powers bloc, and that since they were therefore directly responsible for the Allied victory, they were entitled to gratitude and reward.

"The Bulgar is rapidly recovering the somewhat insolent aplomb which has been characteristic of his official utterances of the past three years," Dansey reported. "He is rapidly forgetting the fact that he has been thoroughly beaten and is at the mercy of the Entente Powers . . . The sliminess and commercial immorality of the Bulgar is a byword among businessmen and there is no reason to suppose that, since the possibility of common action against the Turks has disappeared as a result of the Turkish capitulation, the Bulgar will deal fairly and squarely with the Entente Powers in any affair whatsoever." He continued with a long list of instances of Bulgarian "insolence", starting with the looting of British supply trains.

From Romania, he reported the ominous fact that "French influences are working against the present Government, which they consider pro-British and obstructive, and they want a change". With Allied perfidy linked to Balkan venality, the winter of 1918-19 provided Dansey with a fascinating and valuable exercise in deviousness which would stand him in good stead in the future. It is small wonder that he was later described as a man who thought nine ways at once. By February 1919, however, he had set up the Balkan intelligence organisation and was ready to move on again, back to the very centre of world intrigue.

The Peace Conference opened at the Quai d'Orsay in Paris on 18th January 1919. The Allies gathered in strength – the British delegation alone commandeered four large hotels, using the Majestic as its headquarters. As the wheeling and dealing began, so did the spying. There were so many different interests represented at the Conference that everyone felt the need to discover everyone else's fall-back position in the negotiations. It was rather like a huge poker game – with the intelligence agencies acting as unofficial kibitzers.

Naturally, no side acknowledged that spying was taking place. The British Government simply regularised the position by appointing a Chief of Security. During the preparations for the Conference and during its first four weeks, Dansey's former associate from Scotland Yard, Sir Basil Thomson, was in charge. It soon became apparent, however, that someone with a more direct knowledge of intelligence was needed. Thomson was replaced by Major Stewart Menzies, who had served with Field Intelligence in France and later with the Secret Intelligence Service in Whitehall Court. But Menzies lasted only two weeks before Arthur Balfour, who was heading the delegation, ordered a further reshuffle. Menzies was replaced by a senior and more experienced officer, Lieutenant-Colonel Claude Dansey.

Dansey took up his duties at the end of February. There had been a sharp reminder of the importance of the security aspect of the job when, on 19th February, a young French anarchist named Cottin narrowly failed to assassinate the French Prime Minister, Georges Clemenceau. He fired several revolver shots at the eighty-year-old statesman as he was driving to an appointment at the Ministry of War, hitting him in the shoulder. Clemenceau survived, but the lesson was clear. One of the first things Dansey did was to call for three extra men for the special protection of the British leaders, to add to the chief inspector, two inspectors and twenty-four sergeants and constables on his staff.

It can have been no easy task, looking after a contingent which included such men as T. E. Lawrence and the Emir Feisal among the politicians and civil servants, but Dansey kept security under control with quiet efficiency. He also took the opportunity to make the acquaintance of as many men of power and influence as possible, storing the contacts away for future use, as was his custom.

One of the more pleasant aspects of life at the Conference for Dansey was the presence of many old friends from the Allied intelligence services, most notably the Americans Van Deman and Marlborough Churchill, both newly-promoted brigadier-generals. They must all have enjoyed the irony of a situation where they were busy spying on each other's delegations, particularly when Herbert Yardley made use of the code and cipher breaking skills which Dansey had done so much to promote, to read British cablegrams. Since the British were also intercepting and reading the Americans' messages, there were no hard feelings involved, at least among the professionals.

Dansey and Van Deman had many common concerns, not least the declared intention of President Wilson to have all secret services outlawed throughout the world as part of his plan to create a League of Nations. Fortunately for Dansey, and perhaps for the world, Wilson failed to achieve that part of his aims, though the writing was clearly on the wall for the United States Intelligence Service, which soon found itself fighting a losing battle for its continued existence.

Some of the shared concerns turned out to have lighter endings. On one occasion Van Deman discovered a hidden trapdoor in the main billet of the American delegation in the heart of Paris at 4 Place de la Concorde. Behind it stretched a dark passageway to adjoining buildings. Fearing the worst, Van Deman made his way along the tunnel, noting to his dismay that it had obviously been well used. At the end, he found another trapdoor, through which he crept to find himself in a well-known establishment where, according to one source, "the entertainment was long and greatly varied and the girls' costumes short and simply varied."

When the signing of the Treaty of Versailles on 28th June 1919 ended the Conference, Dansey found himself out of a job, worried once more about his future as he faced another crossroads, this time with a wife and stepdaughter to support. He was forty-three years old, highly experienced, highly skilled and respected throughout the intelligence community. In 1917 his services had been recognised by France with its second highest award as an Officer of the *Légion d'Honneur*, and by Belgium, which made him a Chevalier of the *Ordre Léopold*. In 1918, he had been honoured by his own country with the award of a CMG (Companion of the Order of St Michael and St George), one step short of a knighthood. His position should have been secure.

But with peace, the British intelligence services were being drastically slimmed down. From a total in August 1918 of 557 officers and 919 civilians on salaries of over £250 a year, the strength of the Directorate of Military Intelligence as a whole had shrunk to a mere eighty-nine officers by the beginning of 1920. MI1 (the intelligence-gathering service as a whole) had accounted for sixty-nine officers and ten civilians at the end of the war, and MI5 (the security and counter-intelligence service) for ninety-eight officers and seventeen civilians. By January 1920, MI1c (the SIS) had a full-time staff of only five, including C himself, while MI5 including K numbered twelve.

Some staff had joined the service just for the war. Many of the old professionals, the men who had been in the business from the earliest days, were retired. Others chose to leave the full-time staff and become secret agents again, slipping back into the shadows to work for the SIS at a gentler pace, without the desperate pressures of wartime. Dansey became one of them. Never much of a desk man – even during the second world war those who worked with him commented that he always seemed to be disappearing somewhere, going out alone to secret meetings away from the office – he preferred to be out in the field, where he could enjoy greater independence, free from the bureaucracy which governed the staff of "head office".

Some of his friends deplored what they considered to be a shocking waste of talent and experience. Van Deman wrote to him saying that if the War Office had asked his advice he would have told them that Dansey was the last man they should have allowed to leave the active list. "However," he went on, "you may be sure that you will never be allowed to lose touch with the [American] Intelligence Service; the individual members of that service will see to that . . . If it is any pleasure to you to know it, I can tell you that your name is a household word among the entire Intelligence Service of our Army. There is nothing that you can ask from us that we will not more than gladly give you. Certainly we will keep in touch . . . one of the most pleasant experiences of this war was our friendship. I certainly do not propose to run any chance of losing sight of you."

Leaving the office may have suited Dansey's temperament, but it did pose certain problems. In order to retain his independence, he needed to specialise. But this was not easy: the fields in which he had been most successful were no longer of any use to him. Germany was defeated, supposedly for good; France was now officially an ally; the Irish problem was apparently nearing a solution – or so Downing Street chose to believe. At best the Irish might remain the concern of MI5 and Scotland Yard's Special Branch, but the SIS's Irish role was virtually finished. The fact that his name was, as Van Deman had told him, a household word in American intelligence circles meant that he could never return to work in the USA in his old role.

The prospects did not look promising. Admittedly, a Bolshevik Russia was beginning to be seen as a serious threat, but that was no help to Dansey. His Russian connections were few, and there were others in the SIS who had been involved with the problem since before the Revolution. Where could he turn? He surveyed the situation carefully and logically, and found the solution in typical Dansey fashion.

In the post-war world, Britain had to build for the future. The far-sighted foresaw the end of colonialism which would leave

Britain dependent on its influence and goodwill in what we would nowadays call the developing nations, especially those whose position or natural resources – particularly oil – were likely to have strategic value. What the British Government needed from its intelligence service was information that would put it one step ahead of its competitors.

Dansey was never much bothered about making a fortune for himself. He had had plenty of opportunities to try his luck, from his earliest days in Rhodesia, but his interest lay in other directions. In September 1919, however, he went into business with the backing of Sperlings merchant bank, running a company called the SMA Syndicate Limited from offices in Basildon House, Moorgate, in the City of London. It was the forerunner of several such firms, for Dansey maintained a succession of business "fronts" over the next twenty-five years.

In November, the Foreign Office received anguished messages from Eustace Percy, manager of the Anglo Saxon Petroleum Company in Arabia, saying that two "prospecting geologists" had turned up in Jeddah, despite the fact that his company had the sole oil prospecting concession for the Hejaz, the area alongside the Red Sea and Gulf of Akaba surrounding the holy cities of Mecca and Medina, which was then a separate country. Did the Foreign Office know anything about them? There was a flurry of activity, which ended when the telegrams reached the desk of George Kidston of the Eastern Department, who noted laconically, "I expect this is Colonel Dansey and a companion."

It was indeed Dansey and his assistant, a Major Macdonald. As was Dansey's way, they had arrived with the highest credentials: letters of introduction to King Hussein, the Sherif of Mecca himself, from his son, the Emir Feisal, Lawrence of Arabia's mentor. Dansey had put his time in Paris to good use. The King made him and Macdonald his personal guests during their stay in Jeddah, accommodating them in his palace – something which no doubt irked poor Eustace Percy even more.

Dansey told the King that the SMA Corporation had been formed for the purpose of investing capital in Arabia and Persia. He had, he told Hussein, capital available for railway, harbour, irrigation and water works; electric light and power and other public utility works (shades of Harrison Williams); the search for and development of natural resources, including petroleum, minerals and non-metallic ores such as alkalies, phosphates, coal and so on. Under the terms of the proposed deal, the corporation would receive from the sovereign power a charter for a national bank, which would act in partnership with, and as trustee for, the sovereign power. In addition, the corporation would be prepared to accept a concession to work on and develop a defined and limited area of the state for a specified number of years, sharing the profits with the sovereign power.

It was an audacious plan, and if Hussein had accepted it it would have given the British company a complete stranglehold on his country. It would also have established a permanent relationship with the head of the Hashemites whose sons and family were in the process of taking power in Jordan, Palestine, Syria and Iraq. It might also have had other important consequences. In 1924, Ibn Saud invaded the Hejaz and seized the territory from Hussein, making it part of what was to become Saudi Arabia. If the British had been firmly ensconced, the Saudis might well have thought again about invading, and the shape of the Middle East would have been quite different. In the event, however, Hussein did not accept the deal, and when Ibn Saud ejected him and absorbed his country, it was the American oil companies which finally reaped the benefits. Britain, influenced by Lawrence and his associates, had backed the wrong man.

By then, though, Dansey was long gone and fully occupied elsewhere. He had travelled first to Venezuela, another country with considerable oil potential, and then returned to London and his long-suffering wife and stepdaughter, who must by then have been realising the penalties of having a secret agent as husband and stepfather. But his American wife did ensure that he maintained his transatlantic contacts, including Thomas Fortune Ryan. In 1923, when Dansey's wanderings through the oil world had finished, Ryan came back into his life with a splendid offer: he had decided the time was ripe to fulfil the horse-racing ambitions which had been interrupted by the war: the long-held dream of his horses winning some of the English classics, "more particularly the Derby". This was a project dear to Ryan's heart, and one which he and Dansey had discussed as long ago as 1913. Now he wanted to see it come true. Would Dansey take charge? Dansey was delighted to oblige.

While Thomas Ryan was never as enthusiastic an owner as his late associate, William C. Whitney, founder of the famous Whitney racing stables, he had set up a stud and racing stable on his property at Oak Ridge, Virginia. Ryan had enjoyed considerable success on American tracks and, along with his ever-growing art collection, horses more and more came to dominate his last years. In 1923 he was seventy-two, and although he had not actually retired, he was growing bored with Wall Street. He had done all there was to do.

He was worth over $300 million; his children had grown up; he was enjoying a second marriage; he felt in the mood to play. And what better playground for a wealthy man than the lush green race courses of England?

Did Ryan know that Dansey was a British Secret Service agent? In our view, there can be no doubt that he did, and that after a while Dansey probably made little attempt to conceal the fact from him. Why should he? He had too much to gain from the relationship to jeopardise it by stupid conceit.

Unlike so many of the better-known US robber barons, Thomas Fortune Ryan was subtle, complex and secretive. His perspectives were international. In today's jargon his business would no doubt be described as a multi-national conglomerate: he had fingers in a dozen different financial pies in half a dozen different countries. In the course of his career he had dominated the copper industry, rubber, insurance, the New York transit system, tobacco, coal, iron and steel. It is difficult, therefore, to believe that he would not have rumbled Dansey back in 1911.

Dansey, for all his undoubted talent and considerable experience at that time, had never met anyone like Ryan before. Ryan, however, had survived for over thirty years – and prospered mightily – in the Wall Street jungle. He had not achieved his impressive reputation by being either gullible or a poor judge of character. In any case, from Dansey's point of view, it would have been insane to prejudice his most valuable contact in America by trying to be too clever by half; far better to allow the truth to emerge gradually.

The relationship was symbiotic, both men deriving advantage from it. Dansey, for his part, gained entrée to circles of international political and financial power such as few have ever aspired to; Ryan got an excellent fixer – a perfect instrument backed by the mysterious prestige of the British Secret Service. Despite the hiatus caused by the war, they never lost touch with each other.

Early in 1923, Ryan cabled Dansey in London asking him to buy six colts and have them shipped to New York. A superb horseman himself from his Rhodesian and South African days, Dansey was always a fine judge of horseflesh. He visited various sales and scouted around his racing connections, and by August had found three colts which he deemed suitable for American racing conditions. Then Ryan altered his instructions: he wanted Dansey to find eight, not six, colts, one of which "was to be selected with a view to racing in the Derby", and have them trained in England. By the end of the year, Dansey, now officially manager of Ryan's racing enterprises, had delivered all eight horses to the famous trainer "Atty" Persse, at Chaltis Hill, near Stockbridge, Hampshire.

Henry Seymour "Atty" Persse was one of the great characters of the Turf. A jovial, friendly Irishman with an inexhaustible fund of racing and hunting stories, he was noted for his ability to spot talent not only in two-year-olds but also in young jockeys as well. He was the first English trainer to offer a retainer to the young Steve Donoghue, later Champion Jockey for fifteen years, but then at the beginning of his English career.

Donoghue and Persse provided a strong Irish-American connection which no doubt appealed to Ryan – and probably Dansey too. The jockey had ridden for "Boss" Croker, the notorious boss of Tammany Hall. One American reporter described Croker as "a king and New York was his kingdom", but he was a king who owed allegiance, as did so many officials of the Democratic Party, to Thomas Ryan. When Croker retired from politics, he decided to return to his homeland – he had been born in Clonakilty, County Cork – to devote the rest of his life to enjoying his considerable wealth and indulging in his hobby, racing.

Claude was already putting his post as manager of the Ryan racing stables to good use. Trading on Ryan's name and reputation, he had made a host of new contacts amongst those who controlled the world of international big business and finance, and who turned to the Turf for relaxation. There were many owners like Ryan, nursing slightly improbable racing ambitions, who were flattered to make the acquaintance of the charming retired colonel with the professional eye for a good horse. Dansey made use of Epsom and Ascot and Newmarket, the English racing scene, as he had once used the Sleepy Hollow Country Club – only now he was ten years older and wiser and wilier.

It was Victor Cavendish-Bentinck (now 9th Duke of Portland), chairman of the Joint Intelligence Committee during the second world war, who put the matter most concisely. "Dansey," he told the authors, "always operated at the top." But to do that successfully, you must know the top men personally, you must have established a friendly relationship with them. And there is no better way of discovering what makes a man tick than studying him while he is relaxed and at play. If he is an owner and a keen racing man, then study him at the track.

By the end of the 1924 season, seven of Ryan's two-year-olds had run, winning five races between them and gaining three seconds and four thirds; their winnings for the year totalled £2,840. But money was of secondary importance to Ryan: his gaze was fixed firmly on winning the greatest of the English classics.

Now, thanks to Persse and Dansey, that had begun to seem a real possibility.

Persse and Dansey had found a colt called The Virginian. They had paid 2,200 guineas of Ryan's money – a fair price at the time – for the two-year-old, and at a secret trial the horse performed magnificently. Indeed, so successful was the trial that they both came to the conclusion that the colt just might have an outside chance of winning; certainly he ought to be worth a place.

The 1925 Derby was to be long remembered, but not for the quality of the racing. For one thing, there was an unusually large field: twenty-seven runners were due to line up at the start. But in the opinion of the "fancy", there was no outstanding horse that year; they were all much of a muchness. The *Times* racing correspondent called it "the 'If' Derby" – by which he meant "if" Cross-Bow proved a stayer, "if" Manna had the speed, etc., one of them, or almost any of the twenty-seven horses, could win.

The bookmakers, however, did not agree. They made Lord Astor's Cross-Bow favourite at 9–2 on. Manna, owned by Mr Morriss, a Shanghai bullion broker, stood at 9–1, and the Aga Khan's Zionist (by Spearmint out of Judea) ridden by "Brownie" Carslake, was regarded as a good outside bet at 10–1. The Virginian was quoted at 100–1. In spite of the odds, no expense had been spared in getting the colt ready for the race, and Persse had retained a brilliant young jockey, Harry Beasley, to ride him.

It was not Persse's fault or Dansey's that the 1925 Derby exemplified the truth of Murphy's Law: everything that could go wrong did so – starting with the weather. It rained: in torrents. Gale force winds drove the rain directly into the stands and enclosures, soaking even those who had private boxes. A gipsy caravan was blown over, and the downpour transformed the paddock into a swamp, so that the horses had to parade ankle deep in mud while wearing their waterproof sheets – not that many people left the protection of the stands to see them.

And that was just the beginning. Things got worse.

Even the start of the race was jinxed. One of the webbing tapes of the starting gate snapped as it was going up. The tape struck several of the runners and hit a horse called Solario in the face. Solario's jockey, thinking that the starter had seen the incident, stood his ground when the others took off – until it became obvious that the starter had no intention of re-running the race at all. By that time Solario was twenty lengths in arrears.

But Dansey and Persse were interested only in The Virginian. "At the start," Dansey recorded, "he jumped off in front and raced with the leaders for seven furlongs, after which he began to drop back." The race was won by Manna, who thus gave Steve Donoghue his sixth Derby winner in ten years; second was the Aga Khan's Zionist, and Mr A. K. Macomber's The Sirdar, ridden by A. Easling, was third. The Virginian finished tenth.

Dansey and Persse lost no time in conducting a post-mortem. As *The History of Thomas Fortune Ryan's English Racing Stable* explains: "The Virginian had run so well in the early part of the race that Colonel Dansey, who was managing Mr Ryan's horses in England, and Mr Persse were left wondering if they had been mistaken and that the horse really did not stay 1½ miles." But the reason for The Virginian's failure was soon made clear. When they got him back to his stable at Chaltis Hill, the horse was discovered to be sick. He had "heel-bug", a form of virulent blood poisoning, which was then epidemic in England. The colt was taken out of training for four months, but the damage was done: he never raced again.

Ryan was undeterred by this setback; he was still determined to win the Derby. Meanwhile Dansey and Persse had enjoyed some success with his other horses. Three of them had done well – Conde, Congo (which won the London Autumn Cup followed by the Grosvenor Cup at Liverpool), and Damon (who won the Ascot New Stakes and the Champagne Stakes at Doncaster). Damon, in fact, was regarded as one of the most promising two-year-olds in the country. After he had beaten Call Boy at Doncaster the book-makers made him second favourite for the Derby of 1927.

Then, just before the race, the horse became ill and was later discovered to have an abcess in the head, which eventually killed him.

The following year at the age of seventy-seven Ryan died suddenly at his home at 858 Fifth Avenue, New York City. His sons and heirs did not share their father's passion for racing: they had no burning ambition to win the English Derby; and so in 1929 Clendenin Ryan had all his father's horses shipped to the USA.

Thus, at one stroke, Dansey lost not only a friend and mentor, but also a financially profitable cover for his espionage activities. He was out in the cold once more. But this time there was no point in turning to his other Sleepy Hollow connections for help. It was 1929, the year of the Wall Street crash, when even millionaires had reason to become uneasy.

CHAPTER FIFTEEN

Fighting Fascism

Since officially quitting the Intelligence Service in 1919, Dansey had been fortunate in having a series of extremely enjoyable occupations which not only paid the bills but also provided useful covers for his semi-freelance intelligence activities. Now that Ryan had gone, however, he was forced once more to face economic realities. He had no private income, and the SIS has never been noted for paying its agents too generously, particularly those working on a part-time basis. Happily, however, Admiral Sir Hugh "Quex" Sinclair, the "little man with the face of a faintly surprised frog" who had taken over as Chief of the Secret Service at the age of fifty following the death of the first C, Sir Mansfield Smith Cumming, in 1923, had a job for him. The new, full-time assignment was in Italy, in charge of Passport Control – in other words, head of the Rome station of the SIS.

Rome was a plum posting in 1929, for under Mussolini the city was becoming one of the more sensitive political centres in Europe. *Il Duce*, having ruled Italy for seven years and earned the admiration of many foreigners for making the trains run on time, was now turning his attention to visions of greater glory.

For Italy to be acknowledged as a leading power, it was necessary for her to have an empire, like Britain and France. Unfortunately, all the best territories had already been taken, and however grandiose Mussolini's dreams may have been, they did not encompass trying to oust either of the colonial powers from any of their colonies. Nor did they include the enormous expense of shipping an army halfway round the world to conquer some corner which nobody else wanted. Inevitably, the dictator's eyes settled on easier and cheaper game, nearer home across the Mediterranean.

Italy already had colonies in North Africa. In 1911 she had annexed Tripoli, and earlier still had taken a share of Somalia along with Britain, France and Ethiopia, as Dansey had good cause

163

to remember from his days spent in that inhospitable wilderness fighting the Mad Mullah. But the fact that Ethiopia was one of the partners had always rankled with the Italians, who had been eyeing Ethiopia itself as a potential colony since the late nineteenth century. Their only attempt to gain control had, however, resulted in a humiliating defeat by the Ethiopian tribes at Adowa in 1896. Ever since, the Italians had been waiting to avenge and if possible obliterate what their nationalist poet d'Annunzio described as "a shameful scar". They had already encroached on Ethiopian territory bordering Italian Somaliland in the Ogaden desert, taking over wells used by wandering Somali tribes who were nominally under British protection. It was inevitable that they would eventually attempt a full-scale occupation and conquest.

With such a potential threat to British interests, Italy had to be watched. And who better for the job than Claude Dansey, almost certainly the only officer in the SIS with any knowledge or experience of Somalia and Ethiopia? He accepted the posting eagerly, well aware of its importance not only because of the North African connection but also because Rome housed the Vatican, which spread its tentacles worldwide. The only drawback to the new job was that it meant the final demise of his marriage, for Pauline refused to go to Rome with him.

The marriage had never really worked. There had been friction almost from the beginning, though Dansey could never be persuaded in later years to say much about it. Having a secret agent for a husband, however, cannot be easy. Kim Philby's wife, Eleanor, once wrote: "It is common intelligence practice for a wife to be told that her husband is doing secret work. The men who direct these things know enough about human nature to realise that a wife must be let into the secret. Otherwise, if a husband is always going off on secret jaunts, giving her lame excuses, she will soon think there is another woman and might easily put a private detective on to him. So to avoid any nonsense of this kind, she is usually told just enough to keep her from worrying."

Of course, such knowledge might well give a wife even more cause for worrying – and in any case, it does not alter the fact that the husband *is* always going off on secret jaunts, and leaving her alone. Poor Pauline Dansey could see the prospect of being left for long periods in Rome, where she neither knew anyone nor spoke the language, while Dansey disappeared on clandestine journeys throughout Europe and North Africa. When Ryan was alive, Dansey still had a connection with the United States, and there were regular opportunities for transatlantic visits. The new job meant the end of that, and for Pauline that was the last straw. She packed her bags and took herself and her daughter Elaine back across the Atlantic to New York, where Elaine still lives today, a society matron with a home in the Upper East Side.

The move to Rome in 1929 marked the beginning of another important era in Claude Dansey's life. He was fifty-three years old, and the beefy strength and fitness which had been a physical characteristic of his earlier years was giving way to a more spare appearance. The nose was becoming hawk-like, and the eyes less so, needing the aid of spectacles. They were, however, as penetrat‑ ing and intense as ever, capable of transfixing anyone unfortunate enough to arouse his displeasure. The sardonic humour and acer‑ bic tongue by which so many of his second world war colleagues remember him, were already a prominent part of his armoury, but he was also capable of great warmth and the power of his charm was legendary. What was even more important, his vitality and energy were completely undiminished by the approach of middle age; indeed, they were obviously recharged by his new life, as he entered a decade of amazing activity.

Dansey had hardly settled into his position in Rome, when an event occurred in London which would have important con‑ sequences for his career. On 13th November 1929, Robert Vansit‑ tart was appointed Permanent Under-Secretary at the Foreign Office.

Vansittart was an unusual civil servant with a highly individual style. He dressed fashionably, wrote novels, verse and plays, entertained lavishly in his Mayfair mansion at 44 Park Street, and generally pursued his own inclinations with outspoken tenacity. He was a great sportsman, especially good at tennis – he later became president of the All England Club at Wimbledon – but less so in team games. He was also a keen follower of the Turf and may well have already known Claude Dansey through horse racing, or through the family, since his father, too, had been a cavalry officer. They could also have met in Paris, at the Peace Conference, where Vansittart had achieved some of his earliest diplomatic successes as third secretary in the British delegation. It is not known when their association first began, but they had many friends and acquaint‑ ances in common, most notably Winston Churchill.

Vansittart had a lively mind in most matters, but admitted to being rigid concerning "communism, Deutschism and homo‑ sexuality", a trinity of targets which in hindsight had a certain prophetic irony for the Secret Service. Undoubtedly the strongest of his three hates even in the thirties was Germany, and he determined to do everything in his power to counter the threat of German resurgence. In this he was at odds with his political masters and with many of his colleagues. Yet although he was in a position of great influence at the Foreign Office, as a civil servant he had no direct power. All he could do was advise and argue and try to persuade the government, and for this he needed ammunition in the form of facts and figures.

The amount of information coming in overtly from the Berlin embassy was not satisfactory for Vansittart's purposes. What he needed most was good intelligence about industrial, economic and military matters, and it was precisely in these areas that the Foreign Office machine was most lacking. Until then, economics had been largely ignored by the Foreign Office, and career diplomats had had no incentive to concern themselves with questions of trade or commerce. The service attachés did their best to provide information about military, naval and air strengths, but it was strictly forbidden for any attaché to involve himself in any activity which could be construed as espionage. Attachés, therefore, had to rely for information on what their hosts chose to tell them.

The SIS should have been the natural answer to Vansittart's needs, particularly as it was nominally under Foreign Office control. But by 1929 the service was badly run down, desperately short of funds, and geared to combating Russia and communism rather than Germany and fascism. In any case, the Foreign Office was only one of the SIS's customers, and Vansittart did not have the power to turn it to his own uses. Although he was in charge of the Foreign Office, it was Sir Warren Fisher, the Treasury chief and head of the Civil Service, who was chairman of the Secret Service Committee, and Sir Maurice Hankey, Secretary to the Cabinet, who ran the all-important Committee of Imperial Defence. Neither of them agreed with Vansittart's view of Germany as the greatest threat to peace.

Under these circumstances, Vansittart had to devise other ways of getting information, outside official diplomatic or SIS channels. The answer lay in an area which Claude Dansey had always advocated and utilised: the world of business and commerce. Many British bankers, businessmen, industrialists, merchant navy officers, politicians, journalists and so on visited Germany. Such men often sent in reports to the Foreign Office, or passed on information to embassies or their acquaintances in Whitehall. If such sources could be organised and encouraged, they could provide a great deal of valuable intelligence. For the most part, they would pay their own expenses and would not expect to receive money for doing their patriotic duty – an important consideration when budgets were so tight.

Such an arrangement had another appeal for Vansittart, too. The ministers who were authorised to receive officially-obtained confidential or secret information were for the most part opposed to his beliefs about Germany. The men he had to feed with ammunition which they could use in the political forum, friends such as Winston Churchill, were out of office and therefore not entitled to be given Foreign Office information. The embargo, however, would not apply to intelligence obtained from other sources.

In 1930, Dansey was asked to set up such an independent intelligence service, outside the official SIS, making use of businessmen who were either based in Germany or who made regular visits there. (This would be in addition to and quite separate from his role as station chief in Rome.) It was a job which suited him perfectly, and did not seem particularly unusual. He was always rather independent, regarding the agents he recruited and ran as belonging to him personally, an attitude which he retained right to the end of his career.

The fact that Dansey and Vansittart considered such activities as reasonable is indicative of the state of the SIS at that time. Admiral Sinclair had many good qualities but running a tight ship was not one of them. He allowed his officers to go their own ways and to build their own empires within the organisation, often with no effective supervision except over money. The SIS's total budget had by this time been reduced so drastically that it was only equal to the cost of maintaining one Royal Navy destroyer in Home Waters. Consequently, when Dansey showed he could deliver a steady flow of intelligence at no extra cost to the service – for he naturally copied the independently-obtained material to the SIS – Sinclair was not inclined to ask questions. If Dansey chose to range over the whole of Europe instead of sticking to Italy, that could be regarded as a bonus, for the SIS was actually having to abandon its operations in several countries altogether because it could no longer afford them.

Dansey's connections, built up so painstakingly over the years, now began to bear fruit. His recruits, as we shall see later, included many famous and important men and women, as well as numerous ordinary businessmen. By no means all of them were English. But they all had a common bond, which became stronger and stronger as the thirties progressed and Hitler became Chancellor of Germany in 1933 and then swiftly seized power as dictator: they

167

were all strongly opposed to Naziism and were ready to give their services freely in the fight against it.

This loose association of businessmen and travellers remained informal and was therefore never given any title. However, among those in Parliament, the press and the Foreign Office who were aware of its results if not its methods, it became known as "Vansittart's Private Detective Agency". Dansey's role in it remained, of course, the most private part of all.

Vansittart's first and possibly most important informant was Group-Captain Malcolm Grahame Christie, CMG, DSO, MC, whom he had first met when Christie was air attaché in Washington from 1922–6, while Vansittart himself was heading the American department of the Foreign Office. Christie had gone from Washington to Berlin, where the fact that he was totally bilingual in German and English and had a *Doktor Ingenieur*'s degree from Aachen University meant that he could mix with German aeronautical engineers and technologists as an equal.

He had been a distinguished flyer during the first world war: at one time he had ferried British agents behind German lines, and in 1917 formed the world's first night-bombing squadron. He had earned a certain amount of unpopularity among senior officers by insisting on making his own reconnaissance flights before an action, and then personally leading the squadrons of his wing on raids. A wing-commander was supposed to sit back at base while his men flew the missions and took the risks, but Christie would have none of this.

Although severely hampered by the rules regarding his position as air attaché, Christie was keenly aware of the dangers of German militarism, and did his best to warn others. As early as November 1928 he was writing letters giving long and detailed assessments of German aims, of her intention to avoid paying reparations as well as rearm because the Allies would not disarm. "I suggest," he wrote in one such letter, "that having shorn Samson's locks we should keep his scalp closely cropped until he shows a definite tendency to handle the ass's jawbone in a more delicate manner."

Christie retired from Berlin and from the RAF in 1930 because of ill health, and went to Switzerland to recuperate. It was almost certainly there that he met Dansey and began a fruitful connection which was to last throughout the thirties. Christie had excellent contacts everywhere in Europe, but most especially in Germany, which he was able to pass on to Dansey. He was an extremely wealthy man, and had a house on the Dutch-German border, a perfect base for secret operations and a most valuable addition to Dansey's organisation. He became general manager and director of Otto Coke Oven Limited of Leeds and president of Otto Coke Oven, New York, a genuine position which gave him a bona fide reason to travel and to seek information about all manner of industrial concerns which might be potential customers.

He was able to move easily in official and society circles in Berlin, especially those connected with flying, and was on the closest of terms with Goering and with General Milch, who became Goering's adjutant and was Inspector General of the Luftwaffe from 1939–45. In the early thirties, Milch was basically pro-British and was quite happy to provide Christie with a great deal of information. The German air force, he envisaged, would be equipped with mainly short-range aircraft incapable of operating as far afield as the British Isles: they were to be aimed eastwards. Goering and Milch were exceptions among Christie's contacts, however. Most of these were traditional, conservative Germans and he particularly cultivated those who were fiercely anti-Nazi.

By 1935, the loose association of businessmen and other informants run by Dansey and Christie was well established and operating smoothly, though still on a very informal basis. The intelligence they provided supplemented that obtained by the official SIS, notably by the then Squadron-Leader F. W. Winterbotham, head of the Air Section, who was himself doing remarkable work in penetrating the higher echelons of the Third Reich. It gave clear warnings of German aims in Central Europe, and of the rate of rearmament, particularly in the air.

Reports from Christie dated 23rd and 25th November 1935, and never before revealed, state that German aircraft factories, working on a three-shift system and given sufficient raw materials, were capable of producing 400 bombers a month. There were about thirty factories producing aircraft, employing a total of at least 40,000 men. The German Air Ministry was also expanding swiftly, and by the next April would be occupying some 2,500 rooms – an oddly German statistic. In addition, the reports said, German munition factories were producing large quantities of incendiary bombs.

Another, fuller report soon afterwards enlarged on these figures and gave a complete breakdown of the organisation of the German air force at the end of 1935. This report stated that 9,800 aircraft of all types had been built in the last three years, of which 5,668 were "first line" machines for purely military use, while the remainder included instructional and advanced training machines as well as commercial and "sporting" planes. To accommodate the aircraft, there were plans for some 300 wartime airfields, camouflaged as farms and in many cases with underground or semi-underground repair and servicing depots. About 150 of these airfields had already been selected and prepared by December 1935.

Anti-aircraft artillery was also being manufactured at an impressive rate, including the revolutionary 88 mm weapon which could also be used as a field gun and which was to prove one of the most successful pieces of armament in the second world war. The production programme allowed for 522 anti-aircraft batteries of 88 mm guns to be ready for use by the end of 1938, plus a considerable number of light anti-aircraft guns.

Intelligence obtained by Dansey's irregulars was not confined to air matters, however. There was a constant flow of economic, industrial and political information, as well as military and naval. In the same reports quoted above, there are warnings that Germany was building two aircraft carriers, each of 12,000 tons and capable of carrying "several squadrons of diving bombers" for use against the fleet or special targets. Since there was little or no need for these in the Baltic, it was thought they were to menace Britain. The German shipyards, the report said, were also building 700-ton long-range submarines, and battleships and cruisers.

On the political front, there were warnings of three-cornered proposals by Germany, Hungary and Poland to seize Memel, Czechoslovakia and Austria simultaneously and so present a *fait accompli* to Britain, France and the League of Nations. Poland was reported as having spoiled the plan by getting cold feet. It is interesting to note that in 1935, Poland was prepared to act as an ally of Germany, in order to grab part of Czechoslovakia for herself. No doubt this helps to explain the dislike and distrust of Poland which Dansey would display in 1939, when Britain was preparing to go to war on her behalf.

Dansey, meanwhile, was still carrying on his official secret work in Rome. This reached its climax in 1935, when the Italians finally invaded Ethiopia, and the focus of world attention shifted temporarily away from Germany. By now, however, Dansey had seen and heard enough to convince him that Hitler, not Mussolini, was the major danger to world peace. He was also becoming uncomfortably aware of other, more personal dangers to himself and his colleagues.

CHAPTER SIXTEEN

Z

In 1936, as the conflict in Ethiopia was winding down, the intelligence world was shaken by the news that Claude Dansey had been recalled to London by Admiral Sinclair, and that after a short investigation into his affairs he had been banished from the service for some unspeakable offence, said to involve large sums of SIS money. The word of his disgrace spread swiftly through the Secret Service, and rumour and gossip flourished in the intelligence community of Europe. No doubt there were many who rejoiced at the downfall of a man who was accepted as the most expert and experienced agent and spymaster in the business. Dansey himself, apparently bearing his troubles bravely, returned to Rome for a while to clear up his affairs, before taking refuge in peaceful Switzerland, beside the lake in Zurich. But all was not what it seemed.

Dansey had discovered in 1936, through anti-Nazi contacts in the Abwehr, that the Continental Secret Service had been seriously exposed. He had been aware for some time that the cover of Passport Control Officer, which he himself had invented during the first world war, was wearing thin. Now his contacts brought alarming news. For the past year, the Germans had been watching the office at Scheveningen in the Dutch capital, The Hague. From a barge moored on a canal less than thirty yards from the British Intelligence headquarters at 57 Niewe Parklaan they had filmed the comings and goings of everyone who visited it.

"Unfortunately, it was only a silent film," Hermann Giskes, chief of Abwehr counter-intelligence in Holland during the second world war recalled, "but the captions recorded with complete accuracy the names, cover names, assigned duties, activities and contacts of every one of the involuntary film stars. It scarcely needs saying that the British agents in Germany who operated from this headquarters had a warm reception, unless, of course, they prefer-

171

red to get the intelligence required of them direct from the German counter-espionage authorities, against a decent sum of money to be paid in by the recipients, naturally!"

The Germans had a department of the Abwehr, Section IIID, which was employed solely in providing false or doctored information, to be fed to enemy agents. Giskes says the trade in misinformation was very useful in providing extra funds for the German counter-espionage organisation when it ran short, as it frequently did.

The obvious solution for the SIS would have been to close down the Scheveningen office, sever connections with every agent who had been blown, and start again somewhere else. But in the game of bluff and double bluff which Dansey was used to playing, such a move was unthinkable. Dansey had one inviolable rule which he followed throughout his long career: whatever happens, however disastrous it may appear, you must always look for a way of turning it to your own advantage, even though it may mean making considerable sacrifices.

Dansey's disgrace and banishment were part of a startling proposal he put to Sinclair: his official dismissal would be a front, another of Dansey's covers, intended to confuse the enemy. It is a mark of his dedication, and of the seriousness of the position, that he should be prepared to subject himself to shame and humiliation in order to achieve his purpose. That purpose, quite simply, was to create a complete alternative Intelligence Service in Europe, in parallel with and quite separate from the SIS. This doubly-secret service was to be known as the Z Organisation. Dansey's own code name in the SIS would be, quite simply, Z.

The object of the Z Organisation was not merely to supplement the official SIS, but to replace it completely if either the country or the service were overrun by an enemy. Consequently, it had to be kept completely apart, with only the "expelled" Dansey as a link. There were to be no records or references to it in SIS files, and no other SIS officer should be aware of its existence. There was, of course, one exception to this: C, Admiral Sinclair himself, who was the joint author of the scheme with Dansey (and later, C would second another SIS man to act as Dansey's deputy, but that did not happen immediately).

Sinclair agreed to allocate SIS money to Dansey to use entirely as he saw fit, with no questions asked. It would not in itself be sufficient for his purposes, but he could raise additional finance from other sources to supplement it, through both Vansittart and his own contacts. The richest of these stretched way back into his

Z

past, to his very beginnings: the South African diamond business.
In addition to De Beers, Dansey's friends in diamonds included two colourful characters whom he knew from South Africa, the Joel brothers, Solly and Jack. Born in the East End of London, where their father kept The King of Prussia public house, they had sailed to the Cape in their early twenties to join their elder brother and uncle in the business. Their uncle, Barney Barnato, had been Cecil Rhodes's partner and himself became one of the barons of the diamond industry. Solly and Jack were millionaires in their own right by the time they were thirty, and after the death of their uncle and the assassination of their elder brother, they inherited the Barnato empire.

Like Thomas Fortune Ryan, Solly Joel also had an interest in the Angolan diamond fields, so he had a certain amount in common with Dansey, who had performed various mysterious deeds for Ryan in that country. But the friendship with the Joels was sealed on the racecourse: the Joels were among the five or six most successful racehorse owners in England during the twenties and thirties.

The Joels had been putting money into Dansey's unofficial activities for some time, motivated by patriotism and by hatred of the Nazis. Now, along with De Beers, they were prepared to make greater contributions, and to back him generously. Together with other, lesser sources, and the SIS money, Dansey's new organisation would be financially viable – particularly since many of his agents were rich men who needed no payment from him.

The proposition which Dansey put to Sinclair had been planned in great detail. The Passport Control Office in The Hague should be kept running as though head office was unaware that it had been penetrated. The agents working from it would go on exactly as before. Neither they nor their bosses were to be told of the new Z Organisation – it had to remain a secret.

Twenty years before, Dansey had propounded the principle of making use of enemy agents rather than exposing them – turning them or controlling them while allowing their masters to believe they were still secure. It was a principle which was to reach perfection with the "double cross" system four years later, but for now it was the Germans who were trying to use it against the British. Dansey proposed to take the system one important step further, into a triple cross. As long as the Germans could be made to believe that the British were unaware of what was going on, the blown elements of the SIS could be isolated and used as a perfect decoy. If they did not know that the British were setting up a

173

replacement organisation, the Abwehr would have no reason to go looking for it, but would be content to concentrate on their "successful" surveillance and misinformation operation.

Dansey's new organisation would be built around the existing businessmen, politicians and public figures who were already working for him on an informal basis as part of Vansittart's "Private Detective Agency". In addition to Christie, the Britons involved included Frederick "Fanny" Vanden Heuvel, who was a director of Eno's Fruit Salts and later of the Beecham pharmaceutical group and also a Papal count with strong connections in the Vatican; Guy Vansittart, Sir Robert's brother, who was European manager for General Motors; Sigismund Payne Best, who had known Dansey while serving with Military Intelligence in the first world war and now owned a pharmaceutical and chemical agency in Holland; Rex Pearson, another first world war intelligence officer who was based in Switzerland as a representative for Unilever; Victor Farrell, Professor of English at the St Cyr military academy in France; and Sir Frank Nelson, who had made a fortune early in life as a partner in the merchant firm of Symons, Barlow and Company in Bombay. Dansey also had several British newspapermen working for him, most notably Gibson of *The Times*, Hillard of the *Manchester Guardian* and Maitland, second correspondent in Vienna and south-east Europe for the *Daily Express*.

From the world of oil, there were Calouste Gulbenkian, his son Nubar and daughter Rita, and Henri Deterding of Royal Dutch Shell, plus several lesser names. There were also at least two prominent American businessmen, J. B. "Dutch" Kindelberger, an aircraft manufacturer who had actually employed two of the fathers of the Luftwaffe, Ernst Udet and Erhard Milch, in his Los Angeles factory, and James D. Mooney, Guy Vansittart's boss as president of General Motors Overseas Corporation, who later operated under the code name "Stallforth". From Australia there was W. S. Robinson, a prominent businessman then resident in Europe.

The most important connections, however, were probably the Germans who helped Dansey and Vansittart. These included prominent men from industry, diplomacy and the armed service: Hans Ritter, a former German Air Force pilot and member of the General Staff, serving then as adviser to the Junkers aircraft company and in an honorary capacity as assistant to the air and military attachés in Paris; Carl Goerdeler, Chief Burgermeister of Leipzig, who was later to be recognised as the leader of the German Resistance movement; Robert Bosch, founder of the Bosch precision machines and electrical company, inventor of the

Bosch spark plug, magneto and lamp; Theo Kordt, Counsellor at the German Embassy in London, and his brother Erich, Senior Counsellor at the German Foreign Office; Major Ewald von Kleist-Schwenzin, a member of the German General Staff and a close personal friend of Abwehr chief Admiral Canaris; "Klop" Ustinov, father of Peter and one-time press attaché in the German Embassy in London, who later took British citizenship; and Wolfgang Gans Edler zu Putlitz, another diplomat then in the London embassy, who later moved to The Hague before fleeing back to London to seek Vansittart's personal protection.

These Germans were among the bravest of Dansey's collaborators. Several of them were later caught and executed by the Nazis, but they and their friends continued to the bitter end to struggle for peace, working for much of the time through their links with Dansey.

Another prominent British businessman working for Dansey was Ralph Glyn, an important figure in the City of London and a director of many companies. Glyn had many connections, but probably the most valuable service he performed for Dansey was to introduce him to William Stephenson, a Canadian businessman. Stephenson, who went to New York in the second world war to follow in Dansey's footsteps as liaison with American Intelligence and to set up and run "British Security Co-ordination", was another rich man who wanted to put his wealth and abilities at Britain's service. Many wildly exaggerated claims have been made about Stephenson's role in the war, sometimes giving the impression that he was in complete charge of British Intelligence, counter-intelligence, Special Operations Executive, political warfare and almost everything else in the clandestine sphere. Such claims do a disservice to Stephenson's genuine achievements, which were considerable, and to those who were actually responsible for the other areas and operations concerned. In fact, Stephenson was at all times subordinate and answerable to Dansey and to C.

Stephenson's principal contribution in the early years of his association with the Z Organisation and the SIS was concerned with iron and steel. Among the many companies he owned or controlled was the Pressed Steel Company, which at the time made the bodies for many British motor cars. While regularly visiting Germany to buy steel, he discovered that almost the entire output of the German steel industry was going into arms and munitions, even though the Treaty of Versailles expressly forbade Germany from rearming. Stephenson backed up this information with secretly obtained copies of the accounts and balance sheets of the Ruhr steel firms.

Stephenson's material, along with the information Dansey was obtaining from his various other agents, was fed to Vansittart and to Desmond Morton's Industrial Intelligence Centre, which had been set up by the British Government in 1931 to analyse and assess economic and industrial data. There, the most valuable information was passed surreptitiously to the few politicians – particularly Winston Churchill – ready and willing to make the fullest public use of it.

A prime example of the sort of material Dansey and his friends provided came in April 1936, when they revealed that Germany was spending £800 million a year on military preparations of all kinds, including the building of strategic roads. This was a vast sum at the time, when the British Government's entire budget for all purposes was less than £750 million. Churchill was quick to make sure this information was made public by using it in a parliamentary question on the floor of the House of Commons to the then Chancellor of the Exchequer, Neville Chamberlain. Chamberlain was unable to deny the accuracy of the information, since it was, of course, exactly the same as that provided to the government through the Intelligence Service. Tragically, he and his fellow appeasers seemed incapable of learning anything from such intelligence, and Hitler was allowed to continue along his path to war.

Although Malcolm Christie and William Stephenson were invaluable suppliers of information and contacts, another man was even more important to Dansey personally, particularly in terms of providing physical assistance to the organisation of Dansey's activities outside the official SIS. Not only was this man the most valuable, he was also the most unlikely. Sandor Laszlo Kellner was neither British nor German; he had no military knowledge and no previous background in intelligence; he had no direct connections with governments or with strategic industries; he was not even rich. But he was to become Dansey's closest "civilian" collaborator and probably his closest personal friend for the last twelve years of his life. A Hungarian Jew born in 1893 in a tiny peasant village some eighty miles east of Budapest on the dusty Magyar plains, he was better known to the world as Alexander Korda.

At the time the Z Organisation was set up, Korda was at the height of his fame as a film producer. *The Private Life of Henry VIII* had been a tremendous success critically and commercially around the world. Many of the films that followed also did well: *The Girl From Maxim's*, *The Private Life of Don Juan*, *Catherine the Great*, *The Scarlet Pimpernel*, *Sanders of the River* (*Bomsambo*

in the USA), and *The Ghost Goes West* among them, all within the
space of two years. In 1936, he was working on at least nine new
productions, including *Rembrandt* and H. G. Wells's *Things to
come*. But somehow, in the midst of all this frenetic activity, he
found time to work with Dansey.

Korda was a fanatical anglophile, who had chosen to live and
work in England after twenty years of film making in Hungary,
Vienna, Berlin, Hollywood and Paris. Keen to do anything he
could for his adopted country, he was personally attracted to the
shady world of espionage and intrigue. He hinted obliquely in
conversation, and specifically in an interview in the *Observer* on
22nd April 1951 that a British agent had helped him escape from
Hungary in 1919, after he had been imprisoned by Admiral
Horthy's government. He gave no reason why the British should
have gone to such trouble or of whether he maintained any
connection with the Secret Service afterwards.

Why then should Korda have helped Dansey and the two
organisations? There was one overpowering reason: without Dansey none of Korda's successful films would have been possible. His
association with Dansey, and with Vansittart, had started in 1931,
when the Hungarian was searching for a new base. He was then in
Paris, dreaming of starting his own company but without any
money to pay for it, when he was offered a two-picture directing
contract by Paramount-British. In fact, he completed only one
picture, *Service for Ladies* (*Reserved for Ladies* in the USA),
which was polished and professional but otherwise completely
forgettable apart from the fact that it was the first time Korda
worked with the actor Leslie Howard, who would also be drawn
into Dansey's net. It was the first time he had worked in England,
and he took to the country, and to London, immediately. By a lucky
chance (one presumes), an accident in a Paramount car injured
him just enough to let him out of his contract, and he was free.

Soon afterwards, early in 1932, Korda's brothers Vincent and
Zoltan, who were working in Paris and Hollywood respectively,
were astonished to receive a summons from him to come to
London, where he was setting up his own company, London Film
Productions. Vincent and Zoltan hurried to join him, and to find
out where he could possibly have got the money to finance such a
company, since he had none of his own. Somehow, he had managed to persuade various interests to invest sufficient funds to
finance the company's incorporation: they included City banker
Leopold Sutro, the French Pathé company, George Grossmith,
Captain A. S. N. Dixie and Lord Lurgan. But Korda himself had
put up a substantial share. Where had it come from?

The answer was that he had obtained it by courtesy of the SIS, through Claude Dansey and Sir Robert Vansittart. They had seen the possible value of Korda as a cosmopolitan character who was known to travel widely and who, as a film maker, had a perfect excuse for carrying out reconnaissances for possible locations, talking to financiers and generally asking questions about anything and everything.

Korda took a luxurious five-roomed office in a mews behind number 22 Grosvenor Street, in the heart of Mayfair, and set about producing films. Significantly, his first, *Wedding Rehearsal*, was an idea suggested by Vansittart. This was followed swiftly by five British quota films (pictures made simply to maintain the legally required proportion of British films shown in British cinemas) made under contract for Paramount. Then came *The Private Life of Henry VIII*, which won an Oscar for Charles Laughton and became one of the most successful British films of its time. From being a minor director who had flopped in Hollywood, Korda was suddenly an international celebrity.

The success of *Henry VIII* changed the nature and the requirements of London Films and of its chief. Korda moved out of his suite at the Dorchester Hotel and bought himself a palatial house in Avenue Road, St John's Wood. Being in the big time, he began looking for a bigger source of finance, to pay for an ambitious and continuous production programme. But even in the thirties, British banks and businessmen were loath to take the risk of putting money into films, especially when the producer was a wild man from Hungary with a reputation for flamboyant extravagance. Once again, Dansey came to the rescue.

Dansey's secret funds – and even those of the Secret Service as a whole – though sufficient to pay Korda's share in setting up a company, could not possibly stretch to the scale he now needed. However, among the businessmen providing Dansey with information and assistance was Sir Connop Guthrie, chairman of the giant Prudential Assurance. The Pru had over a million pounds a day to be invested, and a great deal of it was going abroad, into Europe – one of the reasons, of course, why Guthrie was so valuable to Dansey. It did not take a great deal of persuasion from Dansey and his other friends – notably Vansittart, Churchill and an Australian businessman called Montagu Marks – to convince Guthrie that it was his patriotic duty to channel some of those funds into London Films, which could be relied on to promote Britain's image around the world and be valuable in other, more secret ways, too.

In late summer 1934, the Pru's first cheque arrived at the

Grosvenor Street offices. It was for £250,000 and was received with appropriate excitement. With Guthrie on the board and Montagu Marks as general manager, London Films was in business. In 1940, when William Stephenson was sent to New York to set up the British Security Co-ordination headquarters in the Rockefeller Centre, Guthrie went with him to become head of the security division. (Korda's offices in the Empire State Building had already been working for Dansey for some time by then, but with the start of the war the SIS needed to have an official and full-time presence as well.) Dansey's connection with the film company had to be kept strictly secret, of course. He had to wait for his reward until he retired at the end of the war, when he was immediately appointed to the board of British Lion Films, which was by then Korda's principal company.

Korda also helped Winston Churchill, who was at that time not only in the political wilderness but also short of money, by employing him as a writer for several projects, most of which he had no intention of ever making, including a film about Marlborough, Churchill's illustrious ancestor, for which Korda paid him £10,000. Such loyalty both to friends and to the cause was a quality which Dansey prized among those who worked with him.

Korda made many propaganda pictures as part of his loyalty to his adopted country. He used his company and his skills in other useful ways, too, by shooting film as a pictorial record of possible future war zones. One in particular was a mysterious film he shot for Dansey shortly before the war, called *King Pausole*. Dansey's experiences in Africa and in Rome watching Mussolini's progress in Tripoli and Ethiopia had convinced him that when war came North Africa would be an important battle area, and he was naturally aware of the vital importance of the Suez Canal to Britain. But Britain had only scanty information about much of the coastline which she might one day need to invade. Korda, as it happened, already owned a property – a French film by Alexis Granowsky called *Les Aventures du roi Pausole*, shown for one day only in London in 1933 – which would provide the perfect excuse for shooting North African locations. Using French technicians, he shot thousands of feet of film, recording details of the coastline with scantily-clad girls cavorting on the beaches to hide his real purpose. The film was, of course, never completed. The footage disappeared into the vaults, to provide much valuable information when the Allies began preparing for the Anglo-American landings of Operation Torch.

In 1936, faced with the task of creating an integrated intelligence service from scratch, Dansey turned to Korda for assistance. Sitting with his friend in their favourite haunt, the Hotel Bauer au Lac in Zurich, he outlined his problems and his plan. The Z Organisation would not be able to use any of the official British resources for cover, accommodation or communication. Its agents would be forbidden to have any contact with British embassies and consulates. They would not be able to use radios, or to send messages back to London in the safety of diplomatic bags. Dansey's existing informants and agents were all essentially part-timers, picking up what they could while travelling on genuine business. They would go on doing so, but it would also be necessary to set up local stations, manned by specially recruited agents who would be responsible for creating their own networks of spies and informers.

Some agents could operate from established bases. Sigismund Payne Best in Holland, for example, already had the perfect cover and was eager to co-operate. So, too, were other first world war veterans such as Rex Pearson, representing Unilever in Switzerland. But the new recruits would need a cover. Dansey did not take long to work out the answer: how about Korda's London Films? The new recruits would become representatives of this rapidly growing empire, ostensibly running its local offices. They could use the company's name and its communications, and could move around their territories quite openly. Naturally, they would need to learn a little about the film business, but this could be easily arranged – Korda could provide them with training courses at his newly-completed studios at Denham. Korda agreed with enthusiasm – indeed, he entered into the spirit of the idea with such eagerness that some of those who came into contact with the organisation later, such as Frederick Winterbotham, had the impression it was as much Korda's as Dansey's. Those directly involved in it, however, suffered no such delusions. Although Korda was a powerful and ebullient personality, the Z Organisation had only one boss, and that boss was always Claude Dansey.

CHAPTER SEVENTEEN

In Business

Dansey's first intention had been to run the Z Organisation from Rome, but it quickly became clear that this was impracticable. Not only was he too well known there, but when war with Germany came, Mussolini was likely to throw in his lot with Hitler rather than remaining neutral or siding with Britain. And finally, communications had to be maintained with C and with Vansittart: there was no point in collecting information if it could not be processed and used. Although the organisation itself must remain separate from the official SIS, intelligence obtained had to be fed into it.

Dansey decided therefore to set up his head office in London for peacetime operations, with a plan to move it to Switzerland in the event of war. Not only was Switzerland the country most likely to remain genuinely neutral, it was also conveniently situated in the heart of Europe with direct access to Germany, Italy, Austria and France.

Having made contingency arrangements in Switzerland, he set about finding suitable premises in London. He chose a suite of offices on the eighth floor of the north-west wing of Bush House, the mammoth office block in the Aldwych which also housed many Russian concerns such as Intourist and the news agency TASS, and the BBC's overseas services. The Z offices were rented under the name of "C. E. Moore" (could it be pure coincidence that the initials C. E. M. were Dansey's own?) and adjoined the rooms occupied by Geoffrey Duveen and Company Limited, described as a finance corporation. While this was a genuine firm, Geoffrey Duveen (later Sir Geoffrey) was a barrister friend of Dansey's, who also worked for him. He was the nephew of Lord Duveen, the art dealer, but had spent only one year in the family business before deciding the art world was not for him. His uncle insisted he find himself an occupation, so he became a barrister instead. No

181

doubt Dansey found it convenient to have a lawyer – to say nothing of his finance corporation – in the organisation, and to have the use of his offices. In the best Secret Service tradition, Dansey's office suite had two entrances: one of its own and another, more discreetly, through Geoffrey Duveen's rooms.

Dansey still needed a good cover, however, for he could not operate in London as part of Korda's film company. Instead, his office became the export department of a diamond company, part of the Joel brothers' empire, which had genuine premises on the floor below. Once again, Dansey's ability to make and keep friends in useful positions was paying dividends. The diamond connection had other advantages, too – diamonds were an excellent way of moving money across frontiers, both in peace and in war.

As the business of recruiting got under way, Sinclair kept his promise to provide an assistant. Commander Kenneth Cohen, RN, a tall, lean man with aquiline features and a razor-sharp mind, was for the next three or four years Dansey's extremely able deputy, before going on to distinguish himself even further in Portugal and then as the SIS's principal liaison officer with the French. He was, and remained for many years after the war, one of the most respected of the regular SIS officers.

The remainder of Dansey's head office staff at the beginning consisted of Dansey's secretary, an attractive and vivacious redhead called Sheila Deane, Norman Wells, a former Royal Navy chief petty officer who had served on the royal yacht, who acted as major-domo and general factotum, and an ex-policeman, Victor Auger, who looked after the vetting of candidates, among other duties.

One of the first recruits was a young man called Andrew King, who gives the lie to the statement Dansey made during the war that he would never knowingly employ a university graduate. No doubt Dansey was being provocative when he said it, employing his sardonic tongue at the expense of some of the academics who joined the SIS during the war. Not only was King a Cambridge graduate, he was also recruited through the University Appointments Board – a service run by Oxford and Cambridge to help graduates find jobs. King had been going to teach English in East Prussia, but was informed at the last minute that the Germans were cutting back on their spending on education and the job had been cancelled. Shortly afterwards he received a letter from something called "The Albany Syndicate" – oddly reminiscent of the "SMA Syndicate" which had been Dansey's front in 1919 when he visited King Hussein – at Room 624, Abbey House, London, SW1. The letter said the Appointments Board had given his name as a young man who was interested in travelling abroad and using languages. Would he care to attend an interview, with a Mr Haywood, for possible employment?

King attended the interview, and found himself in a bare room, furnished with only a desk, two chairs and a telephone, talking to a man aged about sixty, with a hawk nose, dark-rimmed glasses, a small moustache and incredibly piercing eyes. Mr Haywood – in reality Claude Dansey – questioned him about his views and his background, and told him he was looking for a young man to travel on the Continent to promote British goods and services. Was he interested? King said he was. Mr Haywood said in that case he would be considered, and would be called for another interview in six weeks time, if all was well. With that he shook hands and showed him out.

King, who had a private income, was not worried about the delay, and took the opportunity to go off on holiday. When he returned he found another letter waiting, asking him to attend for a second interview in a few days' time, at what he thought the odd hour of 1 p.m. In the creaky lift to the sixth floor, the lift operator asked him where he was going. When King told him he had an appointment with Mr Haywood, the man sniffed disdainfully and said: "Oh, 'im! 'E's never there." Sure enough, when King tried the door of Room 624, it was locked, and there was no reply to his knock.

By now, he was beginning to think there was something strange about the Albany Syndicate and its job, but as he turned away a tall, lean figure came hurrying down the corridor, asked if he was King, and then handed him a letter. In it Mr Haywood apologised for failing to keep the appointment, but introduced the tall, lean figure as "Mr Crane", his assistant. Crane – in reality, Commander Cohen – took him off to the Berkeley Grill for lunch, questioning him further and telling him the job involved representing and promoting British films. It sounded plausible, and it was only towards the end of lunch, and further questioning, that King began to suspect the real purpose of the interview. When he had accepted the post, Crane confirmed that he was indeed being invited to join a branch of the Secret Service. The six weeks between interviews had given Victor Auger time to carry out a check on him and his family.

King was told to report to the office in Bush House. His recruitment seems to have been typical for the time – as was his training. In the use of codes, ciphers, secret ink, and so on, the instruction seems to have been almost nil. Indeed, King says his only formal training was being taken round the City one afternoon by Norman Wells and shown how to spot and lose anyone trying to follow him. His main training was an enjoyable two months at Denham Studios learning his cover story before being sent out around Europe as a Z Organisation courier, collecting and delivering its messages, which could not be sent through the normal clandestine routes used by the official SIS.

By the beginning of 1938, the Z Organisation had men in place all over Europe – a remarkable achievement in the time. In Zurich were the veteran Rex Pearson, officially representing Unilever, and Basil Fenwick of the Royal Dutch Shell oil company. In Austria, at Kitzbuhel, Dansey's man was a lively character called Conrad O'Brien ffrench, who later escaped when the Nazis were about to arrest him, by walking over the mountains to Switzerland. He put the office funds, amounting to several thousand schillings, in the heel of his boot for safety, but found when he arrived that the banknotes had all been worn away – an unfortunate piece of bad luck which he had great difficulty in explaining to Dansey.

In Rome, the Z man was another intelligence veteran, Graham Maingot, a short, stocky man with prematurely white hair and the looks of a romantic film star, who was fluent in French and Italian and had an impressive range of contacts in both countries. During the war he was to work mainly in Portugal. The Prague representative was John Evans, a journalist who was married to a delightful Czech blonde called Vlasta, and who later worked in Yugoslavia. In Holland, as well as Payne Best in The Hague, the organisation was represented in Rotterdam by another of Dansey's first world war intelligence officers, Richard Tinsley of the Uranium Steamship Company.

In Berlin, Victor Auger's son operated under the London Films cover, and in Vienna there was Frederick Voight, the Central European Correspondent of the *Manchester Guardian*. Dansey's man in Riga, Latvia, was an American, another old hand at espionage, who later moved to Munich. He had an attractive wife who was, according to Andrew King, "adept at sleeping with SS men and getting all sorts of useful information out of them".

When the Nazis uncovered O'Brien ffrench, Voight and the official SIS station in Vienna, King was switched from his job as courier and sent there as Korda's representative, with instructions to establish a new network of agents on the ground. The situation in Austria was extremely difficult, however, with most of the suitable people either imprisoned or in exile, and he recalls that his efforts were mainly unsuccessful.

184

Other agents recruited in London soon after King came from a variety of sources. Major (later Colonel) John Codrington, for example, was a regular soldier who had just retired from the Coldstream Guards. He regarded his cover as being flimsy indeed, and something for which he was ill-equipped, "not knowing a film star from a race-horse owner". He underwent the training period with Korda, however, and says: "Somehow, it seemed to work, though I insisted that one of my brothers should know what I was really doing, as he had been in the Foreign Office and could help with the over-curious, for in those days it would have seemed strange for a major with twenty years' army service suddenly to become 'something in films'." Codrington joined the head office staff, working under Cohen and making frequent trips to Europe.

Another agent was Richard Arnold-Baker, who had a family connection with Dansey. Arnold-Baker was in fact the son of a German general called von Blumenthal and had been born and educated in Germany. When his parents separated, his mother returned to England where she remarried, and Richard went with her and took his stepfather's name. He still had a considerable number of friends in German high places, however, and therefore was a particularly valuable member of the organisation.

To supplement London Films, the Bush House office and the Albany Trust, Dansey also operated through several other firms and addresses in London. These included a pharmaceutical and general import-export firm called Menoline Limited, with offices at 24 Maple Street, off London's Tottenham Court Road, and mainly the responsibility of Cohen and his personal secretary, Doreen Bett. The company also had a Dutch subsidiary through which Payne Best, who was a director, carried out most of his dealings with London. Yet such was the Z Organisation's security that although Best was quite a senior member of the organisation, he only knew Cohen under one of his pseudonyms – Lieutenant-Commander Cowan.

Another firm which provided cover was the highly respectable and respected wine shippers, H. Sichel and Sons, while transport and assistance with courier services came from a bona fide travel company, Lammin Tours, based in Highgate, north London. Andrew King and other couriers often travelled about Europe on Lammin's long-distance coaches, with their secret messages and documents hidden under a seat. There was also a naval section of Z, working through the General Steamship Navigation Company under Ian Hooper. His special assignment from Dansey was the recruitment of ship's officers and masters as agents, along with any other bright seamen who could be trusted, and who visited foreign ports as a regular part of their occupation.

During 1938 and 1939, Dansey extended the scope of the Z Organisation. His agents interviewed the rapidly growing number of refugees from Nazi oppression after they had crossed the frontiers. This was achieved in close co-operation with Korda, who had a special affinity for refugees, being himself an exile. He made himself responsible for finding and selecting suitable subjects for questioning about economic, social and, where possible, Germany's military affairs. Although much of what they could tell was useless or already known, it could be valuable in providing confirmation or cross-referencing.

Not everyone was pleased with what the refugees provided, however. Frederick Winterbotham for one was decidedly unimpressed, complaining at the low standard of information passed to him as head of the Air Section of the SIS. He was asked to prepare questionnaires for the agents carrying out the interviews, setting out the specific areas in which he was interested.

"Korda supplied the refugees, Dansey the money," he recalls. "I asked for details of aircraft and so on, and of the underground airfields which some of them reported. Some of the refugees, who were paid handsomely for their information, provided many details – though I knew there were no such things. One of the locations I was given was in an area I knew was a swamp."

Of course, such inventions are only to be expected of people who are eager to say what they think their benefactors wish to hear, especially when there is money in it. Dansey was certainly aware of this, for it was something he had warned his American students about while lecturing them in 1917. There may, however, have been more truth in their observations in this instance than Winterbotham was prepared to acknowledge, for earlier and well-authenticated reports from Group-Captain Christie among others had, as we have seen, told of underground repair and servicing facilities at some German airfields.

Winterbotham was also scornful of Dansey for paying a well-known British artist fairly large sums of money to tour Germany sketching and painting airfields and other military installations, much as Baden-Powell had done forty or fifty years before. Dansey was well pleased with the results, but Winterbotham was busy developing aerial photographic reconnaissance, which he had himself pioneered during the first world war, and regarded this as the only modern and satisfactory way of obtaining pictorial intelligence. But air photographs still had plenty of teething troubles, and it may well be that Dansey saw a need for the old-fashioned but tried-and-tested method, if only to supplement and back up Winterbotham's efforts. In doing so, however, he was spending money which Winterbotham could have used in buying and developing new equipment for his unit.

Money was one of the main sources of friction between Dansey and the rest of the SIS during the pre-war period. Winterbotham and many of his colleagues were upset that Dansey was always a law unto himself and that he had his own allocation of money, paid directly into his own fund in lump sums to do with as he liked. In the SIS, however, every penny had to be accounted for.

As Dansey had always seen the Z Organisation as a complete and self-contained intelligence-gathering service, he felt it should not be directed only at Germany but able to cover other threats, too. Like Vansittart, he regarded fascism and communism as merely "different symptoms of the same disease". From the very beginning, he had also been recruiting and posting men to fight against communism and the Soviet *apparat* in the west, though his resources would not allow for any attempt to penetrate the Soviet Union itself, at least at that stage.

There has always been a suspicion that Z was also expected to perform other functions within the intelligence community, not least as a "dirty tricks" department, used even by C, Admiral Sinclair, as a last resort in enforcing discipline by disposing of troublesome or dangerous agents suspected of treachery. Such a role makes sense, given that the original purpose of the organisation was to operate in double secrecy outside but alongside an official service which had been penetrated or blown in certain areas. Certainly, Dansey ordered the death of traitors and informers in both world wars, but although it is just as likely that he would be no more squeamish at other times of crisis, there is no proof that he did so between the wars.

This is hardly surprising. Dansey always worked on the principle of "need to know". With Dansey, the old adage of the left hand not knowing what the right hand was up to was carried to the nth degree. Only the brain knew everything, and the brain was solely Claude Dansey. In the latter part of the war, General Sir James Marshall-Cornwall spent the best part of two years as Dansey's deputy and understudy (although he was the senior general in the British army and Dansey was a mere lieutenant-colonel), but confesses that even when he was standing in for Uncle Claude, he was told hardly anything. He never knew, for instance, the identities of most of the agents working for Dansey, for they were very much Dansey's own.

The Germans, however, had a shrewd idea of its function when they discovered the existence of the Z Organisation after the war had started. One of the documents given to the Dutch Minister in Berlin by German Foreign Minister Ribbentrop on 10th May 1940, when the Germans invaded Holland and Belgium, was one signed by Himmler himself accusing the Dutch of breaching their neutrality by harbouring and supporting the British Secret Service. Part of this document says:

An important addition to the official Intelligence Service of the PCO [Passport Control Office] is a special branch of the Secret Intelligence Service which is directed from London – sometimes called the Z Organisation – in which a former Passport Control Officer, Colonel Dansey, who is now in Switzerland, plays the leading role. This special organisation plays an important part in political matters whilst *it also carries out certain internal control over the activities of other branches of the service.* (Authors' italics.) In peacetime the Z Organisation has no connection of any kind with the PCO Service, but, if necessary in wartime, can obtain its assistance for the provision of courier services and its co-operation in avoiding any duplication of agents.

The events in Holland which led to this document being produced, and to the Germans finding out about the Z Organisation, are dealt with in the next chapter. In fact, by the time the document was written on 29th March 1940, Dansey was not in Switzerland, but back in London. Although there was by then no way in which the German intelligence services could get genuine information out of Britain, there is no reason to doubt the accuracy of the rest of Himmler's statement, including the Z Organisation's role in "internal control".

On 1st September 1939, the event which Dansey had been predicting and preparing for finally happened. Germany invaded Poland, and Europe was plunged into war.Dansey had not only predicted the invasion, he had also warned the British Government about it with quite specific details of German intentions and plans. But when Vansittart – who had been removed from his position in 1938 and "promoted" sideways into a non-job as Chief Diplomatic Adviser because of his troublesome views – took the information to his successor as Permanent Under-Secretary at the Foreign Office, telling him he had evidence that Hitler would strike before the end of the month, Sir Alexander Cadogan's reaction was dismissive. "This is the beginning of the 'War of Nerves'," he noted. "And I have seen the first casualty."

For Dansey, however, there was no time for recriminations. He had vital work to do. At the same time as the German army was moving into Poland, the Z Organisation's head office was moving to its battle stations in France and Switzerland, travelling by road and carrying its books and equipment in King's Messenger diplomatic bags. One section, led by Kenneth Cohen and John Codrington, made for Paris, where they set themselves up in parallel with the official SIS office run by Commander Wilfred Dunderdale. The main party drove to Switzerland, a group consisting of Dansey, Andrew King, Richard Arnold-Baker, Norman Wells, the major-domo, Sheila Deane, and a newly-recruited secretary, Joanna Shuckburgh.

The new girl had been found through her sister, who worked as a secretary at Chatham House, headquarters of the Royal Institute of International Affairs. Chatham House had had a long association with the Z Organisation, providing information, advice and contacts to Dansey and to Christie. According to Joanna Shuckburgh, someone walked into her sister's office one day and asked if anyone could do German shorthand. Her sister said she couldn't, but Joanna could. Shortly afterwards, Joanna was invited to tea at the Waldorf Hotel, conveniently just across the road from Bush House, and interviewed there by "two extremely charming gentlemen", whom she later knew as Cohen and Dansey. They were impressed by her and by her family connections with the Foreign Office and the Diplomatic Service, and told her to report to them when war broke out. In fact, she was contacted before the event, and on the day war was officially declared found herself in Switzerland.

Dansey set up shop in Zurich, where the party was joined by the resident Z man, Rex Pearson. For the first two weeks they sat in boredom at the Peterhof Hotel, while Dansey shuttled to and fro between there and the legation in Berne, who at first wanted nothing to do with him or the Z Organisation. Eventually, it was agreed that Dansey's team should become the legation's visa section, with diplomatic cover. Dansey found two flats in the best part of Zurich, one immediately above the other in the luxury Schloss am Mythenquai, overlooking the lake. The top flat was used as living quarters, so that there need be no reason for anyone to leave the building.

Dansey proved to be a hard taskmaster, insisting that work must come before everything at all times, and strongly discouraging any other activity. While waiting for clearance to set up offices and begin work, Andrew King and Joanna Shuckburgh had booked tickets for a Beethoven concert conducted by Furtwängler. It turned out to be on the very night they moved into their new premises, and King asked Dansey if he could slip out to the concert hall to try to return the tickets. Dansey refused, and told him to get on with his job. About an hour later, however, he called all the staff together and gave them a stiff lecture on the importance of their work. In a very disparaging tone he said that two members of the staff had chosen this day of all days to get tickets to go to a concert. What was even worse, he snarled, was that not only was the music German, but so was the conductor! However, since they had already paid for their tickets, he would give them permission to go – but there was to be no repetition of such unpatriotic behaviour.

King and Shuckburgh went to their concert, in some humiliation, and thoroughly enjoyed it. But from then on, they found themselves virtually prisoners of the flat. Only Pearson, who already had his own place in Zurich, was allowed out. The others even had to eat together, with Dansey sitting in state at the head of the table, which tended to restrict conversation. It also restricted the menu, for Dansey had by then succumbed to the occupational disease of espionage, stomach ulcers, and was reduced to a diet – shared by everyone at the table – of what King recalls as seeming to consist mainly of muesli.

Surprisingly, it was Norman Wells who finally rebelled. One evening, at the end of dinner, he startled everyone by pushing his chair back, standing up and announcing boldly that he was going out for a breath of air. Dansey was taken aback, then angry. He said he knew there had to be another reason, and demanded to be told what it was. Wells retorted that there was indeed another reason. He was going round the corner to get himself "a bloody great steak", as he simply had to have something he could get his teeth into. He got his steak, and made his point – after that, the diet improved considerably.

Within a few days, information on German movements, strengths and intentions started to flow in from contacts in Switzerland, notably from private intelligence organisations and from Allied intelligence services, particularly the exiled Czechs, who had an important representative in Zurich, Karel Sedlacek, who was posing as a newspaper correspondent. Dansey also had close connections with Colonel Roger Masson, the very capable chief of Swiss Intelligence, whom he had known for many years, but this had to be handled with extreme delicacy, to protect Switzerland's precious neutrality. What was more important, however, was the information coming directly from Dansey's agents and anti-Nazis in Germany itself. Dansey had spent a great deal of care and effort in establishing his lines into Germany, and these now had to be fully activated and developed. While the Nazis and everyone else were encouraged to believe that Britain's main intelligence base in Europe was at The Hague – a ploy which was so successful that even now historians still refer to it as the headquarters of the Continental Secret Service responsible for all SIS activities in Europe – the true centre in Switzerland was gearing itself up. Dansey had deliberately held back, keeping his staff based in Bush House, until the war actually started, in order to reduce the danger of discovery and penetration by the enemy.

In addition to Zurich, Dansey also had Z men in place in Basle, Berne, Geneva, Lausanne and Lugano. In Basle, Sir Frank Nelson controlled the vitally important border station, dealing with the flow of people and information from France and Germany until June 1940, when he returned to England and became the first head of the newly-formed Special Operations Executive – the British sabotage and subversion organisation which we shall encounter later – being replaced by L. A. "Tim" Frenken. In Berne, Frederick "Fanny" Vanden Heuvel suavely held sway, aided by the fact that he had grown up there and could speak Schweitzer-Deutsch like a native. In Geneva, Victor Farrell had been made consul, providing the vital link across the lake into France, the country where he had spent many years as a professor of English at the St Cyr military academy. To complete the picture, there was Hugh Whittall in Lausanne and Lance de Garston in Lugano.

In Geneva the SIS had a small official station based on the Passport Control Office – the pre-war British minister had banned the service from operating near the Legation in Berne. This was run by Acton Burnell, an old SIS hand, who was absorbed into Dansey's organisation when Z officially took over all secret activities in Switzerland.

Everything was falling neatly into place, when news suddenly came from England which completely changed Dansey's plans. His friend and chief, Admiral Sinclair, was dying. For the moment, Sinclair's deputy, Colonel Stewart Menzies, was running the show, but it looked as though the position of C was open for the taking. Leaving Rex Pearson in charge in Zurich, Dansey caught the first train out and headed back to London.

Part Four

The World at War Again

CHAPTER EIGHTEEN

The Succession

Dansey arrived back in London to find the SIS in a state of turmoil. The offices at Broadway were full of new faces, recruited for wartime operation. But it was the old established faces that Dansey had come to see, and for the moment they were more concerned with the succession to the post of C than they were with the war in Europe.

The principal candidates were Colonel Stewart Menzies, Sinclair's deputy chief, and Rear-Admiral John Godfrey, Director of Naval Intelligence since January, plus what might be described in racing parlance as a rank outsider, Claude Dansey himself. He certainly regarded himself as a serious candidate for the post. When he left Zurich in October, he gave the group of Z men who saw him off at the station the impression that he expected shortly to be appointed the new C.

In many ways Dansey would have been an excellent choice. There can have been few men in the British intelligence community who could boast thirty-seven years' experience in so many different aspects of intelligence work. In some ways, however, that was a disadvantage: he had been in the business too long, made too many enemies. The odds were stacked heavily against him. He had always been a maverick, preferring to go his own way and not caring whose susceptibilities he offended in the process; he had never been much of a desk man; he carried the stigma of his supposed disgrace and banishment, so that in many eyes he was something of a bounder; he was sixty-three years old and his health was beginning to fail. In addition to his stomach ulcers he was starting to have trouble with his heart, another result of the stress he had subjected himself to for so many years.

In the cold light of a November dawn in London it must have soon become clear to Dansey that what had seemed possible in Zurich now looked more and more like wishful thinking. But

Dansey was always a realist. As we have seen, one of his greatest strengths lay in his refusal to be overwhelmed by adversity, plus a capacity to turn it to his own advantage where possible, and that is precisely what he began doing now.

The Admiralty were already conducting a powerful campaign to have Godfrey installed over Menzies's head as the new chief. They argued that the position was traditionally occupied by the senior service – though in fact it had been agreed when the SIS was reorganised after the first world war that the post should rotate between the navy, the army and the air force. But such considerations could be easily brushed aside. There had only been two previous occupants, and both were admirals, therefore a tradition had been established and should be respected.

For Dansey, such a move would have been a disaster. Sinclair had certainly been a sailor, but he had also been a professional and a friend. Godfrey was a completely unknown factor, who had only been in intelligence for ten months. He was a regular naval officer, and there was no guarantee whatever that he would allow Dansey the freedom of action and the independence he was used to and enjoyed. No, if Dansey could not have the job himself, he must do everything in his power to make sure it stayed inside the SIS and went to Menzies.

Graham Stewart Menzies was born on 30th January 1890 into a famous Scottish family whose wealth came from whisky and gin distilling on his father's side and from shipping on his mother's. Being Scottish, they pronounced their name "Ming-iss", the sort of quirk which always confuses foreigners and sorts out those Britons from the inferior orders who are not aware of such unwritten rules. His parents had vast estates in the Highlands of Scotland, and moved in the highest of late Victorian high society, as members of the Prince of Wales's set. Indeed, it was always said that Stewart Menzies was the son of the future King Edward VII, who was notorious for seducing the wives of his friends and who had an affair with Mrs Menzies. Menzies himself did nothing to deny the rumour. He always had a portrait of the King in his office, showing the monarch dressed in tweeds and a hunting cap, a shotgun in one hand and a brace of grouse in the other, with a gundog playing in the heather by his feet. In his entry in *Who's Who*, Menzies listed only one parent, his mother. Whether the story was true or not, he certainly seems to have shared King Edward's fondness for the opposite sex, and for pleasuring the wives of his friends.

After her first husband's death in 1910, Menzies's mother married Lieutenant-Colonel Sir George Holford, commander of the

1st Life Guards – the same position Dansey's father had held some years earlier. Holford was also a Silver Stick, the officer whose duties were "to guard the very person of the King from actual bodily injury, against personal attack, and to do so with his own hands and body". For nearly thirty years he was equerry to successive monarchs: Victoria, Edward VII, George V and Edward VIII. Menzies's mother in her turn became a lady-in-waiting to Queen Mary. Holford owned two of England's greatest houses, Westonbirt in Gloucestershire and Dorchester House in Park Lane – demolished in the thirties to make way for the Dorchester Hotel – where he had one of the world's finest art collections.

Menzies grew up and spent his early manhood, therefore, among the richest and most privileged of Britain's ruling class. At Eton, although no intellectual, he had won the Prince Consort Prizes for German and French, became president of Pop, the influential school society, and was an outstanding athlete and sportsman. He became master of the Eton College Beagles, and also established himself early in his lifelong passion of riding to hounds.

From Eton he took a familiar route, into the Grenadier Guards, then transferred to his stepfather's regiment, the Life Guards, where he rode beside the King on ceremonial occasions, resplendent in silver helmet and cuirass, white plume, scarlet tunic, white breeches and gleaming black thigh boots, his sabre at the ready on his shoulder. In 1911, while Dansey was shaking the dust of Somaliland from his feet and carrying out espionage missions in Morocco and Mexico, the young Lieutenant Menzies was enjoying a moment of glory as commander of the Regalia Escort, the guard on the Crown Jewels, during the coronation of the man who may have been his half-brother, King George V.

In 1914, however, the glittering pageantry of life in the peacetime Household Cavalry had to be put aside. The scarlet tunics were exchanged for khaki, the plumed helmets for more practical and prosaic tin hats, and the parks and parade grounds of London for the mud and blood of Flanders. By November, Menzies was involved in the first Battle of Ypres, and distinguished himself in the taking of Hill 60, a piece of high ground which commanded the entire Allied front. Most of his fellow officers and men were killed in this action, which almost completely destroyed the Life Guards, but the survivors took and held the position. Menzies was awarded Britain's second highest military decoration, the Distinguished Service Order, which he received from the King at a ceremony in the field on 2nd December 1914. Swiftly promoted to captain and made adjutant of the regiment, he saw further action, was wounded and won the Military Cross, and then on 8th December 1915, at the age of twenty-five, he was transferred to a safe desk job at GHQ, with Military Intelligence.

It was here that he first met Claude Dansey professionally, though they may have known each other socially before then. Dansey was nearly forty years old, and already one of the most experienced operators in the business. It is small wonder that the nature of their relationship should be master craftsman and green apprentice. What is surprising is that it appeared to remain that way for the rest of Dansey's career. Several of those who knew them both well recall that Menzies hero-worshipped Dansey, and always deferred to him.

After the first world war, while Dansey went out into the field again, Menzies stayed on in the London headquarters and rose steadily through the service. He became head of the army section in the late twenties, took charge of the German section in the mid-thirties, and shortly afterwards was appointed deputy chief, still with responsibility for intelligence concerning Germany and thus working in parallel with Dansey and the Z Organisation.

Unfortunately Menzies was neither liked nor respected in the service. Many of his contemporaries – men such as Reggie Drake, Rex Pearson, Sigismund Payne Best and later arrivals such as Frederick Winterbotham – considered him a lightweight, a social butterfly who had drifted into intelligence work because it provided him with a pleasant adjunct to his social life. They regarded him with contempt, knowing that he lacked vital practical experience in the field and thus knew little of the harsh realities of espionage.

Menzies was, however, an adept politician, more than able to look after his own interests in the corridors of power – under normal circumstances. But the circumstances in October and November 1939 were not normal. The war had just started, and therefore the choice of the new C could be vital. The authorities were in a quandary: they were faced with a difficult decision. Should they confirm Menzies in the job he was already doing? Should they choose a newcomer (Godfrey), or a well-known maverick (Dansey), whose reputation admittedly stood high? The appointment of the Chief of the Secret Service was by tradition in the royal prerogative for the post gave its holder the right of direct access to the monarch. Menzies should, therefore, have had a head start over his rivals, but George VI had been a naval officer, and was sure to listen sympathetically to the Admiralty. In practice, however, the sovereign makes such appointments on the recommendation of the Prime Minister and Cabinet.

The old C, Admiral Sinclair, had been a sick man for some time, and only the dangerous political situation in Europe had kept him at his post. For much of the time in the months before his death, Menzies had had to stand in for him, and had taken the opportunity to establish a relationship with Neville Chamberlain which would count heavily in his favour. In addition, he had been the SIS officer in charge of Ultra, the operation to break the German Enigma machine ciphers, and although it was still far from certain that the cryptanalysts at the Government Code and Cipher School would be successful in their efforts, this clearly had the potential of becoming the most important weapon in the intelligence war.

As far as Dansey was concerned, if he was not to get the coveted post himself, then it had to go to his ex-apprentice, Menzies. He had no doubt whatever that he would be able to continue to manipulate the man and turn him into his willing tool. Indeed, he foresaw a situation which suited his tastes and inclinations admirably, for as J. M. Langley has recorded: "Dansey was in fact one of those powerful men who prefer to keep their power hidden; an *éminence grise* rather than a ruling monarch, but a highly influential personage for all that. What Dansey wanted done was done, and what he wanted undone was undone."

So Dansey went into action in support of Menzies, pulling every one of the considerable number of strings which he had attached to men in positions of power during his long career. It was not for nothing that such influential men as Victor Cavendish-Bentinck, and General Sir James Marshall-Cornwall recall with some awe that "he had some remarkable connections" and "always operated at the very highest levels, right at the top". Theoretically Godfrey, the Admiralty candidate, would have the support in Cabinet of the First Sea Lord. But the new incumbent in this ancient job was none other than Dansey's old friend Winston Churchill. Whether or not Dansey applied any pressure on the man he had so ably supported during the wilderness years we shall never know. Certainly Churchill owed him a great deal and it would be reasonable to suppose that a shrewd operator like Dansey would not hesitate to collect such debts when it suited him. In any event, support for Godfrey withered and it was soon clear that Menzies would be confirmed in the post.

Before Menzies could safely accept the "Ivory" (the small plaque which is handed to the Chief of the Secret Service by the monarch as a token of office and as a pass giving access in times of trouble) there was one more matter to be cleared up. Dansey had been horrified on his return to find that Menzies had involved not only the official SIS head of station at The Hague but also the resident Z man there in an operation which had disaster written clearly all over it, and was now rapidly turning sour. It not only threatened Menzies's chances of becoming C, but, since Claude had lit the fuse himself two years before, his own career could be prematurely cut short when the operation blew up in their faces, which could happen at any time. The problem was further complicated by the fact that no less a person than Neville Chamberlain, the Prime Minister, was committed to the operation. Indeed, the orders came direct from Downing Street for what has gone down in history as the Venlo Incident.

CHAPTER NINETEEN
Heydrich's Play

The Venlo Incident has all the qualities of a first rate thriller – a tortuous plot made memorable by a rich cast of characters, many of whom were rogues and crooks and changed identities as casually as most men change their ties.

It began when Claude Dansey made contact with a distinguished German refugee in Paris.

Dr Klaus Spieker (or Spiecker) was forced to leave Germany when the Nazis came to power in 1933. During the Weimar Republic he had served as Director of Press Information to two Chancellors, Joseph Werth and Wilhelm Marx. But he earned the hatred of the newly-emerged National Socialist Party when, in 1930, he had been head of the section of the Ministry of the Interior whose job it was, like Scotland Yard's Special Branch, to keep track of subversive radical movements of both right and left.

Once in Paris Dr Spieker joined the *Deutsche Freiheits Partei* (German Freedom Party), a broadly-based social democratic refugee organisation. The DFP waged a propaganda war against the Nazis, smuggling leaflets into Germany, and for a time they even ran a clandestine short wave radio transmitter from a fishing vessel in the English Channel. Late in 1939, following the declaration of war the whole operation moved to just outside Paris where it was taken under the wing of Jean Giraudoux, the French playwright, who had been appointed Minister of Information. In 1940 Dr Spieker, who had become one of the DFP's regular broadcasters, went to England where he was recruited into Department EH broadcasting "black" propaganda from Woburn Abbey. The Department's technical staff and transmitting facilities were provided not by the Ministry of Information or the BBC, but through the good services of Colonel Richard Gambier-Parry, the SIS Controller of Wireless Communications. The Department was yet another intelligence pie in which Claude Dansey had a finger. Later, in

1941, Dr Spieker moved to Canada, where he seems to have ended up working for Sir William Stephenson.

Dansey was impressed with Dr Spieker when they first met in the mid-thirties. For some time he had been cautiously sniffing round several German émigré organisations in France and Switzerland, looking for a man who possessed all the right qualifications. Dr Spieker seemed ideal. He had a reputation as a well-known and dedicated anti-Nazi whose sincerity was beyond question. He was also a man of wide experience who knew how the wheels of power moved, and he had many useful contacts both in the political and business fields. But perhaps best of all, as far as Dansey was concerned, Dr Spieker possessed an invaluable knowledge of subversive movements inside Nazi Germany, and these Dansey planned to exploit. The doctor therefore seemed the ideal recruiting sergeant and contact man for the espionage network Dansey was trying to set up inside Germany.

Anyone as well known as Spieker would, however, be bound to attract the attention of Nazi Counter-Intelligence. Spieker was not a professional spy. He was an honourable man dedicated to a cause, with little capacity for guile. So when Dr Franz Fischer, a fellow refugee, came to him with a letter of introduction from one of his friends, the writer Emil Ludwig, Spieker took the man at his face value. And that was to prove a mistake of monumental proportions.

Dr Fischer was not lying when he described himself as a refugee. But he omitted to explain that he was a refugee from the German criminal police, not from Nazi persecution. In 1933, while head of a Frankfurt fuel distribution centre, he had misappropriated some DM 350,000. Indicted for embezzlement, he fled to Switzerland with the police hot on his trail. They began extradition proceedings against him, but the Swiss wanted nothing to do with a runaway embezzler, and promptly expelled him from their country. Fischer surfaced again in Paris, where he remained for the next two or three years, eking out a precarious existence and living on his wits.

In about 1937 Fischer either offered his services to SS Counter-Intelligence (SD), or else was recruited by Obersturmführer Dr Helmut Knochen, one of the clever young men with whom the head of the SD, Reinhard Heydrich, had surrounded himself. Knochen was to go far in the intelligence game. In 1940 he was sent secretly to Paris by Himmler to set up a Gestapo organisation in occupied France under the noses of the Wehrmacht generals who were determined to confine the activities of the Gestapo to Germany and Poland.

In return for spying on his fellow exiles, Fischer sought to have his conviction for embezzlement quashed. The SD were interested, and agreed that if he proved satisfactory they would arrange for his safe return to Germany, where he would probably have to stand trial but would be guaranteed the minimum sentence. Hauptsturmführer Alfred Ulenberg and later his superior, Standartenführer Bohme, of Section VI of the RSHA, took over his case from Dr Knochen and ran him as an agent.

At this stage no one in the SD had any elaborate game plan in mind: there was no plot, no conspiracy. Fischer's job was simply to penetrate émigré circles. It was a routine intelligence-gathering operation. But then Heydrich took a hand, introducing one of his best agents into the game.

Johannes (Hans) Travaglio was so unlikely a spy that he could only exist in real life. A retired tenor who had sung in opera and operetta, he was born in Frankfurt in 1892, the product of a liaison between the famous Bavarian painter Franz von Lenbach and an Italian opera singer. During the first world war he joined the Luftwaffe, rising to the rank of captain. But the stage was in his blood, and after the war he attempted to follow in his mother's footsteps and become an opera singer. He had a pleasant voice, but neither voice nor talent were sufficiently remarkable to guarantee him anything more than an undistinguished musical career. Instead he concentrated on the production side of the theatre, becoming for a time stage manager at the Prinz Regenten Theatre in Munich and working as assistant to Max Fischer, the man whose production of *The Merry Widow* so enchanted Adolf Hitler that he saw it again and again.

When in 1935 Hitler, in defiance of the Versailles peace treaty, began secretly to rearm Germany and expand the armed forces, Travaglio – then forty-two and growing increasingly weary of the insecurities of stage life – applied for a commission in the newly-formed Luftwaffe. Considered too old for flying duties, he was given a staff job instead. But Travaglio wasn't satisfied. Perhaps he was looking for more excitement, perhaps he was merely trying to provide a second string to his bow, at any rate he obtained an introduction to Admiral Canaris, the head of the Abwehr, who in turn introduced him to his SS colleagues.

Travaglio possessed all the attributes of a first-class spy. Quick witted, charming, and widely travelled, he was also a professional actor of some considerable experience. Operating under the *nom de guerre* of "Major Solms", Travaglio was sent at first to the Netherlands to penetrate émigré circles and spy on their activities. His role was to be that of a dedicated anti-Nazi seeking out like-minded fellow countrymen who had fled Germany when Hitler came to power and who now intrigued against the regime from the security of a neutral country. He was subsequently teamed with one of the SD's small-time agents – none other than Dr Franz Fischer, who was incidentally the brother of Travaglio's last employer, the producer of the Prinz Regenten Theatre.

It was through Fischer that Hans Travaglio met Dr Spieker at the Carlton Hotel, Amsterdam, in January 1938. Travaglio, in his role as Major Solms, arrived in the company of two "friends", Major Dibitsch and Dr Kuhner, whom he brought along no doubt as protection in case the meeting proved to be a British set-up. But realising that his bodyguards were unnecessary, Dibitsch and Kuhner were left behind for all future meetings. Thereafter Spieker and Travaglio met regularly, often in the company of Franz Fischer.

In the autumn of 1938 – that is, about the time of the Czechoslovakian crisis, when Hitler was preparing to invade the Sudetenland – the group was enlarged by the addition of a Dr Strauss, who seems to have been a friend of Dr Spieker. Strauss was a businessman who boasted of his British connections, and once told Fischer that he had access to sources of money in London available to support any active opposition to Hitler. Presumably he, too, was an associate of Dansey's.

Travaglio and Fischer continued their double act. They succeeded in convincing Spieker that they were sincere, reliable and represented a group of senior officers of the Wehrmacht – General von Fritsch, General Wietersheim and Field Marshal von Rundstedt were the names mentioned – who were totally opposed to Naziism and eager to see the end of the Führer's regime. These men, they told Spieker, believed that Hitler's war plans would prove disastrous for Germany. At all costs he must be stopped. This was of course precisely the kind of talk that Spieker liked to hear for, like all political exiles, he tended to live on a diet of dreams and wishful thinking. Between them, Fischer and Travaglio continued to feed Spieker's illusions, so that before long he was able to tell Claude Dansey that he had made contact with an important opposition group inside Germany. There was no reason why Dansey's suspicions should be aroused. Over the years the British had had knowledge of a number of German anti-Hitler plots, involving such diverse conspirators as Admiral Canaris (the Abwehr chief), Ulrich von Hassell (a former German Ambassador in Rome), and the Kordt brothers, who were also in the German Foreign Office. Indeed in 1938, during the Czech crisis, Colonel-General Halder, Chief of the Army General Staff, had sent his own emissary, Bohm-Tettelback, to London to put out feelers amongst people in government circles. But the British Government chose to ignore all approaches. Reinhard Heydrich, director of the SD, decided to exploit this general climate of appeasement.

Heydrich had been a naval officer, but after a dishonourable discharge on account of some sexual peccadillo, he had joined the SS when it was still in its infancy. At thirty-five he had already proved himself to be a born intelligence officer. Totally ruthless, he has been described as "a living card-index, a brain which held all the threads and wove them all together". His second-in-command, Walter Schellenberg, regarded him as "a predatory animal, always alert to danger and ready to act swiftly and ruthlessly".

Heydrich was later to refer to Venlo as his "play". No doubt he overstated his case, but there can be no doubt that he wrote the scenario and that Travaglio and Fischer were his actors.

Following classic espionage procedure – the need-to-know principle which he had employed throughout his own career – Dansey did not meet either Fischer or Travaglio. Had he done so, the Venlo Incident, as it became known, might have been stillborn, because Dansey had a lifetime's experience in spotting wrong-uns. However, there was no necessity for a meeting and every reason against one. The two men were Spieker's contacts, and Dansey considered it advisable to distance himself and his own organisation from the doctor's attempts at conspiracy. All the same, something about the business must have worried him, because he had second thoughts and suggested to Sigismund Payne Best, his chief Z man in Holland, that Franz Fischer might be of some use to him. Probably he just wanted Best's opinion of the man, or it is possible that he hoped to use Best to prise Fischer off Spieker.

Tall, monocled, with an aristocratic air, Sigismund Payne Best looked the perfect caricature of the traditional English gentleman. In fact, he had been educated in Germany, and for the past twenty years had lived on the Continent, mostly in Holland, where he ran a small company, *N. V. Handelsdienst voor het Continent* (Continental Trade Service Limited), which specialised in the import and export of chemical and pharmaceutical products. He was married to a Dutch woman, a portrait painter, the daughter of the late General van Rees, and thanks to her family and his own business connections, he was on friendly terms with many people in the Dutch military and political establishment. He was also a talented viola player, and he was much in demand as a musician. Because of its relative unpopularity as an instrument, amateur string quartets are always in need of viola players, so it was through his music-making that Best gained entrée to the Dutch court and became personally acquainted with members of the royal family.

Having worked for Claude Dansey during the first world war, Best had been involved with him on and off ever since. At various times, from about 1930, Dansey is known to have indulged in what were called "Claude's private ventures" – a euphemism for what seem to have been freelance operations organised and run by Dansey himself and employing his own men, or members of Vansittart's "Private Detective Agency", rather than SIS regulars. Presumably these ventures had the blessing of Admiral Sinclair and Vansittart, though with Dansey almost anything is possible. At any rate Best was involved in spying for Dansey long before he was officially recruited into the Z Organisation in 1935–36.

Taking note of his chief's suggestion, Best discreetly checked up on Franz Fischer. What he discovered confirmed his worst suspicions: the man was little better than a crook and totally untrustworthy. He therefore refrained from making contact.

By now Heydrich must have begun to wonder if the curtain would ever rise on his "play". But then fate, in the shape of Stewart Menzies and Neville Chamberlain, took a hand.

There was now a definite sense of urgency in the SIS. Everyone knew that war could not be long delayed: it was only a matter of time before Hitler decided to invade Poland or commit some outrage that would put an end to peace. Dansey was in Zurich busy setting up the Swiss end of the Z Organisation, and therefore had more important tasks than keeping track of Dr Spieker's intrigues. He was out of touch with the subsequent events in Holland and no longer in personal contact with either Spieker or Best. It was to prove a major error of judgement.

In August 1939 Best was asked by Menzies in London to make contact with Franz Fischer. Although distinctly uneasy, Best arranged a meeting at The Hague.

"I had the damn fellow up to my office," Best complained in a letter to an old friend, Colonel Reggie Drake, several years after the war, "and spent a morning interrogating him. He told me a very long story to the effect that he had always been fighting Hitler and that he had fled to Holland to escape death at the hands of the Gestapo and how eager he was to help the Allies in the fight against Naziism: just the sort of story that one would expect of an *agent provocateur*." The result of the meeting was that Best wrote "a most damning report on him to London", complained bitterly that his position had been compromised by being put in contact with this man and made an urgent plea that he might be allowed "to induce Fischer to visit London where he could be safely jailed".

London, however, paid no attention. Indeed, far from respecting the instincts of the man on the ground, as Claude Dansey would undoubtedly have done, Menzies pooh-poohed Best's suspicions. "I was told that my ideas were all wet, that . . . Dr Spieker knew Fischer well and that he was quite trustworthy . . . From that time on, Fischer simply haunted my office and came in almost daily on some excuse or other."

Best did not reveal that he was working for the Secret Service and gave Fischer the impression that he was somehow vaguely connected with the Foreign Office. In any case, Fischer proved once again, that he was no more than the stalking horse for Hans Travaglio (Major Solms), whom he arranged for the Englishman to meet at the Hotel Wilhemina at Venlo on the German border. "Solms," he told Best, "was adjutant to General Geyl of the Luftwaffe." Fischer did not attend the meeting himself, but gave Best a description of the man he was to meet, so that he would recognise him when he saw him. He described Major Solms as looking like "a well-fed French abbé wearing a Basque beret" Best's own description of the Luftwaffe major is not surprisingly rather more sour. He was, he wrote, "a big, bluff, self-confident fellow, a Bavarian, and inclined to talk as big as he looked".

He also came to the conclusion that Solms was little more than an errand boy for more important people in the background. On being confronted, Solms confessed that "he could not say much until he had reported to his chief about our meeting". Since his chief was Reinhard Heydrich, this was no doubt literally true. Nonetheless, Best was sufficently impressed to agree to meet Solms once again, a week hence. Best may have been suspicious of Fischer, but he was completely taken in by Solms.

On 1st September 1939 Germany invaded Poland. Two days later Britain and France declared war on Germany. The day afterwards, 4th September, obeying orders from London, Best made a phone call to the Passport Control Officer at the British Embassy in The Hague and asked him to come to his office, Nieuwe Uitleg 15. Major Stevens, the PCO, was expecting the call. He had been alerted by a cable from London, which read:

> You (are to) place yourself in touch with Captain S. Payne Best and give him all facilities which he may require in regard to communications and otherwise and also any money that he may want. Captain Best is a highly experienced man of great ability. Beyond giving your services you are not to interfere in his

arrangements. He can himself deal direct with Dutch military and other authorities.

Although he was the "official" head of the SIS in Holland, Stevens had never met Best nor, for that matter, did he know of the existence of the Z Organisation. In this he was not alone.

The Z Organisation remained secret largely because its members were not given radios. Therefore the decoders and radio men in London were unaware of any extra radio traffic, nor were any foreign listening posts. Instead Best and his fellow Z men kept in touch with Dansey by means of the mail. They sent their reports through the post to one of his many clandestine letter drops, or used couriers such as Dansey's young "film company executives" or the captains of Rhine barges one of whom was a character named, ironically, for an anti-Nazi, Goebbels. But he did sterling work bringing messages and information out of Germany until 1939, when he suddenly disappeared.

At first the two men hit it off. "Stevens," wrote Best, "is a very pleasant little man, full of good stories and something of an amateur actor. He has a wonderful gift for languages of which he speaks some ten." But Best's initial enthusiasm for his new helper was soon to be tempered with doubt.

Stevens's military career, it transpired, had been spent in the Indian army, where he had been a staff officer, with only brief spells of regimental duty. He was now eighteen months away from promotion to lieutenant-colonel, and in order to fill in his time before he got his battalion, he had begged a friend from the Indian army, General Sir Claude Auchinleck, to help him find some congenial post. Because of his abilities as a linguist, Auchinleck recommended him to MI6, and so Stevens had ended up in Holland. "He knew nothing about [Secret Service] work," wrote Best, "and less about Passport Control; worst of all, he had absolutely no judgement of people or of their characters." In fact, he was "altogether the Staff Officer and was only happy when holding a conference; he even used to get all his agents in for Staff Talks!" But without doubt the clincher for Best came when he discovered that Stevens was half-Greek – cursed with "the qualities and weaknesses of the Levantine".

However, in the euphoria of the moment, perhaps induced by too many jinevers, the two men decided to join forces and amalgamate their two organisations. It is, of course, most unlikely that Dansey was party to this decision, since it went against all his experience and all the canons of espionage. But in view of the fact that there is no record of his reaction, which one would expect to be blistering, the probability is that he was abroad in Switzerland or France when he heard the news, and by then it was too late to stop the process.

Nevertheless, the proposal was not without merit, particularly in the light of Best's experience in the first world war, when separate Allied intelligence agencies in Holland had competed desperately with each other for both agents and information. It had been chaos, and Best did not want to repeat the errors of yesteryear.

Amalgamation of the "official" SIS and Z Organisation would at least reduce the wearisome duplication of effort and minimise the possibility of friction between the two groups. In any case, since they were both going to be using the same line of communication to London – Stevens's short wave radio – it was obvious that neither service would have been able indefinitely to preserve its virginity: some degree of intimacy would be inevitable.

What Stevens did not know was that the British Passport Control Office in The Hague was under constant German surveillance: they even filmed everyone who went in and out of the building. Dansey, in typical fashion, had chosen to exploit this fact. He permitted – even encouraged – the Germans to keep watch on Major Stevens and the PCO staff, in order to distract the opposition from the more important activities of the secret Z Organisation. It was also the reason why Best had made a point of persuading Stevens to come to his own office at Nieuwe Uitleg 15, rather than putting in an appearance himself at the Passport Control Office, where he ran the risk of being identified by the Germans.

Shortly after the meeting with Stevens, Best received orders from Menzies – orders that went contrary to all his vast experience of espionage procedure. Menzies instructed him to send to London a list of all his agents and their various operational areas, plus a report on the present state of the Z Organisation in Holland.

Best was furious – and deeply worried. He knew Dansey would never have sanctioned such an enterprise. Reliable agents were too valuable for their security to be jeopardised needlessly on the whim of some empire-builder in London. But what was he to do? Dansey was in Switzerland and out of contact with Best. Meanwhile orders were orders, and Menzies was growing increasingly impatient at the delay. Something had to be done. In the end Best compromised – he gave Stevens his report and a list of his agents to take with him to London. Unknown to both Stevens and Menzies, all the names on the list were fictitious. Best preserved the security of his own agents, but at the cost of deliberately mis-informing the acting chief of the Secret Service. Stevens returned from London in a state of high excitement and in the company of what Best calls "a very big noise". The name of the noise was Major Haddon Hall who seems to have acted as Menzies's emissary. Stevens, Best and Hall met in the Passport Control Office in The Hague, a location which suggests that under pressure of events – the war was only a few days old – even Best was becoming less security-conscious than usual.

As a result of that meeting Best was given a new and important role. After extolling the importance of the Z man's contribution to the British intelligence effort, Haddon Hall declared that London was now relying on Best to provide reliable advance information of any German intention to attack the Allied left flank through Holland and Belgium. It had also been decided in London that there would be no change of status for Best's and Stevens's organisations. Z and the "official" Secret Service in Holland would continue to act independently of each other, but they would remain in close liaison. This, it was hoped, would do much to prevent any possibility of friction. Lastly, Best and Stevens were to continue their meetings with Major Solms, who had started to provide what was considered to be valuable technical information about the Luftwaffe. But it was the group of high-ranking Wehrmacht dissidents in which the powers-that-be in London were particularly interested. They were determined to remain in contact with these men. War, however, made communication between France and Germany difficult: Solms could no longer journey from Berlin to Paris for his meetings with Dr Spieker. Since a new venue would have to be found – what better than a neutral country, such as Holland? Thus Best and Stevens were ordered to take over from Dr Spieker as contact with Major Solms. They soon discovered that they were acting as go-betweens for no less a person than the Prime Minister, Neville Chamberlain.

For some time Chamberlain, with Sir Horace Wilson, the Chief Industrial Adviser to the government, as his guide, had been conducting his own foreign policy, without regard to the Foreign Office. It was a state of affairs that had not gone unnoticed. Ivan Maisky, the Soviet Ambassador to Britain, summed up the situation with devastating accuracy: "The Prime Minister . . . usurped control of British foreign policy, and reduced the Foreign Office to the condition of a mere diplomatic chancery attached to his own person. To avoid any complications, the important post of Permanent Under-Secretary for Foreign Affairs, taken from Vansittart, was given [on 1st January 1938] to Alexander Cadogan, who could be relied upon not to provide any unexpected surprises."

210

Although neither Chamberlain nor Wilson had any knowledge or experience of foreign affairs, the Prime Minister was determined to keep control of foreign policy in his own hands. He believed that another Anglo-German war would destroy the very fabric of Western Europe and leave it a prey to bolshevism. Not surprisingly Maxim Litvinoff, Soviet Foreign Minister until 1939, was convinced "that Chamberlain's basic policy was to save England by inducing Germany to fight Russia".

Chamberlain had done everything in his power to avoid war. He had made concession after concession to Hitler. And even now, at this late stage, with German forces invading Poland, he was still prepared to follow up any peace initiative.

It took sixty-two German divisions just four weeks to crush all resistance in Poland. Meanwhile Germany's western borders were defended by a mere forty-four divisions, of which only twelve were regulars; the rest were category two, three and four formations, strengthened by labour service conscripts and workers from the Todt Organisation. (This organisation, founded by Fritz Todt, was responsible for all military construction.) It was a scratch force sufficient, it was hoped, to halt any Allied attack but unable to indulge in any military adventures on its own.

On 17th September the Red Army invaded Poland from the east. On the twenty-seventh Warsaw fell. Final agreement between Germany and the Soviet Union on the division of the country was reached just over a week later. The transfer of German troops from east to west started before the end of September, but it was to be May 1940 before the German General Staff felt ready to mount a major assault in France, an uneasy seven months which came to be called the "phoney war".

Chamberlain and his adviser believed – no doubt rightly – that any successful opposition to Hitler within Germany could come from just one source. Only the armed forces possessed the military muscle and the moral authority to overthrow the Third Reich and sue for peace. But time was running out. By September 1939 the Prime Minister and those around him were ready to clutch at straws. They desperately wanted peace, and were predisposed to look kindly upon any Wehrmacht plot – even one fronted by the dubious Major Solms. Chamberlain closed his mind to the possibility of treachery.

With Dansey safely occupied in Switzerland, Stewart Menzies saw his chance to establish himself with the Prime Minister as the rightful heir to the post of C before Admiral Sinclair, the present incumbent, either died or was forced by his doctors to retire. Everyone who knew the state of the admiral's health realised that

211

his departure could not be long delayed. Menzies, following Chamberlain's instructions, ordered Best and Stevens to press on with a view to opening possible negotiations with Major Solms's principals. Best's account of the subsequent proceedings is, it must be said, suspect, being written eight years after the event and therefore enjoying the benefit of hindsight. Moreover, Best was not unnaturally eager to absolve himself from blame and concerned to rescue his reputation from any mud that might be flung. Nevertheless his is the only account written by any of those concerned with the Venlo Incident, and until it can be proved to be false, then he must be given the benefit of any doubt. Best claims that from the second meeting he began to suspect that Solms was not all he claimed to be. Another rendezvous had been arranged at Venlo, but this time the Luftwaffe major did not turn up. Instead, he sent a man to drive Best to a new meeting place closer to the German border. Fearing a trap – it would have been easy for anyone to drive straight across the border at that point – the Englishman refused the change of venue and stayed where he was. After a while, he says, Solms himself put in a belated appearance.

At the meeting Solms was much more forthcoming about his principals. They were, he declared, a group of high-ranking Wehrmacht officers, patriots all, who were convinced that for the sake of Germany and the future of Europe Hitler must be overthrown. However, the major refused to divulge any further details of the conspiracy, saying that these officers would only deal with Best direct.

Disturbed by the course of events, Best wrote once again to London expressing his distrust of the whole business, but he was reassured when he received a communication from Dansey himself asking him to continue the meetings with the two Germans.

Whether it was a result of Best's suspicious attitude, or whether the Germans feared that the perfidious British might be planning a double bluff themselves, or whether it was all part of the original games plan, we do not know – but suddenly Fischer and Solms threatened to break off contact. Their principals, they declared, were unhappy with the British attitude and demanded a token of good faith: they needed some reassurance that "they were really dealing with British Government representatives".

It was a shrewd move because it transferred the burden of suspicion to the other side and thereby unsettled London's judgement of events. It also enhanced the credibility of the Wehrmacht plotters in British eyes. We are risking our necks in all this, the plotters were in effect saying, prove that you are serious. Thus, forced unexpectedly on to the defensive and finding themselves to be somehow morally in the wrong, the British rushed to justify themselves. How could they demonstrate their good faith?

The two Germans proposed a simple but effective test. They asked that the BBC should broadcast a certain bulletin in its German transmission. This would prove government involvement in the affair. On 6th October Dr Fischer handed Best the text of the message to be broadcast, and three days later in Berlin Reinhard Heydrich must have rubbed his hands with glee when he heard the text read out not once, but twice, in the course of the day.

On 13th October Stevens received cabled instructions from London that the meetings were to proceed as planned. But first Best and Stevens decided to clear the decks with Major-General J. W. van Oorschot, Chief of the Dutch Intelligence Service.

It was a sensible move because the Dutch were determined to remain neutral, as in the first world war, and the Ministry of Justice was therefore interpreting international laws of neutrality in the strictest possible manner. Although the war was only six weeks old, Mr Rhodes, a member of Major Stevens's staff, had already been expelled for espionage activity; while one of Best's men had also been arrested. The last thing the two Englishmen wanted was for the negotiations to collapse because some of the people involved were in Dutch police cells.

General van Oorschot was President of the Netherlands-English Society, and a man whose anglophilia had even extended to marrying an Englishwoman. According to a subsequent German report of doubtful veracity, the general spent his holidays in England and was on friendly terms with Admiral Sinclair himself. The Germans even went so far as to claim that the head of Dutch Intelligence appeared on Passport Control Office records as Agent 930. However unlikely the story, by the time it was put out by the Germans the waters had been so muddied that the Dutch public were prepared to believe almost anything.

Van Oorschot was already on friendly terms with Stevens, with whom he had had professional dealings in the past. But Best was unknown to him – even though the man had been operating a secret intelligence service in Holland for several years.

Best, acting as spokesman, explained the situation to the general, who was prepared to be helpful. "I was willing," wrote van Oorschot in a letter to him in 1948, "to assist Stevens in having talks – on Dutch territory – with . . . people in Germany, who intended to try and convince their government of the desirability of starting peace negotiations . . . these people wanted to know whether terms could be found which would be satisfactory to both sides."

When Best went on to point out the possible danger of the negotiations breaking down because of some over-keen policeman or frontier guard, van Oorschot decided to detail one of his men, Lieutenant Dirk Klop, to accompany the Englishmen and guarantee their safe passage. Later the general was to declare that Lieutenant Klop had exceeded his instructions. Best, however, always insisted that Klop was present at all their conversations and knew the state of play as well as they did themselves. Klop spoke perfect English, and they decided to pass him off to the Germans as an English officer.

By now Reinhard Heydrich knew that the British had taken the bait even if they were not yet hooked. It would, he thought, take one of his best men to drive the hook well home. On 15th October he therefore put Walter Schellenberg in charge of the operation. Schellenberg, a young lawyer from Saarbrucken, had joined the SD when he was twenty-four. He soon proved to be one of their high flyers, becoming the youngest general in the SS at the age of thirty-one. At the time of Venlo he was twenty-nine years old.

With this final addition to the leading characters, the stage was set for the last act of Heydrich's "play".

CHAPTER TWENTY

"An Unexplained Incident at Blerik"

The first contact with the Germans was to have taken place at 10 a.m. on 20th October at Dinxperlo, a small village on the frontier, and some 120 miles from The Hague. The party, consisting of Best, Stevens, Lieutenant Klop and Dr Franz Fischer, set off bright and early in Best's car, a 1937 Lincoln Zephyr. At 8 a.m. they reached the small town of Zutphen, where Best and Stevens decided on a change in plan. They stopped at a café for breakfast, while Klop and Fischer went on by taxi to Dinxperlo to pick up the Germans.

It was not until noon that Klop phoned to say that the two men had at last crossed the border and that he was bringing them back to Zutphen. Fischer identified the men as Captain von Seidlitz (real name Sturmbannführer von Salisch) and Lieutenant Grosch (Hauptsturmführer Christiansen). He said that he knew both men personally and could vouch for them.

The location for the discussions was to be a safe house in Amsterdam, but when the Germans explained that they had to be back across the frontier by 8 p.m., it was obvious that this would be unsuitable. Best therefore had only a short time to arrange another safe house within easy reach of Zutphen. He drove them to an isolated roadside café where they had lunch, while he made some phone calls. A cousin of his wife's lived in a house in Arnhem: Best asked him if they might use his dining-room for their meeting; the cousin agreed.

By now Best had formed the opinion that the men they were dealing with were Nazis and probably SS officers at that. Nevertheless this did not surprise him since "it did not seem at all unlikely that Hitler might be trying to pull off a deal with [the British] at the expense of the left wing of [the Nazi Party]".

The negotiations went well. Stewart Menzies had previously briefed Stevens as to the terms which the British Government considered acceptable. These included the evacuation of Bohe-

215

mia, Moravia and Slovakia (parts of Czechoslovakia) and of Poland, as far as was possible in view of the Russian annexation. The meeting was cut short when Best's Dutch cousin-in-law came into the room to inform them that the house was surrounded by police who were enquiring about the presence of the Germans. Apparently two Dutch soldiers had overheard their conversation in the café and had reported the matter to the police. While Lieutenant Klop was sent out to deal with the local gendarmerie, Best attempted to get the negotiations going again. But not surprisingly the sudden advent of the police had ruined any chance of further discussions. However, they were able to arrange the date and place for another meeting – 25th October, The Hague – when it was hoped that General von Wietinghof, one of the principal conspirators, would be able to attend in person. Best then asked Klop to take the Germans back to the frontier; Fischer was put on the train to The Hague.

When von Salisch and Christiansen returned to their headquarters in Dusseldorf, they were debriefed by Schellenberg himself. Later the young SD officer returned to Berlin to consult with Heydrich. The latter ordered him to continue with the operation and to choose his own collaborators for the next move in the game.

Schellenberg turned to an old friend of his, Professor Max de Crinis, a psychiatrist who was also director of the Charité Hospital in Berlin, and persuaded him to play one of the roles in Heydrich's drama. De Crinis was a tall, distinguished-looking Austrian who held the rank of colonel in the German Army Medical Corps. He was older than Schellenberg and looked every inch the "right-hand man to the leader of the Opposition".

Schellenberg decided that the German delegation would be led by de Crinis posing as Colonel Martini, but he would also require two aides to accompany him. One of these would be Christiansen who, as Lieutenant Grosch, was already known to the Englishmen. The third member of the party would be Captain Schaemmel of the Army Transport Command – and this role would be played by Schellenberg himself.

It must have required considerable courage on Schellenberg's part to go into the lion's cage with the others. He was the one most at risk. It was unlikely that the Englishmen would be able to identify a Berlin psychiatrist or even a junior SD officer, but Schellenberg was one of the rising stars in the SD, and there was a real possibility that he might be recognised. No doubt this was the reason why he assiduously practised wearing a monocle during the days before the meeting. Other precautions were taken, of course. Had Best or Stevens chosen to check the identity of Captain

Schaemmel, they would have found that he existed: his name was on army records. However, the real Schaemmel was far away from the Dutch frontier and had no idea that his name was being used.

The first meeting had been fraught with difficulty, so it was perhaps not surprising that on the twenty-fifth the British received a cable from the Germans which read: "Wedding postponed". This was the code agreed between them to indicate a temporary delay. Four days later another cable arrived which said: "Wedding Monday" – meaning that the meeting would be on Monday, 30th October.

Best and Stevens waited at the office of the Continental Trade Service Company in The Hague, while Best's Dutch chauffeur, a man he trusted implicitly, drove Klop to Dinxperlo to pick up the German delegation. They returned to The Hague at 3.30 p.m.

The Englishmen were disappointed to discover that General von Wietinghof was not amongst the party, but the charming Captain Schaemmel made his excuses for their leader. It was impossible for the general to leave Berlin at the moment since he was expecting to be called to a conference with the Führer. Best was impressed with the young captain, who he soon realised was in *de facto* command of the delegation, in spite of the fact that Colonel Martini (de Crinis) was the senior officer present.

They got down to the discussions immediately. The captain began the proceedings in a business-like manner by giving a résumé of present conditions in Germany. The army, he said, had suffered considerable losses during the Polish campaign, but Hitler still refused to listen to the warnings of the General Staff and was determined to pursue the war in the west to the bitter end. This could only lead Germany to disaster. The three men represented a powerful group of Wehrmacht officers who intended to take over power from the Nazi Party. Their plans involved arresting Hitler at a General Staff meeting, while, at the same time, in a series of raids, troops would occupy all government offices and arrest the other Nazi leaders.

The plan seemed to have been carefully thought out, and in theory at any rate would appear to have every chance of success. A protocol was therefore drawn up at the conference in Best's office. It laid out the basis of the peace proposals put forward by the Germans. They offered a number of concessions in return for a solid commitment by the Allies to negotiate the handing back to Germany of the colonies taken from her by the Versailles Treaty after the first world war. The concessions included the evacuation of Czechoslovakia, the Sudetenland and Danzig, plus the rescinding of all anti-Jewish legislation in Germany and the disbandment of all Nazi para-military groups.

The Germans, for their part, wanted to know if representatives of the British and French Governments would be prepared to come to Holland to negotiate terms for an armistice. In which event, they asked, which German leader would be acceptable to both governments as head of the German delegation? Göering's name was suggested; alternatively, no doubt some member of the ex-royal family could be conscripted for the task.

Best quotes Schaemmel as saying: "We are Germans and have to think of the interests of our own country first. Before we take any steps against Hitler we want to know whether England and France are ready to grant us a peace which is both just and honourable." The Englishmen had every reason to be pleased at the outcome of these talks, which had been conducted in a business-like and professional manner. Of course, there was a long way to go yet, but they had started well. Afterwards Best entertained the Germans to an excellent dinner in his own home, and then arranged accommodation for them at the house of a friend. Stevens meanwhile sent a long cable to London giving details of the protocol.

Since the British would require time to consider the document and the Germans said they had to be back across the frontier before noon the following day, it was decided that some reliable method of communication between the two sides was urgently required. Major Stevens therefore gave Captain Schaemmel a British two-way radio and arranged a code and transmission times.

London's reply to the cable of 30th October did not arrive until a week later, the delay being due to the need to consult the French Government. The reply, when it came, was deliberately non-committal, but over the phone Stevens was told by Menzies that "the matter must be prosecuted with energy". In other words, someone – presumably Chamberlain – was sufficiently heartened to press on with the talks.

In the interim the Germans had sent their first radio message proposing another meeting on 7th November, but this time it was to be at Blerik near Venlo. Best and Stevens drove to Venlo intending to wait for the Germans at the Hotel Wilhemina. Klop, as before, was to escort them from the frontier and bring them to the hotel, which unfortunately turned out to be busy and noisy. The two delegations were bound to attract unwelcome attention, so somewhere else had to be found for the meeting – and quickly.

After reconnoitring the frontier post at Blerik, Klop phoned Best and Stevens suggesting that the talks were held in a café only

200 yards from the black and white painted barrier that marked the German border. The Café Backus was quiet and, because of its nearness to the frontier, poorly patronised these days. Lieutenant Klop could not have made a worse choice. Backus himself, the owner of the café, was a dubious character well known to the local police and suspected of being a smuggler. But at the time no one seems to have been aware of the fact, least of all Lieutenant Klop.

The café was a red brick building with a verandah and a large parking area. At the back there was a garden with a children's playground with swings and seesaws. Facing the café, on the opposite side of the road, stood the Dutch customs house.

When the Englishmen arrived, they found Klop and the two Germans, Schaemmel and Grosch (Schellenberg and Christiansen), waiting for them, but no general; he, it seemed, was still unavailable. They got down to business immediately.

Best and Stevens outlined the British reply to the German document, and it was clear from their reaction that the Germans were disappointed. Obviously they had expected something far more positive. However, they asked for another meeting on the following day, when General Wietinghof would definitely put in an appearance. He was anxious to meet the two Englishmen and wished to entrust some secret papers to them for safe-keeping. Best and Stevens interpreted this as meaning that the general was getting cold feet and was hoping that the British would offer him sanctuary should his plans for revolt fail. The Englishmen agreed to the meeting.

Heydrich was now under pressure from Himmler to wind up the whole affair: it had gone on long enough; it was time to act. At this point Heydrich called in one of his most trusted officers, Alfred Naujocks, an SS man who had already demonstrated a unique talent for what would be described in today's jargon as covert operations. A street fighter from the early days of the party, Naujocks was the man who had led Operation Canned Goods, the raid on the Gleiwitz radio transmitter, which had provided Hitler with the technical excuse to invade Poland. After being briefed by Schellenberg, Naujocks studied what could be seen of the terrain around the café from the German side of the border. He liked what he saw. It would be risky, but with the advantage of surprise he saw no reason why his plan would not work.

The meeting at the Café Backus on the eighth was attended only by Captain Schaemmel, who apologised for the continued absence of the general. The Queen of the Netherlands and the King of the Belgians had made a joint appeal for peace, and as a result, Hitler had decided to summon the General Staff to a conference in

Munich, a conference the general must attend. However, the following day – the ninth – he would be free to come to the café in person.

Something else happened on the eighth, also in Munich, which was to affect the future of the two Englishmen. Every year the Führer celebrated the anniversary of the 1923 Munich Putsch, the Nazis' first attempt to overthrow the government by force. It had failed, and Hitler had been sent to prison. Nevertheless it remained a holy day in the party calendar. This year, as on all the others, Hitler was booked to make a speech to the faithful in the Bürgerbraukeller in Munich, a place also sacred in the eyes of the party. On this occasion Hitler had finished speaking and had left the cellar, when a bomb hidden inside one of the pillars exploded, killing and maiming many people.

The morning of 9th November 1939 was dull and cold, with a threat of rain in the air. Best was kept busy in his office and was unable to join Stevens until after ten o'clock. While they were waiting for Klop to arrive, Stevens produced a couple of Browning automatics and offered one to Best – just in case things went wrong. Best took the gun. He claims to have had a sense of impending disaster.

Since everyone seemed tired after their recent travelling to and from the border Best asked his chauffeur, Jan Lemmens, to drive them to Blerik. On the way they stopped at a roadside café near s'Hertogenbosch for lunch, and over the meal they discussed the possible danger of being kidnapped. Klop dismissed their fears: he had arranged for a stronger guard at the frontier post, and with the customs house just across the road from the café, he was sure the Germans would never attempt anything in broad daylight.

In the car Best and Stevens discussed what action they ought to take if Germany should suddenly invade Holland. For some reason Stevens there and then took out a sheet of paper and began to make a list of names of British agents and sympathisers whom he thought would be at risk in the event of an invasion. He tucked the list into his pocket as they neared the café. Because of the traffic they were already three-quarters of an hour late for the appointment, and as a result they did not bother to stop and check if the police guard at the frontier had been increased. It hadn't; Klop had forgotten to phone.

Everything looked quiet and peaceful in Blerik. A little girl played with a ball and a big black dog in the roadway in front of the café. The only other person in sight was a German customs officer. It was then that Best noted a curious fact – the black and white barrier on the German side of the frontier was raised.

220

Best, who was now driving the car, reversed into the car park at the side of the café. As he did so, they saw Schaemmel standing on the verandah, chatting to Backus and his wife. Schaemmel waved to them, or at any rate made some sort of sign. They thought it meant that the elusive general was waiting for them inside the café. Best switched off the engine, and as they got out of the car, all hell broke loose. There was shouting and shots were fired. A large open touring car, which had been hidden out of sight behind the German frontier post, drove round the corner, across the Dutch frontier and into the café car park, where it screeched to a halt with its bumpers touching Best's Lincoln Zephyr. There were seven men in the car, some standing on the running boards. All were armed with machine pistols which they fired over the heads of the British party, who didn't have a chance to draw their guns. Lieutenant Klop, under cover of the open car door, broke away and ran towards the road firing his revolver as he went. Two of his bullets struck the German car, shattering the windscreen. There was a rattle of shots from the machine pistols as some of the Germans fired back. Klop was hit in the head and right shoulder and collapsed in a heap on the grass.

Best, Stevens and Jan Lemmens, the chauffeur, were swiftly handcuffed and thrust into the Germans' car. Klop, mortally wounded and covered in blood, was thrown into Best's Lincoln, and then both cars were driven at top speed back across the border.

The Dutch press was quick off the mark. On 10th November 1939 several newspapers carried an ANP (General Netherlands Press Agency) report concerning "an unexplained incident on the German frontier" which had occurred the previous day. "On the afternoon of 9 November shots were fired on the German frontier near Blerik in which people wearing civilian clothing were involved. It appears that one person was shot whilst the others were taken across the frontier."

Thus, in the neutral language of a press agency report, the world received the first news about what is now known as the Venlo Incident. The confusion even about where it happened seems typical of the obfuscation and mismanagement of the whole affair. Yet it still remains a sensitive subject in British intelligence circles – so sensitive, in fact, that the official papers will not be available for scrutiny until the year 2015 at the earliest.

CHAPTER TWENTY-ONE

Tea at White's

On the face of it, Venlo was a major disaster. Less than three months after a declaration of war both the Z and official espionage networks in Holland had been smashed by the SD, their best agents "*brûlé*", to use Rex Pearson's phrase – "burned" in the jargon of espionage. Two senior British Secret Service men had been abducted, and in the course of interrogation, had given their captors a considerable amount of information. British radio codes and procedures had been handed to the enemy, who had at the same time gained valuable insights into the organisation of British espionage methods. Lord Dacre, who was recruited into the intelligence service during the war, even goes so far as to say that "our entire espionage system in Western Europe was mopped up by the German Secret Service in a single swoop, at Venlo on the Dutch frontier".

All this suggests a disaster of Wagnerian proportions, and yet one must ask why was it not a great deal worse?

Lord Dacre goes some way towards giving an answer. He says: "I have always regarded it [Venlo] as a blessing in disguise. The Germans . . . destroyed a rotten body which, had it survived, would have destroyed us. Through it, they could have controlled our Secret Service, as we controlled theirs." Instead fresh blood had to be brought into the incestuous world of the pre-war Secret Service, new networks had to be set up. At times it almost looked as if the traditional Secret Service were being replaced by a mirror of the Z Organisation – with Dansey still at the helm.

In spite of the disaster no heads rolled amongst the upper echelons of the SIS in London. Menzies remained as C (there was no attempt to unseat him), Dansey became his deputy, and it was soon noticed that his domination of the younger man now seemed total. It became almost impossible to see Menzies, even in his own

222

office, without Dansey being present; most operational decisions were made with Dansey at his elbow. In due course, thanks to his hold on Menzies, Dansey effectively controlled MI6 and MI9 (the escape organisation), and his fine Italian hand can even be detected in some of the affairs of the French section of the SOE. Dansey thus became the single most powerful figure in British Intelligence: in Colonel Langley's words, "what Claude wanted done was done".

The besetting sin of all intelligence work is that in the last analysis it is all too often profoundly frivolous. Any espionage operation, no matter how ingenious or how skilfully conducted, has no value unless it performs a specific function or is part of a larger strategy. The game of foxes can too easily become just that – a game. Intrigue for intrigue's sake, with no object other than to demonstrate the intriguer's own brilliance. The history of espionage is littered with the bones of white elephants – schemes of mindboggling deviousness which achieved little more than wasting the time of the various Secret Services involved. The Venlo Incident is a classic example of the species.

Venlo was a brilliantly conceived espionage game brought to a satisfactory conclusion by Heydrich and Schellenberg. Yet (*pace* Lord Dacre) it achieved little beyond the borders of Holland, where admittedly the consequences of the operation led to the tragic failure of British Intelligence, which contributed to a series of intelligence and military disasters in the Netherlands throughout the war.

Heydrich possessed a unique talent for intrigue, which he could never resist the opportunity to show off. He also nursed, as did Schellenberg, romantic notions about the British Secret Service, and inspired by Kipling-esque tales of the Great Game, he longed to match himself against the men whom he regarded as the masters of espionage, and whom he credited with a subtlety they did not possess. In the end the temptation to make a fool of the British overcame all other considerations.

It was at the meeting at Zutphen on 20th October 1939 that Heydrich made a positive move to change the status of the game. What had hitherto been merely low-level meetings – they could not be described as negotiations – were now elevated into something much more significant. By introducing a supposed Staff colonel (Professor de Crinis alias Colonel Martini), who was to be followed in due course by no less than a general, the Germans made it clear that as far as they were concerned, negotiations were now to be

223

conducted at a more senior level. He was, in fact, inviting a positive response from the British.

How did the British react? In one sense, as positively as Heydrich could have wished. As we have seen, on 30th October the secret message, which signalled their desire to continue the negotiations, was read out twice on BBC European broadcasts, and on 6th November they agreed to a further series of meetings, beginning the following day. Yet it is significant that in the interim the British changed neither the status nor the personnel of their negotiating team. They continued to rely on Best and Stevens, an elderly captain and an Indian army major, both of whose intelligence activities in Holland were now well and truly blown as far as the enemy was concerned. Indeed, it is hard to believe that the two men were ever in a position to conduct much in the way of negotiations. Best records the almost laughable occasion when, on the seventh, in talks with Schaemmel (Schellenberg), he strayed from the terms of his original brief and in error demanded that the Germans should quit the whole of Czechoslovakia and not just Bohemia, Moravia and Slovakia, as the British Government were suggesting. Menzies was furious, but Captain Schaemmel did not bat an eyelid.

It is clear that some time after the thirtieth and before the sixth there was a change of heart at SIS headquarters. Menzies was committed to obeying the orders from Downing Street – what else could he do? – but suddenly there seems to have been a greater sense of caution and much less enthusiasm for the whole project. It is more than likely that this emanated from Dansey. Only he possessed the moral authority with Menzies to influence him to that extent.

Dansey's intervention almost certainly prevented a greater disaster. Schellenberg is on record as saying that he hoped to get to London in the course of the negotiations and penetrate the British Secret Service on its own ground. But a more likely possibility is that some senior diplomatic or military figures, chosen to conduct negotiations once the SIS had completed the preliminaries, would have been the kidnap victims – instead of Best and Stevens. There is no doubt that Heydrich was after bigger game than he eventually bagged. Thanks to Dansey, his efforts were frustrated.

Thanks also to Dansey, Menzies survived to fight another day, with his reputation more or less intact. He had been saved from the folly of his own lack of experience and his misreading of the situation, and could point to the politicians for their errors of judgement. Whereas only Dansey and possibly Best – and he was in Sachsenhausen concentration camp – knew of Menzies's own errors. Nevertheless his confidence had been badly shaken. He had never found it easy to make decisions. He had always had a tendency to avoid committing himself to a particular course of action, hoping that the problem would meanwhile somehow go away. Frequently it did, of course – which earned him a reputation for shrewdness with certain of his colleagues. And it is true that in peacetime there is much to be said for periods of masterly inactivity in the intelligence field. But in wartime operational decisions have to be made. What Menzies needed was someone to make them for him. Partly out of gratitude, partly out of genuine admiration for the man, partly out of fear that news of his bungling might be leaked to his political masters, Menzies chose Dansey.

As for the unfortunate victims of the Incident:

Lieutenant Klop died of his wounds within an hour or two of the shooting, though the Gestapo went to the trouble of manufacturing the macabre fiction that he survived long enough to dictate a statement. Jan Lemmens was interrogated and eventually repatriated to Holland, where in due course he distinguished himself in the Dutch Resistance. When Stevens was searched, his list of agents was found, and he and Best were interrogated by the SD. In all intelligence work there is a time to be a hero and a time to be sensible, and Best never made any bones about the fact that he told his interrogators what it was clear that they knew already. He guessed that Heydrich's "play" could only have been put into production because the Germans had inside information about all British Intelligence activities in Holland, his own included.

Best and Stevens were incarcerated in a special compound in Sachsenhausen concentration camp, where Best in particular had a hard time, spending the first year or two in chains. Towards the end of the war they were removed to Buchenwald, both men being repatriated in 1945.

There is no doubt that they owed their continued survival to the man who had built and planted the bomb which exploded in the Bürgerbraukeller in Munich on the day before they were abducted at Venlo. The man's name was George Elser.

Elser had spent two years in Dachau concentration camp when, in October 1939, his talents as a carpenter and model maker came to the attention of the SS. Before the war he had at one time been a model maker for BMW cars. He was approached by two men who told him that the SS had uncovered a plot to shoot Hitler after he had made his speech of commemoration in the beer cellar. Since the authorities did not want the scandal of a big treason trial only six weeks after the declaration of war, it had been decided to assassinate the would-be assassins by means of a bomb which could be exploded the minute Hitler had been spirited out of the cellar. They wanted Elser to place the bomb inside one of the pillars. In return for his co-operation they offered him his freedom and a large sum of money.

Of course, Elser didn't believe a word of all this, but since it was a choice of do what they wanted or, in the grim vernacular of the inmates of Dachau, "go up the chimney", he agreed to plant the bomb which, as we know, exploded as planned.

To Elser's astonishment the following night the two SS men drove him to the Swiss frontier at Bregens at the western end of Lake Constance. They stopped 400 yards from the frontier post, handed him a large envelope full of German and Swiss currency, and gave him a postcard of the Bürgerbraukeller with the exploding pillar marked with an X. The German frontier guard, they told him, had orders to let anyone through carrying such a card. Elser, who had expected a bullet in his head, couldn't believe his luck. But he should have known better, because when he approached the frontier guard, the man seemed to know nothing about any such arrangement and arrested him as a currency smuggler.

The incriminating postcard led him back into the clutches of the Gestapo, but even when badly beaten up, he continued to deny that he had any accomplices in placing the bomb. He reasoned that if he kept his mouth shut about SS involvement, he might be permitted to survive. And he was. Then like the traditional bad fairies, the two SS men turned up yet again. This time they wanted him to identify an Englishman they would point out to him. Why not, thought Elser? So, he pointed out the man as the one who had bribed him to place the bomb in the Bürgerbraukeller. It was Sigismund Payne Best, who had never met Elser in his life, though he was to learn his story at Sachsenhausen.

Instead of gaining his freedom, as he had been promised, Elser was locked away in a large attic at Gestapo headquarters, with a workbench, a set of tools and a supply of wood to keep him happy. To pass the time, he had made himself a zither. After about ten months, he was transferred to a large cell in Sachsenhausen, where he remained until 1945, making furniture for the guards and visiting their brothel twice a week. He was kept alive by Walter Schellenberg, who planned to use his evidence in a show trial once the war was won. Best and Stevens, and through them the British Government, would be accused of the assassination plot, and Elser, the man who had planted the bomb, would give evidence against them. With the war lost, however, Elser became an embarrassment. On 9th April 1945, one month before the German surrender, Schellenberg sent orders to shoot him. Best and Stevens were allowed to survive, as useful examples to any war-crimes trial of Schellenberg's clemency.

During his captivity, Best discovered that the original plan for the explosion in the beer cellar had come from Nazi Propaganda Minister Josef Goebbels. Goebbels had felt in the autumn of 1939 that the German people were markedly unenthusiastic about the war. The Third Reich did not seem to be under any great threat from its enemies. Poland had been crushed, Russia pacified by the non-aggression pact with Stalin, and the rulers of Britain and France were still dithering and looking for ways of making peace rather than war. What was needed was something dramatic to convince the people that Germany was in danger. An assassination attempt on the beloved Führer was just the thing to create a mood of national solidarity, particularly if it could be linked to an event of such emotional significance as the annual rally in the Munich beer cellar.

Goebbels naturally turned to Himmler and his SS to carry out the plan. A bomb was to be concealed in the cellar, timed to go off as soon as possible after Hitler had left. It did not matter how many of the party faithful were killed – the more deaths, the bigger the outrage. Could Himmler arrange this, and lay the blame at the door of the notorious British Secret Service? Himmler could do even better: he could produce the "organisers" of the affair, two of the leading British agents in Europe. They were, he knew, being worked on by his SD subordinates, Heydrich and Schellenberg, who were playing some sort of game with them. The specific objects of the game were not clear to Himmler, though Schellenberg had some hopes of being able to penetrate to the very heart of British Intelligence by being invited to London for "peace talks" with senior officials. Whatever the plans, Himmler felt they were less important than the valuable propaganda success which would be gained by capturing the British agents and charging them with the assassination attempt. So it was that in the middle of one dark November night Schellenberg was awakened by the telephone, to find Reichsführer Himmler himself on the line, giving him his orders. He was to forget his plans for the deep penetration of British Intelligence, and bring in Best and Stevens – but not until 9th November, the day after the Munich rally.

Whatever his reservations, and however disappointed he must have been to abandon an operation which was looking so promising, Schellenberg had no option but to carry out his orders.

227

In 1945, at the end of the war, there was a considerable flutter in Broadway Buildings when they received the news that Sigismund Payne Best had surfaced in Naples. Although sick and frail, and after an extraordinary journey across Europe he was still – amazingly – alive. Menzies and Dansey had believed he was dead. Indeed, he ought to have been. He was sixty when he was captured at Blerik, and looked like a walking skeleton when he was released. Neither Dansey nor Menzies was pleased to see him: he was the death's head at the feast. They immediately packed him off on indefinite leave.

"Claude was obviously very badly scared when I first saw him," Best wrote in a letter to Colonel Drake a few months after Dansey's death, "and made a half-hearted suggestion that I might like to write an account of the events which led to my capture to be placed on record. When I answered that I saw no reason for raking up past history nor for washing our dirty linen in public, he seemed relieved and since then our relations were always most cordial."*

And why should they not have been? It must have been clear to Dansey from that first meeting that Best had no idea that he had been sacrificed. Or perhaps he did suspect something. In any case, Best was not a man to be ungrateful. After all, Dansey had been responsible for getting Best's Dutch wife out of Holland before the German invasion of 1940, and he had seen to it that she was looked after in England all through the war.

According to Lady Dansey, her husband once confessed to her that he felt badly about poor Best. And so he should have done. He had used Best and Stevens as if they were pawns in some complex game. And pawns, as any chess player knows, are expendable.

"I am sure that [Claude] wished me well," wrote Best, "though perhaps he still more wished me well away."

By late 1947 Dansey was dead and Best was at last recovering his shattered health. Best's business in Holland had been taken over by the Germans, his house at The Hague had been destroyed, and he was at that time living in Devon in reduced circumstances. He therefore approached Stewart Menzies for some form of compensation for his loss of capital and loss of livelihood. The figure he suggested was in the region of £15,000. At first he got nowhere. However, knowing Menzies of old, he invoked the assistance of Colonel Reggie Drake, the intelligence officer who had been one

---

* Best was not being completely straightforward with Reggie Drake. He had in fact written a secret report about his capture and captivity for Menzies, and subsequently he gave a radio broadcast and published a book about his experiences.

of Menzies's superiors in world war one, and who was then living in Bournemouth. Between them they concocted a letter skilfully designed to scare Menzies into coughing up some cash. Not to put too fine a point on it, they were proposing to blackmail the man – though they kept assuring each other that they were not.

A meeting was arranged. Best and Menzies met at the latter's club, White's, in St James's Street, at 4 p.m. on 24th September 1947. They had tea together in a corner of the billiard room, where they discussed the question of compensation.

"I always relied on Claude's promise that I should be well looked after," declared Best, who wrote a verbatim account immediately after the meeting. ". . . I refuse to accept any responsibility for the [Venlo] business – I simply obeyed orders after I had repeatedly warned Claude and your office that the people with whom I had been put in touch were phony."

Menzies attempted to wriggle out of any commitment, but when it became clear that Best was prepared to make trouble, his attitude gradually changed. His first offer of £1,000 was turned down, and a figure of £2,000 was mentioned. This grew into £3,000 and eventually £4,000 which, as Drake pointed out in a subsequent letter, was about all the money Menzies could lay his hands on within the department, without going to the government for more. It is not clear if this was the final figure. In some tapes he recorded at the end of his life Best mentions a figure of £6,000, but this may have included money from the compensation paid by the German Government to non-Jewish concentration camp survivors.

It is perhaps appropriate that the Venlo Incident should end over a cup of tea in White's – not with a bang, but in a whimpering altercation about money.

CHAPTER TWENTY-TWO

Eminence Grise

Immediately Stewart Menzies's appointment as C was confirmed on 28th November 1939, he asked Claude Dansey to return to London as assistant chief. It was an astute move; Menzies knew he was too weak to run the SIS on his own. Dansey naturally accepted. He would be conveniently placed at his protégé's shoulder, gaining effective control of the Intelligence Service as a whole during its most crucial period of rapid expansion.

Officially, Dansey was to be in charge of two crucial areas, the G sections and the circulating sections, which meant that he would be in command of intelligence gathering and assessment throughout the world, apart from Ultra, which was the personal responsibility of Menzies as C. It was a formidable enough task in itself, without the added burden of supporting Menzies and organising and reorganising the entire service. Time was, as usual, not on his side, but also as usual, he approached the challenge with calm confidence.

Before taking on his new role, Dansey had to return to Switzerland for a hectic two weeks of tying up all the loose ends of the Z Organisation. That he would no longer be in Zurich but would himself be running the operational side of the official SIS changed everything. In any case, the Venlo disaster had made his original plan for a completely separate organisation impossible to sustain. He decided, therefore, that the main body of Z should now be incorporated into the official service as its Swiss section, absorbing the existing office in Geneva, answerable only to himself. From Switzerland it would run most of the lines and agents which he had set up in Europe, and especially those into Germany. Some individual agents, however, would remain his personal concern, known to no one else in the SIS.

With his new status, Dansey was able to bring much greater influence to bear on the British diplomats in Berne, ensuring that

230

his people would be guaranteed autonomy, freedom from any interference, and support when necessary.

He was also able to achieve a similar arrangement with the Swiss authorities, through his good friend Colonel Roger Masson, head of Swiss Intelligence.

At the beginning of December 1939, with everything taken care of, Dansey said farewell to his little private army in Zurich, and returned to London for good. The staff were genuinely sad to see him go, despite his authoritarian rule in the office and at the dinner table. The legendary Dansey charm seems to have worked its wonders, for both King and Shuckburgh recall that when they gathered at the railway station to see him off, several of them – and not only the women – were in tears.

Dansey left Rex Pearson in charge. It was a natural move, for Pearson had long experience and Zurich had been his patch for several years. However, it soon became painfully apparent that he was not up to the job. Those who were there recall that he made a total botch of it, creating chaos and confusion. On one occasion he even sent Andrew King and Joanna Shuckburgh separately to meet the same contact at the same rendezvous – a display of inefficiency and a breach of security which would have had Dansey breathing fire and brimstone had he been there. But word got back to London, and at the beginning of February 1940, Claude sent Frederick "Fanny" Vanden Heuvel to take command.

Vanden Heuvel, another old intelligence hand from the first world war, had been with the Z Organisation since its inception. But unlike Pearson he was still only fifty-five and in full command of his faculties. Tall, slim, elegant and immensely courteous, Vanden Heuvel looked every inch the old-style diplomat, always impeccably dressed and with a penchant for wearing lavender spats with his morning suits. The son of a papal count, he had excellent connections with the Catholic Church, but in spite of his Flemish name was British, although with strong Swiss connections. He had been educated privately, in Berne and in England, before taking a science degree at University College, London. He had been a director of several companies and was managing director of Eno's Fruit Salts until it was taken over by a Canadian company, in the early 1930s. He proved to be an excellent chief, and remained in charge of Switzerland for the rest of the war as Dansey's principal lieutenant in Europe. After the war, he stayed in the service until he reached retirement age, following once more in Dansey's footsteps, as head of station in Rome.

Back in London, Dansey settled into a flat at 3 Albemarle Street, immediately across Piccadilly from St James's Street and barely a hundred yards from his club, Boodle's, where according to another member of that time, Ian Fleming, the food was the best in London. He studiously avoided White's club, which lay halfway between his flat and Boodle's. There Menzies held court in its bar, displaying an indiscretion with his cronies which was anathema to Dansey. Among others, Group Captain Frederick Winterbotham, who was then head of Section IV, Air Intelligence, remembers how Menzies, always a terrible judge of character, was forever trying to find jobs in the SIS for totally unsuitable acquaintances from White's, and his subordinates would then have to turn them away with as much tact as possible. Dansey kept well clear, believing firmly in the old adage that a Secret Service should above all else be kept secret.

A further hundred yards or so down St James's street, above Overton's Restaurant and Oyster Bar was another flat, which the service had bought from William Stephenson. Dansey used this flat regularly for meetings over tea and toast in the comfortable chintz-covered armchairs and settees. He never, of course, allowed anybody from outside the service to get anywhere near the office in Broadway.

For the most part, Dansey lived quietly. He generally took breakfast and weekend meals in a modest and unsmart little Italian restaurant. He dined regularly – sometimes as often as two or three times a week – with Alexander Korda, first at his home in St John's Wood until it was bombed and then in Korda's suite at Claridge's Hotel. For lunch his favourite haunt was the Savoy, where the *maître d'hôtel* was an Italian called Manetta, who looked after Dansey and his guests assiduously, providing them with such wartime rarities as fillet steak and ripe Stilton cheese, in the belief that Dansey had the power to protect or condemn his Italian friends and relatives interned on the Isle of Man when Italy entered the war. Dansey did nothing to disabuse Manetta of this belief.

If Manetta did not know exactly who Dansey was, he had no doubts as to his importance, and in wartime London one did not ask questions. The aura of danger and power which surrounded Dansey always assured him of excellent service wherever he was – the slightest snap of his fingers was enough to bring waiters scurrying to his side. "The response to his signal," said Jimmy Langley, remembering his first encounter with Dansey at the Savoy, "was as swift as a guardsman responding to a shout from the regimental sergeant-major!"

SIS headquarters was at Broadway Buildings, 54 Broadway,

opposite St James's Park Underground station, a little over half a mile from Albemarle Street and in good weather a pleasant stroll for Dansey across the Mall and the park. The brass plate on the wall outside proclaimed it as the headquarters of the Minimax Fire Extinguisher Company. Later, it was also labelled "Government Communications Department". Today, the building houses the legal and public health departments of the Thames Water Authority, and the visible security arrangements'are much more impressive than they were in SIS days. Then, the innocuous-looking lobby was manned by two ordinary-seeming commissionaires at the reception desk, and passers-by often sheltered from the rain – as long as they did not try to penetrate any further into the building, they were generally left undisturbed. In the best Secret Service tradition, there were two other concealed entrances to the upper floors where Menzies and his senior officers resided. One was a private staircase leading to and from C's own room, so that he could come and go if he chose without being seen.

This staircase led to a corridor which ran from the rear of the building to connect up with an attractive period house, built in 1704, number 21 Queen Anne's Gate, which provided comfortable living accommodation for C in town. Since this was in the next street, Menzies and his senior officers could enter and leave the main building without even going near Broadway.

As the service expanded, it overflowed into other buildings nearby, including the St Ermin's Hotel just around the corner from Broadway Buildings. The indicators in the hotel lifts showed only four floors. New recruits, recalled Noel Coward who was one of them, were surprised when they were whisked past the supposed limit, up to the fifth and sixth floors, which had been commandeered by the SIS for the duration.

For the most part, the interior of 54 Broadway was a dusty warren of dingy corridors and offices, divided by plywood and frosted-glass partitions. The most senior officers, however, fared rather better. C's room was a thickly carpeted and elegantly furnished office on the fourth floor, where he presided from behind a huge antique desk brought from the old Admiralty by the first incumbent, Mansfield Cumming. A blue light shone outside the door in the corridor, and two secretaries occupied the ante-room to the inner sanctum itself. Dansey moved into a nearby room and made himself comfortable, but he was not often to be found there. He also used other offices in the building and in other SIS premises in London, and even more often conducted his business from the flat at 5 St James's Street or from one of several other flats kept as safe houses and meeting places. Vansittart's stepson, Cecil Barclay, who joined the service in 1939, recalls that Dansey always seemed to be leaving Broadway for secret meetings elsewhere, conspiratorially wrapped in a long dark overcoat.

Dansey was, however, invariably in the office in the early evening, at 6 p.m., when he spent an hour or more closeted with Menzies, going through the events of the day and guiding the chief in any decisions that needed to be taken. Menzies was not good at taking firm decisions. According to several senior officers from those days he would never give a straight answer if he could possibly avoid it, but would sit behind the great desk, fiddling with his pen – filled with the green ink he used to scrawl illegible notes on his vivid blue stationery – and procrastinate. His usual response was, "Leave it with me," and he would then do nothing until reminded, when he would say, "Oh, well, I suppose you'd better do it, then, but see to it all yourself. Don't involve me." "Menzies was a great buck passer," recalls Frederick Winterbotham, who regarded him as untrustworthy, never standing by his people as a good chief should. Winterbotham did not have a very high opinion of Dansey, either. He considered him old-fashioned and stuck in his habits, particularly in the way he clung to his faith in the agent in the field. To Winterbotham, the advent of aerial photography and the reading of the enemy's signals through Ultra made the secret agent obsolete. To Dansey, mechanical methods of obtaining information were valuable aids but could never replace the human element completely.

With two such strong personalities as Winterbotham and Dansey differing so radically in their approaches to intelligence gathering, it is hardly surprising that there was little love lost. Fortunately, as the war progressed, Winterbotham found himself fully occupied with the vital task of running the distribution of Ultra intelligence and so had few dealings with Dansey, leaving such contact as was necessary to his deputy, John Perkins.

In the early days of Dansey's time back in London, however, Winterbotham particularly resented his habit of monopolising Menzies every evening. When Sinclair was still the chief, Winterbotham had been in the habit of dropping in each evening for half an hour or so to discuss the day's happenings. With Menzies so completely dominated by Dansey, he was now denied the opportunity.

One man who was even more put out by the situation was Lieutenant-Colonel Valentine Vivian. Vivian, known as Vee-Vee, was now actually deputy chief and therefore technically senior to Dansey, though his areas of responsibility were nothing like as great. He was in charge of security and counter-espionage overseas, where MI5's writ did not run. He was thin and elegant, wore a monocle and "carefully dressed crinkles in his hair", had wet eyes and cringed before Dansey's frequent put-downs. The son of a well-known Victorian portrait painter, Comley Vivian, he had served in the Indian Police before joining SIS in 1925, and is chiefly remembered now as the man who brought Kim Philby into the service.

Dansey regarded Vivian with utter contempt and generally refused even to speak to him, making him the target of a continuous stream of barbed memos and the principal butt of his sardonic wit. He referred to Vivian's staff as "a lot of old women in red flannel knickers", and when the question of colour codes to represent the various sections in the filing system was being considered wrote in the margin against Vivian's counter-espionage section: "I suggest yellow would be a suitable colour for this section."

Vivian was eventually shunted sideways with the meaningless title of Chief Security Adviser, while Dansey was given the new designation of Vice-Chief of the Secret Service. Vivian, demoralised and defeated but still clinging to a vestige of pride, always arranged his leave periods to coincide with Menzies's absences, in order to avoid having to take direct orders from Dansey.

The feud between Dansey and Vivian has been described by many former SIS officers, most graphically by Kim Philby in his book, *My Silent War*. Philby's book is very much a personal account, of course, and his views are highly coloured by his own part in the proceedings and by his ambitions at the time. Sir Maurice Oldfield, a later C, has described the book as "largely true as far as it goes, but cleverly peppered with disinformation and mischief". Certainly, the element of mischief can be seen in Philby's references to other involvements with Dansey, which we will come to later, but it was probably a lack of understanding and knowledge which led him to declare that Dansey regarded counter-espionage as a waste of effort in wartime.

In truth, Dansey was always extremely conscious of the value of counter-espionage, having himself worked in that area during the first world war and earlier. But it was an important part of the image he presented to the world that he should display his personal dislikes – which were indeed many and various – as powerfully as possible. To have admitted the usefulness of Vivian's section and its work would have weakened his attack against the man, therefore everything he was responsible for had to be denigrated.

It was an approach which created many false impressions during Dansey's life, often quite deliberately. It made him many enemies, too, but to Dansey all that mattered was whether or not he obtained his long-term objectives. Usually, he did. If he wished to disarm or unmake an enemy, all he needed to do was turn on the celebrated charm. His victims were usually so pleased to think they had won him round that they capitulated completely.

Even Philby succumbed. He confessed himself surprised by the courtesy Dansey showed him, particularly in view of Dansey's reputation for "unnecessary combativeness", and his loudly expressed disdain for counter-espionage and all involved in it. Philby did not, however, seem to appreciate the large element of theatrical performance in Dansey's nature, even when he had penetrated behind the public mask.

"Dansey was a man who preferred to scatter his venom at long range, by telephone or on paper," he wrote. "The only way to deal with him was to beard him in his office; a personal confrontation lowered the temperature and made it possible to talk common sense. As soon as I grasped this I had little difficulty with him."

Although Dansey was resented by some of the older hands at Broadway, many of whom suffered under the lash of his withering scorn, he quickly won the respect and admiration of most of the younger men and women who were entering the service. The university intellectuals never found him to their taste and often cordially detested him – a feeling which in some cases was heartily reciprocated. But many other young men and women formed an entirely different impression, which resulted in a name which was to stick to him for the rest of his days. They dubbed him, affectionately, "Uncle Claude".

One of them, Philip Johns, whom Dansey sent in 1941 to be head of station in Lisbon, wrote:

At first approach he could be quite frightening to a junior officer, but he would suddenly relax and his smile would flash out in reassurance. Apart from all his other qualifications he had the uncontested ability of putting his finger immediately on any weak points of a scheme or project submitted to him for assessment. More than once I would go away with my tail between my legs and with a determination to put forward a cast-iron proposal for the next time.

There was a love/hate feeling for him within the organisation, but he was unquestionably a pillar of strength. Provided one could tolerate his pungent wit and criticism, often deliberately assumed to provoke a subordinate, he could be a most likeable character and a good and helpful friend. One of his pearls of

236

wisdom: "In this Service, always be 100 per cent sure, and if possible 150 per cent, before you trust *anybody*."

The first four or five months of Dansey's time back in London were spent against the background of the phoney war. Hitler was still occupied with events in the East, completing the subjugation of Poland and only gradually bringing his forces back in preparation for the war in the West. It was a strange, uneasy period, when there still seemed to some people the chance that peace might yet be achieved. Chamberlain remained Prime Minister, wringing his hands and keeping Churchill waiting in the wings.

The SIS continued recruiting, gearing itself up for the coming conflict. It concentrated its main effort on obtaining accurate information on German intentions, and in this it was partly successful. The politicians and generals, however, failed to believe the warnings and when the Germans struck through the Low Countries on 10th May, going round the fortified Maginot Line instead of battering themselves against it, there was dismay and confusion. Worse was to follow. While Dansey's agents had accurately foretold German plans, they had failed to report on something equally vital. Sir Maurice Oldfield, a post-war C, regarded it as Britain's major intelligence failure of the second world war: not knowing that France did not have the political will to resist the Germans.

The collapse of France and the need to evacuate the British Expeditionary Force from Dunkirk in June 1940 was a military disaster. It was also a disaster for the Intelligence Service. They had not been prepared for a war in which France, Belgium, Holland, Luxembourg and Denmark – the entire mainland of Western Europe with the exception of Switzerland and the Iberian Peninsula – would become occupied territory within the space of a few weeks.

With the main thrust of their effort directed at obtaining information from Germany itself, the SIS had failed to set up networks to obtain information in what had been Allied or neutral countries. There were some agents on the ground, part of the lines out of Germany, and plenty of people willing to help, if they could be located and organised. But a desperate shortage of radio sets in 1939 and 1940 meant they had no means of communicating with London, and the SIS had therefore based its plans on the use of couriers for the passing of information. Now, suddenly, those lines had been cut. Dansey and his colleagues would have to start again in occupied Europe, virtually from scratch.

CHAPTER TWENTY-THREE

An Island in a Sea of Troubles

Although he had agents and stations in every continent except Antarctica, Dansey's most important station – particularly in the early part of the war – remained Switzerland. It was, after all, the only neutral state which bordered on to Germany itself, as well as having land frontiers with Austria, Italy and France. Fortunately, Dansey's preparations had been thorough, and with Vanden Heuvel safely installed at its head, the intelligence apparatus developed from the Z Organisation was able to function extremely well.

Initially, Vanden Heuvel continued to work out of Zurich, from offices near the central railway station at 16 Bahnhofstrasse. As cover for his activities he was appointed vice-consul in Zurich on 5th March 1940, and raised to the rank of consul on 31st May. He soon found it safer and more convenient, however, to leave Zurich in the capable hands of Eric Grant Cable, and move the main base of the operation to Geneva, in French-speaking Switzerland. There was too much pro-Nazi feeling in the German-speaking cantons at that stage of the war. Based beside Lake Leman at 41 Quai Wilson, Vanden Heuvel became consul there, too, until the beginning of 1941, when he passed on the title to another Z man, Victor Farrell, while he assumed the unlikely role of assistant press attaché in Berne.

When Germany put an end to the phoney war and began its attack on the West, there was a brief period of confusion. It seemed probable for a time that Hitler would even invade Switzerland, tossing aside its neutrality with the same contempt he had shown Holland and Belgium. Dansey sent an order for his people to prepare to leave in order to avoid capture and internment. Shortly afterwards, reassured by new information from Germany, he told them to stay put. The immediate threat to Switzerland had passed. But some members of the team had already left, notably

238

Richard Arnold-Baker and two redoubtable women, Ena Moles-worth and Marguerita "Rita" Winsor, who made their way from Switzerland to Bordeaux on bicycles. Rita Winsor had previously held an important position in Passport Control in Berlin. Knowing all about the SIS's connections in Germany, she was a sad loss to the Swiss operation, but Dansey was quick to welcome her safely back to London, and to reassign her first as head of the secretariat and then as a fully-fledged officer of SIS in her own right in Lisbon, where she became invaluable to the new head of station, Commander Philip Johns.

Johns describes her as being dark, quite tall, with an attractive personality and "an exceedingly genuine sense of the ridiculous". And continues: "I could have imagined her in fancy dress as a sort of gipsy queen. She was particularly suited to the job, quick thinking and with just that devious approach to problems so important in our operations." When the anti-Nazi officers behind the 1944 plot to kill Hitler sent Otto John to Lisbon to sound out the Allies about peace terms, it was Rita Winsor who dealt with him, driving him in a closed car through the darkened night-time streets while listening to his proposals, which were then relayed via Dansey to the British Government. After the war she left the service and with Ena Molesworth set up the highly-successful International Travel Service in London's Haymarket.

Back in Switzerland, Vanden Heuvel and his people found themselves marooned for the duration. The only way out for couriers, escapers or anyone else was the hazardous land route through southern France to Spain, using all the cloak-and-dagger paraphernalia of disguises, false names and forged papers. Radio sets were still in short supply, and in any case the Swiss, ever fearful for their precious neutrality, did not welcome the transmission of secret information which might be intercepted by the Germans and used as an excuse for invasion. Because of this, the British Legation had to be extremely careful to distance itself from any espionage activities. The SIS therefore had only one available radio transmitter, located in Victor Farrell's office in Geneva. This was used for urgent communications; anything less vital was sent as telegrams through the Swiss Post Office over the normal telegraph lines, enciphered by the one-time pad method, the safest of all systems since it involves a completely random and unique arrangement of letters on a pad, the only duplicate of which is held by the person receiving the message. Each pad can be used once only, and is then destroyed, hence the name.

After the fall of France, lines were soon operating into Switzerland from agents left behind by the British and from French patriots involved in the early stages of resistance. Before the war, Kenneth Cohen for the Z Organisation and Commander Wilfred Dunderdale for the official SIS had busied themselves establishing connections with French Intelligence and with useful individuals and organisations. In the chaos of summer 1940, many of these contacts turned to Switzerland as the best route for re-establishing communications with the British. Soon, there was a steady flow of information from France into Geneva, Berne and Basle.

Berne and Basle, however, had other connections which were even more vital. Supported by the Zurich sub-station, they were responsible for running the lines into and out of Germany itself.

The world has been encouraged by official historians to believe that during the second world war Britain had no spies, no agents, within the Third Reich itself. Those anti-Nazi Germans who were brave enough to make contact with the Allies either to warn them of impending events or to try to establish peace initiatives in return for support in overthrowing Hitler have been acknowledged and praised. But they were not agents actively working for British Intelligence on a regular basis. These anti-Nazi resisters, who constantly risked their lives, are never spoken of. Dansey did have agents in Germany, sending vital information out through Switzerland, but he and his successors chose to protect them in the best possible way: by denying they ever existed. It is best left that way, for the sake of themselves and their families.

Perhaps the most bizarre of Dansey's informants was none other than Admiral Wilhelm Canaris, chief of the German Abwehr and therefore Dansey's principal opponent. There has been speculation for many years that Canaris was a British agent and this speculation has led to a number of extremely far-fetched stories. As a dedicated anti-Nazi Canaris eventually paid the ultimate penalty for his views. But he was never a traitor, and cannot be said to have worked for the enemy. There can be no truth, for example, in claims that he personally informed Britain of the plans and order of battle for Barbarossa, the German invasion of Russia. He would have known that Britain would pass on the information immediately to the Russians, and this would cost the lives of thousands of German soldiers. (Britain did know about Barbarossa, and did try to inform Stalin, but this is a different story, which we shall come to shortly.)

What Canaris did do was to pass on political information which he felt might possibly be used to help overthrow Hitler, and which might also temper Britain's attitude to the German people as a whole. As a go-between, Canaris used a Polish woman, Halina Szymanska, wife of the former Polish military attaché in Berlin. Her husband had been arrested, and was imprisoned in Russia, but Canaris, who had known the couple in Berlin, arranged for Madame Szymanska and her three children to leave the ruins of Poznan and travel across Germany to Switzerland, where she made contact with Vanden Heuvel.

Dansey checked out Madame Szymanska with the Polish authorities in London, and found she was genuine. On his initiative, she was given a cover job as a typist in the Polish Legation in Berne. Vanden Heuvel was deputed to deal with her personally, to provide her with extra financial help, and to promise her a safe home after the war for herself and her family in England.

For his part, Canaris sent Hans Bernd Gisevius, one of his personal aides in the Abwehr, to be vice-consul in Zurich, to protect and keep an eye on her. Gisevius had worked for Dansey for a short time in 1939, but had been dropped as a suspected double agent soon after Venlo. Later in the war, when the American OSS arrived in Switzerland, he supplied them with much valuable information.

Canaris made at least one clandestine visit to Halina Szymanska in Switzerland, but for the most part she travelled abroad to meet him, in Paris or Italy. Dansey arranged for her to be provided with a French identity card, numbered 596 and apparently issued on 5th June 1940 by the French Government, but in reality forged by his SIS documents department. According to this card, she was Marie Clenat, born in Strasbourg and living in Lyons.

Claude enjoyed his indirect contacts with Canaris. They had been on opposite sides of the fence ever since 1935, when Canaris took up his post, and Dansey became head of the Z Organisation. Dansey had a great respect for Canaris's abilities. "After the war we will have a great deal to talk about," he told the French agent Colonel Rémy. "There are so many things I would like to know." But the meeting was fated never to take place. Implicated in the Generals' Plot of 20th July 1944, Canaris was arrested, tortured, and eventually executed at Flossenburg concentration camp.

One of the most puzzling mysteries in which Dansey and his Swiss organisation were concerned was the flight to England of Rudolf Hess, Deputy Führer of Germany, on the night of 10th May 1941 – the anniversary of the invasion of the Low Countries and therefore of the effective start of the war in the West.

There are two principal unanswered questions in the affair. The first is why Hess should have made the journey at all. He was certainly interested in the idea of securing a separate peace with Britain: he believed Britons and Germans came from the same racial stock, and found it difficult to understand why their two countries should not be able to have the same sort of special relationship as Britain enjoyed with America. But why did he choose that particular time?

Hess discussed his ideas many times with his friend and intellectual mentor, Professor-General Karl Haushofer, the apostle of geopolitics, a great proponent of the notion of brotherhood between the two countries, and with Haushofer's son, Albrecht. At Albrecht's suggestion he wrote a long letter to the Duke of Hamilton, who he believed would be sympathetic and who had access to Churchill and even to the King, suggesting a meeting in neutral Lisbon. He also sent Albrecht to Geneva to meet Dr Carl Burckhardt, President of the Swiss Red Cross, asking him to act as an intermediary in arranging a meeting between Hess and Sir Samuel Hoare, the British Ambassador in Madrid.

With arrangements being made for meetings on neutral grounds, it seems extremely odd that Hess should suddenly decide to fly himself to Scotland and there make his first parachute jump although there was a perfectly good landing strip near the Duke of Hamilton's house. Did Dansey have a hand in this? Lisbon and Geneva were both very much Dansey territory – indeed, it would have been difficult for anyone in any branch of British Intelligence to have made a move in either place without Dansey's express permission. Sir Samuel Hoare was himself a former member of the Secret Service and was in regular communication with London. By coincidence, Burckhardt, the Swiss intermediary, had just returned from a visit to London when he was approached. What is more, Hess's letter to the Duke of Hamilton had been intercepted and opened. So Dansey must have known all about Hess's plans and hopes. Did he do anything to lure Hess to Britain? Could it have been Dansey's way of levelling the score after Venlo?

A further, intriguing, complication to the affair is that Hess had his own intelligence organisation which he set up in competition with the Abwehr and the SD, and according to a later C, Sir Maurice Oldfield, its head was in reality an agent of the Russian KGB. Oldfield suggested that this man also had a hand in Hess's flight to Britain, and that this may be one of the reasons why the Russians have proved so intent on keeping Hess in Spandau jail until he dies. Did the Russians believe that if they could stop the war between Germany and Britain, then it might be possible to reach an accommodation among the three powers, with Hitler continuing to honour his non-aggression pact with Stalin? A possibility, but it does not seem very likely. In any event, the supposed KGB agent does not appear to have been one of those who warned the Kremlin about the invasion plans, so there must be some doubt as to whom he was actually working for. He would not have been the first Russian agent to have been turned to work for the Germans – or for the British. And at that point in the war, it was very much in Britain's interests that Germany should attack Russia and thus bring her into the conflict.

The second major area of mystery is whether the man who landed in Scotland and who is now imprisoned in Spandau jail, is actually Rudolf Hess. Hess definitely took off from Augsburg near Munich in a Messerschmitt 110D at 5.45 p.m. on Saturday, 10th May 1941. But there is evidence to suggest that the aircraft which crashed into a Scottish field at 11.09 p.m. that night was not the same machine, and that the man who parachuted to earth, although looking like Rudolf Hess, was wearing a different flying suit and carrying no identification documents. A British surgeon, Hugh Thomas, who examined him in Spandau, states in his book *The Murder of Rudolf Hess* that Prisoner Number Seven could not under any circumstances be Hess, since he does not have the scars, either external or internal, from the severe bullet wounds which Hess received during the first world war, and which Frau Hess has confirmed her husband bore.

Thomas repeats the general belief that Hess – or the man who landed in Scotland – was for some reason never subjected to proper interrogation by the intelligence services. In fact, Dansey had Hess interrogated, for three weeks by Richard Arnold-Baker. What emerged from those three weeks we shall probably never know. It seems most unlikely, either, that we shall ever know Dansey's exact role or purpose in the affair. But involved he certainly was.

Dansey was also involved in another puzzling affair which remained one of the war's greatest intelligence mysteries for many years – a spy network known as the Lucy Ring. Yet it played a significant role in changing the course of the war.

"Lucy" was the code name of a small, asthmatic, bespectacled German refugee called Rudolf Rössler. His code name derived from the fact that he lived and worked in the city of Lucerne, where he ran an anti-Nazi publishing house called Vita Nova. He was a quiet, insignificant little man who rarely moved far from his house or office. Yet he has gone down in history as one of the greatest masterspies of all time. From 1941 until October 1943 he and the Lucy Ring provided the Soviet General Staff with a constant flow of incredibly detailed, accurate and up-to-the-minute intelligence. The Russians fought the Battle of the Kursk, the biggest tank battle in history and arguably the most decisive battle of the second world war on direct information from Lucy. The ring supplied Centre, the Soviet Intelligence headquarters, with everything from technical data about the new German Tiger and Panther tanks to the answers to such questions as, "At precisely what point of the southern section of the Eastern Front is the German offensive to open?"

Whatever the demands made upon it by Centre, Lucy always seemed able to come up with the right answer in a remarkably short time. Then, in October 1943, the flow stopped when the Swiss authorities moved in on the ring and broke it up. But it had done its job: the Battle of Kursk had been won, the tide of war on the Eastern Front had been turned so decisively that Russia's victory was now inevitable, whatever happened elsewhere.

Where had Lucy obtained his wonderful intelligence? Did he really, as was later claimed, have a group of ten highly placed officers in the German High Command who fed him with information, in the belief that only by losing the war could Germany rid itself of Hitler and the Nazi Party? Rössler himself always said he did not know. He also disclaimed being a spy. Of course, no one believed him: everyone knew the incredible results he had achieved. When he died, in October 1958, the world assumed that he had taken his secret with him to the grave – and went on hunting the ten German generals.

But Rössler was telling the truth. He really did not know where the information came from. He did not know anything about a group of German generals. He did not know that, indirectly, the man for whom he had been working during those two and a half hectic years was none other than an ageing lieutenant-colonel in London, Claude Dansey.

The story of how Dansey came to be running the most important Russian spy of the second world war is complicated, but it shows him at his most devious and his most impressive.

Stalin always distrusted the perfidious British, and with good reason. In 1919, British troops as well as contingents of Czechs, Japanese, French, Americans and Poles, had invaded Russia with the aim of defeating bolshevism. They had failed. But the result of their actions was to encourage Russian xenophobia and fuel Joseph Stalin's paranoia. Thereafter, in Stalin's eyes western governments and particularly the British were never to be trusted. When on 12th June 1941, Anthony Eden, the British Foreign

Secretary, and Victor Cavendish-Bentinck, head of the Joint Intelligence Committee, tried for the last time to convince Ivan Maisky, the Soviet Ambassador to London, that a German invasion of his country was imminent, he brushed their warnings aside. Stalin himself was even more obdurate. He refused to believe that the Nazi-Soviet Pact which he had worked so hard to achieve was about to become a dead letter. "Nothing that any of us could do," wrote Churchill, "pierced the purblind prejudice and fixed ideas that Stalin had raised between himself and the terrible truth." Even when the Germans did invade, thus proving the accuracy of British Intelligence, Stalin still remained if anything even more suspicious of Churchill's motives.

The Russians refused to act on any information unless they knew its source to be reliable. Churchill, on the other hand, refused to permit his Intelligence Service chiefs to give the provenance of their information, because they would then be forced to reveal to the Russians that they had broken the German Enigma machine cipher. The Ultra secret had to be protected at all costs. If the Germans realised that the cipher had been broken, they would change their system and the huge advantage the British enjoyed would be lost, perhaps for ever.

Churchill, in common with Dansey, had a very low opinion of Soviet security methods and feared quite rightly that the quickest way to inform the enemy that the British were able to decipher his messages was to tell the Russians. Nonetheless, it was obvious to everyone that the Russians could not be left in ignorance of intelligence vital to their own survival. If Russia fell, then Britain's chances of defeating Germany could be rated as little better than nil.

The problem of passing information to the Russians without their questioning its provenance was handed over to Claude Dansey. He came up with a typically Dansey solution. It was as elegant as it was devious. He proposed to feed the Russians with disguised Enigma and other intelligence using one of their own spy rings to authenticate the material. And it so happened that Dansey knew of just the right ring – and even had one of his own men on the inside.

In 1936, Dansey had recruited an English adventurer, Alexander Allan Foote, into his Z Organisation. Foote, the son of a failed Yorkshire chicken farmer, was one of the few Z men who came from a working-class background. He was not the product of a university or a good regiment, but a council-school boy who had had to leave at the age of fourteen and go to work in a corn chandler's. He had joined the RAF at the age of thirty, and was an AC1 fitter when he came to the notice of Dansey, who was looking for men with suitable qualifications to infiltrate communist spy rings. Foote was ideal material. He had joined the RAF seeking adventure, but had seen precious little of it, and was eager for a change. Dansey arranged for him to leave the air force, posing as a deserter though he was assured no charges would ever be brought against him. He sent him to Spain to join the International Brigade and fight for the left in the civil war, thereby establishing his bona fides with the Russians.

The plan succeeded brilliantly. At the end of the civil war Allan Foote was inducted into the GRU, Soviet Military Intelligence, and was sent to Switzerland for training, where Soviet spy rings had operated ever since Lenin's day. But they had never been particularly active or important, mostly playing a counter-intelligence role, keeping an eye on the Russian émigrés who had made their homes in the country after the Revolution.

In 1938, the head of the network was a woman calling herself Ursula-Maria Hamburger, an attractive German in her early thirties with, according to Foote, "a good figure and even better legs". She worked under the code name "Sonia", but her real name was Ruth Kuczynski and her father was a well-known German Jewish economist who had taken refuge from Hitler in Oxford.

It was Sonia's job to train Foote in the use of codes, wireless, and the general business of espionage. He was an apt pupil, and proved so successful as a Soviet spy in Germany and Switzerland that by the fall of France he had worked himself up to the position of second-in-command of the network and had become Sonia's principal radio operator. When she was subsequently posted to England, Foote had every reason to believe that he would take over as head of the network, to the delight of Dansey. But their hopes were dashed when he discovered, to his alarm, that a Hungarian who was running another Russian ring in Switzerland was to be Moscow's choice as a resident director, with Foote remaining second-in-command.

Foote's new chief was Sándor Radó, a distinguished geographer and mapmaker who had written the first guidebook to the Soviet Union – a name he claimed to have coined as an acceptable shorthand for the full title, Union of Soviet Socialist Republics. A dedicated communist since his teens, Radó had offered his services as a spy on a visit to Moscow in October 1933. He was initially sent to work in Brussels, but the Belgian authorities, suspicious of his motives, refused him permission to set up a business there. On

Moscow's instructions, therefore, he moved with his wife and family to Switzerland, and having taken on board two Swiss sleeping partners (one of them a well-known supporter of Hitler!) as the law required, he set up an agency in Geneva to supply specialist maps to the European press. Under this effective cover he organised a small spy network, operating under the code names "Dora" to Moscow, and "Albert" to his own agents.

Although Foote was not to be in charge of the combined network, the merging of the two groups was a useful bonus to Dansey, since it widened the scope of the operation and gave him additional control and information. An even bigger bonus was the fact that Radó had no radio set, having until then relied on couriers to carry his messages to Russia, or at least to Soviet embassies in Western Europe. As the war developed, however, this method became too unreliable and everything had to be sent by radio – which meant that Foote had control of all the network's communications, and with his assistance they could be monitored by the British.

With Allan Foote in such a vital position, Dansey could be well pleased with the state of this little corner of his empire. But there was even better to come. A third Soviet spy ring operated in Switzerland, in the International Labour Office in Geneva. This was run by a remarkable German woman called Rachel Dübendorfer, who worked under the code name of "Sissy". Sissy, too, was ordered by Moscow to merge her group with Radó's, which she duly did. She was, in fact, an old friend of the Radós, and was herself a well-known communist. Although she had a radio set, she was unable to work it, and so her communications, too, were to be channelled through Allan Foote.

As it happened, Dansey did not need to listen to Foote's transmissions to discover what Sissy was up to, for she was already working for British Intelligence anyway. Her reason was quite simple: she needed the money which Victor Farrell regularly paid her. She had managed to become a Swiss citizen by a marriage of convenience with a Swiss national called Dübendorfer, whom she subsequently divorced. This enabled her to live in Geneva with her lover, an unpleasant character called Paul Böttcher, a former minister in the communist government of Saxony. Neither of them, of course, could return to Germany, but Böttcher was living in Switzerland without a permit, and therefore could not work.

Sissy earned only a pittance as a secretary at the ILO, but even with the little she received from her Soviet masters at Moscow Centre, she could not make enough to keep herself and Böttcher. It seems likely, too, that she had to pay hush money to Dübendorfer and several others. In such circumstances, Dansey's offer of financial help must have seemed a godsend. She could also square her conscience with the thought that Dansey was not asking her to betray her other employers, merely to join him in the fight against the common enemy, fascism. She accepted readily.

Sissy was always regarded as a minor and unimportant member of the Soviet network in Switzerland. The ILO, after all, was something of a backwater. But in fact, she became the most vital link in the chain which became known as the Lucy Ring, for it was she who introduced Rudolf Rössler, Lucy himself, to the network.

Rössler was born in 1897 at the Bavarian town of Augsburg, and educated at the *Realgymnasium* there at the same time as Bertholt Brecht. He served in the army in the first world war, developing a profound horror of German militarism. After the war he worked as a journalist in Munich, then moved to Berlin to become the manager of the *Bühnenvolksbund*, an organisation which combined the roles of theatrical producer, agent, ticket agency and publisher.

In 1933, the year the Nazis came to power, Rössler made friends with a young Swiss law student at Berlin University. Xaver Schnieper, twelve years younger than Rössler, was dazzled by the older man's intellectual brilliance. When the Nazis decided to take over the profitable activities of the *Bühnenvolksbund*, ousting Rössler from his position, Schnieper persuaded him to flee to Switzerland. Rössler and his wife rented a small villa on the outskirts of Lucerne, Schnieper's home town, where his father was a minister in the cantonal government. With the help of the Schniepers he set up a publishing house devoted to anti-fascist literature.

In 1936, Rössler started to publish a magazine called *Die Entscheidung* (*The Decision*), the mouthpiece of a similarly named group of young Swiss Catholic liberal intellectuals with whom he became associated. For this magazine, Rössler began writing political and military evaluations of events inside Germany. The evaluations were brilliant, and attracted considerable attention, revealing the quiet German as a man with remarkable abilities in this field.

Rössler had almost total recall of everything he read, especially military and political information. Mention any unit in the German army and Rössler could rattle off the name of its commanding officer, where it was presently stationed, its duties, and the names of most of its officers. He was a walking card-index. Combined

248

with his analytical ability, this was a gift no intelligence service could afford to ignore. When Xaver Schnieper was called up into the Intelligence Corps when the Swiss army mobilised in 1939, he naturally told his chief about his friend's extraordinary talent. It is hardly surprising that the chief wasted no time in taking Rössler on to his payroll.

Rössler's new employer was a wealthy dealer in photographic and optical equipment called Hans Hausamann. Hausamann, under the system whereby all able-bodied Swiss men of fighting age are part-time members of the army, held the rank of captain and took an active interest in military affairs. His story has an oddly familiar ring to it: like many businessmen who could see what was happening in Europe, he had been appalled at his country's unpreparedness. During the depression, the Swiss had economised on their army with disastrous effects on its efficiency. Nowhere was this more evident than in intelligence. From 1930 to 1935, the Swiss army's intelligence department consisted of just two officers with an annual budget of 30,000 Swiss francs, the equivalent then of about £1,500 or $7,000. This was the subject of some wry humour: if one man was ill and the other away on business, it was pointed out, the telephone remained unanswered and Swiss Military Intelligence was out of action!

Hausamann was determined to do what he could to rectify this state of affairs. He decided to use his money and his business connections to set up an intelligence organisation at his own expense. He called it the Bureau Ha – "Ha" being the German pronunciation of the letter H, which in this instance stood for Hausamann. At first, the Bureau occupied three rooms in his own home in Teufen, in the eastern canton of Appenzall. With a staff of three, including Hausamann's brother-in-law, it was already fifty per cent larger than the official Military Intelligence Department which it supplied with information.

The Bureau Ha was essentially an intelligence gathering organisation, relying mainly on reports from businessmen visiting Germany and the rest of Europe. In 1937, however, Hausamann also established a close-working relationship with Czech Intelligence, then under the command of General Frantisek Moravek, an old friend of Claude Dansey's. As a favour to Moravek, Hausamann took a Czech agent, Karel Sedlacek, into his home, giving him cover and sharing intelligence with him. Sedlacek was also known to Dansey, and was feeding valuable information to the Z Organisation in Switzerland, including reports from an agent who was a senior officer in the German Abwehr. Hausamann was therefore already an established figure in the tangled web of

European intelligence when the Bureau Ha became part of Swiss Military Intelligence in 1939, and employed Rudolf Rössler as an evaluator.

In addition to his evaluation work, Rössler was able to supply some information himself. Friends of his in Germany who shared his anti-fascist views began sending him intelligence on military and political matters, and this he passed on to the Bureau. After a while, however, he became uneasy about the effectiveness of his work. He was growing increasingly concerned by the attitude of the Swiss Government. There was, he perceived, a large pro-Nazi element in the country – an element which was encouraged by the Swiss Federal President, Pilet-Golaz, and his party, many of whom were obvious appeasers, or "adjustors" as they were called. He came to the conclusion that the cause of anti-fascism could only be advanced if something more positive was done. It was not enough just to provide information and prepare evaluations for Hans Hausamann.

The opportunity to do something more positive was not long in presenting itself. It came from an unexpected quarter. With all the work he was doing for the Bureau Ha, Rössler found it difficult to continue running his publishing house virtually single-handed. He therefore advertised for someone to read proofs and do part-time editorial work. The advertisement was answered by a professional translator called Christian Schneider, who worked for the International Labour Office in Geneva. Rössler was delighted to discover that the man seemed to share many of his political views. Before long, he was confiding to Schneider his profound dissatisfaction with his work for the Bureau Ha.

Rössler was particularly incensed by the fact that he had never met Hausamann face to face. "He treats me like a machine," he complained. Following classic espionage procedures, Hausamann preferred to deal with Rössler only through Xaver Schnieper. But more importantly, Rössler felt that much valuable intelligence material was wasted simply because the Swiss refused to pass it on to the Allies, preferring just to sit on it lest they offend the Germans and breach their neutrality.

In fact, Rössler was wrong. Not only was Swiss Military Intelligence secretly sharing material with the British, but Hausamann was also passing on his evaluations direct. Andrew King recalls that Hausamann used to send them huge wads of paper flimsies giving details of German plans. It is clear from the wording of these that they must have been copies of Rössler's evaluations. To King's surprise, Dansey later ordered his people to ignore this material, and not to pass it to him in London. By then, as we shall see,

Dansey had his reasons for looking this particular gift horse in the mouth.

Schneider was sympathetic and helpful. He offered Rössler a solution to his problem. He was, he said, a spy himself, working for a small Soviet ring based in the offices of the ILO. If Rössler ever wanted to pass intelligence to the Russians, he could do it through Schneider, who would see that it was radioed immediately to Moscow. What Schneider did not say, of course, was that his answering of Rössler's newspaper advertisement could hardly have been a coincidence, but must have been done on the instructions of the leader of the spy ring, a lady who worked under the code name of Sissy. Nor did Schneider know that Sissy was being paid by Claude Dansey.

Rössler eagerly accepted Schneider's offer, and began feeding him important information, which Schneider gave to Sissy, who in turn passed it to Radó for transmission by Allan Foote to Moscow. As a *quid pro quo*, Schneider also began giving Rössler information which he could feed into Swiss Intelligence via the Bureau Ha. Everyone seemed to be happy. Rössler's only condition was that Schneider should not reveal his identity to anyone. When Sissy passed the material to Radó, therefore, she could tell him only that it came from an unknown source in Lucerne. Radó, needing a label of some sort for this new source of intelligence, dubbed it "Lucy". The stage was set, and the characters were in position for one of Dansey's most masterly deception acts.

On the morning of 17th June 1941, Sissy went to see Radó. She was very excited. She had information from Lucy that about 100 German infantry divisions were in position a few miles from the Soviet frontier. Radó, like a good communist, followed Stalin's line and refused to believe that Hitler had any intention of invading the Soviet Union. Any reports to this effect were dismissed as attempts by the desperate British to cause trouble between Russia and Germany in order to relieve the pressure on Britain itself.

But not much more than twenty-four hours later, Sissy was back with yet more material from Lucy. This time it gave not only the date and time of the forthcoming German attack – dawn on 22nd June – but also the German order of battle and a list of primary objectives for various army groups. The detail was incredible.

This new development placed Radó in a quandary. Lucy's earlier reports had not found favour in Moscow. They were regarded as unreliable. But this new material was different. It was almost too good to be true: it was as if someone on the German General Staff were feeding the mysterious Lucy direct with up-to-the-minute information. Radó phoned Foote and arranged a hurried meeting to discuss the implications of Lucy's new intelligence. It is perhaps not surprising that Foote backed Lucy, and persuaded the Hungarian to let him encode and transmit the report immediately to Moscow.

Everything in Lucy's report was corroborated by Moscow Centre's other sources of information. But they were powerless to make use of it because Stalin refused to listen. He could not believe that Hitler would double-cross him. However, the accuracy and detail of Lucy's information was appreciated by Centre, particularly after the invasion itself provided total confirmation. Of all the many sources of intelligence around the world, Lucy had been far and away the best. None of the others even began to compare with it. From that point on, the Russians decided to trust this mysterious Swiss supplier.

The second Lucy report had, of course, originated with Claude Dansey. Information from Bletchley Park and other sources was fed by his agents into the Lucy Ring. Because it came via Sissy, who was Radó's sole means of contact with Rössler, Radó accepted it as authentic. Although Stalin refused to believe the information and did not alert his troops to the forthcoming invasion, it had served its long-term purpose: Lucy had been validated as an exceptional and reliable intelligence source. Dansey could now feed whatever information he wished into the network, giving it Lucy's imprimatur whether Rössler had seen it or not, and know that the Soviets would accept it as gospel.

Churchill was paranoid about Ultra: he was terrified that the secret might be accidentally revealed to the enemy. Thanks to Dansey's deviousness, there was little chance of anyone uncovering the truth about Ultra from the operations of the Lucy Ring.

The Lucy Ring was like some vast and complex machine. It was a series of interlocking spy networks, each separate from the others, yet each feeding intelligence into a central cell run by Radó. Not all the material, of course, came from London. The various groups all had their own, perfectly genuine, sources.

Radó and Sissy continued to work their own agents, and Foote, too, ran his own small network, which he had inherited from Sonia. He had agents in Germany as well as in Zurich and Basle, and also had control of the supply of passports and false documents for the entire ring.

The situation was further complicated by the fact that several intelligence services operated in Switzerland. Sometimes they co-operated with each other; frequently they did not. Swiss Intelligence and the Bureau Ha continued their activities both alongside and independently of the British. The Czechs, too, continued running their own agents in occupied Europe.

There was also another independent network in Switzerland, run from Berne by a Swiss journalist called Otto Pünter, whose code name was "Pakbo". Pünter had been involved in espionage since 1926. Through his wife, Marta, an Italian Swiss from the Ticino, he had many family connections in Italy, and when Mussolini came to power he found himself drawn into Italian opposition to fascism. Since he was active during the time Claude Dansey was head of station in Rome, Dansey would have become aware of him then, though they never met.

When the Spanish civil war started, Pünter became press representative for the Republican Government. He saw this as a continuation of his struggle against international fascism, and during the civil war began to organise a network of like-minded friends and agents opposed to the Nazis, whose growing influence amongst German Swiss he deplored. By the time the second world war started, Pünter's network was already widespread, and with the fall of France it grew even bigger. At its height, intelligence was flowing in from well over a hundred agents, including many Vichy French diplomats and Free French sympathisers. At least three of his most important suppliers – Leon Sousse ("Salter"), a Vichy diplomat, Georges Blun ("Long"), a French journalist and one-time agent of the *Deuxième Bureau*, and a member of the Bir Hakeim Resistance group code named "Nègre" – had had dealings with British Intelligence prior to the war, and Sousse was still working for them.

Dansey, of course, was happy to receive intelligence from these various sources, but the Lucy Ring's principal value to him was as a channel to Moscow. Sissy was the easiest and swiftest point of entry for him. She was, we have been told, constantly in and out of Victor Farrell's office in Geneva, with its direct radio link with London. All that was required of her was that she should send the material given her by Farrell to Rössler via Schneider for evaluation, and then pass Rössler's reports to Radó. But in order to maintain the camouflage, Dansey also used the various other routes to Rössler and Radó: Sedlacek, Foote, Pünter, and the official Swiss and British intelligence organisations all played their parts in his master plan.

The Lucy Ring became a kind of giant carousel, where information went around and around until no one, least of all the Soviets, could ever know precisely where it originated. The biggest irony of it all is that Rudolf Rössler, Lucy himself, never was a spy and had no idea of the use made of his name and reputation. He was merely a pawn used by Claude Dansey to convince Moscow Centre that the information he sent them was genuine. Had they ever realised that much of it originated in London, they would have ignored the material, and the Battle of the Kursk Salient, the turning point of the second world war, might have had a different outcome.

CHAPTER TWENTY-FOUR

Friends and Relations

When the Germans overran Western Europe during the summer of 1940, most of Dansey's networks and lines of communication had been severely disrupted, if not actually destroyed. The speed with which Hitler's armies had smashed the Allied forces had taken everybody – even the Germans themselves – by surprise. The intelligence services had suffered like everyone else from the general chaos and confusion: the *blitzkrieg* advance had left them no time to reorganise for the new situation. It was fortunate that the Swiss station was intact and in good order, but from June 1940, Dansey's chief priority was to re-establish his lines into occupied Europe.

At the same time, however, there were important developments taking place in other parts of the secret world. All of them would inevitably affect the work of the SIS. Obtaining accurate and reliable intelligence was more vital than ever to the war effort, and remained the prime objective. But it was no longer the only one. Two other areas in particular had to be developed immediately: first, escape and evasion, and second, sabotage and subversion. This meant the creation of two new organisations, MI9 and the Special Operations Executive, SOE.

Dansey did not welcome either. Sabotage he regarded as crude and noisy; escaping prisoners and shot-down aircrew were nuisances, more trouble than they were worth. "Escapers don't win wars," he proclaimed. "Intelligence does." Both new organisations could be guaranteed to work against the interests of intelligence agents in the field, since they were bound to draw unwelcome attention from the Germans. In addition, their head offices were likely to be staffed by people who had had little or no experience of the extreme secrecy demanded by the SIS. Many of them would undoubtedly be not only amateur but also wild.

Dansey, therefore, had two essential requirements for the new

255

outfits: they should be kept completely apart from the SIS, knowing nothing about it or its operations; and yet, the SIS – meaning specifically Claude Dansey – should know everything about them and if possible should actually control them. From the moment of their inception, he set out to ensure, with varying degrees of success, that MI9 and SOE fulfilled both conditions.

SOE and MI9 both had their origins with the same man, a Royal Engineers lieutenant–colonel, J. C. F. Holland, who had been too ill to take a regimental command when due for one. Instead, he had been given a one-man department in the War Office, labelled GS(R), with instructions to study and report to the General Staff on any military subject which appealed to him. He chose to research irregular warfare, which he had experienced first-hand from both rebelling and controlling sides – first with Lawrence in Arabia and then in Ireland during the Troubles in 1919–20 when he was seriously wounded by the IRA.

This remarkable man had also won the Distinguished Flying Cross during the first world war, when he had flown some of the earliest bombers, dropping grenades and rudimentary bombs on the enemy by hand from an open cockpit. He had an agile and extremely sharp mind, a vivid imagination and a fiery temper. Chain-smoking continuously he argued and explored, and produced a stream of papers. Besides SOE and MI9, he was also responsible for the creation of the Commandos and various other unorthodox outfits, and was a great believer in the future of the helicopter, though in this his advice went unheeded for many years.

As war approached, his department expanded to take in three or four other officers with similar minds, most notably Major (later General) Colin Gubbins, RA. In 1939, GS (R) was renamed MIR and moved from the War Office to the SIS to link up with the Intelligence Service's existing Section D (for Destruction), which had been set up a year earlier under Colonel Lawrence Grand. Section D's brief was "to investigate every possibility of attacking potential enemies by means other than the operations of military forces".

Holland and Grand were as unlike each other as is possible for two Royal Engineers colonels. Holland was serious and intense, "an unsmiling visionary" as his one-time secretary, Joan Bright Astley, described him, though she also said he had a loving and poetic heart. Grand, on the other hand, was a "volatile dreamer". Another officer who worked with him in those days was more forthright: "Grand was mad as a hatter. He'd blow up anything, given half the chance!" Somehow, the two men managed to work alongside each other, and both found themselves under Dansey's sway, to the disgust of Holland, who would have much preferred to stay in the War Office.

The first of Holland's proposed new organisations to come into existence was MI9. Holland had prepared a paper for the Joint Intelligence Committee in October 1939, setting out proposals for a new body to be responsible for the hundreds of thousands of prisoners who might be taken by the enemy during the war, and any evaders who might find themselves trapped behind enemy lines. On 23rd December 1939, only two or three weeks after Dansey returned to London to take up his new position, MI9 was officially created. At Holland's suggestion, Lieutenant-Colonel Norman R. Crockatt, DSO, MC, a former infantry officer with a distinguished first war record, was given command and a single large room from which to operate, Room 424 of the former Metropole Hotel off Trafalgar Square in Northumberland Avenue. Eventually, MI9 outgrew Room 424 and moved to permanent headquarters at Wilton Park, Beaconsfield, but its early days were spent with everyone crowded together in the one room.

The new body incorporated another War Office department which had been set up independently of and with no knowledge of GS(R) or MIR. This was MI1A, a revival of the section with the same name during the first world war, which was commanded by an officer who had served in it then, Captain (later Lieutenant-Colonel) A. R. Rawlinson.

When Rawlinson was belatedly informed that MI1A was to be replaced by an entirely new section, he made himself known to Crockatt, agreeing to serve under his command. Crockatt, who divided MI9 into two halves, one to deal with British and Commonwealth prisoners, escapers and evaders, the other with handling and interrogating enemy prisoners, put Rawlinson in charge of the latter and of the Combined Services Detailed Interrogation Centre. In 1941, this part of the organisation became a separate department, still under Rawlinson and answerable to Crockatt, as MI19. Naturally, it was of great interest to Dansey, since its job was to obtain information from enemy prisoners, and he therefore kept a close eye on its activities.

He also watched over the arrangements for escape and evasion (evasion being the attempts by aircrew or other personnel to avoid being taken prisoner and if possible to make their way home to fight again), suspicious that they might overlap or interfere with the work of his own agents. He was particularly nervous that MI9

257

would be using women in its escape lines. Dansey did not like the idea of employing women in the field. He felt they were more vulnerable than men, and should not be exposed to the risks of capture, torture and possible execution. He was perhaps too much a gentleman of the old school, what we would now call a male chauvinist. More likely, he was influenced by the Cavell experience during the first world war, an attitude recorded by Crockatt when writing his summary of MI9's achievements.

"The oft repeated statements," wrote Crockatt, "that Nurse Edith Cavell, who apparently worked for SIS during the last war, had been discovered through assisting a prisoner of war seemed to dictate the whole attitude of the SIS towards the section [MI9]. They were determined to prevent evaders and escapers from involving them in any way. This attitude may have been correct from their own security aspect, but it was a terrific handicap for those trying to build up an organisation."

If Dansey's attitude in the early months was unhelpful, there was little Crockatt could do. As M. R. D. Foot and J. M. Langley say in their history of MI9, Dansey "could have broken Crockatt, or anyone else in MI9, as easily as he blew his own nose; and Crockatt knew it".

With the fall of France, however, Dansey suddenly seemed to have a change of heart. Thousands of men had been left behind when the BEF was evacuated from Dunkirk, and their numbers were swelled by RAF aircrew shot down over the newly-occupied territory. Those who were not caught by the Germans headed for unoccupied southern France, where the Vichy Government interned them in Marseilles. To everyone's surprise, on 6th August 1940, Dansey suddenly offered to set up an escape line to run from Marseilles into Spain. Crockatt knew that to accept would be to place MI9 into Dansey's hands. He also knew it was an offer he could not refuse, since it was the only immediately practicable solution to the problem of rescuing the interned men. He accepted gratefully and graciously.

Dansey was in fact offering the services of Donald Darling, a young man on his staff whom he had just asked to go to Spain and Portugal to repair the overland courier links with France and northern Europe. Darling was an excellent choice. He was fit, strong and resourceful, spoke good French and Spanish, having lived in both countries, and was familiar with the Pyrenees which anyone making for Spain would have to cross. Dansey told him to set about establishing escape lines into Spain, offering guides a fixed fee which he had negotiated with the Treasury of £40 for each officer and £20 each for other ranks delivered at the British Consulate in Barcelona or elsewhere.

Darling went out to Spain, where he was made distinctly unwelcome not only by the Spanish authorities, who made no secret of their preference for Germany rather than Britain, but also by the British Ambassador, Sir Samuel Hoare (later Lord Templewood). Hoare had been one of the political leaders opposed to both the work and the ideas of Vansittart and Dansey during the thirties, and in spite of having at one time served in intelligence was generally unsympathetic. He was determined to stick rigidly to his brief from Churchill: to keep Spain neutral, avoiding any provocation which might drive Franco further into Hitler's arms. He had just had to endure a scandal when the military attaché had been caught trying to obtain strategic information and had been declared *persona non grata*, and he was taking good care such a thing would not happen again. He had Darling escorted out of Spain by one of his diplomats the day after he arrived.

Barcelona was obviously out of the question, so Darling turned to Lisbon, with considerably more success. He sent Dansey a blistering report on the treatment he had received in Spain, and was gratified a little later when Hoare visited Lisbon and greeted him effusively, promising to do anything he possibly could to help, within the confines of his diplomatic status. The ambassador had clearly received a powerful rocket – Dansey's arm could be impressively long when dealing with anyone who crossed him or any of his people!

Lisbon was very much Dansey territory. He had several agents there, performing different roles, and used it as an important staging post for the Mediterranean, North Africa and the Americas. It was also full of enemy agents.

Darling was happy to settle for Lisbon as a comfortable and practical base. He worked under the cover of vice-consul in charge of repatriation, a genuine position in which he was responsible for looking after civilians who were allowed to leave Vichy France in the early part of the war, and servicemen who were repatriated by the Germans on medical grounds. It had the added value that many of those who came out in this way could give him useful information about conditions in France, Germany and the Low Countries, and some of them even brought messages from Marseilles, where a young Scottish captain in the Seaforth Highlanders, Ian Garrow, had taken charge of escape operations.

As soon as he was safely installed, Darling set about making contact with pre-war friends in Spain and France, to put together the beginnings of an escape organisation. Some of his contacts were vetoed by Dansey. Others he kept to himself. In order to communicate, however, he needed neutral citizens who could travel into and out of France. Here he was fortunate in making friends with the American Jewish Aid Organisation, which was working from Lisbon managing the escape from France of prominent Jews. The Americans were happy to carry messages and money from him to Garrow, and soon things began to move. Darling was also helped by another American, the aptly named Dr Joy, a Unitarian minister engaged in extricating people from occupied Europe.

The first escapers were led across the Pyrenees by smugglers. As the lines became better established, however, Darling was able to rely more and more on his own guides. He soon had a flourishing traffic connecting with the lines which ran down through Holland, Belgium and France. By the time the Americans entered the war in December 1941, he was ready to move on to establish a new base in Gibraltar, leaving his Lisbon post in the capable hands of Dorothy Johns, wife of the SIS head of station there, Philip Johns.

Among the couriers and agents who passed through Darling's hands while he was still in Lisbon, both for the MI9 side of his business and for straight intelligence, were several of Dansey's old friends. One of the most prominent of these was Nubar Gulbenkian, who was known in the service by the code name "Orchid", since he always wore one in his buttonhole, even on the hunting field. Gulbenkian was pleased to carry messages and money into France, to which he had access as a neutral Iranian citizen. His value was very high, since not only was his sister Rita allowed by the Germans to stay in Paris, but his father, Calouste, was at that time Iranian ambassador in Vichy. All three Gulbenkians had been involved with the Z Organisation from its earliest days, providing Dansey with valuable information gleaned from their connections in the worlds of oil, finance, diplomacy and high society, so Nubar's visits to them were particularly worthwhile.

On one of his trips, Nubar was delayed in Lisbon for several weeks. Growing increasingly restless and worried that his personal affairs were being neglected, he asked Darling to signal London asking for his personal secretary to be sent out to him, saying that she was a key person. Dansey himself replied to the request, with a typically dry response: "For what purpose is key person?" Dansey knew his friends only too well!

——

Having assured himself of control over escape and evasion inside Europe, Dansey turned his attention to the London end of the organisation. In the spring of 1941, he interviewed a young captain in the Coldstream Guards who had been repatriated from Marseilles as unfit for further military service. The young man was Jimmy Langley, whose father had worked for Dansey in Switzerland in 1917 and 1918. Langley junior had lost an arm fighting a rearguard action to hold off the Germans while the remnants of the British army were evacuated from Dunkirk the previous June. Because there was no room on the little boats for his stretcher, he had to be left behind, and was captured by the Germans. In spite of his terrible injury, he had managed to escape from hospital in Lille and then to make his way down virtually the entire length of France to Marseilles. There he had made himself useful to Ian Garrow, playing on the sympathy aroused by a young man with only one arm in order to avoid suspicion while carrying money and messages, until the Mixed Medical Commission board of six doctors – two appointed by the Americans to represent the Germans, two by the Swiss to represent the British and two by the Vichy French Government – sent him home.

Typically, Dansey's first meeting with Langley was over lunch in the Savoy Hotel, a meeting which Langley describes in his autobiographical book, *Fight Another Day*. His colonel notified him of the appointment with ominous foreboding.

"You are well aware of the immense power of the Brigade of Guards in all matters concerning the employment of its officers?" he asked. "As a last resort, we can always appeal to the Monarch. However, in your case, we can do nothing and I am further informed that the Monarch would be powerless to intervene. It goes without saying that I personally can do no more than give you the orders I received yesterday by telephone."

The orders were that Langley was to go at 12.30 p.m. to the Savoy, where in the foyer opposite the restaurant he would see a man dressed in a dark suit, wearing a red carnation, and with a folded copy of *The Times* on the table at which he was seated. He was to make himself known to him.

Langley followed his orders, and duly met Dansey, who looked him sharply up and down, grunted his approval, and said, "F. O. L.'s son and wounded. What a bit of luck!" He then proceeded to ask what decorations Langley wanted – the same question, he said, as he had asked his father, F. O. Langley, when he had joined his staff nearly a quarter of a century before. Langley said he did not understand. Dansey looked at him with exasperation.

"Surely I make myself plain?" he barked. "It is always much

easier if you get what you want before you start working, then you don't spend half your time worrying about your possible award. Now, an MC or an OBE? A DSO is more difficult and you're too young for a CBE. However, there are plenty of foreign decorations available. I'm told the Poles have the nicest ribbons – the Order of Stanislaus or some such outlandish name is very sought after. I call it 'Pologna Prostituta' as it is immensely popular with the women. Take your choice, but be quick about it."

Langley replied that he did not want anything.

"Just like your father," Dansey snorted. "Well, don't come complaining to me that you have not been properly looked after!"

Then they enjoyed an excellent lunch, with Dansey apparently preferring to eat in silence, snapping caustic answers to Langley's cautious questions and saying he never talked business in public. At the end of the meal, having obviously made up his mind, he told Langley to report to him next day, relenting grudgingly when the young man said he had had only five days' leave and that in any case the next day was Saturday.

"All right," he conceded, "I suppose Monday will do, but don't forget we are at war. Report at 10 o'clock Monday at this address."

He took a visiting card from his wallet and scribbled the address of SIS headquarters on the back before dismissing him with a curt: "I've got some more work to do." Langley glanced at the name on the card. To his surprise it read: "Captain James Pomfret-Seymour, CBE, DSO, RN, The Naval and Military Club, Piccadilly" – Dansey's choice of alias for the day.

Langley duly reported for duty at Broadway, where he was initiated into the mysteries of the SIS and given a brief lecture by Dansey. Langley's own description of the event is well worth repeating here:

Uncle Claude, as Colonel Dansey was widely called, wasted no time in getting down to business. "Just listen to me and don't ask any damned silly questions," he said. "The likes of you are causing me considerable trouble, which is being made worse by the apparent inability of the RAF to remain airborne over enemy-occupied territory. My job, and that of my agents, is to collect information, not to act as nursemaids to people who seem incapable of doing much to get back on their own." He pressed the bell for his secretary.

"Miss Reade, who controls Hengist?"

The pretty red-headed girl replied, "Captain Caines, sir."

"Right. Ask him to come to my office, please."

Captain Edward Caines was obviously somewhat apprehensive of the reason for this sudden summons.

"Good morning, Teddy. If I read your messages right, Hengist has picked up another pilot. From the way he rakes them in you might think he is a homosexual. Rare, I know, in France but always possible. Is he one, by any chance?"

"He is not a he, sir. He is a she."

Uncle Claude slammed the desk with his fist.

"How many times have I told you not to go recruiting women and above all not without my agreement? A fine fool I'd have looked if I'd recommended him for the DSO and he turned out to be a woman."

"I didn't recruit her, she recruited herself when Horsa was caught."

"That is beside the point. I will not have any of your organisation run by a woman. They are simply not trustworthy. Do you understand?"

"Yes, sir."

"Right. Now, what are you going to do about the pilot?"

"I don't know."

"I thought so. Well, this is Captain Langley who has recently escaped from Lille and knows all about the escape lines in France. His job will be to take over all British service personnel who come into the hands of our people and arrange for them to be sent back here. Tell Hengist to hide the pilot for a couple of weeks, when Langley will take him over."

Teddy Caines withdrew and Uncle Claude turned to me. "You understand now what you have to do?"

"Yes, sir."

"Good. Then let's get one or two further points clear. Theoretically, you will be on loan from MI9, which is commanded by Colonel Crockatt. In practice you will be on my staff and under my orders in MI6. Is this clear?"

"Yes, sir."

"While you will liaise with Colonel Crockatt on routine matters you will not give him any detailed report of your activities without my agreement."

"Yes, sir."

"Now, I suppose we must fit you in here."

Langley was fitted in, and for the next four hectic years worked under the code name IVZ, running a section designated P15. He managed successfully to serve his two masters, representing Dansey in MI9 and MI9 to Dansey. It was not always easy, particularly

263

as he admits that in his early days Dansey reduced him to "a petrified jelly which had great difficulty in even saying the required 'Yes' or 'No' ". However, he gained confidence, aided by the arrival a few months later of Airey Neave, who had escaped from Colditz and was posted to join him and contribute his own practical experience of escape and evasion to the section.

The work of the underground lines and exploits of the brave men and women who sheltered, tended and guided literally thousands of Allied escapers and airmen during the remainder of the war have been widely chronicled. It seems invidious to single out any of them for particular mention without including others, but there are two individuals who deserve at least a brief word for the special parts they played. Both were Belgian, and both were recruited only after grudging approval from Dansey, who remained deeply suspicious of anyone who could not be checked out one hundred per cent.

The first was a doctor, Albert-Marie Guérisse, who had served with a Belgian cavalry regiment before his country was over-run, had then escaped to England and managed to join the crew of a buccaneering Q ship, a French vessel which had been taken over by the British, crew and all, and renamed HMS *Fidelity*. The French captain insisted on keeping his girl friend aboard, despite British naval regulations, and had her commissioned into the Royal Navy along with himself. Guérisse became first officer and was made a lieutenant-commander RN. Disguised as a harmless merchant-man, the heavily-armed *Fidelity* was used for various secret purposes, including transporting agents and equipment into Europe. On one of these missions, Guérisse was rowing a skiff back to the ship after putting two agents ashore when it overturned in a squall. He managed to swim ashore, was caught and arrested by the Vichy French police but posed as an evading French-Canadian airman and was sent to Marseilles, as a prisoner of war. Here, he immediately and enthusiastically set about helping Ian Garrow.

In June 1941, Garrow sent a message to London via Donald Darling, asking for security clearance and permission to enrol a man calling himself Patrick Albert O'Leary. Langley managed to confirm that O'Leary was in fact Guérisse, and that he had served as a first officer on the *Fidelity*. But Dansey alone could grant permission for him to join the organisation. Unfortunately, his real identity could only be confirmed by consulting the Belgian authorities in London, and this Dansey flatly forbade. He had the lowest possible opinion of the security of most of the governments in exile.

"Once the Belgians know we are interested in Guérisse," he

said, "they will guess he is working for us and it is merely a matter of time before the news gets back to Belgium and the Germans."

Knowing Uncle Claude's obsession with security, Langley thought that would be the end of the matter. But he had reckoned without his chief's powers of reasoning. Dansey knew all about the *Fidelity*, of course, and was well aware of the personality of its captain. Serving in the same ship as him was one of the surest security checks imaginable – anyone with the remotest trace of Nazi sympathies would not have survived longer than a few hours in his company. Guérisse had managed several months. What was more, Dansey reasoned, if he had been a German agent, Guérisse already knew more than enough to have gone straight to Berlin, rather than to internment in Marseilles. As far as Dansey was concerned, nobody in the world was perfectly secure other than himself and possibly the King, but he decided Guérisse would do. With the proviso that the man should be given a code name for use in the field and a different one for London, and that no one should ever, under any circumstances, refer to him by his real name, Dansey gave his permission. It was one of his wisest decisions in the entire war.

As Pat O'Leary, Guérisse was a tower of strength to Garrow and when the Scot was arrested and sentenced to ten years in a concentration camp in October 1941, he took over sole command. One of the first things he did as chief was to organise Garrow's escape and despatch him over the mountains and back to safety in London. The line was then officially named PAO, after his ficti-tious initials, but was known as "Pat" by most of those involved. Between then and March 1943, when he was himself caught and sent to Dachau concentration camp, Guérisse was responsible for getting some 600 escapers and evaders to freedom.

Guérisse's capture was the result of a rare piece of bad judge-ment by Dansey. One of the helpers in the line was an Englishman named Harold Cole. He turned out to be an embezzler and confidence-trickster with a long criminal record, wanted by the British civil police on a charge of manslaughter and by the military police for absconding with the funds of a sergeants' mess. Despite growing suspicions about him by Guérisse and others, Dansey at first refused to give permission for him to be eliminated. It proved a costly mistake, for Cole turned traitor and betrayed the line to the Gestapo. By then, Dansey had been persuaded of the man's real character, and had ordered him to be shot on sight. But it was too late. The damage was done, and Cole survived, working for German Intelligence until the end of the war, and even then conning his way into an American army unit posing as a major in intelligence, before finally being killed in a shoot-out with the French police.

Dansey was less squeamish about another traitor, who was known to have betrayed several members of the escape lines to the Gestapo. The man was spotted in Lisbon, in the company of German SD officers. Philip Johns, as head of station, signalled London for instructions. Dansey's reply was immediate and unequivocal: "Kill him repeat kill him." The man vanished without trace.

An incident which occurred when the Germans captured Guérisse's radio operator, Tom Groome, provides a good illustration of Dansey's habit of thinking in several different directions at the same time. The Germans tried to "play back" Groome, forcing him with a revolver in his back to transmit to London. Being a well-trained agent, Groome kept his head and warned London of the situation by omitting his security check. Dansey was informed at once, and the next time Groome came on the air he directed the reply personally. A message was sent to Groome telling him to go to Ventimiglia, just over the border on the Italian Riviera. There he was to get in touch with the chief of police in Genoa, who was hiding several Allied escapers. There were no escapers, of course, but the message achieved several satisfactory results: first, it settled a personal score by causing serious trouble for the Genoese police chief, who had crossed Dansey in some unrecorded way before the war; second, it directed attention towards the opposite end of the Riviera from all the genuine escape routes; third, it tied up enemy security forces in searching for the fictitious escapers; fourth, it caused friction between the German and Italian police forces; and fifth, it encouraged the Germans to continue using Groome's set in a *funkspiel* which Dansey could turn back against them in a triple-cross operation. As a bonus, it also meant that the Germans had to keep Groome alive since the listeners in London would be certain to notice the change in touch if anyone else tried to use his set. It was an object lesson in making the fullest use of a disaster, as Dansey had done so often in the past.

The second major figure in the escape lines who must be mentioned was an attractive twenty-five-year-old Belgian girl called Andrée de Jongh, who was known as "Dedée". She entered the service by the simple expedient of turning up at the British Consulate in Bilbao with one British evader and two escaping Belgian officers whom she had brought all the way from Brussels. She explained that she, her family and friends had been assisting escapers and evaders ever since Dunkirk, and that she had managed to set up a chain of safe houses between Brussels and the western Pyrenees. There were a number of men waiting all along the chain. Could she come back to Bilbao again, bringing more of them? And could the British provide funds, she asked rather apologetically, to cover some of the expenses involved? She wanted nothing more.

Andrée de Jongh was almost the victim of another error of judgement by Dansey. His immediate and understandable reaction when her actions and her requests were reported to him was that she must be a German plant, intended to infiltrate the organisation and send enemy agents into Britain – a perpetual worry. He signalled that she was to be treated with the greatest suspicion. The fact that she was a beautiful young woman who had had the strength and determination in spite of her apparent frailty to travel down the length of France and then across the Pyrenees the hard way merely strengthened his suspicions. When he learned that she claimed to be a schoolmaster's daughter, a commercial artist but with some training as a nurse, and that she had been brought up to revere the memory of Edith Cavell, his fears grew. She sounded, quite simply, too good to be true.

Eventually, however, he was persuaded that she was genuine and valuable, and reluctantly gave his permission. He appointed one of his men in Spain, Michael Cresswell, then operating as an attaché at the embassy, to be her contact and collaborator, responsible for ferrying escapers through Spain and delivering them to Gibraltar for return to Britain. So, Andrée de Jongh and her friends were in business. As they referred to the men they delivered as "parcels", the line was first given the code name "Postman". This was later changed to "Comète", which was to become one of the most famous names of the secret war in Europe.

On sixteen separate two-way crossings of the harsh and forbidding mountains, Dedée herself ferried 118 people to safety, before being captured and sent to Ravensbrück concentration camp. She suffered great hardship and personal tragedies: her sister died in another concentration camp, her father was shot for his part in helping Allied airmen, and many of her closest friends also lost their lives. But Andrée de Jongh never gave in. She emerged at the end of the war to receive the gratitude of those she had helped, the George Medal from the British Government, and Dansey's unhesitating admission that his earlier doubts about her had been completely wrong. She now works in a leper colony in Africa.

For the record, Albert-Marie Guérisse also emerged safely from Dachau, and was awarded the George Cross by the British, to go with the DSO he had already been given in 1942. He returned to the Belgian army and became a major-general, commanding the military medical service.

Many of those who worked in the escape and evasion lines were strong personalities, who could only be controlled with difficulty. In every case, the final decisions regarding their recruitment and use lay with Dansey. Security was always one of his main concerns, not for the sake of the agents themselves, but for the danger to others if they were captured. In the ruthless tradition of the world of espionage, any agent who gets caught is on his or her own. They know the score when they take on the job, and must be prepared to pay the penalty if anything goes wrong. Dansey always felt that any attempt to change the rules in wartime would only be setting a very dangerous precedent, and he resisted any suggestion of trading with the enemy either for exchange or clemency.

It was for this reason that he was always extremely chary of sending back into the field any agent who had had a narrow escape. Those who had once been caught by the Gestapo and had then escaped were automatically suspect, for there was always the lurking possibility that they might have been turned. The double agent is one of the hazards of the secret war. Normally, therefore, he refused permission for such people to be returned to the field, no matter how good they were. In any case, once they had been captured their identities were known, and they were bound to be at risk.

There were a few exceptions to Dansey's rule, depending on individual circumstances. One of the most individual was a redoubtable lady called Mary Lindell, who had lived in France for many years as the Comtesse de Milleville. She had escorted several British officers across the demarcation line to safety before she was caught by the Gestapo and sentenced to nine months in Fresnes prison. On her release, completely undaunted, she crossed into Spain disguised as an elderly governess and finally reached London in July 1942, where she got in touch with Langley and Airey Neave, demanding to be sent back at once to organise an escape line. Langley and Neave were extremely dubious, but found her adamant. They consulted Dansey, who said he would personally inform the lady that he would not sanction her return.

For once, Uncle Claude met his match. Mary Lindell was utterly impervious to his charm and refused even to listen to his orders. When he tried to explain that he was trying to save her life, she retorted that it was not her life he was concerned about but his own reputation. She then went on to inform him in detail of all his shortcomings. Langley was highly amused to see Dansey coming off second best for once, and to a mere female. When the interview was over, Dansey ordered him to spare no effort to get Mary Lindell back to France as soon as it was humanly possible!

To Dansey, MI9 was always a sideshow, something which he supervised, controlled and kept a wary eye on while continuing to conduct the more important business of the SIS. But ultimately, even he had to admit that it was extremely valuable. By the end of the war in Europe it had been responsible, both on its own and later in conjunction with the American MIS-X, for bringing home over 7,000 escapers and evaders from Western Europe alone, not counting those who reached Switzerland or those in the Mediterranean area.

Co-operation between the SIS and MI9 had been both amicable and fruitful. So, too, had the co-operation with the Americans: almost half of those 7,000 – 3,415 of them to be precise – were United States citizens, the largest individual national grouping. World-wide, the grand total of British, Commonwealth and American evaders and escapers was over 35,000, the equivalent of three fighting divisions. No doubt that final statistic was what made it all worthwhile to Dansey. He would never have admitted to deriving any satisfaction from the purely humanitarian aspect of rescuing so many men and women – his final words to Jimmy Langley when the latter departed after D-day to set up a new MI9 section in Europe, were typical of the impression he liked to create: "Your trouble is, Jimmy, that you love your agents." The odd thing is that so many of his agents loved Uncle Claude.

While relations between MI9 and the SIS were mainly amicable, the same cannot be said for Colonel Holland's other brain-child, the Special Operations Executive. From the very beginning Dansey was doubtful about both the wisdom and the value of such an organisation, and he was at all times extremely aware of the dangers it presented to his networks in the field. He recoiled in horror from Churchill's famous exhortation when SOE was officially created on 22nd July 1940: "And now set Europe ablaze!" The last thing he wanted for his intelligence agents was the glaring light of fires. The really successful intelligence operation is the one where the enemy is totally unaware that his secrets have been discovered or even that there is an agent at work in the area. A sabotage operation, on the other hand, cannot usually be regarded as successful unless the enemy is made painfully aware of what has happened. With two such opposing aims it was hardly surprising that there should be friction.

Dansey would have liked to control SOE as he did MI9, keeping it firmly in its place as a sideshoot of the SIS. But Churchill gave overall responsibility not to the Foreign Office but to Hugh Dalton, the Minister of Economic Warfare, and Dalton was too strong a personality and too experienced a politician to be bamboozled or browbeaten. As usual, however, Dansey did not accept defeat easily. If the government in its wisdom had seen fit to place the new body outside the SIS and away from either the Foreign Office or the War Office, where he could have brought some influence to bear, he would have to use other methods.

Initially, it looked as though he had succeeded. The first head of SOE was Sir Frank Nelson, Dansey's Z man from Basle. As Nelson was an old friend, it seemed natural to assume that he would be prepared to co-operate, as indeed he did – to a certain extent. His first recruits for senior positions were given clear instructions that they were to liaise closely with the SIS, and those being posted to neutral countries – such as J. G. Beevor to Lisbon and John McCaffery to Switzerland – were interviewed by Dansey, who advised them to contact the SIS representatives in those countries and not to recruit anybody or make any move without consulting them. The SOE men were quick to realise that this would mean giving the SIS a veto on all their activities, but they also realised the wisdom behind it and did their best to follow his advice. Relations between the two services in those countries remained generally good throughout the war.

While these arrangements were promising, they did depend on the personal goodwill of the people involved, and Dansey knew that this was an insubstantial foundation on which to build. He wanted something more reliable, and soon found it: he proposed that in order to avoid confusion the SOE should use the SIS's own signals, coding and communications organisation. There were, of course, very good practical reasons for this, as Dansey was at pains to point out. But it was a master stroke, all the same. For the next two years, until the volume of traffic became too great, a copy of every signal that was sent or received on behalf of SOE was placed on Dansey's desk. The only exceptions were personal messages to the director – though it is probable that Dansey made sure of seeing these, too. Since hardly anyone in SOE was aware of this, it made a most valuable source of information for Dansey, not only on SOE activities but also on its agents' attitudes and intentions regarding SIS as well as the common enemy.

The early promise of a workable if rather uneasy relationship was not to last. Apart from the basic differences in aims and philosophies, there were other sources of friction. The two organisations were inevitably in competition with each other for facilities and resources which were in desperately short supply. The first and most important of these was people, for they were both trying to recruit in the same areas. Later, there were constant problems over the sharing of aircraft and boats needed to ferry agents and supplies into and out of the occupied countries.

Nelson, unfortunately for Dansey, did not last long. He was forced to retire at the beginning of 1942 because of ill-health, and was succeeded by Sir Charles Hambro, a merchant banker, an old friend of Dansey's, but one who refused to be browbeaten. Hambro, in turn, was succeeded in 1943 by Major-General Colin Gubbins, one of the original members of Holland's MIR, a strong character who was determined to keep SOE out of the hands of SIS at all costs.

As relations became steadily worse, Dansey's attitude and behaviour towards SOE became more and more outrageous. He publicly rechristened it "Stately 'Omes of England", as a sharp comment on the rate at which it was occupying country houses. He lost no opportunity of gloating over any disaster which befell the younger organisation – and there were several during the early stages. When he heard that the French passenger liner *Normandie* had been accidentally destroyed by fire in New York harbour he immediately called up the senior officer on duty at SOE headquarters and congratulated him on their "latest battle honour", urging him to keep up the good work. When he visited the Baker Street offices of SOE, he made a habit of raising his hat to every junior officer he met in the corridors, saying that anyone in SOE who managed to stay a mere lieutenant for more than twenty-four hours deserved "a congratulatory salutation".

Things became so bad – largely due to Dansey – that at the end of 1942 General Sir James Marshall-Cornwall, then the senior general in the British army and former Vice-Chief of the Imperial General Staff, was sent in to try to sort things out. He was told to spend six months in each organisation, discover the facts, and "knock their heads together". It sounded a sensible proposition. In the event, it did not prove to be so easy.

Marshall-Cornwall thoroughly enjoyed his time with SOE, where he got on famously with Gubbins, who was a former Gunner like himself. Having learned all about SOE and its problems, he then arrived in SIS, where in six months with Dansey, he learnt absolutely nothing. Nevertheless, he developed a great affection for Dansey, saying that he "greatly appreciated his sardonic humour, enlivened by his somewhat bitter tongue". He admired Dansey's ability to keep everything in absolutely watertight compartments. "Only Dansey," he says, "knew anything about 'his' agents, who remained very much his own."

The six months became two years, during which time Marshall-Cornwall, despite his high rank, was happy to serve under Dansey, who was still a lieutenant-colonel. (He did, however, remove one of his general's pips to avoid embarrassing Menzies, who by then was a major-general, and cared about such things.) Later when Dansey's health was failing, Marshall-Cornwall stood in as acting vice-chief, but he still never found out everything about Dansey's activities – and he certainly never managed to knock SOE's and SIS's heads together. As for Dansey, he maintained to the end that SOE was filled with undisciplined amateurs who were more dangerous to his agents than they were to the enemy, and were therefore to be avoided and frustrated at every opportunity.

Part Five

The Allies

CHAPTER TWENTY-FIVE

The Exiles

It has been stated repeatedly that in 1940 Britain stood alone
against Hitler and the Axis powers. For all practical purposes that
is quite true. This does, however, ignore the fact that although the
Nazis had overrun and now occupied the whole of Europe apart
from the neutral countries, most of the occupied nations were still
at war with Germany. Only the French signed an armistice with the
conqueror – under the most humiliating terms and conditions.
Thus only France had a genuine national government still in
power. The governments of most of the other nations were in exile
in London. With them were their military high commands – and
their intelligence services. Since they were all guests of the British
Government, the intelligence organisations functioned only with
its express permission. This placed Claude Dansey, as SIS chief
responsible for operations (and of course as the *éminence grise*
behind Menzies) in a uniquely powerful position.

Dansey had the effective power of veto over Allied governments
for any secret operations or activities. They had to rely on Britain
for funds, communications systems and transport by sea or air to
maintain any contact with their homelands – and Dansey had the
authority to deny them these essentials. He found himself, therefore, with power over Secret Services of Belgium, Holland, Norway, Poland, Czechoslovakia and, later, of the Free French. There
was also a further "national" intelligence service, known as "The
Friends", operated by the Jewish agency and involving such figures
as David Ben Gurion, Berl Locker and Moshe Shertock (who later
changed his name to Sharret), which co-operated closely with the
SIS during the war.

The Czechs were the first intelligence service to arrive. Eleven
men under the command of Colonel (later General) Frantisek
Moravec flew into Croydon Airport on 14th March 1939, in a KLM
aircraft arranged by the SIS. Moravec had brought with him about

£32,000 in cash, and during the preceding months of crisis had secretly transferred nearly a million pounds sterling to London banks. His important files and papers had been brought out of Prague by the SIS in British Embassy bags. The rest had been burned, so that when Abwehr chief Admiral Canaris rushed to Moravec's office as German troops marched into Prague on 15th March, all he found were empty cupboards and ashes.

Moravec was an old friend of Dansey, since he had been working with him personally and with British Intelligence in general for several years. The two services enjoyed excellent co-operation, sharing technical research as well as intelligence, and working so closely together at times that they might well have been affiliated to each other. As we have seen, Moravec had been especially active in Switzerland, where his chief agent, Karel Sedlacek, worked with the Z Organisation and the Bureau Ha, and was to become a valuable link with the Lucy Ring.

Through Moravec, Dansey had access to one of the most important individual spies of the second world war, Paul Thümmel, a senior official in the Abwehr, whom Moravec code named "Agent A54". Thümmel provided vital intelligence on a variety of subjects ranging from invasion plans to the first intimations of the developing German V1 and V2 weapons. He worked unceasingly from his first contact in 1937 until he was caught in March 1942.

Moravec himself described the co-operation between his service and the British:

We provided the British with the intelligence received from our agents' network, and they reciprocated. We received from them also technical assistance, from help in setting up our radio centre at Woldingham to such things as preparing courier documents, personal papers and passports. I maintained personal contact with the chiefs of MI5 and MI6, and liaison officers from these departments and the War Office were assigned to us. Later, the British trained our parachutists and special groups for tasks inside enemy territory.

One of the "tasks" was the assassination of SS Obergruppenführer Reinhard Heydrich, Chief of the Nazi Security Service and Gauleiter of Bohemia. The SIS were called upon to provide training, transport, weapons and facilities for the assassination squad. It must have gone very much against Dansey's better judgement, bearing in mind his aversion to sabotage and assassination, which he always regarded as counterproductive. But the Czechs were determined, and succeeded in winning high-level support for their operation.

The results proved Dansey's point. Hitler took appalling revenge on the Czech people for the killing of Heydrich. Hundreds were arrested and executed. The entire population of the village of Lidice was slaughtered as a reprisal. In the ruthless security sweep, Moravec's networks were virtually annihilated: the flow of intelligence dried up and the Czech Intelligence Service never regained its position of importance in the Allied set-up.

Perhaps the only satisfaction Dansey could derive from the whole sorry business was the thought that Heydrich had been the originator of the Venlo Incident. But even for that, it was an expensive revenge.

With the possible exception of the Norwegians whose most notable achievement was providing the vital information on the heavy water plant at Vermork that resulted in it, and Germany's atomic bomb programme, being destroyed, Dansey's relationship with the Czechs was closer and happier while it lasted than with any of the other services in exile. His recent experience with Dr Spieker had made him deeply suspicious of all émigré organisations. From the security point of view they leaked like sieves, and they attracted more than their fair share of odd-balls and misfits. Men and women of every shade of political persuasion who, in normal times and in their own countries, would have been happily at each other's throats, had in wartime and in a foreign country to try to work with each other.

This combination of personality clashes and internal political divisions inevitably imposed strains on any such organisation – strains which Dansey believed were detrimental to good intelligence gathering and assessment. The idea of sharing secret information with them filled him with horror, so little did he trust them. "You might as well hand any intelligence straight to the Gestapo," he once sarcastically remarked.

Dansey was determined to keep track of all Allied intelligence activity, partly for his own information but also because he believed that far too many of those involved in intelligence on behalf of the various governments were, in fact, amateurs. Dansey detested amateurs. He disliked them even more than he hated Poles and over-eager Americans. In his view, they were a menace to good intelligence work, and he had no intention of permitting any well-meaning innocent to endanger the safety or the smooth running of his own networks. He was, above all, determined to protect his own agents at any cost.

277

But life was not made easy for Dansey – particularly as far as the Poles were concerned. Like the Czechs, the Poles had had longer to organise themselves than other governments, having been invaded earlier, and as a result they arrived in London with intelligence and resistance networks already in place in their own countries, and with spy rings operating in several other countries, too. Only the Poles and the Czechs enjoyed the privilege of using their own codes, ciphers and radio links which meant that Dansey's power of veto over them was considerably weakened.

The Poles have always enjoyed the game of espionage. As a former Polish Intelligence chief once remarked: "If you live trapped between the two wheels of a grindstone [Germany and Russia], you have to learn how to keep from being crushed." The Poles therefore made it their business to learn what the two giants on their borders were planning. Espionage became almost their national sport – and they did not propose to give it up at the behest of the British. They made it clear they were not prepared to play according to Dansey's rules. Dansey, for his part, distrusted the traditional Polish *spymanie* (spy mania).

Eventually, an agreement was reached. The Polish Government would "hand over to the SIS all the intelligence it gathered, except that dealing with Poland's internal affairs". In theory, this was admirable. In practice, it meant that the Poles handed over to the British just what they wanted the British to know – anything else was regarded as being a purely Polish concern.

The Belgians had two separate intelligence services which, according to Philip Johns, regarded each other with "almost paranoic suspicion and jealousy . . . exacerbated by the fact that the two services fought bitterly for larger sections of the 'cake', the cake being the facilities put at our disposal [by the SIS] for our joint missions to Belgium".

The principal service was run by a thirty-five-year-old lawyer, Baron Fernand Lepage. He started by recruiting mostly members of the Brussels Sûreté, but soon discovered that policemen do not make good spies, and replaced them with fellow lawyers and officers of the reserve who were willing to return to occupied Belgium as agents. Lepage had been in business for several weeks before he was contacted by British Intelligence in the form of a mysterious Englishman calling himself Captain Page, who later took him to the flat at 5 St James's Street, where he was confronted by an intimidating, white-haired gentleman who demanded: "Do you realise, Lepage, that you are endangering the security of the realm?"

Lepage was not clear how he had achieved this distinction, and it was to be some time before he learned that this was Claude Dansey. However, he confessed that he knew nothing about intelligence but was willing to learn, and to co-operate with the British in any way he could. Dansey's attitude softened. Eventually, he and Lepage were to conclude a written agreement that all information which was of concern to both parties should be shared.

Co-operation continued amicably throughout the rest of the war. Like many of the young turks recruited into intelligence, Lepage came to regard Dansey with affection and respect. Whenever he was faced with a particularly tough problem, he would turn to Dansey for help. He was rarely disappointed. On one occasion, he hit upon the idea of raising money for an operation, which required a great deal of immediate cash by selling diamonds on the black market in Belgium. He appealed to Dansey, who came round to his office personally within a day or two and poured some £10–12,000 worth of uncut stones on to Lepage's desk.

When the Americans tried to set up their own network in Belgium in 1942, to the dismay of Lepage who already had to contend with the Poles operating on his territory without his consent and feared for the security of his own networks, Dansey went with him to the US Embassy and put a stop to the plan.

In April 1944 a directive was issued that all Allied diplomatic bags should be opened first by the British, as one of the precautions to protect the security of the Normandy invasion. But Lepage was concerned for the safety of his own agents; an inadvertent leak could endanger them. He appealed again to Dansey, who quickly saw his point and found a way of getting round the directive: in future, he decreed, Belgian bags would remain sealed until Lepage opened them on the big table in his Belgrave Square headquarters, in the presence of Captain Page.

Of all the Allied countries, the one with the greatest strategic importance, and therefore the one which remained Dansey's principal concern from 1940 until 1944, was France. It was also the country which posed most political problems. Other nations were troubled by internal conflicts within their governments in exile – dealing with such organisations was never easy. But Dansey soon found it was mere child's play compared with the difficulties of dealing with the French.

The psychological blow of the collapse of France left its people shattered and confused. The country was riven by dozens of different factions, all at bitter odds with each other. Most of them found it difficult if not impossible to comprehend the scale of the

279

tragedy that had overtaken their nation, and under such circumstances it is hardly surprising that there should be lack of agreement on how to relate to those still carrying on the struggle.

The policy of the Vichy Government was, in Pierre Laval's words, "to gain a peace that will hurt France the least". In a radio broadcast on 14th October 1940, after meeting Hitler at Montoire, Pétain at last put a name to this policy: "I am today," he said, "embarking on a path of collaboration." In yet another radio broadcast he told the French people: "Our honour is safe."

Unfortunately many of his countrymen and women disagreed with him. Unable or unwilling to flee to Britain, they were still determined to continue the war against the enemy. They therefore joined what came to be known as the Resistance.

The expression is, of course, generic. The French Resistance was a loose collection of many disparate groups, each owing allegiance to different political groupings inside and outside France, from Gaullist to communist. Politically the groups had nothing in common. The only political aim they shared was a determination to drive the Germans out of France.

Forty years after the event, the subject of the Resistance is still a sensitive issue in France. The divisions between the various Resistance groups are reflected even today in the dialectic of French political life. The subject was a minefield with which Dansey became only too familiar. In one way or another he had to deal with all the factions, and in this he demonstrated not only the familiar Dansey deviousness and ruthlessness, but also a remarkable talent for diplomacy.

CHAPTER TWENTY-SIX

Passy and Rémy

In 1940 Charles de Gaulle was a temporary brigadier-general who had successfully commanded a French armoured division and later in the same year, served briefly as Under-Secretary for War in the government of Paul Reynaud. When France collapsed, he escaped to England and became the first *résistant*. He arrived in London determined to act not merely as the general commanding Free French Forces, but as putative head of the French state. But his dual role won him few friends. Both Churchill and Roosevelt found his attitude frequently exasperating, and it confirmed the American President in his profound distrust of the man who came to be seen as the embodiment of France.

Roosevelt regarded de Gaulle as a dictator in embryo; he refused to grant diplomatic recognition to the Free French in London, even though he recognised all the other governments in exile. To de Gaulle's fury, the United States granted recognition to Pétain's government in Vichy, and subsequently tried to set up the "non-political" General Giraud as leader of the Free French, though the scheme came to nothing.

On 18th June 1940 de Gaulle made the first of his famous broadcasts over the BBC, calling on the French to continue the struggle against the Germans. Today, the anniversary of the speech on 18th June is marked by ceremonies throughout France. At the time, it was so little regarded that the BBC did not even trouble to record it as it went out live. De Gaulle, conscious as always of history being made, was incensed.

De Gaulle was determined to demonstrate to the world his independence, even though he was totally dependent on the British for funds and facilities. He chose, however, to ignore this inconvenient fact. As a soldier, he understood the value of intelligence, and as head of state (albeit self-proclaimed), he insisted on having his own intelligence service under French command and run by his own men. He believed it was vital that he remain directly in touch with events inside France. He wanted information to flow direct to his staff rather than arrive through the filter of British Intelligence which, not without reason, he did not wholly trust.

Having no one with any experience of intelligence work on his staff, he picked out a bright young captain from the engineering corps, André Dewavrin, to take on the task of building an intelligence service from scratch.

It was an excellent choice. Dewavrin spoke perfect English and possessed a first-class brain. He was a graduate of that peculiarly French institution, the *École Polytechnique*, which these days moulds a self-generating élite of technocrats to run French industry and some branches of French government. Until the outbreak of war he had held – in spite of his youth (he was born in 1911) – the post of professor of fortification at the *École Militaire Spéciale de Saint Cyr*, France's most prestigious military academy. Furthermore, Dewavrin shared many of de Gaulle's prejudices, including a leaning towards authoritarian solutions to political problems and a profound contempt for the politicians of the Third Republic.

With no previous experience, no staff and no agents, Dewavrin set out to create his new intelligence service. It says much for him that, from these inauspicious beginnings, the service grew rapidly, so that by 1942 it had become the BCRA (*Bureau Central des Renseignements et d'Action*), an organisation which, as its name suggests, combined intelligence-gathering with sabotage.

To protect their families and friends still in France from German retaliation, Dewavrin and his agents adopted code names derived from stations on the Paris Métro. While the first two agents became Saint-Jacques and Corvisart, Dewavrin himself chose Passy.

Shortly after setting up his organisation, Dewavrin was visited by an elderly, white-haired English gentleman, with pebble glasses and a small military moustache, who looked rather like a retired bank manager.

Dansey and Dewavrin took to each other. Dansey put himself out to be charming, helpful and courteous, while always remaining, as Dewavrin told us, "the most professional intelligence officer I ever met". They would remain on excellent terms even when their masters, Churchill and de Gaulle, were engaged in one of their frequent feuds. Perhaps they sensed in each other the same qualities of commitment and dedication and ruthlessness.

Dansey offered the fledgling Gaullist organisation the full co-operation of the British Secret Service. But the Frenchman was under no illusions. He knew that any failure to co-operate on his part would mean that all his efforts would be nullified. The SIS –

which meant Dansey – controlled codes, the supply of radios, and most important of all, the means of landing agents in France.

On occasion the co-operation between Dansey and Dewavrin could lead in surprising and sinister directions. In Lyons, for example, there was a brothel which had been taken over for the exclusive use of senior German officers. The owner of the establishment was a patriotic Frenchman who had fled to Lisbon late in 1942, with the aim of eventually offering his services to de Gaulle in London. Vetted by Dewavrin's Lisbon agents, he confessed that he was worried about his girls, and also about his daughter who had been forced to stay behind in Lyons.

The prospect of controlling a senior German officers' brothel was irresistible. Dansey and Dewavrin discussed ways of best exploiting this valuable windfall. It would not have been the first brothel to play a role in an intelligence operation. In Berlin the notorious Salon Kitty, the establishment at 11 Giesebrechtstrasse, much patronised by foreign diplomats, businessmen and other visiting luminaries, operated under the aegis of SS Counter Intelligence. It was the brain-child of Walter Schellenberg (of Venlo fame). Every room in the place was bugged – in particular the seven bedrooms – and many of the girls were specially recruited agents temporarily attached to the Waffen SS. For a while, until it was bombed in 1942, Salon Kitty provided Schellenberg and Heydrich, his chief, with much valuable intelligence, as well as enough blackmail material to put many of its clients in their power.

Dansey and Dewavrin were not quite so fortunate. As the brothel was in occupied France, there was no possibility of their organising any complicated bugging system or staffing the place with their own agents. However, one item of information supplied by the co-operative proprietor did cause Dansey's eyes to light up. The man reported that some of the German officers went there not merely to relax in the arms of compliant whores, but also to take drugs.

Dansey therefore arranged to keep the brothel well supplied with heroin, as well as other drugs, acquired from a source in Marseilles. The drug habit of any senior German officer was encouraged. The scheme was highly successful, as Dewavrin recalls: "We got a number of them hooked on drugs." This not only reduced their military efficiency but also made them dependent on the brothel, and therefore on Dansey, for supplies. On their regular return visits, the officers got to know the girls well and, as a result, tended to drop their guard, often letting slip valuable information.

While Dansey was prepared to exploit the weaknesses of his

enemies, he expected his own associates to avoid emotional entanglements of any sort. He once saw Dewavrin dining in a restaurant in Dover Street with an attractive English girl. Later he warned him against such frivolity. *"Mon cher ami,"* he said, "don't forget that France fell because of a woman."* His lectures to his own staff followed similar lines: "I can't have sex interfering with our work," he used to tell them.

On another occasion, when Dewavrin slipped secretly into France, he found the whole Paris network in a state of uproar. The Germans had clamped down in the city; travel had become extremely difficult. This meant that some ninety Allied evaders and escapers were trapped in the city, unable to move south along the usual escape lines. They were young, high-spirited, and bored with the discomfort of hiding out in attics and cellars. Many of them grew careless; some left their hiding places and went for walks and even visited cafés and clubs, while waiting to be moved. Their Resistance hosts were horrified. It only needed one man to be stopped by the police and questioned and the whole network could be in jeopardy. The Resistance workers turned to Dewavrin for advice: what could they do? They had no authority over the men. Dewavrin radioed Dansey. After all, most of the men were British and American, and MI9 was his responsibility. Dansey's reply was short and to the point. It consisted only of two words: "Kill them". Fortunately the Germans relaxed their grip on the city before Dewavrin had to decide whether to follow Dansey's advice.

Dewavrin's chief agent in France was a man whom Dansey once described as "the greatest spy I have ever known" – high praise indeed from the most experienced spymaster in the world. His name was Gilbert Renault. He was a Breton and a Catholic by birth and a film producer by profession, and until 1940 he had never been involved in anything more sinister than in raising co-production money for his movies – not a bad training ground for a spy.

Renault, however, does not welcome Dansey's description of his role. He does not like the word "spy" which he feels – no doubt rightly – is a pejorative expression and should be applied solely to someone who operates on foreign territory. How can he, he argues, a loyal Frenchman defending his own country from the invader, be described as a spy? He considers the word an insult to the memory of those comrades in the Resistance who met their

---

* Presumably he was referring to the Comtesse de Portes, Paul Reynaud's mistress, who was in favour of peace at any price.

deaths at the hands of the Germans. He prefers therefore to be known as a "secret agent".

Where Dewavrin won fame during the war under his code name "Colonel Passy", Gilbert Renault made his mark in the history of intelligence as "Colonel Rémy". It is by this name we will refer to him in future.

A stocky, energetic man with enormous charm, Rémy during the course of his career had worked on many different film projects with, amongst others, the late Abel Gance of *Napoleon* fame. In 1940 he was in Spain trying to organise a co-production for an historical movie based on the life of Christopher Columbus.

At the time of the fall of France, he returned home to his wife who was expecting their fifth child. He was determined to serve his country in some manner. But how? He discussed the matter with his wife, and it was agreed that he should leave France and offer his services to whatever French government was set up in exile, wherever it might be.

The whole Renault family responded with equal enthusiasm. Philippe, the youngest brother, had joined the Marines and was already at sea. Rémy was never to see him again. Claude, his twenty-year-old brother, who was later to serve with distinction as the ADC of General Koenig of 1st Free French Brigade at Bir-Hacheim, North Africa, decided to accompany Rémy on his quest.

Rémy and Claude managed to obtain passage from Lorient, Brittany, on *La Barbue*, an old fishing trawler, which was carrying in her holds some 5,000 million French francs in notes being shipped out of the country by the Bank of France.

At the mouth of the River Gironde *La Barbue* was ordered to off-load her valuable cargo into a more appropriate vessel, the *Clairvoyant*, bound for Morocco, where it was confidently expected that a government in exile would be set up. The two Renault brothers begged the captain of the *Clairvoyant* to take them with him, but he refused. His orders were to carry no civilians. Had he agreed and had they gone to Morocco, then Rémy's subsequent career would have been very different.

In the event the brothers made their way to London, where twenty-year-old Claude immediately joined the Free French forces. But Rémy himself was forced to cool his heels for a while. He was thirty-six years old, and his last experience of military life had been at least fifteen years before when he did his military service in the artillery. Despairing of ever seeing active service, Rémy asked for an appointment with General de Gaulle's recently appointed head of the *Deuxième Bureau* (Intelligence) and

285

Troisième Bureau (Operations), then Captain (later Colonel) Passy.

What initially intrigued Passy – and subsequently, Dansey, though Rémy did not meet him till later – was not the man, but his passport. It contained an up-to-date Spanish visa. Rémy could therefore enter Spain quite legally, and from there – also legally – proceed to France. Whereas other agents at that time had to be smuggled in.

"What sort of information do you think you will be able to get?" asked Dansey's assistant, Lieutenant-Commander Cohen, at that point Rémy's sole connection with the SIS.

Rémy had no idea, nor at that time did he know how he was going to get any information back to Britain. He was a complete tyro at intelligence work, but he learned quickly.

His first task was to up-date SIS maps of France. Until then, because of a general shortage, the Secret Service had been forced to work with tourist maps put out by the Michelin Tyre Company. Rémy arranged to buy a complete set of so-called "General Staff" maps from the official cartography office in Rue La Boétie, Paris, and sent them to London. Unfortunately the purchase attracted the attention of SS Counter-Intelligence, but by then the maps were in Britain.

Rémy soon found himself faced with the task of organising clandestine intelligence networks in France. So short was the BCRA of reliable people, that Dewavrin put him in command of networks in an area stretching from the Spanish border in the south to the port of Brest in the north-west. Later, in preparation for D-day, he was given control of the vital Channel coast of France, from Brest to the Belgian border.

As a result of his Resistance activities, Rémy was soon on the Gestapo wanted list. They arrested his mother and five sisters, two of whom (Maisie and Isabelle) were eventually sent to Ravensbrück concentration camp, from where they were rescued by the Swedish Count Bernadotte. When London heard that the Gestapo were searching for Rémy's wife and children to use as hostages, arrangements were made to bring them out of France. So at dawn on 17th June 1942 a boat, *Les Deux-Anges*, slipped out of Pont-Aven harbour, Finistère, with Rémy and his family aboard. After transferring to a trawler they were then taken on board an MTB two days later off the Iles Glénan and brought to Britain. Rémy did not travel empty-handed, even then. He brought with him copies of the plans for all German defence installations on the Channel coast, which one of his men had stolen – a major prize and a most welcome present for Dewavrin and Dansey.

In England complications arose when Edith gave birth to their son, Ian, just over a year later. Rémy had been given a Canadian identity card in the name of Georges Roulier: for security purposes he did not use his own name. When the child's birth was registered, Edith could only give the name of his father as Roulier, thus making her son illegitimate. It was only after the war that the child was legitimised, and then Rémy was forced to change his own name by deed poll to Renault-Roulier.

Rémy's remarkable success as an intelligence chief and leader of a Resistance network is the result of personal chemistry, rather than military discipline. People liked him and trusted him. He was a civilian to his finger tips, and above all a patriot; and he understood his fellow countrymen in a way that soldiers rarely do.

Soldiers give orders and expect them to be obeyed; such is the nature of military life. But no civilian Resistance movement can operate in a purely military manner. People cannot be ordered to risk death. However patriotic they may be, they have wives and children and loved ones who could suffer for their actions. Their area of operation is proscribed by their domestic commitments. They may be prepared to die for their country, but until such time they have to get back home and collect the children from school or feed the chickens. Life has to go on, even in wartime, even under enemy occupation. Rémy appreciated this and allowed for it. It was one of the qualities in him that Dansey admired.

Rémy first met Dansey at the end of March 1942, just after the Bruneval Raid, in which both men had been involved, though at that point Rémy was not aware of Dansey's part in the operation.

The Bruneval Raid was of historic importance. It was the first raid in which British forces and the French Resistance co-operated, one supplying the military muscle, the other the detailed local intelligence. Success was vital for the morale of any future operations. An initial failure would have had disastrous consequences for the future of resistance on the continent of Europe.

Whether it was an RAF pilot who first noticed the curious metal construction on the cliffs near the village of Bruneval on the French coast between Le Havre and Dieppe or whether, as some historians state, it was a French air force officer, Roger Dumont (code name "Pol"), a member of Rémy's own network, the Confrérie Nôtre-Dame, who first took note of the structure, is open to question.

Photo reconnaissance established that the object was a Wurzburg radar apparatus which, in conjunction with the Freya system, enabled the Luftwaffe to track Allied aircraft. German nightfighters directed on to their targets by Wurzburgs were taking heavy toll of RAF bombers. But before they could combat this threat the British boffins needed to know precisely how the Wurzburg worked, which meant getting experts to the installation to examine it and, if possible, bring bits of it back to England for further analysis. Aerial photographs are excellent at giving the lie of the land. But they do not provide the kind of information about the enemy's defences that a raiding force needs to know in order to guarantee success. Only an agent on the ground can supply that sort of detail – and that was where Claude Dansey came in.

Rémy was ordered to provide a team to reconnoitre the Wurzburg installation. He selected two of his best men for the job – Pol, of course, who was later caught and executed for his part in the operation, and Charles Chauveau ("Charlemagne"), a Le Havre garage proprietor.

They ascertained the composition and frequency of German patrols in the neighbourhood, the position of enemy strong points, access to and from the installation. But perhaps most important of all, they discovered that the beach at the foot of the cliffs where the Wurzburg was positioned – contrary to notices put up by Germans – was not mined. Therefore any raiding force could be evacuated by sea.

On the night of 27th February 1942, 120 paratroops, commanded by Major J. D. Frost, were dropped in three groups inland of the village of Bruneval and the installation on the cliffs. In spite of unforeseen problems – one "stick" of paras was dropped one and a half miles south of their intended position – the raid was a total success. Parts of the Wurzburg were removed and brought back to England when the paras were evacuated by the 14th Flotilla of the Royal Australian Navy early the following morning. Their losses were two killed, six wounded and six missing.

While the intelligence gained from the seizure of the Wurzburg apparatus was invaluable, as Professor R. V. Jones has explained in his book *Most Secret War*, British boffins had already more or less worked out how the system operated: the raid merely confirmed their theories. But for the French, both those with de Gaulle in Britain and the thousands in France who later heard rumours of the landing, it represented an historic feat of arms, an achievement beyond mere intelligence gathering. The Bruneval Raid was the first time since the fall of France that an Allied force had set foot on French soil. It was a symbol to France that all was not lost, that even in the dark days of 1942 there was hope.

Rémy learned of the successful outcome of the raid the following day when he returned to England, and a friend showed him a copy of the London *Evening Standard* which headlined the good news.

288

A little while later he was invited to be guest of honour at a dinner party given by Stewart Menzies at Brown's Hotel, Dover Street. In the course of a pleasant evening Rémy was introduced by someone – with, as he says, an air of "affectionate deference" – to an elderly gentleman who seemed to be known as Uncle Claude.

The two men got on famously together– in spite of the fact that, as Rémy was to discover later, Dansey did not like or trust General de Gaulle. He believed that the French leader was too ready to use intelligence as a political bargaining counter against his allies, rather than employ the knowledge as a weapon against the enemy. In this Dansey was either being naive, or else was conveniently ignoring those occasions when the British and the Americans committed similar abuses. Dansey, like almost everyone else, found it hard to get on with *le roi Charles*.

At the end of the meal Dansey told Rémy, "We have been thinking of an operation which we believe would have a great effect on the morale of our friends in Paris." The operation in question involved nothing more than shooting up a mounted German military band which every day at noon rode down the Champs-Élysées, with fifes and drums blaring – to the considerable annoyance of the Parisians. The plan was to send a fighter to machine-gun the band in mid-concert. Of course, the whole operation required split-second timing. The pilot of the plane needed to know the exact time the band left the Arc de Triomphe to commence its musical ride. Rémy was therefore asked to supply a precise timing of the whole procession from beginning to end. For several days his men studied the proceedings, stop-watches in hand. Eventually they concluded that the safest place for the attack, where there was least chance of innocent Parisians being accidentally killed, was when the band had reached a point between the Rond-Point and the Place de la Concorde.

In the event the operation misfired. Owing to an unexpected change in the timetable, the band did not appear at noon. When a Beaufighter, flown by A. Kitchener Gatward, dived out of the sky, there was no band in sight. Undeterred by this disappointment, Gatward dropped a French tricolour at the Arc de Triomphe, flew the length of the Champs-Élysées to the Place de la Concorde, where he shot up the Navy Ministry building and dropped a second tricolour.

From the end of 1942 and throughout 1943 the long Gestapo campaign against the Resistance in northern France began to bear fruit. Arrests were made, many people were interrogated and tortured. Some talked, some turned traitor. As the arrests mounted, so inevitably the flow of counter-intelligence to the Germans increased, and several networks, including the communist FTPF (*Francs Tireurs et Partisans Français*), which in the end was forced to throw in with de Gaulle, came under severe pressure.

Experience had taught Dansey that the life expectancy of a Resistance leader was no more than six months, and he believed that Rémy was now into borrowed time. So while Rémy was on one of his periodic trips to London, Dansey decided to veto the possibility of any return to France. It was too dangerous. Dansey had learned that a Gestapo agent was living in the house in Vannes, Brittany, directly opposite from where Rémy's mother and three of his sisters were staying. The Germans were simply waiting to pick him up should he put in an appearance. Dansey did not propose to risk one of his most important agents falling into enemy hands, and since he controlled the means of transport across the Channel, it seemed that Dewavrin and Rémy had no alternative but to accept his decision.

Rémy, however, had other ideas. Suppose he could so disguise himself that no one – not even his own mother – would recognise him? Dansey somewhat sceptically agreed to consider any possible transformation that the experts might effect. A make-up man from Denham Film Studios (courtesy of Alexander Korda) was called in and went to work on Rémy in MI9's offices in St James's Street.

Dansey was astounded at the results. Rémy made a most convincing old man. Indeed, so successful did the disguise prove to be that not only did Uncle Claude relent and allow him to return to France, but when he was travelling on the Paris Métro a middle-aged German soldier actually took pity on the poor old Frenchman and gave him his seat.

Rémy played the part to the hilt; he enjoyed such encounters. There was always a touch of the Scarlet Pimpernel about him – as on the occasion when, much to the horror and indignation of Fernand Grenier, the communist Deputy, who was sent to England by fishing boat to make peace with de Gaulle on behalf of the FTPF, Rémy chose that particular trip to smuggle a three-foot azalea bush, purchased from a fashionable Paris florist's, into Britain for Madame de Gaulle. Grenier, who had no sense of humour and in any case suffered from appalling sea-sickness in the cramped space where he was hidden, was not amused. Suppose a German patrol boat stopped and searched the vessel? Even if the Germans failed to discover Rémy and Grenier in their hiding place, they were unlikely to overlook a three-foot azalea bush which was hardly standard equipment aboard a trawler. But then

Rémy had made the trip half a dozen times before and had grown blasé about the risks involved.

In his brief career Rémy revealed a quite exceptional flair for intelligence work – not only of the cloak-and-dagger variety, but also in the field of information-gathering. And of course, he enjoyed more than his fair share of luck. In his conversations with the authors, and in his many letters to them, Rémy always speaks affectionately of Uncle Claude, a man who "understood as few others have done the difficult business of espionage", a man who "hid a genuine kindliness behind a sardonic exterior". Most of Uncle Claude's contemporaries did not, however, share Rémy's roseate view of the man.

CHAPTER TWENTY-SEVEN

Marie-Madeleine and Alliance

While the Gaullist Free French organised and ran the BCRA from London, various other factions and groups worked in France itself. Some got their information out through embassies in Vichy, some through Spain, some through Switzerland: but no matter what the route, all their intelligence was eventually destined for Claude Dansey's desk in London.

The most important spy ring – indeed, it became the exclusive adjunct of British Intelligence – was what came to be known as the Alliance network, later dubbed by the Gestapo "Noah's Ark", because most of the agents had animal code names. Madame Marie-Madeleine Fourcade, who became head of the network, was "Hedgehog". Other code names ranged alphabetically from "Alligator" (Captain Crèmieu) to "Zebra" (Arnold Gartner), and included most of the animal kingdom in between.

The Alliance was the brain-child of Commandant (Major) Georges Loustanau-Lacau. Born in Pau, in the Pyrenees near the Spanish border, he entered the French Military Academy of St Cyr in October 1913, and nine months later, in white gloves and plumed shako, he went marching off to war. Unlike so many of his contemporaries at the Academy, he survived four years in the trenches – only to emerge, at the age of twenty-four, bitter and with his illusions shattered. He remained in the army, however, and was sent to the *École Supérieure de Guerre* (War College), where he was in the same class as a young captain, recently released from a German prisoner-of-war camp: Charles de Gaulle.

It was while serving on Pétain's staff in 1935, that Loustanau-Lacau enjoyed his first real taste of clandestinity and like so many others, he found it irresistible. It must also have been about this time that he came to the attention of Dansey and Wilfred Dunderdale, then SIS head of station in Paris.

Loustanau-Lacau organised *Corvignolles*, a kind of secret

society of right-wing officers, dedicated to purging the French army of "subversion, indiscipline and anti-militarism", for which they believed the Communist Party was responsible. The aim of the communists was to destroy army morale and "ruin the confidence of the soldiers in their commanders". In spite of holding such views Loustanau-Lacau, unlike many of his background and class, was neither fascist nor anti-semitic. .

In 1938 one of Loustanau-Lacau's agents, a reserve officer from Nancy, growing uneasy about the activities of *Corvignolles*, informed the police. After an investigation the authorities decided that the time had come to put an end to the commandant's army career: Loustanau-Lacau was transferred to the non-active list and forced to leave Pétain's staff. Refusing to be downcast by this setback, he threw himself in his usual energetic manner into setting up a publishing house which was to be devoted to publishing political magazines. One of these, *L'Ordre National*, was edited by the executive secretary of the company, a petite, attractive, dark-haired Parisienne in her early thirties, Marie-Madeleine Fourcade.

More than ever convinced of the German menace, Loustanau-Lacau foresaw the need for precise intelligence in the war which he knew could not be long delayed. Rather like Hans Hausamann in Switzerland, he began setting up his own intelligence organisation which operated not only in France but also inside Germany itself.

So effective were his sources of information that on the eve of the war he was able to publish in *L'Ordre National* the entire order of battle of the Germany army, navy and air force. This was compiled from intelligence reports sent by his agents. The compiler was his friend Bertold Jacob, a French Jew who – to complete the comparison with the Lucy Ring – seems to have been an assessor of intelligence almost in the same class as Lucy himself.

When war was declared, the fiery commandant rushed to rejoin the army – which showed an understandable reluctance to have the troublemaker back again. However, after a month's intensive lobbying of political and military contacts, it was agreed that he should return to active duty. In view of his experience of intelligence work, he was posted to the *Deuxième Bureau* (Military Intelligence) of General Corap's 9th Army which held the Meuse Line in the Ardennes. But at the last minute the posting was changed, and he found himself commanding a battalion in the Maginot Line. Early in July 1940 he was severely wounded by machine-gun fire when leading his battalion in a hopeless attack on a German tank column. He was captured and spent some weeks in a POW hospital at Châlons-sur-Marne.

Marie-Madeleine, who had fled with her two children to Loustanau-Lacau's home at Oloron-Ste-Marie in the Pyrenees near Pau, heard that he had persuaded the hospital commandant to release him and had crossed the border into unoccupied France on 20th August.

Loustanau-Lacau lost no time in getting back into the war. A great bull of a man, he possessed an air of authority which impressed the bureaucrats, and his record was such that no one, not even the most rabid right winger, could accuse him of being a communist sympathiser. He also had a little money. He therefore rented the Hotel des Sports in Vichy to house ex-soldiers, of which there were many roaming around the country and of whom a number still longed for a chance to get back at the enemy in some way. He even persuaded his old chief, Pétain, to appoint him his delegate to the *Légion Français Combattants*, a Vichy-sponsored veterans' organisation. By bringing all veterans' organisations under one umbrella – theirs – Pétain's advisers hoped to be able to impose some degree of political control over a group which the French public regarded with great sympathy.

Although Loustanau-Lacau planned to use his own connection with the veterans' organisations in order to recruit men for a Resistance movement, he was aware that this would create problems. He explained the situation to Marie-Madeleine: "For the next few months I'm going to let myself be seen among that bunch of ninnies, see the Marshal in order to do what the old hypocrite has asked me to do, let him know what is happening to his 'dear old soldiers'. I must be absolutely above suspicion." While he was busy playing the political game in Vichy, he needed someone to run the clandestine side of the growing organisation. But it had to be someone he could trust. He chose Marie-Madeleine.

In her book, *Noah's Ark*, Marie-Madeleine quotes herself as greeting the proposition with the words: "But Navarre [Loustanau-Lacau's code name], I'm only a woman!" It is the only thing in her story we find it hard to believe. No one who has met her can ever imagine her reacting with such timidity!

By Christmas 1940, Loustanau-Lacau's Resistance group, which he had christened the Crusade, had grown from an initial six volunteers to a total of fifty people. It was enough to provide the basis for a real intelligence network, and was obtaining excellent information. The only problems that remained were how to obtain secure communications and sufficient funds with which to operate – and what to do with the intelligence once they got it. Perhaps he knew *le roi Charles* too well from their days at the *École Supérieure de Guerre* ever to be a true worshipper at their particular shrine. Loustanau-Lacau was never a Gaullist. Nevertheless, he was prepared to deal with his former classmate, and tried to enlist his support in London. De Gaulle is reported to have rebuffed him in a typically haughty letter with the words: "Who is not with me is against me". Loustanau-Lacau responded to the rebuff by turning to the British. Using Marie-Madeleine's brother as an intermediary he renewed his earlier contacts with Dansey.

Dansey, already having problems with de Gaulle, was quick to realise the value of the network and of the intelligence it was able to supply. He arranged a meeting in early 1941 between Loustanau-Lacau and Lieutenant-Commander Kenneth Cohen, who had been his second-in-command of the Z Organisation. The two men met in Lisbon, and together worked out the details of the future operation of the network. The British would supply radios, codes and full communications support, plus an initial five million francs (or just under £30,000) to grease the wheels of espionage. In return, Loustanau-Lacau's network would come under the direct command of Claude Dansey and the British SIS. In one move, Dansey had outflanked de Gaulle and acquired control of the most important intelligence network in France, while the troublesome French leader was still struggling to establish the nucleus of his own organisation. De Gaulle was furious at what he considered a defection to the perfidious British. But Loustanau-Lacau's time was running out. He was simply too visible, and in the end too imprudent, to survive in the world of espionage. For a long time he had nursed the idea of organising a military coup amongst dissident officers stationed in Algiers. His plan was to arrest the Pétainists and eventually take control of French North Africa. He had sent Commandant Léon Faye (code name "Eagle") to recruit reliable men for the coup, and when Eagle advised him that all was ready, Loustanau-Lacau immediately set out for Algiers, where he arrived on 5th May 1941.

If the coup were successful, he believed that it would forestall the possibility of an Allied invasion of North Africa, in which a French colony would inevitably be treated as conquered territory. An uprising would, he thought, also inspire his fellow countrymen to acts of resistance against the Germans.

In Algiers he met an old army friend, once a classmate at Saint-Cyr, now a colonel and Deputy Chief of Staff of the 19th Army Corps. Having every confidence in the man, he told him the purpose of his mission. The colonel made all the right noises and offered his whole-hearted support. A couple of hours later Loustanau-Lacau and his fellow conspirators were arrested by the French police. The colonel had betrayed them.

A few weeks later Marie-Madeleine was travelling from Pau to Marseilles, when she was astonished to meet her old chief aboard the same train. He had escaped from prison in Algiers, thanks to the help of another old army friend, now the local police commissioner. But Loustanau-Lacau was not at large for long. Marie-Madeleine went to his home in Pau to warn him that the police were closing in on him; he must leave immediately. But Loustanau-Lacau insisted on saying good-bye to his wife who was staying with her parents in a nearby village. The police followed Annick Loustanau-Lacau to the pension where her husband was waiting for her. He was arrested, and tried before a tribunal at Clermont-Ferrand, which sentenced him to two years' imprisonment and the confiscation of his possessions. After serving fifteen months of his sentence the Vichy Government handed him over to the Gestapo who kept him on bread and water for six months before sending him to Mauthausen concentration camp with an NN (*Nacht und Nebel*) sign against his name. This meant that he was supposed to disappear without trace. Typically, he survived – to turn up after the war as a witness in the trial of Marshal Pétain.

The imprisonment of Loustanau-Lacau placed the whole Alliance network, at one of the most crucial moments of the war, in the hands of a young Parisian matron: Marie-Madeleine was now in charge. The network was no longer small. Indeed, it was growing fast – too fast, Marie-Madeleine believed. At its height she commanded at least 3,000 agents, which must make her not only the greatest female spy of the second world war, but probably the greatest female spymaster of all time.

Shortly after the capture of Loustanau-Lacau, the following decoded radio message landed on Claude Dansey's desk: "NI arrested this morning stop network intact stop everything continuing stop best postpone parachuting next moon stop Turenne patrol leaves for Paris tonight stop confidence unshakable stop regards POZ 55 end." POZ 55, Marie-Madeleine's radio-call sign, had not been previously used in messages to London. In reply, after the usual expressions of regret at the arrest of the network's leader, London asked the pertinent question: "Who is taking over command?" "I am," replied Marie-Madeleine with a confidence she did not feel.

London did not know at that time that POZ 55 was a woman. But they need not have worried because her next move revealed a talent for clandestinity which even Dansey would have admired and which had been so sadly lacking in Loustanau-Lacau himself.

Marie-Madeleine arranged to rent a house in Pau where she

installed some of the network's agents who had travelled the 500 miles from Paris. She was determined that it would be business as usual for the Alliance in spite of the arrest of their leader. She reasoned that the authorities, flushed with their success in capturing Loustanau-Lacau in Pau, would expect the *résistants* to go into hiding. They would not expect the network to continue operating in the very same place as if nothing had happened. At the same time, in order to spread the risk in case someone figured out what she was up to, she decided to maintain her other operational centre in Marseilles.

Marie-Madeleine's nerve was very soon put to a severe test with one of Dansey's most serious mistakes. One must assume that this error of judgement which almost brought total disaster to the Alliance network was caused by the grave shortage of fully-trained, French-speaking British agents at the time. But when one considers Dansey's fanatical obsession with security, it is hard to explain or to understand how he could approve the sending of an agent called Blanchet, code named "Bla", even though the man had lived for many years in France before the war. Nevertheless, approve it he did, and Bla was parachuted in to teach the network the latest ciphering and communications techniques, after which he was to proceed to Normandy and there set up a group of his own.

Bla was a sight to behold when they brought him to Marie-Madeleine. He was "attired as if for a village wedding – short jacket and waistcoat, striped trousers, a spotted cravat, a stiff shirt with cutaway collar beneath a little goatee beard, a pair of pince-nez, and as a crowning glory, a bowler hat". In addition he spoke perfect French but with a broad Cockney accent. Marie-Madeleine told him to shave off his beard and get a complete change of clothes.

The following day there was more bad news. Bla had gone down with acute appendicitis and a temperature of 104. In the face of opposition from members of her group who were prepared to let the man die, Marie-Madeleine got him admitted to the local hospital. However, she took the precaution of sending a female agent in with him to act as his wife. The danger period would be when he began to come out of the anaesthetic after the operation. If he began to talk English, then all could be lost. The "wife" was to throw herself on him and smother him with kisses until he was clear-headed enough to remember that he was supposed to be French.

The ploy was successful. No one in hospital suspected. But it meant that Marie-Madeleine had to keep Bla longer in Pau than she had anticipated, and his behaviour continued to be a worry. The man was becoming too interested in everyone who came to see her at the Villa Etchebaster, Marie-Madeleine's headquarters. He was asking altogether too many questions. He even approached one of her agents with an offer to buy information from him for a series of articles for one of the English newspapers. However, eventually, voluble as ever, Bla departed for Normandy to work with other networks.

By now Marie-Madeleine's suspicions were thoroughly aroused. After a series of arrests of members of the network in Paris, she became convinced that Bla was to blame. He had to be a traitor.

Meanwhile Major Richards, the network's London contact, wanted to arrange a meeting with the new leader of the Alliance, the mysterious POZ 55. But it was difficult. Richards did not want to come to France and Marie-Madeleine had no intention of going to London. Spain was the nearest neutral country, so Madrid was chosen to be the rendezvous.

Marie-Madeleine was smuggled across the Spanish border, doubled up and half-naked, in a four-foot by two-foot mail bag. Richards was astonished to discover that the formidable POZ 55 was an attractive young woman. However, he had fresh orders for the network and much new information to impart. Amidst their discussions about air operations, selection of landing places, etc – the minutiae of a successful Resistance movement – Marie-Madeleine raised the question of Bla. Had he been sent to test them in some way, or was he a traitor?

Richards was surprised. The British were pleased with the man's work. His radio was operating from Normandy and he was sending some first-class information to London. Marie-Madeleine was able to inform Richards that to her certain knowledge the man was not in Normandy at all, but in Paris.

The arrests continued and soon the network had no doubt that Bla had betrayed them to the Germans. Further messages were despatched to London, giving all the evidence they had against the man and demanding positive action. Finally a reply came from London: "No 218 for POZ 55: You were right stop Bla a traitor stop working for the Gestapo stop secure everything he knows about that is still intact stop we are issuing execution order stop Richards." It was arranged that the treasurer of the network, Marc Mesnard, code named "the Bishop", would contact Bla as if nothing had happened and arrange to meet him in Lyons. There the Bishop would kill him. Mesnard waited at the appointed meeting place for three hours, but the other man never showed up.

298

Instead three Abwehr thugs appeared and attempted to kidnap the would-be assassin.

For a time it seemed as if Bla had vanished. Then one day an agent, code named "Heron", but actually an Englishman by the name of Crawley, chanced to bump into the man at the railway station in Marseilles. The two men knew each other since they had met on the same course for radio operators in London.

Bla seemed delighted to see his colleague. He accounted for his presence in Marseilles by telling a marvellous tale of derring-do, a hairbreadth escape from the Gestapo and the subsequent smashing of his Resistance group. Now he was broke, at a loose end, and looking for another underground organisation to join.

Heron had the presence of mind to act as if he knew nothing about the other's treachery, and he persuaded the man to meet him later in a bar in the Rue de Paradis. Meanwhile he got in touch with Commandant Léon Faye (Eagle), Marie-Madeleine's second-in-command.

The network wanted to get their hands on the traitor, but they knew it was not going to be easy. Although kidnapping may look simple on the movies, in reality many things can go wrong even in the most meticulously planned operation. Somehow Bla had to be persuaded to accompany Heron to a place where they could interrogate him at their leisure; Bla had to be persuaded to go there of his own free will.

The two men met as arranged, and when Heron was satisfied that the other had come alone to the meeting, he suggested they moved into the street where they could talk with no danger of anyone overhearing their conversation. While they were thus discussing the possibility of Heron finding his colleague a place in a new network, a couple of Alliance heavies dressed like detectives "in khaki-coloured raincoats, their hats pulled down over their faces", came up to them and demanded to see their identity cards. Heron began to protest loudly. Bla, convinced they were genuine, was much more amenable. The "detectives" insisted that the two men accompany them to their office. Bla had no objections: he knew he had nothing to fear from the French police or the DST (*Direction de la Surveillance Térritoire*) the French counter-espionage and internal security agency. "You'll see," he told Heron, "it'll be cleared up in no time."

The "detectives" took them to a block of middle-class flats, such as was frequently used by the DST for interrogations or temporary headquarters. When Bla walked through the front door of one of the flats, he found Commandant Faye and several others waiting for him.

It was vital for the network to find out whom he had betrayed, who had been arrested in Paris, and precisely what he had told the Germans. But Bla proved to be tougher than anyone had ever expected: he refused to talk and kept denying that he was Blanchet.

Eventually Marie-Madeleine went to see him herself. At that point he could not continue to deny his identity. He began to talk – indeed it became almost impossible to stop him: everything came out. He admitted that he was a member of Mosley's British Fascist organisation before the war and that he had succeeded in infiltrating British Intelligence. He also admitted that he had betrayed everyone in the network. He had even operated his radio, not from Normandy, as Major Richards believed, but from Abwehr headquarters in Paris.

Marie-Madeleine radioed London that Bla was now in their hands and that they awaited further orders. The reply from Dansey came promptly: "Well played confirm execution order." This was easier said than done. The trouble is that in real life murder is apt to be both noisy and messy: people scream and tend to bleed all over the floor. And a block of flats, with respectable tenants on all sides of you, is not a recommended execution ground, particularly if you wish to kill your victim secretly and in silence.

Bla had to be killed – but how?

Monsieur Albert (code name "Mastiff") had a solution. On his last trip to London he had been given a tube containing white "L" tablets. These were for agents who feared that they would not be able to withstand torture. One tablet was guaranteed to kill a man.

They had brought some food with them – bread and soup – which they offered to share with the traitor. He accepted eagerly; he was hungry. In Bla's plate of soup, however, they carefully dissolved three of the deadly white tablets – and waited. And waited. But nothing happened. Then suddenly – to everyone's relief – he stood up and clutched his stomach, complaining of pains. He lay down, and everybody waited for his imminent demise. However, in spite of his stomach ache, Bla continued to chat to them; he told dirty stories, and even at one point got up to demonstrate the latest dance steps.

Three hours later the apparently indestructible Bla, although complaining of pain, was still alive.

Gabriel Rivière (code name "Wolf") had another suggestion. He had connections with some local gangsters who in turn had connections with some of the fishermen from the Old Port. They agreed to take the man out to sea with them that night and allow the group to finish him off at sea and slip his body overboard.

300

Marie-Madeleine agreed to the plan. But once again the gods smiled on the traitor. It was a beautiful night, bright and calm and peaceful. Afraid that they might be seen by German patrols picking up someone, the fishermen left Bla and his executioners on shore.

Eventually Commandant Faye and Lieutenant Pilote Poulard (code name "Jack Tar"), after offering the man the consolation of a last confession with a priest – which he refused – took Bla out into the country, shot him and dumped his body into the sea.

In spite of pressure from subordinates Marie-Madeleine was loath to expand the network still further – partly because of the danger of infiltration and betrayal by Gestapo informers, but also because the job of administering the whole operation was becoming increasingly complex.

By July 1943 the pressure on the network, both from within and without, was intense. The Gestapo and the French Police were active and had already enjoyed several notable successes against the various Resistance movements. Bertie Albrecht, Henri Frenay's assistant in the Combat Resistance network, had been captured and died in Fresnes prison; Jean Moulin, de Gaulle's representative and founder of the National Council of the Resistance (CNR) had been tortured to death; and General Delestraint, the first head of the Secret Army, had fallen into the hands of Klaus Barbie, the notorious "Butcher of Lyons".

In addition, Marie-Madeleine found herself faced with the task of making a number of important military decisions which were pressed on her by her subordinates. Georges Lamarque ("Petrel"), head of the Druid section of Alliance, in preparation for the expected Allied landings in France, wanted to arm 17,000 men of the Compagnons de France, a Pétainist organisation heavily infiltrated by Alliance. Commandant Faye, who was an air force officer, had plans for preventing many vital French air force personnel from being drafted for forced labour in Germany. There were also plans to arm the *Pompiers de l'Air* and the *Jeunesse et Montagne*, another Pétainist organisation. In all, the Alliance needed weapons for 30,000 men. Could London supply them? And if so, how?

It soon became obvious that Marie-Madeleine must go to London herself to discuss strategy with the man under whose orders she had worked, the man responsible for supplying Alliance with arms and money – Claude Dansey. A Lysander picked her up just after 1 a.m. from an improvised landing strip a mere twenty-five miles from Paris. A couple of hours later she was being welcomed at an airfield in southern England by Major Richards. He took her to a house near Chichester where she had a meal, and at 11 a.m. precisely Dansey arrived in person to greet her.

Dansey never confessed to Marie-Madeleine how shocked he had been when he first learned from Major Richards that POZ 55, Hedgehog, the leader of one of the most successful of his French networks, was an attractive young woman with two children. However, she was now in England, and he had decided that here she would stay until the cessation of hostilities: her espionage career was over. Someone else could run Alliance for the time being.

Of course, Marie-Madeleine at no time was aware of Dansey's views. To her he was a charming uncle, and she still recalls him with the greatest affection. At the same time she must have had an inkling of what he intended.

"My haunting fear of not being able to return to France had begun to quicken again at the sight of the man who could do everything," she wrote.

"We'll see, we'll see," Dansey responded when she spoke of returning to her country. "You've gone on long past the safety limits. According to the law of averages, an underground leader can't last more than six months. You've lasted over two and a half years . . ."

"You mean you're not going to let me go back?" she demanded.

Dansey treated her to one of his most charming smiles. But to her dismay, he remained adamant. She was to stay in London.

Determined to take her mind off events in France as much as possible, Dansey arranged for her to contact her children whom she had sent to Switzerland for the duration for safety. He even provided a secretary to take her shopping around the London stores.

There was plenty for Marie-Madeleine to do in London. Dansey provided her with headquarters in Carlyle Square, off the King's Road in Chelsea, which was quickly named Alliance House. She spent all her time there, sleeping in the office, worrying over her colleagues still in France, directing their activities as far as she was able, and collecting and passing the vital intelligence they sent. The camp bed she slept on could not have helped the pain she suffered in her back and hip, as a result of her journeys across the Pyrenees and through France in mail bags and car boots. Dansey was particularly solicitous, and arranged for her to have treatment from an attractive young woman physiotherapist, Frances Rylander, who was to play an increasingly important role in his own life in the few years that remained to him.

One of the Alliance's best-known contributions to the war effort was their infiltration of the Peenemunde rocket research establishment. They were able to provide accurate intelligence on the early development of the V1 and V2 weapons. They were, in fact, one of three British intelligence sources on Hitler's secret weapons.

Marie-Madeleine and Commandant Faye, who had joined her in London, discovered amongst a pile of Alliance intelligence material forwarded to London a report sent by Georges Lamarque, a university mathematician and statistician. One of his best agents, an attractive young woman called Jeanne Rousseau (Amniarix), who spoke five languages, was working for a group of French industrialists in 1943 when she came into contact with a new German research organisation, said to be working on secret weapons. She succeeded in getting a job as translator in the purchasing department of the new organisation, and for a while, thanks to her friendship with a German officer working in the establishment, sent back first quality intelligence material to Petrel.

Elated by this discovery, Marie-Madeleine turned the material over to Dansey. But she did not find out until much later if it was ever put to any use. It is her only complaint against Dansey – he never told her anything. He was, she says, "over-secretive". She need not have worried. The material was in good hands and was used to excellent effect against the German terror weapons.

During the summer and autumn of 1943, the long Gestapo campaign against the Resistance at last began to produce results. More and more agents were picked up and tortured; a few, terrified for their lives and their families, even turned informer. Even the Alliance network was seriously hit by defections. But it was imperative that the network should be ready to operate at full scale once the Allies had landed in Normandy. Experienced resistance leaders such as Marie-Madeleine herself and Léon Faye were desperately needed to prepare the network for its new role.

They begged to be allowed to return to France. But Dansey was adamant. He explained his reasons when he invited both of them to lunch at Brown's Hotel. "Your organisation has grown vast," he told them. "You're the only network covering the whole of France." Someone was needed to keep an overall view of the organisation, and the only place anyone could do that from was London.

Faye refused to accept Dansey's verdict. He was determined to get back into the fight. He continued to badger Marie-Madeleine for permission to return. She consulted Dansey again.

"He's going to be captured," he told her, bluntly. "I've been through his file again with my specialists: three arrests, two escapes, three two-way Lysander trips. He's very much in the red." Danscy read an agent's file like one of the racing form books he had used in earlier days – and calculated the odds in much the same way. When capture became an odds-on certainty, it was time to stop gambling.

In the end, however, Marie-Madeleine had no option but to agree to Faye's return. Things were beginning to go badly wrong for the network in France. Marie-Madeleine needed someone over there in whom she had complete confidence. It was a difficult and fateful decision, but when she tried to discuss it with Dansey he brusquely washed his hands of the matter, telling her it was up to her. "If you order him not to return, Poz," he said, "we won't provide him with a Lysander. I'm putting his fate in your hands."

Marie-Madeleine made her decision. Faye returned to France. A few days after landing he was betrayed by an old comrade and captured by the Gestapo, who tortured him. Tried before a tribunal in the fortress of Bruchsal, he was condemned to death. While awaiting execution in a prison near Kustrin on the River Oder, he had the final misfortune to be one of 819 prisoners massacred by the guards the day before Soviet troops marched in; the others managed to escape. Much later, when his old comrades wanted to take his body back to France, they were unable to identify him. The mass grave was full of blackened, charred corpses. The guards had attempted to destroy all traces of their handiwork by burning. To his great credit, Dansey did not say, "I told you so."

Throughout her stay in London, Dansey kept in close touch with Marie-Madeleine. He was at his most thoughtful and charming, sending her red roses on her birthday and taking her to lunch at the Ivy, the famous theatrical restaurant off the Charing Cross Road. Throughout the same period and in spite of constant harassment and Gestapo arrests, Alliance under Marie-Madeleine's direction remained in business and kept up a remarkable flow of vital intelligence to London ranging from assessments of the state of the Luftwaffe in France to the movements of submarines and torpedo boats. The demand from London for detailed information never slackened. London wanted to know the identities of the commanders of German warships based between Calais and Brest, the list of vessels in Marseilles harbour, the position of new defences and fortifications: everything the agents could discover.

With the approach of the Allied invasion of Europe, Alliance was able to provide one of the most valuable and amazing single intelligence coups of the war. Ironically, in the age of the computer and Ultra, it was produced by the same methods practised by Baden-Powell at the time of Dansey's first introduction to intelligence: a wandering artist painting harmless and attractive landscapes. Dansey's critics had derided his use of an artist in Germany in the years before the second world war as being useless and out of date. In 1944, the old way was still proving its worth.

In this case, the painter was Maurice Dounin, art teacher at the lycée in Caen. Over a period of time, partly on foot and partly by bicycle, he had managed to traverse the entire coastline from the mouth of the Dives to the Contentin Peninsula. From the sketches and notes he made, he was able to draw a huge map, which was proudly carried to London in March 1944 by the man who had recruited him, the chief of his group, Jean Sainteny. When it was unrolled in Marie-Madeleine's office before Dansey's delighted gaze, the map was found to be some fifty-five feet long and showed the position of every German gun emplacement, fortification and beach obstacle along the coast, plus details of all military units and their strengths. It proved to be an invaluable aid to the Allied commanders.

Sadly, Dounin himself did not live to see the triumph of his brain-child. With some fifteen other Resistance agents he was captured by the Gestapo and on 7th June, the day after the landings, he was shot. On the same day, Sainteny, who had returned to France after delivering the map, to take command of Alliance operations north of the Loire, was arrested in Paris with most of the leading members of the Paris network. He was the third Alliance leader to be taken in less than a year.

"Your famous law of averages is all wrong," Marie-Madeleine complained to Dansey. "Paul Bernard lasted six months. Dragon (Sainteny) only six weeks. I must go and take their place."

But Dansey had no intention of allowing Marie-Madeleine to return to France. "Unless security is cast-iron, Poz," he told her, "you won't last six days."

Marie-Madeleine persisted, however, and eventually succeeded in persuading de Gaulle's intelligence chief, André Dewavrin (Colonel Passy), to permit her to go, protected by a remarkable disguise and two different identity cards. Dansey was ill at the time, and therefore unable to interfere, but he seems to have acknowledged that the situation had by then become so desperate that they had no alternative but to use Marie-Madeleine again in an active role.

His concern for her was undiminished, however, and he told her that if she were captured she should use his name.

305

"If they arrest you, my dear," he instructed her, "tell them that I sent you to France to watch the Communist Party. They know my name. They won't dare touch you."

The political differences between the Gaullists and communists were well known to the Gestapo and were frequently exploited by them. Dansey believed that the Germans would be unable to resist the chance of acquiring one of his agents who could be turned and used against the FTPF. There was little more he could do for her except to wish her well. When she flew out of Britain he went to the airfield in person to see her board the black Lysander aircraft, and as a parting gift handed her his own rabbit's-foot charm for good luck.

Dansey's grim warning about Marie-Madeleine's chances of survival were to be proved correct. She had only been in Aix-en-Provence a few days when the flats where she was hiding were raided by the Germans. The Gestapo had followed one of her agents, Captain le Comte Helen des Isnards (Grand Duke), to the rendezvous. Their business soon over, he had left by a back way a few minutes before the Germans broke down the front door.

Desperately wishing to gain time in order to warn the rest of the network, Marie-Madeleine convinced the Gestapo men who had arrested her that she was a double agent. She refused to divulge her real identity to them: she would speak only with the local Gestapo chief. Fortunately for her, he was out of town and not due to return for twenty-four hours. Not quite sure of how to handle her, the Gestapo men took her to Miollis barracks in Aix instead of the prison, and locked her in one of the guardroom cells, having first kicked out the German soldiers being held there.

It was five hours till daybreak. Marie-Madeleine had just five hours to effect her escape.

An investigation of the window of her cell revealed that the glass had been broken long ago – all that remained were iron bars and a thick wooden plank screwed horizontally across the opening. Marie-Madeleine is a small woman, and in those days she was almost painfully thin. Stripped naked, she succeeded in getting into the space between the board and the iron bars. She thought that she just might be thin enough to squeeze through two of the bars. She was in the throes of this agonising operation when a German military convoy drew up outside her cell window. She managed to get back inside and had to stand, naked, trapped like a beetle against the plank behind her, while the German convoy commander got fresh directions from one of the guards. When the convoy moved off again, she was at last able to force herself

306

through the bars and drop down to the street below, holding her clothes between her teeth, and complete her escape. Next day, she made contact with her friends, resumed her control of the network and continued to direct it until the Liberation was complete. She had proved Dansey both right and wrong – she was taken, but she survived. Maybe his lucky rabbit's foot actually worked.

Today, Marie-Madeleine is in her early seventies, and still remarkably active. She is a Gaullist Member of the European Parliament, dividing her time between Brussels, Strasbourg and her elegant apartment on the Quai d'Orsay in Paris, as always battling fiercely for those causes which are dear to her heart. At the moment, her dearest cause is the fate of the Polish people. She remains a woman of great intelligence and immense energy.

Her last meeting with Claude Dansey was sad. It occurred immediately after the war when he had just retired. He seemed, she told us, depressed almost to the point of tears. With Europe divided and conflict growing between the superpowers, it seemed to him that everything they had fought for was about to be destroyed. The world had changed irrevocably. The war had been fought in vain.

CHAPTER TWENTY-EIGHT

The Yanks Are Coming – Again

As in the first world war, the last of the major Allies to enter the conflict was the United States. As in the first world war, they had to start from scratch in setting up an intelligence service. And as in the first world war, it was Claude Dansey who provided them with advice and a blueprint from which to build.

Although the US was technically neutral for the first two and a quarter years of the war, unofficial collaboration between America and Britain in the intelligence sphere had been growing steadily since 1939. Dansey, of course, already had his own Z Organisation base in New York, in Alexander Korda's Empire State Building office. Through it he was in touch with old friends from earlier days, such as Marlborough Churchill, Ralph Van Deman and J. Edgar Hoover. Early in 1940, further advances were made when President Roosevelt gave his personal permission for Hoover's FBI to maintain informal contact with the SIS, and for Sir William Stephenson to be sent out to America in May as SIS liaison officer.

In July, the President sent a special envoy to Europe. He had two main tasks: to investigate the causes of the French collapse, and to assess the determination and the ability of the British to continue the war. The man Roosevelt selected for this important mission seemed an unlikely choice: he was a right-wing Republican, which should have made him unacceptable to the New Deal Democratic Administration in Washington; he was an Irish Catholic, which should have made him suspect in the eyes of the British, smarting under the hostility of an Irish Catholic American Ambassador, Joseph P. Kennedy, who was openly anti-British.

But Roosevelt's special envoy was also a special man, and an old friend of both Stephenson and Dansey. He was William Joseph "Wild Bill" Donovan, a millionaire Wall Street lawyer whose clients included Standard Oil of New Jersey, large New York banks and many leading international companies. During the first

308

world war Donovan had commanded one of America's most famous regiments, the Fighting Sixty-Ninth, and had emerged with three wounds, the Congressional Medal of Honour and several other medals, as one of the most decorated heroes in American history. For a time after the war he had been Deputy Attorney-General, before starting his private law practice.

Donovan was a large, stocky man, fifty-eight years old, with silver hair and pale blue eyes. He was an independent thinker, and very much his own man. Roosevelt, crippled and confined to a wheel-chair by polio, called him "my secret legs", and on 14th July 1940 sent him to Europe without telling either Kennedy in London or the equally defeatist ambassador in France, William Bullitt. Inevitably, Kennedy soon discovered Donovan's presence in London, and reacted furiously, doing his best to sabotage the mission. But there was little he could do about it. Since Donovan's visit was unofficial and informal he did not have to be officially received by the British Government, but was free as a private citizen to talk to whoever he chose. And one of the first people he chose was his old friend Claude Dansey.

Dansey swiftly gave him an accurate picture of the situation in both France and Britain, contributing to the impressions Donovan was building and which he would incorporate in his report to the President in August.

The views Donovan presented of the two countries were radically different. France, he reported, had "cracked morally". The French establishment, disenchanted with the Republic and democracy, had become attracted to the authoritarianism of the fascist regimes. He believed that French politicians, industrialists and many senior army officers had been more interested in defending their privileges of wealth and power than in defending their country. It was a shattering analysis and bore out the views of French communist and liberal intellectuals who blamed the right for the fall of France. There can be no doubt that Donovan's report coloured many of Roosevelt's later policies, and sowed the seeds of his antagonism to General de Gaulle.

For Britain, however, Donovan had an entirely different assessment. Britain, he reported, would fight on, whatever happened – and America should be prepared to support her. On moral grounds, America was bound to side with democracy against dictatorship. On practical grounds, support for Britain was essential because it was America's own first line of defence. "If the British are reduced to guerilla campaigns against a Nazi occupation," he wrote, "it will take Americans a generation to regain a foothold in Europe. And from what I have learned here about Nazi fifth-column methods, we in America by then may find it's too late to save ourselves."

Aid to Britain was stepped up, and preparations were started – in the strictest secrecy – for the creation of a new American intelligence organisation, in readiness for the time when the United States would have to join the fight. More immediately, it was agreed that the time had already arrived when there should be a full and free exchange of intelligence between Britain and America. Initially, the British were disappointed with the quality of the information supplied by the Americans, who were finding it extremely difficult to collect reliable intelligence, particularly from the Axis and occupied countries, without an organisation or agents. But the important thing was that the two great nations were once again co-operating. It was twenty-three years since Dansey had gone to Washington to help set up a military intelligence service for the USA. Now, he was instrumental in getting a new service started, on an even grander scale. When Donovan talked to Dansey in the summer of 1940, Dansey impressed on him the need to create a new, centralised intelligence agency as quickly as possible. Donovan agreed wholeheartedly, but it was not so easy to put their ideas into practice in 1940, while the United States was still neutral. There were powerful forces in favour of isolationism and of keeping America out of Europe's war whatever happened. Popular voices such as those of Charles Lindbergh and Father Charles Coughlin were raised clamorously and incessantly against giving any help to Britain. Many influential figures, too, still held the same views as Woodrow Wilson had had on intelligence and espionage. To crown it all, 1940 was a Presidential election year, and Wendell Willkie was pressing Roosevelt hard on an anti-war platform.

Under such circumstances, progress was inevitably slow and cautious. Nevertheless, it was made. And after the election, with Roosevelt safely back in the White House, the preparations accelerated. In February 1941, Donovan's first two recruits were sent to London under the guise of FBI officers, to be trained by the SIS under Dansey's direction. Soon, military missions were exchanged which included intelligence officers. In London, the embryo intelligence service of the United States watched, listened, talked and learned the rudiments of the business under their innocuous title of the "United States Special Observers Group".

On 11th July 1941, Roosevelt created the Office of the Coordination of Information (COI) under Donovan, a name which was to be changed a year later to the Office of Strategic Services (OSS). Following Dansey's advice, the two main components were kept separate: Secret Intelligence (SI) was the equivalent of the SIS "G" sections, responsible for intelligence gathering; Secret Operations (SO) was the equivalent of the SOE. There were also three other branches: Research and Analysis; Morale Operations, responsible for black propaganda; and X-2, responsible for counter-intelligence. The Americans were officially back in business.

The new organisation expanded at an astounding rate. By 1944 it had reached a strength of 15,000 men and women, with a budget of nearly $57 million. In the early days, most of the training was done by the British, either in London or, after November 1941, in a special camp in Canada. But soon it became self-generating, and eager to be free from its foster parent's domination. Inevitably, friction between the two bodies grew. The British reaction to the mushrooming growth of its counterpart was similar to that expressed by the Royal Navy when the US Navy outstripped it for size. "How's the world's second biggest navy?" an American warship taunted as it passed a British destroyer at sea. "Fine," came the reply. "How's the second best?"

Malcolm Muggeridge, who served in SIS during the war, says,

They came among us, these aspiring American spymasters, like innocent girls from a finishing school anxious to learn the seasoned demi-mondaine ways of old practitioners – in this case, the legendary British Secret Service. . . . Alas, the period of tutelage lasted all too short a time. The first feeling of awe and respect soon evaporated; and it turned out that the finishing school products had learnt all the tricks and devices of the old practitioners in no time at all, and were operating on their own, sustained by lavish supplies of money whose reckless dispensing sent up the accepted tariff of bribes to astronomical proportions everywhere.

Donovan always openly regarded Dansey as "the Master", and was grateful to him for his help and guidance. But it soon became clear that he was not prepared to accept the subordinate role which Dansey seems to have assumed the American organisation would play. Dansey was horrified to discover that the COI, even before it became the OSS, had been in direct contact with the other Allied intelligence services in London, without telling him. He was alarmed at the opportunities for confusion created by such independent action, and pointed out the dangers to Donovan, who agreed that, although American Intelligence could not be controlled by the authorities of another state, he would take care to maintain the closest collaboration with the SIS.

This early squall gave Donovan a warning of the stormy waters that lay ahead, and of the need for a good pilot to steer the OSS through them. In the late summer of 1942 he appointed a man he thought would be exactly right for the task, to be OSS chief in Europe. This was David Kirkpatrick Este Bruce, forty-four years old, tall, lean and elegant, a prominent member of an old American family. His social qualifications were undoubtedly excellent for dealing with men like Menzies and Dansey. He was a millionaire in his own right, and married to the daughter of one of the world's richest men, steel magnate and former Republican Secretary of the Treasury, Andrew Mellon. He was himself the son of a United States senator and had served as a Democratic member of the state legislatures of Maryland and Virginia.

Bruce was a charming, intelligent and diplomatic man. He had been recruited by Donovan in 1941 while representing the American Red Cross in London. In the post-war years he was to become, among other things, a highly successful ambassador to London, Paris and Bonn, head of the US delegation to the Vietnam peace conference and of the first US mission to China. He found no difficulty in getting on splendidly with Menzies, who treated him with his usual smooth, polished charm.

But Dansey, it seemed, was a different matter. Bruce later described him as "a crusty old curmudgeon who could not stand interference or rivalry from the Americans – indeed, we could hardly do anything right in old Claude's eyes". Bruce's bewilderment at Dansey's attitude displays a naivety which was typical of the OSS at that time – even those who, like Bruce, regarded themselves as sophisticated men of the world. In his eagerness to get things done and to be in the thick of the action, he overlooked one essential point: although he was chief of all OSS activities in Europe, he had been in the business for less than a year, and had no practical experience whatever – and neither had his chief. Dansey had been in it for forty-five years, more than half of them at the top, and his practical experience was immeasurable. It is hardly surprising that he was not disposed to treat Bruce as an equal.

As fast as OSS grew, so did Dansey's forebodings and fears. Donovan had a brilliant mind, but it was a highly unorthodox one, and most of the people he recruited were also unorthodox. They were impatient, often brash, and almost always totally scornful of authority or military discipline. Agents on the ground regularly chose to go their own way, ignoring any orders from above and regardless of overall political or military objectives. Where Dansey

312

instinctively chose the most devious method of doing anything, the American freshmen usually went bull-headed for the most direct and obvious, heedless of the security dangers involved.

A former British attaché who was in Switzerland when the first OSS men arrived has described their approach as being like a man with a loud handbell, which he rang as hard as he could in the town square while shouting his wares and calling for customers. An SIS man in Geneva was horrified when a newly-arrived American threw open his suitcase to reveal that it was literally packed with money, which he planned to use to buy agents and information.

When, later in the war, the OSS decided to seek agents to go into Germany itself – having been led to accept the erroneous belief that Britain had no one inside the Reich – they decided to make use of a category of refugee in London which had not been exploited by the British: the communists of the Free Germany Committee. In spite of warnings that this could be dangerous and shortsighted, Donovan gave the order to go ahead. The OSS was essentially a short-term organisation, with only one objective: the winning of the war. What happened afterwards was not its concern – unlike the permanent SIS, to whom the war was just an interruption to its normal job of keeping track of all enemies and potential enemies.

The job of making contact with the German communists was given to a young lieutenant, Joseph Gould, who had formerly worked as a motion-picture publicist in New York. His method was so direct and simple that it must have given Dansey an attack of apoplexy. He sought out London's main left-wing political bookshop, walked in and announced himself. He asked who was important in the Free Germany Committee, and was given the name of a man who could help him. He went to the man's flat, and explained to him that he was looking for agents capable of undertaking delicate missions inside Germany. The German refugee was delighted. He told Gould he was the first intelligence officer of any Allied nation to approach him. He said he knew exactly what was wanted, and would be glad to help, and he was as good as his word.

The man who helped Gould was Jurgen Kuczynski. He was brother of Ruth Kuczynski, alias Sonia, Allan Foote's original GRU boss in Switzerland, first head of the Soviet network which became the Lucy Ring, who was now in Oxford, spying on Britain for the Russians. Sonia was then running Klaus Fuchs, an atomic scientist who was giving her vital information on the development of the atom bomb for transmission to Moscow. She had other agents, too, working against Britain and America. Jurgen was also spying for the Russians – indeed he had introduced Fuchs to his sister – and so was their father, Professor René Kuczynski, who supplied secret political information which he obtained through conversations with Sir Stafford Cripps, then a member of the War Cabinet.

American naivety at that time was further demonstrated to Dansey by a report from Washington which had a more humorous turn. Leonard Miall – later the BBC's American Correspondent, and incidentally the man who had failed to record de Gaulle's 18th June speech – was then working for the Ministry of Economic Warfare. While in Washington he dined with the President, Cordell Hull and various other dignitaries. Naturally, the main topic of conversation was the war in Europe, and at one point the President turned reassuringly to Miall and told him they knew Germany was about to give in, as America was monitoring a German radio station believed to be somewhere in Bavaria, which broadcast strong anti-Nazi sentiment. "It must be supported by high-ranking and powerful officers," Roosevelt explained, "or it wouldn't be allowed to broadcast so openly and for so long."

Miall kept a straight face but when he got back to his office he sent an immediate cable home, saying it was splendid to fool the Germans, but should we be fooling the US President, too? The radio station was, of course, British black propaganda from England, but this possibility had apparently never occurred to the President or his Secretary of State.

During 1942 and 1943, Dansey's chief problem with his American allies was in restraining them from impulsive actions. The enormous natural energy which Donovan and his men brought into the alliance was a great asset to the weary British warriors, but it was also dangerous. Donovan wanted to put his own agents into Europe as quickly as possible, to run his own intelligence and sabotage operations, independently of the British. Dansey resisted desperately. He had spent two difficult years rebuilding old networks and creating new ones. The situation in France was, as we have seen, extremely complicated, very delicate and very dangerous. There were already too many different organisations at work, and the intrusion of yet another – and one which Dansey still regarded as mainly a bunch of green amateurs with more money than sense – could put everything and everyone at risk.

It is from this period that the legend of Dansey's virulent anti-Americanism stems. When one considers his past, and the intimate connections he had with the United States and with individual Americans over the years, such an accusation seems odd. Nevertheless, he was the man who was seen to be constantly frustrating American efforts to get moving, and therefore became an ogre in the eyes of many. We should bear in mind, too, that much of the evidence of Dansey's anti-American sentiments and actions comes from the writings of Kim Philby, who has always had a vested interest on behalf of his Soviet masters to do everything possible to drive a wedge between Britain and the United States. And we must remember that although America was welcomed into the war, there was often a general resentment by the bruised, battered and battle-weary British people to the sudden appearance in their midst of eager, fresh, affluent American servicemen proclaiming in loud voices that they had come to the rescue. Popular feeling was often summed up in the three-fold complaint about the Yanks – that they were "over-sexed, over-paid and over here".

Fortunately, Bruce's chief of SI for most of the war, Dr William Maddox, understood Dansey's point of view. Maddox, in civilian life a professor of political science, resisted Donovan's urgent directives to set up independent OSS networks in Europe. He pointed out that the British were passing on everything they got from occupied Europe, that it could be counter-productive to try to set up new networks in competition and perhaps at cross purposes with existing Allied networks. In his view, nothing should be done which could endanger close, friendly relations with the British.

This closeness did not extend, however, to sharing codes and a single (SIS) communications system – as Dansey proposed in January 1943. The Americans were quick to realise that this would mean that the SIS could keep its activities secret but would know everything the OSS was doing. Dansey had been successful in pulling this ploy on the SOE, but he was not so lucky with the OSS. The Americans rejected his kind offer out of hand.

For nearly two years, Dansey managed to hold off allowing the OSS to send any agents into France from London. But in the meantime the Americans were given the chance to ease their frustrations in November 1942 when the Allies landed in French north-west Africa with Operation Torch. As this was a US-controlled theatre, they were able to set up an intelligence network in Algiers, running agents in North Africa and the Mediterranean. Dansey did not mind giving the Americans precedence in that part of North Africa, since it was an area which had never particularly interested him. But when they started trying to run agents into southern France from Algiers, there were more squalls.

In July 1943, Henry B. Hyde, head of the OSS's SI branch in Algiers, travelled secretly to London to see Dansey in person, to explain his aims and to try to persuade him to change his attitude. Hyde was a twenty-nine-year-old New York attorney, who had been born and raised in France, where his father had moved after a US Government investigation of his business affairs. He was, naturally, completely bilingual and in addition to his French education had also studied at Cambridge University in England and received a law degree at Harvard in the USA. He was married to the daughter of a French baron and ultra-conservative senator, and his views on French politics were said to border on monarchism. He was pro-Giraud, and violently anti-Gaullist.

After arriving in England inadequately disguised in British uniform, he was detained at Prestwick airport for two days, but was eventually allowed to travel to London to see Dansey. He was taken to Broadway Buildings on a sunny Sunday afternoon by a rather nervous Maddox, who instructed him to forget the address and everything else about the "holy of holies". The two Americans were shown into a rather bare, dusty room on the fourth floor, containing two battered old desks, a Victorian safe and a pre-war map of the world stuck on one wall – the only decoration. It did not compare favourably in Hyde's eyes with Donovan's ultra-modern, comfortable and well-equipped offices back in New York. He was under the impression that this was Dansey's office, but it is more likely it was a deliberately anonymous interview room.

After keeping them waiting for a few minutes, Dansey entered, "a tall, spare man with an air of authority who was obviously used to getting what he wanted". He greeted Hyde politely, but his manner suggested that he would rather have been somewhere else that Sunday afternoon, and he proceeded to question him vigorously. What, he demanded, did Hyde hope to achieve with his agents which was not already being done by the British and French agents in France?

Hyde explained that the American forces appreciated what they were getting from the SIS, but quite naturally they wanted to have their own sources of information which could be asked to provide for their specific needs prior to the invasion of the South of France. Dansey listened impassively, nodding his head as Hyde acknowledged the dangers and the need to ensure that any new agents operated in strict separation from any existing networks, so as to avoid endangering their security. He did his best to assure Dansey that he was well aware of the British chief's fears, and had already made very careful arrangements to cover them.

What Dansey did not tell Hyde was that he already knew about his intentions. He knew too, that Hyde had been receiving emissaries from Marshall Pétain in Vichy and from the German Abwehr, who were hopeful of penetrating the OSS with "peace" proposals. As it happened, Schellenberg and the Nazi SD were also aware of the Abwehr's hopes, and were themselves waiting to move in on the operation.

As the interview progressed, Hyde was pleased to notice that Dansey appeared to be softening. He stopped raising objections and began asking detailed questions about the quality of Hyde's agents and his operational plans. By the time General Sir James Marshall-Cornwall came in, bristling with hostility and the "innate superiority" of a former Vice-Chief of the Imperial General Staff, Hyde was convinced that Dansey was on his side. As Marshall-Cornwall fired off salvo after salvo – all, of course, as previously instructed by Dansey – Hyde played his trump card. Following a tip given to him by David Bruce, he told Dansey that one of the OSS officers in Algiers who would be responsible for Secret Intelligence operations into France was Ted Ryan, grandson of Dansey's old friend Thomas Fortune Ryan. Indeed, Hyde himself had some connection with the Ryans, for his own grandfather had founded the Equitable Life Assurance Company, which Thomas Ryan had owned for a time.

Dansey then actually smiled at Hyde, and talked for a while about his experiences as manager of Ryan's African interests. The Americans went off happily soon afterwards, leaving Dansey to congratulate Marshall-Cornwall on playing his part so well, and helping him to achieve his objectives. It had been a Sunday afternoon well spent for Dansey. He would be able to silence the continuing clamour from the OSS in London to be allowed to send their own agents into France by pointing out that they were already doing so from Algiers. He had managed to off-load the troublesome General Giraud on to the Americans in Algiers, leaving himself free to concentrate on dealing with de Gaulle, who was now quite obviously emerging as the victor in the French political struggles. He had also found out all he needed to know about American plans, and could use Hyde's branch of the OSS as a decoy for German attentions. After a decent interval of three days, he gave his approval.

Hyde proceeded with his plan and sent agents into Vichy France. The result – as Dansey must have anticipated – was a complete disaster. It also contributed in large part to the demise of the Abwehr and the ascendancy of Schellenberg's SD. And it brought about the final downfall of Giraud, leaving de Gaulle – and, more immediately important for Dansey, friends such as Rémy and Passy – in total control of Free French Forces: by some strange chance, the Gaullists seemed to know in advance every move Hyde and Giraud were planning.

Relations between the OSS and SIS were not fraught with friction everywhere in Europe. In most of Dansey's outposts, representatives of the two services got along together extremely well. Nowhere was the harmony greater or more fruitful than in Switzerland.

To a large extent, this was due to happy coincidence in the choice of two key Americans. The head of the OSS in Berne was none other than Allen Dulles, whom Dansey had known there in the first world war. And the American minister in Switzerland was Leland Harrison, who had been Dansey's chief contact in the US State Department in 1917 and 1918. Both were old friends. Both were men with experience of clandestinity and statecraft.

There is a persistent story that Dulles and Dansey were enemies, and that the British and Americans were constantly at loggerheads in Switzerland, but the authors have been unable to find any evidence to substantiate either statement. Instead, they have found considerable evidence to the exact opposite. Indeed, Dulles and Vanden Heuvel, Dansey's SIS chief in Switzerland, became such close friends that for years after the war they visited each other's homes annually, corresponded personally as well as professionally, and always held each other in high esteem. The authors have spoken to many former agents who served in Switzerland during the war, and with only very minor exceptions their recollections are of close, friendly co-operation and collaboration at all times.

The main source of the stories can be traced back, once more, to Kim Philby, another example of his making mischief between Britain and the United States, sowing seeds of doubt and discord for the benefit of his masters in the Kremlin. One story in particular can now be set straight. It concerns a German called Fritz Kolbe, a forty-three-year-old official of the German Foreign Office, who became Dulles's star spy.

Kolbe was a dedicated anti-Nazi, and was determined to do his bit in bringing down the Hitler regime. "It is not enough to clench one's fist and hide it in one's pocket," he explained. "The fist must be used to strike." By 1943, he realised sadly that the best hope for Germany's future would be defeat in the war. That was the only way of ensuring the removal of Naziism. In his job, he regularly handled information which he knew would be of tremendous value to the Allies. If he could get it to them, he would be using his fist to strike a blow for freedom.

By pulling strings within the Foreign Office, he managed to get himself the chance of making regular trips as a courier to Switzerland, on the pretext that he had business interests there. He arrived in Berne on 23rd August 1943 on his first journey, carrying a bundle of secret documents strapped to his leg, and after delivering his diplomatic pouch to the German Embassy he made his way to the British Legation. There, he asked to see the military attaché, assuming that he would be the man who handled intelligence matters.

Unfortunately, Colonel Henry Cartwright did no such thing. In neutral Switzerland he was strictly forbidden any such activity – to his great relief. When Kolbe was brought to his office, and started to explain his purpose, Cartwright panicked and threw him out. He wanted nothing to do with the sleazy business of espionage, and in any event was terrified that the strange little German might be an *agent provocateur*. Had Kolbe found his way to Vanden Heuvel, it might have been a different story, but his abrupt rejection by the stiff-necked Cartwright left him shattered.

Fortunately, a friend persuaded him not to give up, but to try his luck with the Americans, and arranged for him to see Allen Dulles at 23 Herrengasse, the picturesque old house which was the OSS headquarters in the medieval heart of the city. At their first meeting, Kolbe presented Dulles with no less than 186 pages of microfilmed documents from German top secret diplomatic files.

It is at this point that Philby's version veers sharply from the truth, as described to the authors by some of those who were involved on the spot. According to Philby, Dulles "without hesitation . . . decided that the goods were genuine. They shocked him into a lyrical state which was still on him when he drafted his official report to Washington. 'If only,' he wrote, 'you could see these documents in all their pristine freshness!'" The documents were then copied and sent to Washington, and OSS loyally made them available to the SIS. Naturally, the first person they were given to was Dansey, who immediately and without even studying them announced that they were fakes. Philby says Dansey "resented the installation of OSS in Switzerland, and lost no opportunity of belittling Dulles's work. The sight of the Berlin papers must have been a severe shock to him . . . It was clearly impossible that Dulles should have pulled off this spectacular scoop under his nose. The stuff was obviously a plant, and Dulles had fallen for it like a ton of bricks."

However, there was a brilliant man working in Section V, dealing with counter-intelligence, who had the presence of mind to realise that the documents could be genuine, and could be checked by having them compared with Ultra intercepts at Bletchley. Lo and behold, many of them matched precisely – they were original messages of enormous value, and what was more they were rapturously received by the cryptanalysts as a great help in cracking further ciphers which had been causing problems. With infinite care, the brilliant man from Section V approached the appropriate departments in the Foreign Office and the armed services, and obtained equally rapturous reactions from them. All were clamouring for more.

Dansey, of course, was furious. If the documents were genuine, it merely made matters worse. It would encourage OSS to "run riot all over Switzerland, fouling up the whole intelligence field". He was pacified, however, when the young man told him he had circulated the information as coming from a British source, without mentioning the Americans, and that Dansey's stock had risen considerably in consequence. The brilliant young man from Section V, who saved Dansey's bacon, was none other than Kim Philby.

That is the gospel according to Philby. In fact Dulles was by no means foolish enough to accept Kolbe's documents at their face value. He saw immediately that there were at least three possible reasons for either the Abwehr or the SD planting the documents on them. First, it could be a scheme for breaking American codes and ciphers: German cryptanalysts would be able to compare the originals with the enciphered versions which Dulles would radio back to Washington. Second, Kolbe could be an *agent provocateur* who would inform the Swiss security police that Dulles had German documents which would prove he was involved in espionage, and thus have him and his staff expelled from Switzerland. Third, the documents could be "chickenfeed" – genuine information handed to enemy intelligence services to lull them into a false sense of security, so that they would accept false and deliberately misleading information later.

Of course, there was always the fourth possibility: that Kolbe was a genuine anti-Nazi with incredibly good sources, who was prepared to risk all by helping the Allies. Dulles could not forget that twenty-six years before, during his previous stay in Berne, he had missed the chance of meeting an obscure Russian revolutionary called Vladimir Ilyich Lenin. To lose such an opportunity again would be criminal, but at the same time it had to be treated with extreme care. As a sign of good faith, Kolbe told him his real name, address, position and dates of service with the German Foreign Office, details of his first wife, of a young son who was living in South Africa, and of his second wife, who came from Zurich. All these could be checked, and used to identify him to the German authorities and get him hanged. Dulles agreed to take his documents, and for the German to visit him again with another batch when he next came to Berne in about three months' time.

When Kolbe had gone and the documents had been examined, Dulles called his friend Vanden Heuvel and told him what had happened. The two men discussed the various possibilities together. Dulles divided the pile of documents and gave one half to the British, for them to run an independent check while the other half went to Washington. One hundred and eighty-six documents, apart from anything else, represented a considerable task of encipherment and transmission, and the SIS people were delighted to share the load with OSS.

London and Washington naturally provided each other with the other halves. Dansey was deeply suspicious about the documents – they just seemed too good to be true. He gave them, in the normal and proper way to the department responsible for investigating possible plants by hostile intelligence services: Section V. Equally normally, Section V – in the shape of Kim Philby – took the obvious first step of asking Bletchley if they matched any radio intercepts. When they were satisfied that the documents were genuine, and contained material that was too important to have been used as "chickenfeed", Dansey was informed, and he in turn passed on the good news to the OSS.

Kolbe made his second trip to Berne on 7th October 1943, and from then on continued to provide first-class material in considerable quantity. He arranged more direct ways of getting particularly urgent information to Dulles through friends, and also methods for the OSS to contact him should they want information on anything specific. He enlarged his field of operation, spreading from the Foreign Office into industry, the military high command and the Church. By early 1944 he had built up what he described as his "inner circle" of some two dozen reliable and well-connected informants supplying him with secrets.

Kolbe suddenly went silent on 29th July 1944. That was the day a bomb plot narrowly failed to assassinate Hitler. The Gestapo and the SD tore the country apart in their efforts to find all the conspirators and their supporters. Kolbe was not caught, but security became so tight that it was impossible for him to continue. His days as a masterspy were over. It had been a brief but spectacular career: in a little over a year, he had provided more than 1,600 secret documents, on vitally important subjects, to Allen Dulles in Berne. And at all times, throughout the entire operation, the OSS and the SIS had co-operated fully and happily.

By that time, the two organisations were at last working alongside each other, together with the French, inside occupied France in Claude Dansey's last major operation.

CHAPTER TWENTY-NINE

"Sussex"

On 19th June 1943, David Bruce received the following draft plan personally prepared by Claude Dansey:

PLAN "SUSSEX"

(1) To recruit a special unit, actual numbers need not be fixed – nationality French – with knowledge of particular areas and localities. For preference men who have been in France since 1941.

(2) Recruits as far as possible to be chosen from men who have had military training and experience: former officers when possible.

(3) The unit to be formed with the object of placing men in pairs, composed of one observer, who should have good education and be of such a character that he will be able to attract others to work as collectors of information after arrival in France. His companion at time of departure to be a fully qualified W/T operator.

(4) The "Sussex" unit to be held as a formation under discipline, at a point to be selected outside London.

(5) As and when the different theatres of command are established, the unit to be subdivided into two groups,
(A) for operating in the back areas at strategic points, and
(B) forward areas in proximity to the coast for supply of tactical information.

(6) It will probably be advisable to despatch groups under (A) two moon periods in advance of zero-day, groups (B) in the lunar period immediately preceding.

(7) The measures proposed in paras 5 and 6 to be adopted in order to obviate, or at any rate lessen, the danger of the agents becoming too active in advance and to improve their

chances of survival. Groups (B) would probably be not required to operate until X days before zero-day.

(8) Unless there are special reasons, these groups would not be put in touch with organisations at present in existence, as their casualty rates increase each month and security reasons make it undesirable.

(9) Communication lines in detail to be worked out, when the different commands have been allocated according to the wishes of Force Commanders.

For the OSS in London, this was a momentous occasion. The dreaded Colonel Dansey, who had steadily blocked all their efforts to set up an independent intelligence service in Europe, was at last proposing a full partnership. In a covering memo he told Bruce that his plan had the backing of the British authorities, and hoped that OSS would agree to participate and would get the approval of the United States European Theatre commander. He pointed out that it would be necessary for SIS and OSS jointly to obtain general agreement with the French – though at that stage it was still not clear which of the French authorities was the best one to approach. And, to emphasise the co-operative nature of the project he was proposing, he stated that a clear understanding would have to be reached "as to uniform treatment of all men in the proposed unit, as respects discipline, rates of pay, equipment and training". It was a covering memo which shrewdly fingered all the principal danger areas for friction between the partners.

The idea behind Sussex was a very simple one. When the Allied armies landed in Normandy, it would be of great value to them if they had specially trained agents in place behind the German lines, in addition to and separate from any existing Resistance networks, to report by radio on the positions and strengths of German forces, troop movements, supplies and anything else that was requested. To this end, Dansey proposed parachuting a number of two-man teams into France, each comprising an observer and a radio operator. They would be dropped only a short time before the invasion, to lessen the chances of capture, to a number of key points selected by the military commanders.

All the men would be subject to military discipline, though they would be wearing civilian clothes, and they should be genuine Frenchmen, preferably selected from those who had been in their native country during the preceding two years. Ideally, they should have specific knowledge of parts of northern and central France, and they would be sent to areas they knew, though never to their home towns or villages where they could be recognised. The area to be covered was to be split into two zones, roughly divided by the River Seine. The zone to the north was to be the responsibility of the British; that to that south would be in the total control of the OSS. All intelligence messages from either sector were to be transmitted to SHAEF and to the Allied armies in the field, where special liaison units were to be set up. It had taken some time to reach the stage where Dansey could present a firm-outline plan. The OSS, of course, had been pressing for active collaboration with the British ever since it arrived to set up shop at 72 Grosvenor Street. But the SIS had kept its fledgling godchild firmly in its place. Dansey considered the Americans had a great deal to learn before they could safely be let loose.

The SI London Branch Report of 1st May 1943 showed how well he had achieved his object. It stated that "the primary occupation of London SI had been, up to the present, the maintenance of effective liaison with the British and Allied Secret Intelligence Services in London for the purpose of obtaining their intelligence reports, and of disseminating this material (as well as our own SI reports) to the appropriate American and British agencies."

In thwarting Donovan's wish to make SI London an equal rather than a junior partner with the SIS, Dansey found help from an unexpected quarter. Many members of the US military establishment were bitterly opposed to the very existence of the OSS. One of the ways in which they managed to obstruct the activities of what they saw as a dangerous, disorganised and undisciplined outfit was to block all transport facilities to Europe for OSS personnel. This meant that the London office found it almost impossible to expand and since the number of staff it had was "barely adequate to maintain existing liaisons", undertaking new and more positive responsibilities seemed out of the question.

Donovan and his Chief of SI in Washington, Whitney Shepardson, continued, nevertheless, to push the London branch to take a tougher line with the SIS. On 15th May, they instructed Bruce and Maddox to persuade Dansey to let them supply "at least some under cover agents", so that they could get some experience in running them. Realising that Dansey might prove hard to convince, they suggested that Bruce should tell him the OSS was preparing for an independent service on the Continent once the invasion had started. Bruce, however, had learned from bitter experience that it would not be that easy. The only way of achieving the sort of partnership they wanted, he told Donovan, was for SI London to have something tangible to offer. What that could be, though, was more difficult: "Money, neither the British nor the foreign services needed," he wrote later. "SI London had no agents to contribute, since agents recruited in the US would generally have no adequate cover and since foreign prospects were preempted by the British. Having no agents, SI was in no position to compel co-operation by the threat of independent operations."

Shepardson replied that he appreciated the problems, and suggested a different approach. Instead of threats or attempts to buy their way in, why not simply *ask* to be allowed to take part – if need be only as observers to begin with, in order to gain the experience they needed. Surely, he reasoned, Dansey "would prefer the Americans to gain such experience rather than to act later as amateurs". This final point was probably the strongest he could have made, knowing Dansey's views on such matters.

To everyone's surprise, Dansey agreed, and at a meeting on 29th May 1943 suggested Sussex – a major operation in which the SIS and OSS would be equal partners. Perhaps he considered the Americans were ready – or would be by the time of the invasion. Perhaps he simply decided to accept the inevitable. Whatever the reason, the die was cast.

Ironically, once the offer had been made, most of the delays and difficulties came not from the British but from the Americans and the French. Although OSS complained loud and long about British attitudes and obstructions, these were as nothing compared to the hostility shown to "Donovan's Dreamers" by the US military. It took until October for General Jake Devers, US GOC of the European Theatre, to give his consent to Sussex. The OSS champed at the bit and chafed at what they regarded as British reluctance to proceed until then, but Dansey had made it a condition of his offer that it should have the full backing of the military authorities. He had seen too much of the sort of in-fighting between the US army and the OSS which had led General Crockett, chief of US Military Intelligence in London to refer to the OSS as an "irregular trespass on his own orthodox preserves", and for Devers himself to tell Donovan, at a meeting in London, that he did not trust him or his ideas. Donovan responded by saying that unless the general apologised at once he would have to tear him to pieces physically and throw his remains through the windows into Grosvenor Square!

Eventually, however, peace was restored and Devers did consent – after making a hasty apology to Donovan and thus avoiding dismemberment. By that time, OSS Washington had put together a special team to run the American end of Sussex, which had flown into London in mid-September. It was headed by Francis Pickens Miller who had been recruited into the OSS with the rank of lieutenant-colonel on 7th June. Although he was virtually a rookie in the OSS, Miller had many years of overseas experience. He had fought in France in the first world war, been a Rhodes scholar at Oxford and chairman of the World Student Christian Federation in Geneva. He had, like Bruce, been a member of the Virginia legislature, and in 1941 had joined the COI as chairman of the propaganda planning board. As soon as he and his staff arrived in London they began working to establish a genuine partnership with the SIS.

At first, determined to underline their equality and independence, the OSS tried to recruit its Sussex agents from Frenchmen living in the United States, but it soon became obvious that such men were not suitable for the job. Most of them had been out of France for too long and were unfamiliar with current conditions. Nearly all of them were considered too soft after living in comfort in America. OSS was forced to go with the SIS to recruit men from the French forces in Algiers.

The French situation was even more divided and problematic than the American. Passy had agreed to the BCRA joining the OSS and SIS in mounting Sussex, but he had to get approval from the Committee of Liberation in Algiers – where the whole thing became bogged down in the bitter wranglings and strife between the various factions, especially between the two rival leaders, de Gaulle and Giraud. The weeks dragged by, with little hope of a decision, and the state of affairs was made even worse when Donovan impetuously announced his support for Giraud.

Dansey had planned to open the first special training school – SIS was to arrange all training for the operation – at St Albans in early October. But it was the end of that month before a representative of the Committee of Liberation flew into London to assure him that the French would co-operate, and the first few recruits began to arrive. Most of them were totally unsuitable, however, and the school opened, at last, on 15th November, with only a handful of the 100 trainee agents who were needed for the operation. The first drop was scheduled for the March 1944 moon, and time was rushing past.

By then, the SIS and Miller's team were working together in total harmony. After all the previous doubts and difficulties, Miller was delighted to be able to report that "the British were marvellous" and "opened all doors to us". But the flow of recruits was still only a trickle, and it was the end of the year before the situation in Algiers could be sorted out and recruiting put on the urgent footing that was needed.

Suddenly, it was January, and the invasion was no longer "next year" but only a matter of weeks away – at that stage it was still scheduled for the beginning of May. The pressure increased. A tripartite committee was established to concentrate entirely on Sussex. Dansey, of course, though deeply interested in the progress of his brain-child, had far too many other responsibilities to devote himself to Sussex alone: he was still in charge of all SIS operations world-wide, with agents in every continent working at full blast.

His deputy, Commander Kenneth Cohen, therefore became Chairman of the Sussex committee, with the responsibility for overseeing the entire operation. Miller, naturally, was the American representative. The French chief was none other than Gilbert Renault-Roulier, Dansey's friend Rémy. The SIS also provided a major as the secretary of the committee, which was responsible for all important questions of policy. Operational details were to be looked after by a sub-committee of six, two from each nation including Rémy as chairman.

Rémy's appointment was the key which could unlock the recruitment problem. He would be able to go to de Gaulle himself, to get authority to recruit agents directly from the Free French army. In the event, however, it became a close-run thing – de Gaulle's pride almost put a stop to everything, because of what was known as the Dufour affair.

Dansey gave a dinner party for Rémy, on the eve of his departure for Algiers to see de Gaulle. At the dinner, Dansey and one of the other guests, a leading Member of Parliament, asked Rémy to speak to the French leader about an unfortunate affair involving a Frenchman called Dufour. This man had worked for Dansey in France on several occasions, and had offered his services to the BCRA, claiming to be an officer and to hold the *Légion d'honneur*. When Passy discovered he was lying, he suspected him of being an enemy agent, and locked him away in a dungeon in the cellar of his headquarters in Duke Street. Dufour had managed to escape, with the help of a group of anti-Gaullists, had gone to the police and was charging Passy and de Gaulle with unlawful imprisonment. The matter was about to come to court, and de Gaulle was required to appear, to answer the charges. De Gaulle, true to his nature as always, was refusing to appear or even to be represented in a British court.

Dansey explained to Rémy that if de Gaulle did not put in an appearance, either in person or through a lawyer, he would inevitably be found guilty by default. This would certainly please the anti-Gaullists who were behind the whole affair, but it would provide the Germans with an incredible propaganda weapon, which they would use to the full. This was a sensitive time, Dansey reminded Rémy. The effect on French opinion, and on the morale of the Resistance when they heard that de Gaulle had been convicted of a criminal charge against the liberty of the individual, and by a British court, would be disastrous.

Rémy, in consternation, asked Dansey if he could not pull strings to have the business hushed up, and perhaps not reported until later. Dansey's shocked face gave him his answer.

"In this country," Dansey told him, "we have a profound respect for the liberty of the individual. No considerations can be allowed to interfere with the course of justice."

One of the other diners remarked that King Edward VII, when Prince of Wales, had been called to appear in court during a celebrated case, and had complied. Dansey suggested that Rémy might use this information in trying to persuade his chief to change his mind. He begged Rémy to do what he could while he was in Algiers, and explain to de Gaulle that it would be in his own interest, as well as that of France and the Allies.

Rémy promised to do what he could, though he would not hold out much hope. And indeed he was proved right. He braved the General's wrath to present Dansey's message, although de Gaulle forbade any mention of the affair. When all appeals to reason had failed, he tried the incident about King Edward. De Gaulle drew himself up imperiously, gave his desk a tremendous thump and roared, "I am not the Prince of Wales!"

"*Mon général*," pleaded Rémy, "it would be so simple to be legally represented."

"The head of the government of France will never appear before a foreign court not even through an intermediary!" came the furious reply.

Dansey was delighted with the success of Rémy's primary mission – to recruit French volunteers for Sussex – but gloomy about the effects of de Gaulle's rejection of his pleas concerning the court case. "If he refuses to appear before the judge," Dansey told Rémy, "he will certainly be convicted and the consequences will be disastrous. What a cranky man!" The disastrous circumstances never happened, however. Dansey went to his friend Churchill to explain the situation, hoping that between them they could work something out.

"Winston is still a journalist above all things," he told Rémy. "He is also a remarkable actor, and – from time to time – an excellent statesman." No doubt it was the statesman in him which produced a solution. He asked Sir Stafford Cripps, then Minister of Aircraft Production, to approach Dufour and find a way of persuading him to withdraw the charges. Cripps was well-known for his qualities as a negotiator and conciliator, and somehow he succeeded, to everyone's great relief.

Perhaps the only person who remained unaffected was de Gaulle himself. He continued to behave as though the affair had never existed, and when eventually Rémy told him that the charges had been withdrawn, his reaction was typical. He permitted himself a light smile, and said, nonchalantly, "But, of course."

Sussex, meanwhile, was going ahead at full speed. The task of selecting and training some 100 agents to be parachuted in to fifty separate points between the Belgian border and the Atlantic coast south of Brittany was enormous. They had to be completely new to the business, so that there was no chance of their being known either to the Germans or to existing French networks which might have been penetrated. While this was good for security, it vastly increased the problem of training. Each man had to learn everything from scratch: tradecraft, military requirements, how to identify enemy units and all their equipment, armour and aircraft, details of the area to which he was assigned and the specific intelligence objectives there, names and details of people and places to be avoided in the areas, parachute jumping, and such essentials as how to resist torture and interrogation by the Gestapo.

Radio operators had to pass an intensive course in working fast and secretly, and in ciphering techniques. All agents had to learn their personal ciphers and signal plans. And, of course, every single agent had to be provided with authentic clothing and an incredibly detailed personal cover – an identity with a past and a present which would stand up to the most rigorous inspection – complete with every conceivable type of false paper and document, both personal and official. These were provided for the whole operation by the SIS forgers and printing workshop. Every single cover story was different. The only thing they all had in common was that in their fictitious identities every agent was an only child and an orphan.

By the end of January, the first agents were ready, and on 8th and 9th February five Pathfinder agents were dropped into France to prepare the way for the rest of the Sussex mission. Their job was to prepare reception areas for parachuting, safe houses and local experts, all outside the existing French networks. The first operational agent teams were sent in on the night of Sunday, 9th April 1944. By the end of May there were thirteen teams in France. The first intelligence message was received on 16th May. It contained five items of intelligence; the location of two German munitions dumps and a sabotage school, a report on the evacuation of civilians from a town, and the information that another munitions dump supposed to be located in a certain town did not in fact exist. Operation Sussex was well and truly under way.

After the D-day landings in Normandy, the Sussex teams continued to provide vital and constantly up-dated information on enemy movements for the Allied armies battling their way through France. Some of them were caught and executed by the Germans, but the work went on. Even by mid-June, the value of the operation had been proved: a Sussex agent had been the first to identify the movements of the Lehr Panzer Division, and 21st Army Group went on record as saying that the value of that particular piece of information alone was sufficient to justify all the work that had been put into the Sussex operation, even if nothing more were accomplished. But, of course, considerably more *was* accomplished.

By July, the Sussex committee was asking SHAEF to name a further ten points to be covered by the operation, further east, in addition to the fifty which were already being dealt with. By August, the first teams were being overrun by the advancing Allied armies. They were sent back to England to rest and were then either returned to the French army or, if they volunteered for further duties, as most did, were rebriefed and parachuted back into France behind the German lines.

By early October, it was all over. Sussex had triumphantly completed the mission which Dansey had envisaged for it some fifteen months before. The teams had sent in nearly 2,500 separate items of intelligence, covering a variety of subjects ranging from German battle order, airfields, and secret weapons to bombing targets and details of the results of bombing raids. The army commanders were lavish in their praise; undoubtedly, Sussex had made a substantial contribution to the success of Overlord and the liberation of France.

For Dansey, Sussex was something of a grand finale to his career. The wheel had come full circle: Sussex was "hot" intelligence gained by agents operating secretly in enemy territory and supplying vital information to armies in the field, the modern equivalent of the sort of thing he had started out doing in South Africa nearly half a century before. There were only seven months left of the war in Europe, and another three before the Japanese, too, surrendered. He still had agents working in Germany and other parts of occupied Europe. He still had men in position from the northern end of Norway to the southern tip of South America, in Africa and Asia and the Middle East. But there were no new initiatives to be started, and Dansey could afford to start thinking of other things, at last.

One of the first things he thought of was marriage. To almost everyone's surprise, on 1st March 1945 he married Frances Gurney Rylander, formerly Wilson, at Chelsea Register Office. Frances was an attractive young woman, who had been parted from her first husband, a Swedish businessman, for some time. She was the physiotherapist who had treated Marie-Madeleine and others. She also had several things in common with his first wife: both were divorced, both were aged thirty-four at the time they married him, both their previous husbands had been foreign businessmen, both were the daughters of doctors, and each of them had an eight-year-old daughter, who initially resented Dansey's intrusion.

Frances's daughter was a bright, fair-haired girl called Anna. She had been away at boarding school since she was six, because of the dangers of bombing in London, but she still had a very close relationship with her mother. At first, she was determined not to like her new stepfather. "We'd been on our own for a long time," she explains. But it did not take long for the Dansey charm to do its work.

"He used to tell me marvellous stories about Arabs and things," she recalls. "He was great fun, and I was soon completely won over."

Among the wedding presents was what Frances describes as "a wonderful gift from the diamond firm" – Dansey had maintained his contacts with them, since diamonds were a very useful way of moving money about during the war. Diamonds were always good currency, everywhere. "Of course," she says with a laugh, "I never saw them – they went straight in!" At that stage in his life, cash was more valuable to Dansey than precious stones.

If the diamonds were one of the fruits of his career, there were others, too, which Dansey relished. In July 1943 he had been knighted, and was now Sir Claude Dansey, KCMG. A little later he was honoured again by the French, as a Commander of the *Légion d'Honneur*. The decorations poured in.

In 1945, President Truman awarded him the United States Legion of Merit, Degree of Officer. The citation read:

Lieutenant-Colonel Sir Claude E. M. Dansey, KCMG, British Army, from August 1942 to May 1945 was indefatigable in his

331

efforts to ensure the success of Anglo-American cooperation in highly important operations. His enthusiastic interest, unflagging support and superior diplomacy contributed materially to special activities which produced results of great value to the United States and her allies in the defeat of Germany. Harry S. Truman.

Then, suddenly, it was all over. The world was at peace, and Sir Claude, weary and in failing health after the strain of many years, was glad to retire to seek a little peace for himself and the new Lady Dansey. In the countryside near Bath, they found an old house in the warm stone of the region: Bathampton Manor. It was a graceful Georgian building, set in pleasant grounds surrounded by a stone wall, every English gentleman's dream of a retirement haven. There, they settled down. But even at Bathampton it was impossible to escape the past. They had only been living there for a few weeks when they found some mysterious caller had scrawled the letter "Z" on the front door.

Of course, a man who had been as active as Dansey could not cut himself off completely. He still had a wide range of friends, who kept in touch. Alexander Korda – by then also knighted for his secret services to Britain – repaid a little of his early debt by making Dansey a director of what had become his principal company, British Lion Films.

Life in the country was very pleasant. Dansey told Frances this was the happiest time ever for him. But sadly it was not to last for long. His heart had suffered too much during seventy years of intense living, and eventually it gave up the struggle. He died, peacefully, in the Lansdowne Grove Nursing Home, Bath, on 11th June 1947. Frances was at his side. The death certificate gave the causes as coronary thrombosis and myocardial degeneration.

For the world of secret intelligence, the death of Claude Dansey marked the passing of an era. It had witnessed the rise of the British Secret Service to the very peak of its power and success – and the birth of the intelligence service which would supplant it as the principal agency in the West. The CIA was created in Washington under Allen Dulles in the year Dansey died. In many ways, it could be said to have been his bequest to the United States.

Back in Bathampton, Frances had the task of going through his papers to destroy anything which could be a danger to security. There were many reminders of a colourful life, but perhaps the most telling was a pile of at least half a dozen passports in different names. He had remained the model secret agent to the last.

Finding a suitable epitaph for a man such as Claude Dansey is an impossible task. Perhaps the simplest way is to leave the last words to three very different men, who knew and worked with him.

Kim Philby wrote: "It came to me, when I heard he was dead, that I had really rather liked him. Nefarious as his influence on the service was, it gave me a pang to think that that crusty old spirit was still for ever."

Brendan Bracken, former Minster of Information and close supporter and confidant of Churchill, wrote to Frances: "England had in him one of the ablest and most single minded servants she has ever known. Our debt to him is beyond computation."

The Duke of Portland, who as Victor Cavendish-Bentinck was head of the all-powerful Joint Intelligence Committee during the war, was more succinct. He told the authors, quite simply: "Claude Dansey? He was the best of them."

Sources

BIBLIOGRAPHY

Published sources used in the preparation of this book include the following:

Amort, R. and Jedlicka, M., *The Canaris File*, Wingate, London, 1970
Andrzejwski, B. W. and Lewis, I. M., *Somali Poetry, An Introduction*, Oxford University Press, 1964
Anon., *A Short History of Thomas Ryan's English Racing Stable, 1923–28*, privately printed
Anon., *The Sleepy Hollow Country Club*, privately printed, 1919
Anstruther, Ian, *Oscar Browning, A Biography*, John Murray, London, 1983
Aster, S., *The Making of the Second World War*, André Deutsch, London, 1973
Aster, S. (ed), *The 'X' Documents*, André Deutsch, London, 1974
Astley, Joan Bright, *The Inner Circle*, Hutchinson, London, 1971
Barron, Clarence, *They Told Barron*, New York, 1973
Battersby, H. F. Prevost, *Richard Corfield of Somaliland*, Arnold, London, 1914
Beesly, Patrick, *Very Special Intelligence*, Hamish Hamilton, London, 1977
Beevor, J. G., *SOE, Recollections and Reflections, 1940–45*, Bodley Head, London, 1981
Best, S. Payne, *The Venlo Incident*, Hutchinson, London, 1951
Birmingham, Stephen, *Real Lace*, Hamish Hamilton, London, 1974
Blackburn, Douglas, *Secret Service in South Africa*, Cassell, London, 1911
Blythe, Ronald, *The Age of Illusions, 1914-1940*, Hamish Hamilton, London, 1963
Brown, Anthony Cave, *Bodyguard of Lies*, W. H. Allen, London, 1976
Burke's Landed Gentry, London, 1982
Burke's Peerage and Baronetcy, London, 1980
Churchill, Winston S., *London to Ladysmith*, Longman, London, 1900
Churchill, Winston S., *My Early Life*, Thornton Butterworth, London, 1930
Clifford, H., *Sally: a Study*, Blackwood, London, 1904

Bibliography

Coit, Margaret L., *Mr Baruch*, Gollancz, London, 1958
Colvin, Ian, *Vansittart in Office*, Gollancz, London, 1965
Crozier, J., *In the Enemy's Country*, Knopf, New York, 1931
Dank, Milton. *The French Against the French; Collaboration and Resistance*, Cassell, London, 1978
Darling, Donald, *Secret Sunday*, Kimber, London, 1975
Darling, Donald, *Sunday at Large*, Kimber, London, 1977
Davis, John H., *The Guggenheims*, Morrow, New York, 1970
Deacon, Richard, *A History of the British Secret Service*, Granada, London, 1980
Egremont, Max, *Balfour*, Collins, London, 1980
Foot, M. R. D., *SOE in France*, HMSO, London, 1966
Foot, M. R. D., and Langley, J. M., *MI9, Escape and Evasion 1939–1945*, Bodley Head, London, 1979
Fourcade, Marie-Madeleine, *Noah's Ark*, Allen & Unwin, London, 1973
Fuller, J. F. C., *The Last of the Gentleman's Wars*, Faber & Faber, London, 1937
Furze, G. A., *Information in War*, W. Clowes & Sons, London, 1895
Gann, L. H., *A History of Southern Rhodesia*, Chatto & Windus, London, 1965
Gardner, B., *Mafeking, A Victorian Legend*, Cassell, London, 1966
Giskes, H. J., *London Calling North Pole*, Kimber, London, 1953
Goebbels, Josef, *Diaries 1939–41*, André Deutsch, London, 1982
Graham Murray, J., *The Sword and the Umbrella*, Times Press, New York, 1964
Gulbenkian, N. S., *Pantaraxia*, Hutchinson, London, 1971
Haswell, Jock, *British Military Intelligence*, Weidenfeld & Nicolson, London, 1973
Henderson, David, *Field Intelligence, Its Principles and Practice*, HMSO, London, 1904
Hendrick, Burton J., *The Age of Big Business*, Yale University Press, New Haven, 1921
Hewitt, Malyn, *Portugal in Africa*, Hurst, New York, 1981
Hillcourt, W., *Baden-Powell: The Two Lives of a Hero*, Heinemann, London, 1964
Hinsley, F. H., *British Intelligence in the Second World War*, HMSO, London, 1979, 1981
Hoare, Sir Samuel, *The Fourth Seal*, Heinemann, London, 1930
Hoehling, H. A., *Edith Cavell*, Cassell, London, 1958
Höhne, Heinz, *The Order of the Death's Head*, Secker & Warburg, London, 1969
Hollins, Christopher, *The American Heresy*, Sheed & Ward, New York, 1927
Howe, Ellic, *The Black Game*, Michael Joseph, London, 1982
Hyde, H. Montgomery, *The Quiet Canadian*, Hamish Hamilton, London, 1964
Ind, Alison, *A History of Modern Espionage*, Hodder & Stoughton, London, 1965

Bibliography

Inglis, Brian, *Roger Casement*, Hodder & Stoughton, London, 1973
Jardine, Douglas, *The Mad Mullah of Somaliland*, Herbert Jenkins, London, 1923
Jennings and Addison, *With the Abyssinians in Somaliland*, Hodder & Stoughton, London, 1905
Johns, Philip, *Within Two Cloaks*, Kimber, London, 1979
Jong, Louis de, *The German Fifth Column in the Second World War*, Routledge, London, 1956
Kossmann, E. H., *The Low Countries, 1780–1940*, Oxford, 1978
Kulik, K., *Alexander Korda*, W. H. Allen, London, 1975
Langley, J. M., *Fight Another Day*, Collins, London, 1974
Lewis, I. M., *The Modern History of Somaliland, From Nation to State*, Weidenfeld & Nicolson, London, 1965
Liddell Hart, B. H., *A History of World War I*, Cassell, London, 1970
Littlejohn, D., *The Patriotic Traitors*, Heinemann, London, 1965
Lockhart, J. G. and Woodhouse, C. M., *Rhodes*, Hodder & Stoughton, London, 1963
Lockhart, Sir Robert Bruce, (ed. K. Young), *Diaries*, Macmillan, London, 1973
Lockhart, Robin Bruce, *Ace of Spies*, Hodder & Stoughton, London, 1967
Mackenzie, Compton, *Greek Memories*, Chatto & Windus, London, 1932
Maisky, Ivan, *Who Helped Hitler?* Hutchinson, London, 1964
Martelli, George, *Leopold to Lumumba*, Chapman & Hall, London, 1962
Maugham, W. Somerset, *Ashenden*, Heinemann, London, 1928
Maugham, W. Somerset, *The Summing Up*, Heinemann, London, 1938
McNeill, Captain, *In Pursuit of the "Mad" Mullah*, Pearson, London, 1902
Millin, S. G., *Rhodes*, Chatto & Windus, London, 1952
Moravec, Frantisek, *Master of Spies*, Bodley Head, London, 1975
Mosley, Leonard, *Dulles*, Hodder & Stoughton, London, 1978
Mosley, Leonard, *The Reich Marshal*, Weidenfeld & Nicolson, London, 1974
Muggeride, Malcolm, *Chronicles of Wasted Time, Vol. 2: The Infernal Grove*, Collins, London, 1973
Myers, Gustavus, *History of Great American Fortunes*, Random House, New York, 1936
Neave, Airey, *Saturday at MI9*, Hodder & Stoughton, London, 1969
Nutting, Anthony, *The Scramble for Africa*, Constable, London, 1970
Pakenham, Thomas, *The Boer War*, Weidenfeld & Nicolson, London, 1979
Papen, Franz von, *Memoirs*, André Deutsch, London, 1952
Parritt, B. A. H., *The Intelligencers*, privately printed, 1972
Passy, *Deuxième Bureau – Londres*, Paris
Passy, *Missions Secrète en France*, Plon, Paris, 1951
Passy, *10, Duke Street – Londres*, Paris

Bibliography

Persico, Joseph, *Piercing the Reich*, Michael Joseph, London, 1979
Philby, Kim, *My Silent War*, MacGibbon & Kee, London, 1968
Pope, Arthur Lipham, *Maxim Litvinoff*, Secker & Warburg, London, 1943
Putlitz, Wolfgang zu, *The Putlitz Dossier*, Wingate, London, 1957
Rayne, Major J., *Sun, Sand and Somalis – Leaves from the Notebook of a District Commissioner in British Somaliland*, H. F. & G. Witherby, London, 1921
Read, Anthony, and Fisher, David, *Operation Lucy – Most Secret Spy Ring of the Second World War*, Hodder & Stoughton, London, 1980
Rémy, *Mes Grands Hommes et Quelques Autres*, Bernard Grosset, Paris, 1982
Rémy, *On M'Appelait Rémy*, Plon, Paris
Rémy, *Réseaux d'Ombres*, Editions France-Empire, Paris, 1953
Repington, Charles à Court, *Vestigia*, Constable, London, 1919
Rintelen, Franz von, *Memoirs*, André Deutsch, London, 1952
Rose, Norman, *Vansittart, Study of a Diplomat*, Heinemann, London, 1958
Rutter, O., *British North Borneo*, Constable, London, 1922
Rutter, O., *Golden Rain*, T. Fisher Unwin, London, 1928
Schellenberg, Walter, *Memoirs*, André Deutsch, London, 1956
Schoenbrun, David, *Soldiers of the Night*, New American Library, New York, 1980
Seaton, Albert, *The German Army 1933–45*, Weidenfeld & Nicolson, London, 1982
Seth-Smith, Michael, *Steve, The Life and Times of Steven Donaghue*, Faber & Faber, London, 1974
Shirer, William, *The Collapse of the Third Republic*, Simon & Schuster, New York, 1979
Skeat, W. W., *Malay Magic*, Macmillan, London, 1900
Smith, R. Harris, *OSS, The Secret History of America's First Central Intelligence Agency*, University of California Press, Berkeley, 1981
Smyth, B., *The History of the Lancashire Fusiliers*, Sackville Press, London, 1901
Stimson, H. L. & Bundy, McGeorge, *On Active Service in Peace and War*, Harper Brothers, New York, 1949
Stirling, J., *The Colonials in South Africa*, Blackwood, London, 1967
Sullivan, Mark, *Our Times, Pre-war American 1900-25*, Scribner's, New York, 1930
Tarling, N., *Britain, the Brookes and Brunei*, Oxford, 1971
Thomas, Hugh, *The Murder of Rudolf Hess*, Hodder & Stoughton, London, 1978
Thomson, Sir Basil, *The Scene Changes*, Collins, London, 1938
Thwaites, Norman, *Velvet and Vinegar*, Grayson & Grayson, London, 1932
Todd, Judith, *Rhodesia*, MacGibbon & Kee, London, 1966
Tregonning, K. G., *Under Chartered Company Rule (Borneo 1881–1963)*, University of Malaya Press, Kuala Lumpur, 1965

Bibliography

Trythall, Anthony J., *Boney Fuller, the Intellectual General*, Cassell, London, 1977

Tuchman, Barbara W., *The Zimmermann Telegram*, Ballantine Books, New York, 1952

Vandenbosch, Amry, *The Neutrality of the Netherlands During the World War*, Eerdmans, Amsterdam, 1927

Van der Flier, M. J., *War Finances in the Netherlands up to 1918*, Oxford, 1923

West, Nigel, *MI5 – British Security Service Operations 1909–1945*, Bodley Head, London, 1981

Whitehead, Don, *The FBI*, Panther Books, London, 1972

Whiting, Charles, *The Battle for Twelveland*, Leo Cooper, London, 1975

Willert, Sir Arthur, *The Road to Safety*, Derek Verschoyle, London, 1952

Winterbotham, Frederick W., *The Nazi Connection*, Weidenfeld & Nicolson, London, 1978

Yardley, Herbert O., *The American Black Chamber*, Bobbs-Merrill, Indianapolis, 1931

Young, Kenneth, *Balfour*, G. Bell, Edinburgh, 1963

NEWSPAPERS AND MAGAZINES

The Baltimore Sun, 10th May 1931
The Citizen's Register, Ossining, New York, 23rd September 1961
Cosmopolitan, New York, 1908
Great Eastern Railway Magazine, April 1915, September 1916
Journal of the Royal Asiatic Society, Malay Branch, 1965
The King, 24th March 1900
New York Herald Tribune, 10th July 1947
New York Times Magazine, 17th February 1918
Nursing Mirror, 15th September 1982
Saturday Evening Post, 4th April, 18th April, 9th May, 1931
Sunday Star, Washington, 19th February 1922
Sunday Times, 15th March 1981
The Times, May, December, 1925; January 1926
The World's Work, July 1918

UNPUBLISHED DOCUMENTARY SOURCES

Payne Best Papers (Imperial War Museum and Mrs Bridget Payne Best)
Payne Best Tapes (Stewart Steven and Mrs Bridget Payne Best)
Oscar Browning Papers (Ian Anstruther and East Sussex County Library, Lewes)
Captain M. R. K. Burge Papers (Intelligence Corps Archives)
Group-Captain M. G. Christie Papers (Churchill College, Cambridge)
Winston S. Churchill, "A Minute on the Somaliland Protectorate", 24th November 1908 (Public Record Office, London)
Dansey Papers (Mrs Frances Suter)
De Beers Archives (London and Johannesburg)
Colonel R. Drake, Report of Special Intelligence (Intelligence Corps Archives)

338

Bibliography

Allen W. Dulles Papers (Princeton University)
Free State Archives (Bloemfontein)
Intelligence Corps Archives (Ashford, Kent)
Kirke Papers (Intelligence Corps Archives)
Lancashire Fusiliers Archives (Bury, Lancashire)
Jared Louwenstein Collection (Jared Louwenstein, University of Virginia, Charlottesville, Va.)
Memoirs of Sir James Marshall-Cornwall (Intelligence Corps Archives)
Military Report on British Somaliland, 1925 (Public Record Office, London)
Francis P. Miller Papers: War Diary of the OSS, SI Branch, Account of Operation Sussex, (George C. Marshall Research Library, Lexington, Va., USA)
National Army Museum Archives (London)
Parliamentary Commission of the Netherlands States General: "An Inquiry into all Matters of Government Action, 1940–45" Vol. 2B (Netherlands State Institute for War Documentation, Amsterdam)
Public Record Office, London; various papers and files in War Office, Colonial Office, Foreign Office and Cabinet records, including CO 607, CO 713, CAB 37, WO 25, WO 32, WO 76, FO 45, FO 371, FO 372, FO N51
Sleepy Hollow Country Club: Minutes of the Board of Governors, 1911-14 (Sleepy Hollow Country Club, Scarborough on the Hudson, New York)
South African Republic National Archives (Pretoria)
Transvaal Archives (Johannesburg)
US National Archives, Washington, DC: various papers in Military Intelligence records, RG No 165; War Diary of the OSS, SI Branch; War Office (British) Memorandum No 903
Vansittart Papers (Churchill College, Cambridge)
Wellington College Archives (Wellington College, Crowthorne, Berkshire)
Zimbabwe National Archives (Harare, Zimbabwe)

A full list of sources, both published and personal, for matters concerning the Lucy Ring and the situation in Switzerland during the second world war will be found in the authors' previous book, *Operation Lucy*, Hodder & Stoughton, London, 1980.

INTERVIEWS AND CORRESPONDENCE

Professor B. W. Andrzejwski, Mrs Anna Ashton, Mr Cecil Barclay, Mrs Bridget Payne Best, Mrs Eleanor Parke Brady, Colonel Maurice Buckmaster, Mr Harry Chapman-Pincher, Colonel John A. Codrington, Commander Kenneth Cohen, Major Felix Cowgill, Lord Dacre, Lady Duveen, Mr Nicholas Elliott, Mme Marie-Madeleine Fourcade, Lord Gladwyn, Major J. McQ. Hallam, Commander Philip Johns, Mr C. A. B. King, Lieutenant-Colonel J. M. Langley, Mrs Peggy Langley, Baron Fernand Lepage, Mr Jared C. Louwenstein, General Sir James

Marshall-Cornwall, Mr Leonard Miall, Mr Malcolm Muggeridge, Colonel Passy (M André Dewavrin), Duke of Portland, Colonel Rémy (M Gilbert Renault-Roulier), Colonel Felix Robson, Mrs Joanna Simon, Mr Stewart Steven, Mr William G. Stevenson, Mrs Frances Suter, Dr Heather Tomlinson, Mr F. Tyree, Mr Nigel West, Group-Captain Frederick W. Winterbotham, Mrs F. W. Winterbotham, Plus several former members of the intelligence community who do not wish to be identified.

Acknowledgments

Many individuals have given us help and encouragement in the preparation of this book. A list of those who gave their time freely in interviews or correspondence appears elsewhere. We are grateful to them all.

There are some, however, to whom we owe particular thanks: first, Mrs Frances Suter, formerly Lady Dansey, for her kind approval of our plan to write about her late husband, for giving us access to his remaining papers and belongings, and for her continuing encouragement; secondly, the late Lieutenant-Colonel Jimmy Langley, who introduced us to her and opened so many other doors for us, too; Colonel Rémy (Gilbert Renault-Roulier) for his help in guiding us through the intricacies of wartime French politics, for valuable introductions, and for splendid hospitality at his beautiful home in Brittany; Mme Marie-Madeleine Fourcade, for her help and for loaning us personal letters from Colonel Dansey; Mrs Eleanor Parke Brady, for telling us about her grandfather, Thomas Fortune Ryan, for her hospitality during our stay in Virginia, and for allowing us to visit the family estate at Oak Ridge; Mr Jared Louwenstein of the University of Virginia, Charlottesville, for making available to us many documents from his treasured collection of Ryaniana; Mr Stewart Steven, for his help over the Venlo Incident, and for lending us tapes of his interviews with Sigismund Payne Best; Mrs Bridget Payne Best, for talking to us about her late husband and for giving us access to his papers; Mrs Leslie, of the Sleepy Hollow Country Club, for guiding us through the club and its records: Dr Heather Tomlinson, archivist of Wellington College, for her help in piecing together the scarce information about Dansey's schooldays; and Mr Ian Anstruther, who gave us particularly valuable help in revealing other aspects of Dansey's youth and schooling, and also provided additional information about the Dansey family, as, too, did Miss L. Moaby.

Several curators, archivists and librarians were especially helpful. These included Mr Philip Reid and his colleagues at the

Acknowledgments

Imperial War Museum, London; Miss Maida H. Loescher and Mr John E. Taylor, of the US National Archives, Washington, DC; Mr John Jacobs, of the George C. Marshall Research Foundation, Lexington, Virginia; Miss Nancy Bressler, of the Seeley G. Mudd Manuscript Library, Princeton University, New Jersey; Colonel Felix Robson, of the Intelligence Corps Museum, Ashford, Kent; Major J. McQ. Hallam, of the Royal Regiment of Fusiliers, Bury, Lancashire; the librarian and staff of the London Library, Maidenhead (Berkshire) Public Library, Burnham (Buckinghamshire) Public Library, the New York Public Library, and the Public Record Office, Kew, London.

We must also thank Rosemary Read and Barbara Weller, for their amazing patience and unflagging support during the long process of research and writing; Amelia Read, for organising the bibliography and source notes; Sherry Zeffert, for her efficient, speedy and enthusiastic typing; and Helen Baz, for providing, as always, a first-rate index in remarkably quick time.

Finally, we must thank our editors, Ion Trewin in London and Alan D. Williams in New York, for their forbearance, advice, and above all for their iron determination to deny us any indulgence or carelessness in either style or fact. The final shape and quality of this book owe much to their efforts.

Anthony Read & David Fisher

Index

Index

Index

Index

Index

Guérisse, Albert-Marie
Olympic liner, 99
Oorschot, Major-General J.W., van, 213–14
Oppenheim, Major, 142
Orange Free State, 27, 44, 49, 51, 53
Orange River Colony, 49
Orange River Station, 44
L'Ordre National, 293
OSS (US Office of Strategic Services: formerly COI), 14, 135, 241, 310–30; Secret Intelligence (SI), 311, 315, 324; Secret Operations (SO), 311; Research and Analysis, 311; Morale Operations, 311; X-Z (counter-intelligence), 311; David Bruce appointed head of, 312; in Switzerland, 313, 318–21; and Free Germany Committee, 313; in Algiers and Vichy France, 315–17; and Fritz Kolbe, 318–21; Plan "Sussex", 322–30
Ottoman Empire, 151, 153
Overbeck, Baron von, 37

P15 section (MI9), 263
Page, Walter Hines, 88
PAO ("Pat"), escape line, 265
Papen, Franz von, 89, 129
Paris Peace Conference (1919), 152, 153–5, 165
Paris, Z Organisation in, 189
Parker, Mrs Rose Sutton, 128, 129, 130
passeurs ("line-crossers"), 138–9
Passport Control Offices (PCOs), 104, 188; Dansey head of Rome office, 163–5, 170; Scheveningen (The Hague), 171–2, 207–8, 209; Geneva, 191
"Passy", Colonel (André Dewavrin. head of French Intelligence), 282–4, 285, 286, 290, 305, 317, 326, 327
Pau, Alliance network in, 296–8
Peace Conference *see* Paris Peace Conference
Pearson, Rex, 198, 222; and Z Organisation, 174, 180, 184, 189, 190, 191, 231
Peenemunde rocket research establishment, Alliance infiltration of, 303

Percy, Eustace, 157
Pershing, General, 107, 108, 113
Persse, Henry Seymour "Atty", horse trainer, 79, 160, 161–2
Pétain, Marshal Henri-Philippe, 280, 281, 292, 293, 294, 296, 316
Philby, Eleanor (Kim's wife), 164
Philby, Kim, 235; and Dansey, 235, 236, 315, 318, 333; and Fritz Kolbe, 318–20, 321
Piasan (Borneo), Dansey's attack on, 40–1
Pilet-Golaz, Swiss Federal President, 250
Ploesti oilfields, 152
Plumer, Lieutenant-Colonel Herbert, 31, 32, 47; and relief of Mafeking, 44, 45, 46
Poland, 170; Nazi invasion and subjugation of, 188–9, 207, 211, 219, 227, 237; Red Army's invasion of, 211
police force, MI5's relations with, 110–11
Polish Intelligence, 278
Pompiers de l'Air, 301
Portland, Duke of *see* Cavendish-Bentinck, Victor
Portugal, 184, 259–60
"Postman" (later "Comète"), escape line, 267
Poulard, Lieutenant Pilote ("Jack Tar"), 301
Prague, Z Organisation in, 184
Pretoria, 27, 28
Prinsloo, General, 49
prisoners-of-war: escaped, 143, 255, 257–8, 261, 263, 264; interrogation of enemy, 257
"Private Detective Agency", Vansittart's, 167–70, 174, 206
The Private Life of Henry VIII (film), 178
Prudential Assurance, 178–9
Pünter, Marta, 253
Pünter, Otto ("Pakbo"), 253
Pyrenees, escape lines over, 258, 260

Qaadiriya Brotherhood, 58
Queensland Mounted Infantry, 45
Quigg, Lemuel E., 71
Quinn, John, 129
Quinn, Superintendent, 86

355

Index

Index

Ulman, Joseph Stevens, 89
Ulman, Mrs Pauline Monroe Cory
  see Dansey, Mrs
Ultra, code-breaking operation, 199,
  230, 234, 245, 252, 319
Unilever, 180, 184
United States: Forminiére financed
  by private capital from, 72; Irish
  in, 73–4, 77, 94, 120, 124, 128–30;
  Dansey works as Resident
  Secretary of Sleepy Hollow, 67,
  75–81; Military Intelligence Service,
  14, 101–9; Zimmermann telegram,
  95–8; and war declared on
  Germany, 98; Balfour mission to
  Washington, 98–100, 119;
  British–US Intelligence special
  relationship, 105–9, 133; French
  Mission to, 119; enemy agents and
  sabotage in, 120, 122–35; British
  Security Coordination set up
  (1940), 175, 179; Vichy government
  recognised by, 281; and neutrality
  in Second World War, 308, 310; and
  Donovan Mission to Europe, 308–
  10; Roosevelt re-elected President
  (1940), 310; Operation Torch
  (Allied landings in North Africa),
  315; and Allied invasion of
  Normandy, 326–7, 330
United States Special Observers
  Group, 310
University Appointments Board,
  182–3
Uranium Steamship Company, 184
US General Staff, Dansey's lectures
  to, 109, 110–11, 112
US Military Intelligence Division,
  101–9, 119–20, 136, 310; Field
  Intelligence, 108; British
  Intelligence's cooperation with,
  105–9, 133, 144; "The Black
  Chamber", 114–15; New York
  branch office, 126
US Naval Intelligence, 104
US Secret Intelligence Service, 155;
  codes and ciphers ("The Black
  Chamber"), 113–15; secret
  writing, 115; enemy agents, 120,
  122–35; in Holland, 144–5; and in
  Switzerland, 146–8; and British
  Security Coordination, 175, 179;
  OSS liaison with SIS in Second

World War, 308, 310–21; and Plan
  "Sussex", 322–30; see also CIA;
  FBI; OSS
US Steel Corporation, 109
Ustinov, "Klop", 175

V1 and V2 weapons, 276, 303
Van Deman, Major R.H., 100, 113,
  135, 142, 144, 156, 308;
  development of US Military
  Intelligence and role of Dansey,
  101–9, 119–20, 121, 122, 123, 156;
  moves to Europe, 119; "The Black
  Chamber", 114; New York office
  set up by, 126; enemy agents,
  127–8, 131, 132, 133, 134; at Peace
  Conference (1919), 154, 155
Vanderbilt, William H., 75
Vanderlip, Franklin A., 76, 77, 81
Van Leer, Peggy (Mrs Langley), 12n
Vansittart, Guy, 174
Vansittart, Robert, Permanent
  Under-Secretary at Foreign
  Office, 165–8, 175, 210, 259;
  anti-communism of, 165, 187;
  fears about German resurgence,
  166–7; and "Private Detective
  Agency" of, 167–8, 174, 206; and
  Z Organisation, 172, 176, 181;
  Korda's association with, 177, 178;
  "promoted" to Chief Diplomatic
  Adviser, 188; and warns Cagoden
  of German intentions, 188–9
Venezuela, 158
Venlo Incident, 200, 201–22, 222,
  223–5, 227–9, 230, 277
Verdon, Captain, 142
Vermork heavy water plant, 277
Versailles, Treaty of (1919), 155, 175,
  203, 217
Vichy Government/Vichy France,
  239, 258, 259, 260, 261, 264, 280,
  292, 294, 295–6, 299, 316; US
  recognition of, 281; and OSS
  agents sent to, 317
Victoria, Queen, 17, 197
Victorica, Manuel Gustave, 132, 133
Victorica, Madame Maria de, 131–5
Vienna, 184
"The Virginian" (colt), 161–2
Vita Nova, publishers, 243
Vivian, Lieutenant-Colonel
  Valentine (Vee-Vee), feud with

359